Reagan, Congress, and Human Rights

This book traces the role of human rights concerns in US foreign policy during the 1980s, focusing on the struggle between the Reagan administration and members of Congress. It demonstrates how congressional pressure led the administration to reconsider its approach to human rights and craft a conservative human rights policy centered on democracy promotion and anti-communism – a decision that would have profound implications for American attention to human rights. Based on extensive archival research and interviews, Rasmus Sinding Søndergaard combines a comprehensive overview of human rights in American foreign relations with in-depth case studies of how human rights shaped US foreign policy toward Soviet Jewry, South African apartheid, and Nicaragua. Tracing the motivations behind human rights activism, this book demonstrates how liberals, moderates, and conservatives selectively invoked human rights to further their agendas, ultimately contributing to the establishment of human rights as a core moral language in US foreign policy.

RASMUS SINDING SØNDERGAARD is a Marie Skłodowska-Curie Fellow in the Department of History at Lund University. He is a recipient of the Danish Ministry of Higher Education and Science's Elite Research Travel Grant and fellowships from the Carlsberg Foundation, the American-Scandinavian Foundation, and the Society for Historians of American Foreign Relations.

Human Rights in History

Edited by

Stefan-Ludwig Hoffmann, University of California, Berkeley
Samuel Moyn, Yale University, Connecticut

This series showcases new scholarship exploring the backgrounds of human rights today. With an open-ended chronology and international perspective, the series seeks works attentive to the surprises and contingencies in the historical origins and legacies of human rights ideals and interventions. Books in the series will focus not only on the intellectual antecedents and foundations of human rights, but also on the incorporation of the concept by movements, nation-states, international governance, and transnational law.

A full list of titles in the series can be found at:
www.cambridge.org/human-rights-history

Reagan, Congress, and Human Rights

Contesting Morality in US Foreign Policy

Rasmus Sinding Søndergaard

Lund University

CAMBRIDGE
UNIVERSITY PRESS

CAMBRIDGE
UNIVERSITY PRESS

University Printing House, Cambridge CB2 8BS, United Kingdom

One Liberty Plaza, 20th Floor, New York, NY 10006, USA

477 Williamstown Road, Port Melbourne, VIC 3207, Australia

314–321, 3rd Floor, Plot 3, Splendor Forum, Jasola District Centre, New Delhi – 110025, India

79 Anson Road, #06–04/06, Singapore 079906

Cambridge University Press is part of the University of Cambridge.

It furthers the University's mission by disseminating knowledge in the pursuit of education, learning, and research at the highest international levels of excellence.

www.cambridge.org
Information on this title: www.cambridge.org/9781108495639
DOI: 10.1017/9781108862455

First published 2020

Printed in the United Kingdom by TJ International Ltd, Padstow Cornwall

A catalogue record for this publication is available from the British Library.

ISBN 978-1-108-49563-9 Hardback

Contents

Figures

Acknowledgments

This book would not have been possible without the generous support of a number of institutions and people to whom I am now indebted. The following is an attempt to begin the process of paying off this debt by expressing my gratitude and thanks.

In the years predating this book, I have been privileged to develop my ideas and conduct my research at some inspiring academic institutions. In particular, I have benefited from being situated at the Department of History and the Centre for American Studies at the University of Southern Denmark; the Department of History at the University of California, Berkeley; the Danish Institute for International Studies; and the Department of Government at Georgetown University.

I am also grateful to several institutions and foundations for providing me with generous financial support. The Danish Ministry of Higher Education and Science awarded me an Elite Research Travel Grant, which greatly contributed to the research for this book. The American-Scandinavian Foundation gave me a grant to support my stay at the University of California, Berkeley. The Carlsberg Foundation awarded me an Internationalization Fellowship to support a two-year postdoc at Georgetown University, which allowed me to finalize my manuscript alongside working on a new project. In addition, I am grateful for travel grants and fellowships from the Society for Historians of Americans Foreign Relations, the Heidelberg Spring Academy, and the Salzburg Global Seminar.

The real joy of writing this book has been the wonderful people I have met along the way, who have provided me with support, advice, and constructive criticism. My PhD advisor, Niels Bjerre-Poulsen, was a constant source of support and counsel during my years as a graduate student when I began the research for this book. The same goes for my MA advisor, Helle Porsdam, and my academic mentor, Niklas Olsen, who have continued to encourage and advise me throughout the years. Samuel Moyn, Barbara J. Keys, and Casper Sylvest offered valuable suggestions on how to revise the dissertation into a book. Sarah B. Snyder, Carl Bon Tempo, Daniel Sargent, William Michael Schmidli, Robert "KC" Johnson, Steven L. B. Jensen, and Betty Koed helped guide my research and/or provided insightful comments about and criticism of my writing. Moreover, I have received constructive feedback on conference papers and draft book chapters from Robert K. Brigham, Lauren F. Turek, David Prentice, Joost Baarssen, Anders Bo Rasmussen, Hal Friedman, Kelly J. Shannon, Wilfried Mausbach, James Vernon, Vibeke Schou Tjalve, Rosanna Farbøl, Poul Villaume, and Toshihiro Higuchi. Finally, I have received very helpful suggestions from anonymous readers of the manuscript at Cambridge University Press. There is no doubt in my mind that these people have contributed greatly to improve the quality of this book through their criticism and comments. The responsibility for any shortcomings and mistakes is, of course, mine alone.

I am also deeply indebted to a long list of archivists without whose patience and skillful support my archival research across the United States would not have been possible. The list is much too long to mention in full, but I would be remiss not to give thanks to Rodney Ross at the Center for Legislative Archives at the National Archives, the staff at the Bancroft Library at UC Berkeley, and Shelly Williams at the Reagan Presidential Library. I also owe thanks to The Lantos Foundation for granting me exclusive access to the Tom Lantos Papers, covering the work of the Congressional Human Rights Caucus.

These acknowledgments would be incomplete without a word of thanks to the people in one's life who matter the most. While my friends and family may not have contributed directly to the content of this book, they have had a bigger role in its completion than they probably realize. The first in my family to attend university, I would like to thank my family for being supportive of my decision to pursue a career in academia, which at times may appear as a strange and distant world. My parents deserve credit for encouraging my curiosity about the world from an early age. My brother and I have been fortunate to grow up in a household full of books, despite being born in a community where intellectual curiosity is otherwise in relatively short supply. I want to thank my friends for reminding me that there is a world outside of archives and university offices. I am blessed with old friends, who are always ready to pick up where we left off whenever I have returned from my numerous travels over the past years. I am also thankful for all the new friends I have been fortunate to make during the process of writing this book.

   In the end, no one is more deserving of my thanks and gratitude than my wife, Annabel Acs. In important ways, our relationship and this book have developed in tandem over the past years as we have moved back and forth across the Atlantic. Despite suffering through editing and proof-reading the manuscript and enduring my endless talking about the history and politics of her own country, she has blessed me with unwavering support and company along the way. For this, I am profoundly grateful.

Abbreviations

ACOA	American Committee on Africa
AIUSA	Amnesty International USA
ANC	African National Congress
CAAA	Comprehensive Anti-Apartheid Act of 1986
CBC	Congressional Black Caucus
CFHRM	Congressional Friends of Human Rights Monitors
CFW	Committee for the Free World
CHRC	Congressional Human Rights Caucus
CHRF	Congressional Human Rights Foundation
CIA	Central Intelligence Agency
CMO	Congressional Membership Organization
CPD	Committee on the Present Danger
CSCE	Conference on Security and Cooperation in Europe
FDN	Fuerza Democrática Nicaragüense
FSAM	Free South Africa Movement
FSLN	Frente Sandinista de Liberación Nacional
ICCPR	International Covenant on Civil and Political Rights
ICESCR	International Covenant on Economic, Social, and Cultural Rights
ICJ	International Court of Justice
INF	Intermediate-Range Nuclear Forces Treaty
IPG	International Parliamentary Group for Human Rights in the Soviet Union
MAD	Mutually Assured Destruction
NCSJ	National Conference on Soviet Jewry
NED	National Endowment for Democracy
NGO	Non-Governmental Organization
NSA	National Security Advisor
NSDD 17	National Security Decision Directive 17
NSDD 187	National Security Decision Directive 187
NSDD 75	National Security Decision Directive 75
SALT I	Strategic Arms Limitations Treaty I

SALT II	Strategic Arms Limitations Treaty II
SDI	Strategic Defense Initiative
S/LPD	Office of Public Diplomacy for Latin America and the Caribbean
TLHRC	Tom Lantos Human Rights Commission
UCSJ	Union of Councils for Soviet Jews
UDHR	Universal Declaration of Human Rights
UN	United Nations
UNESCO	United Nations Educational, Scientific and Cultural Organization
USIA	United States Information Agency
WOLA	Washington Office on Latin America

Introduction

Commitment to human rights concerns as an important element in US foreign policy hung in the balance in the 1980s. Far from being the tacitly presumed self-evident truths of today, human rights, and the degree to which respect for these ought to inform American foreign relations, was a highly contested subject.[1] The 1970s had witnessed a breakthrough for human rights concerns in US foreign policy, emerging in Congress during the Nixon administration and culminating with the presidency of Jimmy Carter, who made human rights the centerpiece of his foreign policy.[2] At first, it seemed unlikely that the breakthrough would continue in a decade where President Ronald Reagan proclaimed he would undo the human rights-based foreign policy of his predecessor. At the new administration's first National Security Council meeting on February 6, 1981, Reagan declared: "We must change the attitude of our diplomatic corps so that we don't bring down governments in the name of human rights [...] We don't throw out our friends just because they can't pass the 'saliva test' on human rights."[3] In the following months, the administration's rhetoric, diplomacy, and bureaucratic appointments reinforced the intent to downgrade human rights.

Yet, during the 1980s, the administration's approach to human rights changed to such a degree that the journalist Tamar Jacoby observed a

---

[1] Stefan-Ludwig Hoffmann, "Human Rights and History," *Past & Present* 232, no. 1 (2016): 1; Stefan-Ludwig Hoffmann, "Introduction: Genealogies of Human Rights," in *Human Rights in the Twentieth Century*, ed. Stefan-Ludwig Hoffmann (New York: Cambridge University Press, 2010), 2.

[2] For the human rights breakthrough in the 1970s, see Samuel Moyn, *The Last Utopia: Human Rights in History* (Cambridge, MA: Harvard University Press, 2010); Barbara J. Keys, *Reclaiming American Virtue: The Human Rights Revolution of the 1970s* (Cambridge, MA: Harvard University Press, 2014); Jan Eckel and Samuel Moyn, eds., *The Breakthrough: Human Rights in the 1970s* (Philadelphia: University of Pennsylvania Press, 2014).

[3] US Department of State, *Foreign Relations of the United States, 1981–1988, Volume III, Soviet Union, January 1981–January 1983* (Washington, DC: US Government Publishing Office, 2016), Document 15.

"Reagan turnaround on human rights" in 1986.[4] While the administration had initially sought to downgrade the role of human rights concerns in US foreign policy, by 1986 it had incorporated these into its
wider foreign policy agenda. In a speech to Congress in March 1986,
Reagan declared, "We have sought to defend and advance the cause of
democracy, freedom, and human rights throughout the world [...] there
can be no doubt where America stands. The American people believe in
human rights and oppose tyranny in whatever form, whether of the left or
the right."[5] While the administration's commitment to human rights was
more selective and limited than this statement indicated, something its
congressional critics were eager to point out, human rights concerns
played a much more prominent role in US foreign policy by the mid-
1980s than Reagan had initially envisioned.

This book traces the role of human rights concerns in US foreign
policy during the 1980s, focusing on the struggle among the Reagan
administration and members of Congress. Looking beyond the presidency to individual members of Congress holds the key to understanding
"the Reagan turnaround." The book argues that pressure from members
of Congress had the unintended consequence of initiating the administration's creation of a conservative human rights policy centered on
democracy promotion and anti-communism. The administration's decision to proactively craft its own human rights policy had profound
implications for American attention to human rights, as it changed the
conversation from whether human rights concerns should inform US
foreign policy to how they should. The book explores the vital ways in
which relations between the executive and legislative branches of government shaped attention to human rights in US foreign policy and how the
issue of human rights, in turn, impacted executive–legislative relations.

The book examines the varied motivations that led some members of
Congress to champion human rights. At times, members of Congress
shaped US human rights policy to a degree that was disproportionate to
their formal influence on foreign policy. Political scientists Ralph
G. Carter and James M. Scott use the term "foreign policy entrepreneurs" to describe members of Congress who set the political agenda
and drive policymaking on foreign policy.[6] Given that most of the

---

[4] Tamar Jacoby, "The Reagan Turnaround on Human Rights," *Foreign Affairs* 64, no. 5
(1986): 1066–1086.

[5] Ronald Reagan, Message to the Congress on Freedom, Regional Security, and Global
Peace, May 14, 1986. Online by Gerhard Peters and John T. Woolley, The American
Presidency Project, accessed August 7, 2019, www.presidency.ucsb.edu/node/258530.

[6] Ralph G. Carter and James M. Scott, *Choosing to Lead: Understanding Congressional
Foreign Policy Entrepreneurs* (Durham, NC: Duke University Press, 2009), 21.

535 members of Congress have little interest in, or knowledge about, foreign policy, motivated foreign policy entrepreneurs can have a disproportionate impact.[7] As this book shows, such members of Congress concerned with human rights issues were able to draw on information, expertise, and political capital from human rights NGOs and activists, who frequently turned to Congress in their attempt to influence US human rights policy. From this position, members of Congress pressured the administration to put a higher emphasis on protecting the civil and political rights of dissidents, human rights activists, and minorities in communist countries as well as in rightwing dictatorships.[8]

The book covers the period between the 1970s when human rights were elevated to the top of American politics, and the post–Cold War era, when human rights became a near-universally accepted norm in global politics. More specifically, due to its focus on executive–legislative relations, the book opens with the 1980 election and concludes with the end of the Reagan administration and the 100th Congress in January 1989. This period formed a tumultuous setting for American foreign policymakers.[9] On the global scene, the Cold War heated up significantly at the beginning of the decade, heightening the fear of nuclear war, before reaching its rapid and remarkably peaceful conclusion only a few years later. At home, a conservative movement, personified with Reagan's sweeping victory in 1980, arose to challenge the liberal consensus that had come under increasing pressure during the 1970s.[10] In an agenda that was later dubbed the "Reagan Revolution," the new president promised radical change, in the form of less government regulation,

---

[7] Rebecca K. C. Hersman, *Friends and Foes: How Congress and the President Really Make Foreign Policy* (Washington, DC: Brookings Institution Press, 2000), 10; Carter and Scott, *Choosing to Lead*; Burdett A. Loomis, *The Contemporary Congress* (New York: St. Martin's, 1998), 121.

[8] Jacoby, "The Reagan Turnaround"; Joe Renouard, *Human Rights in American Foreign Policy: From the 1960s to the Soviet Collapse*, Pennsylvania Studies in Human Rights (Philadelphia: University of Pennsylvania Press, 2016), 198–207; David P. Forsythe and David Beetham, "Human Rights and US Foreign Policy: Two Levels, Two Worlds," *Political Studies* 43, no. 4 (1995): 122–124.

[9] The 1980s were at the heart of the period that historian Daniel T. Rodgers has described as "the age of fracture." Daniel T. Rodgers, *Age of Fracture* (Cambridge, MA: Harvard University Press, 2011).

[10] Over the course of the 1960s and 1970s, American liberalism experienced a crisis as American society underwent dramatic transformations. Before this crisis of liberalism, scholars such as Louis Hartz had claimed the existence of an underlying liberal consensus in America centered on Lockean ideals of equality, individual freedom, social mobility, and popular democracy. Louis Hartz, *The Liberal Tradition in America: An Interpretation of American Political Thought Since the Revolution* (New York: Harcourt, 1955); Allen J. Matusow, *The Unraveling of America* (New York: Harper & Row, 1984).

lower taxes, and a foreign policy of "peace through strength."[11] In the same election, Republicans won control over the Senate for the first time since 1955, in part due to the rise of a new conservative grassroots coalition known as the New Right.[12] The new political constellation led to an intense politicization of foreign policy, with repeated confrontations between the administration and especially liberal Democrats in the House. Outside of government, Americans increasingly organized on behalf of their favored causes, including a growing body of human rights NGOs, which increasingly turned their attention to Washington.[13]

Rising Cold War hostilities abroad and the politicization of foreign policy at home were critical determinants of human rights policy debates during the first half of the 1980s. Liberal and conservative conceptions of human rights and their appropriate role in US foreign policy clashed as Americans sought to determine how to respond to a changing international environment. The Reagan administration and its conservative allies defined human rights narrowly as civil and political rights and argued that the United States should focus on criticizing human rights violations in communist countries, while ignoring abuses by American allies.[14] Liberals, by contrast, continued to define human rights somewhat more broadly and advocated a human rights policy more evenly applied to allies as well as to adversaries.[15] Throughout the book, I classify policymakers as liberal, moderate, or conservative to describe where they belonged on this continuum of foreign policy worldviews. Unless otherwise specified, the classification does not refer to their

[11] For a discussion of the Reagan Revolution, see W. Elliot Brownlee, "Introduction: Revisiting the Reagan Revolution," in *The Reagan Presidency: Pragmatic Conservatism and Its Legacies*, ed. W. Elliot Brownlee and Hugh Davis Graham (Lawrence: University Press of Kansas, 2003), 1–13.

[12] Religious evangelical leaders of the New Right such as Jerry Falwell and Pat Robertson gained large followings and used their influence to raise money to support conservative politicians, including Ronald Reagan. For more on the rise of the New Right, see Michael Schaller, *Right Turn: American Life in the Reagan–Bush Era, 1980–1992* (New York: Oxford University Press, 2007), 27–48.

[13] According to James M. Lindsay, "The intense politicization of foreign policy during the Reagan years pushed people to organize on behalf of their favored causes." James M. Lindsay, *Congress and the Politics of U.S. Foreign Policy* (Baltimore, MD: Johns Hopkins University Press, 1994), 28.

[14] Reagan's conception drew on a neoconservative understanding of human rights promulgated by figures such as Senator Henry M. Jackson (D-WA) and Jeane Kirkpatrick during the 1970s, which saw human rights as a way to break with détente and restore American leadership in the world.

[15] Keys, *Reclaiming American Virtue*, 221–225. For Republican human rights conceptions of the 1970s, see Carl J. Bon Tempo, "Human Rights and the U.S. Republican Party in the Late 1970s," in *The Breakthrough. Human Rights in the 1970s*, ed. Jan Eckel and Samuel Moyn (Philadelphia: University of Pennsylvania Press, 2014), 146–165.

positions on domestic policy. For members of Congress, the most used categories are liberal Democrats, conservative Republicans, and moderates from both parties. For officials in the administration, the two main categories are moderates and hardliners, with the latter consisting of a combination of Cold War warriors and neoconservatives.[16] All such classifications are constructs used for analytical purposes and do not necessarily reflect the self-identification of the individuals in question.

The contestation over the appropriate role of human rights in US foreign policy strengthened human rights as a language of morality but increased the uncertainty around what a human rights policy entailed. By incorporating human rights concerns into a doctrine aimed at rolling back communism through support for guerrilla groups and right-wing dictatorships, the Reagan administration underlined the concept's flexibility and ambiguity. Carter had adopted human rights as a language to restore America's moral standing in the world after the Vietnam War and had seen it as a way to break with the Cold War dichotomy of East–West contestation.[17] Reagan shared Carter's desire to rehabilitate the international image of the United States, but he employed human rights as an ideological weapon in an attempt to win the Cold War rather than to move beyond it. Shifting coalitions of members of Congress and NGOs challenged the administration's human rights policy, contributing to the increasingly ubiquitous presence of human rights in debates over US foreign policy. This contestation coincided with, and arguably contributed to, the continued institutionalization of human rights concerns into US foreign policy that had begun in the 1970s. In Congress, members of Congress strengthened existing institutions concerned with human rights and formed new ones. In the executive branch, the State Department's Human Rights Bureau underwent a substantial professionalization, and outside of government, human rights NGOs grew in strength and numbers. As a result, by the end of the decade, human rights concerns enjoyed a more firmly established presence in US foreign policy, even as they were as contested more vigorously than ever before.

Scholarship by diplomatic historians in recent years has expanded dramatically as human rights history has emerged as a thriving subfield within the discipline of history.[18] In the words of one the leading scholars

---

[16] The classifications of members of Congress are elaborated further in Chapter 1, while the categories for administration officials are explained in Chapter 2.

[17] David F. Schmitz and Vanessa Walker, "Jimmy Carter and the Foreign Policy of Human Rights: The Development of a Post-Cold War Foreign Policy," *Diplomatic History* 28, no. 1 (2004): 113–143.

[18] Sarah B. Snyder, "Human Rights and U.S. Foreign Relations: A Historiographical Review," *Passport: The Newsletter of the SHAFR* 44 (2013): 16–21.

of human rights history, Samuel Moyn, "It [the history of human rights] came to professional attention from nowhere and extremely rapidly."[19] This book offers three new contributions. First, while the existing scholarship has focused mostly on the breakthroughs of human rights in the 1940s and the 1970s, this book addresses the less studied subject of what happened to human rights concerns in the 1980s after these breakthroughs. Historians of human rights in US foreign relations have been preoccupied with establishing the genesis of modern human rights with the 1940s and the 1970s as the two leading contenders. Arguing for the primacy of the 1940s, Elizabeth Borgwardt proposes that the international human rights pinned down in the Universal Declaration of Human Rights (UDHR) were essentially an expanded version of the New Deal and Four Freedoms launched by US President Franklin D. Roosevelt.[20] Moyn, by contrast, argues that human rights emerged in the 1970s as a "last utopia" in the form of morality-based anti-politics, filling the void after the failure of the omnipotent revolutionary agendas of socialism and anti-colonialism.[21] Challenging both of these breakthroughs, Stefan-Ludwig Hoffmann contends that it does not make sense to speak of human rights as a basic concept in global politics until the 1990s.[22] Recently, Robert Brier and others have urged historians to move beyond the search for a breakthrough, arguing instead that scholars ought to identify the multiple chronologies of postwar human rights history and a focus on the variety of human rights vernaculars.[23] This book, along with other recent publications, embodies this sentiment by tracing multiple conceptions of human rights in American foreign

---

[19] Samuel Moyn, "Substance, Scale, and Salience: The Recent Historiography of Human Rights," *Annual Review of Law and Social Science* 8 (2012): 136. Moyn has professed that after having enjoyed an historiographical victory in recent years, human rights history might soon reach its end because both human rights and its history "become normal and undramatic." Samuel Moyn, "The End of Human Rights History," *Past & Present* 233, no. 1 (2016): 322.

[20] Elizabeth Borgwardt, *A New Deal for the World: America's Vision for Human Rights* (Cambridge, MA: Harvard University Press, 2005). See also Mary Ann Glendon, *A World Made New: Eleanor Roosevelt and the Universal Declaration of Human Rights* (New York: Random House, 2001); Mark Mazower, "The Strange Triumph of Human Rights, 1933–1950," *Historical Journal* 47, no. 2 (2004): 379–398.

[21] Moyn, *Last Utopia*. See also Eckel and Moyn, eds., *The Breakthrough*; Daniel Sargent, *A Superpower Transformed: The Remaking of American Foreign Relations in the 1970s* (Oxford: Oxford University Press, 2015); Keys, *Reclaiming American Virtue*.

[22] Stefan-Ludwig Hoffmann, "Human Rights and History," *Past & Present* 232, no. 1 (2016), 20.

[23] Robert Brier, "Beyond the Quest for a "Breakthrough": Reflections on the Recent Historiography on Human Rights," *European History Yearbook* 16 (2015): 155–173. Moyn likewise warns that "the chronological dispute risks becoming a distraction." Moyn, "Substance, Scale, and Salience," 124.

relations in the 1980s. Taking advantage of the increasing availability of archival material from this decade, historians such as Sarah B. Snyder, Carl J. Bon Tempo, Gregory F. Domber, Christian Philip Peterson, and Joe Renouard have established a fast-growing body of scholarship.[24] Together with this scholarship, this book promises to bridge the extensive research on the 1970s, pioneered by Moyn, and the nascent research on the 1990s, called for by Hoffmann. As such, the book helps us to better understand the evolution of human rights concerns in American foreign relations from their cold war origins to our own time.

Second, while the majority of the existing scholarship has focused on presidents or grassroots movements, this book places individual members of Congress at the center of the narrative, uncovering their significant, but overlooked, contributions to the formation of US human rights policy. Whereas most foreign relations scholarship has focused on the executive branch, recent scholarship inspired by the transnational and cultural turns within diplomatic history has drawn attention to nongovernment actors at the grassroots level such as human rights NGOs, religious groups, and ethnic groups.[25] Still, a middle-layer of actors between presidents and

---

[24] Sarah B. Snyder, *Human Rights Activism and the End of the Cold War: A Transnational History of the Helsinki Network*, Human Rights in History (New York: Cambridge University Press, 2011); Carl J. Bon Tempo, "From the Center-Right: Freedom House and Human Rights in the 1970s and 1980s," in *The Human Rights Revolution: An International History*, ed. Petra Goedde and William Hitchcock (New York: Oxford University Press, 2012); Gregory F. Domber, *Empowering Revolution: America, Poland, and the End of the Cold War*, The New Cold War History (Chapel Hill: University of North Carolina Press, 2014); Christian Philip Peterson, *Globalizing Human Rights: Private Citizens, the Soviet Union, and the West*, Routledge Studies on History and Globalization (New York: Routledge, 2012); Renouard, *Human Rights in American Foreign Policy*. See also the forthcoming book Lauren F. Turek, *To Bring the Good News to All Nations: Evangelicals, Human Rights, and U.S. Foreign Relations* (Ithaca, NY: Cornell University Press, in press).

[25] Thomas W. Zeiler, "The Diplomatic History Bandwagon: A State of the Field," *Journal of American History* 95, no. 4 (2009): 1053–1573. For examples of scholarship on human rights at the grassroots level, see Sarah B. Snyder, *From Selma to Moscow: How Human Rights Activists Transformed U.S. Foreign Policy* (New York: Columbia University Press, 2018); Lauren F. Turek, "To Support a 'Brother in Christ': Evangelical Groups and U.S.–Guatemalan Relations during the Ríos Montt Regime," *Diplomatic History* 39, no. 4 (2015): 689–719; Peter Slezkine, "From Helsinki to Human Rights Watch: How an American Cold War Monitoring Group Became an International Human Rights Institution," *Humanity* 5, no. 3 (2014): 345–370; Barbara J. Keys, "Anti-Torture Politics: Amnesty International, the Greek Junta, and the Origins of the Human Rights 'Boom' in the United States," in *The Human Rights Revolution: An International History*, ed. Akira Iriye, Petra Goedde, and William I. Hitchcock (Oxford: Oxford University Press, 2012), 201–221; Jan Eckel, "The International League for the Rights of Man, Amnesty International, and the Changing Fate of Human Rights Activism from the 1940s through the 1970s," *Humanity* 4, no. 2 (2013): 183–214; Bon Tempo, "From the Center-Right."

grassroots movements, such as members of Congress and career diplomats, remains largely unexamined by historians of American foreign relations concerned with human rights, especially in the 1980s.[26]

Third, this book contributes a new interpretation of the development in the Reagan administration's approach to human rights. Since journalist Tamar Jacoby first pointed to a "Reagan turnaround on human rights" in 1986, scholarly assessments have stressed different factors for this and identified different moments for its occurrence.[27] Beth Fischer argues that the turnaround took place in early 1984, when Reagan softened his approach to the Soviet Union due to heightened fears of nuclear war.[28] Others locate the turnaround during Reagan's second term and explain the change with changes in the foreign policy team as well as Reagan's strengthened position following his reelection and the establishment of a stronger defense posture.[29] Members of Congress are only afforded limited attention in this scholarship. The most notable exception to this is Sarah Snyder, who argues that the Senate Foreign Relations Committee's rejection of Ernest Lefever to head the Human Rights Bureau led the administration to reevaluate its approach to human rights as early as 1981.[30] Building on Snyder's work, this book argues that the administration gradually changed its approach to human rights during 1981. It demonstrates that the seeds for a more assertive human rights policy were present in internal debates in the National Security Council (NSC) as early as February 1981. Finally, it traces how individual members of Congress continued to influence the administration's approach to human rights issues throughout the 1980s.

[26] William Michael Schmidli, *The Fate of Freedom Elsewhere: Human Rights and US Cold War Policy toward Argentina* (Ithaca, NY: Cornell University Press, 2013), 5. The main exceptions are two articles by Barbara J. Keys and Sarah B. Snyder that examines how members of Congress introduced human rights concerns into US foreign policy through hearings and legislation in the 1970s, forcing a reluctant executive branch to employ human rights language. Barbara J. Keys, "Congress, Kissinger, and the Origins of Human Rights Diplomacy," *Diplomatic History* 34, no. 5 (2010): 823–851; Sarah B. Snyder, "'A Call for U.S. Leadership': Congressional Activism on Human Rights," *Diplomatic History* 37, no. 2 (2013): 372–397, as well as two book chapters by Snyder on the 1980s: Snyder, *Human Rights Activism and the End of the Cold War*, 38–52, on the US Helsinki Commission; and Sarah B. Snyder, "The Defeat of Ernest Lefever's Nomination: Keeping Human Rights on the United States Foreign Policy Agenda," in *Challenging U.S. Foreign Policy: America and the World*, ed. Bevan Sewell and Scott Lucas (Basingstoke: Palgrave Macmillan, 2011), 136–161.

[27] Jacoby, "The Reagan Turnaround."

[28] Beth A. Fischer, *The Reagan Reversal: Foreign Policy and the End of the Cold War* (Columbia: University of Missouri Press, 1997), 147–148.

[29] Renouard, *Human Rights in American Foreign Policy*, 198–199. For the latter in relations to Latin America, see Kathryn Sikkink, *Mixed Signals: U.S. Human Rights Policy and Latin America* (Ithaca, NY: Cornell University Press, 2004), 149.

[30] Snyder, "The Defeat of Ernest Lefever's Nomination," 151–152.

Historians have offered a variety of explanations for why Americans began to care about the human rights of people in foreign countries. They have pointed to how the growing human rights consciousness during the 1970s, and one argues in the 1960s, was driven by large transformations abroad and at home. These transformations included decolonization, dissatisfaction with the Vietnam War and US support for anti-communist dictators, the civil rights movement, the rise of human rights NGOs, and increasing interdependence across borders as a result of new technologies.[31] Several of these developments continued to influence American attention to human rights into the 1980s as the salience of human rights reached unprecedented heights in debates over US foreign policy.[32] Moreover, Americans embraced human rights for various ideological, religious, and moral reasons. Often the key motivation was deeply personal brought about by a moving encounter with a victim or a strong identification caused by the person's own lived experience.

Why members of Congress, with busy schedules dominated by constituent concerns and reelection, would devote time to the human rights of people in far-off lands who could not vote for them or make campaign contributions poses an additional puzzle. After all, political scientists in the tradition of rational choice argue that members of Congress are single-minded seekers of reelection and, as a result, we should expect them to devote their time to this objective.[33] Members of Congress are also driven by their desire for power and a wish to do good public policy.[34] Although human rights issues do not appear to fall into either of these categories, a closer look suggests that they can. In some cases, championing a human rights issue could offer political gains with potential electoral rewards if constituents cared sufficiently about the issue. This occurred, in particular, when ethnic and religious groups in home districts mobilized on specific human rights issues.[35] Moreover, some members of Congress had relatively safe seats that allowed them to

---

[31] Keys, *Reclaiming American Virtue*, 3–14; Snyder, *From Selma to Moscow*, 3–6; Mark Philip Bradley, *The World Reimagined: Americans and Human Rights in the Twentieth Century* (New York: Cambridge University Press, 2016), 6–10.

[32] For the importance of the telephone for human rights activism in the 1980s, see Barbara J. Keys, "The Telephone and Its Uses in 1980s U.S. Activism," *The Journal of Interdisciplinary History* 48, no. 4 (2018): 485–509.

[33] David R. Mayhew, *Congress: The Electoral Connection* (New Haven, CT: Yale University Press, 1974).

[34] Richard F. Fenno, *Home Style: House Members in Their Districts* (Boston, MA: Little, Brown, 1978).

[35] Tony Smith, *Foreign Attachments: The Power of Ethnic Groups in the Making of American Foreign Policy* (Cambridge, MA: Harvard University Press, 2000); Andrew Preston, *Sword of the Spirit, Shield of Faith: Religion in American War and Diplomacy* (New York: Alfred A. Knopf, 2012).

dedicate significant attention to their policy interests without concern about reelection. Championing human rights also offered some members of Congress increased political visibility that could translate into both political gains and power.[36] Raising the banner of human rights allowed members to cast themselves as moral leaders in ways that could help them further their political ambitions. In addition, human rights issues offered members interested in foreign affairs a path to shape US foreign policy because Congress had legislated itself into a prominent position on human rights since the mid-1970s. Importantly, several members of Congress genuinely believed the promotion of human rights fell into the category of good public policy. For them, promoting human rights was both morally right and in America's best interest.

Several additional factors shaped how and why members of Congress embraced human rights concerns in general and in specific cases. Just as for ordinary Americans, ideological, religious, and moral reasons informed their positions on human rights issues and often personal experiences was an important catalyst. Moreover, members of Congress had to contend with partisanship, institutional affiliation, and public opinion, which could lead them to both elevate and downplay human rights concerns. Most of the members of Congress and other policy-makers in this book displayed a combination of motivations. This mixture of motivations, and the difficulty of proving their relative importance, makes it difficult to assess the sincerity of human rights activism. A comparison of the case studies reveals a considerable inconsistency in the commitment to human rights from both the Reagan administration and most members of Congress. For most policymakers, human rights essentially constituted a political language that could be invoked to fur-ther specific causes when expedient. Nevertheless, some policymakers were committed to human rights almost across the board. Sometimes opposing sides would both claim to advance the cause of human rights thanks to the flexibility and vagueness of human rights language as well as the complexity of some of the issues.

The book combines chapters on the Reagan administration and the Congressional Human Rights Caucus (CHRC), a new human rights institution created in 1983, with case studies of US policy toward Soviet Jewry, South Africa, and Nicaragua. This structure makes it possible to examine new approaches to human rights in the 1980s in both the executive and legislative branches of government while also analyzing in-depth how members of Congress and the administration contested the

---

[36] David P. Forsythe, *Human Rights and U.S. Foreign Policy: Congress Reconsidered* (Gainesville: University of Florida Press, 1988), 145.

role of human rights in specific foreign policy cases. The purpose of these case study chapters is not primarily to assess the impact of US human rights policy but rather to examine the internal constellation of forces and influences that shaped US human rights policy.[37]

The chosen case studies were among the human rights issues with the strongest resonance in Washington in the 1980s. All three drew considerable attention from members of Congress and the administration and mobilized a range of NGOs and the general public. In short, these cases mattered a great deal to many Americans, and they represent considerable diversity in geographical regions, types of rights, and Cold War positioning, highlighting the range of US human rights policy and revealing similarities and differences. Soviet Jewry represents a human rights issue in the Eastern Bloc very much at the heart of superpower relations, where the key human right in question was the right to emigrate. South Africa exemplifies a human rights issue in an American ally, affected by Cold War contestation but also by decolonization and race, encompassing numerous human rights violations rooted in racial segregation. Nicaragua constitutes a human rights issue steeped in Cold War conflict and the legacy of US interventionism in Latin America, covering a broad range of human rights violations in a region of pivotal concern to the Reagan administration.

The cases also represent different types of human rights policy. In the case of Soviet Jewry, the human rights policy was mostly confined to a combination of diplomacy and condemnation of violations. In the case of South Africa, the debate was over the imposition of economic sanctions. In the case of Nicaragua, human rights were intertwined with debates over foreign aid and US covert operations. Finally, and most importantly for this book, the cases represent different relationships between the Reagan administration and members of Congress. In the selected cases, some members of Congress took very different positions and consequently formed shifting coalitions, depending on the issues. Some members of Congress also changed their positions considerably over time. The diversity of the case studies thus allows the book to demonstrate points of inconsistency and shifting alliances in American policymakers' commitment to human rights. Several other human rights issues

---

[37] Historian Robert McMahon has referred to this approach as the "internalist" approach within diplomatic history, which he contrasts with the "externalist" approach focused on the state and state-to-state relations. Robert J. McMahon, "Diplomatic History and Policy History: Finding Common Ground," *Journal of Policy History* 17, no. 1 (2005): 97. For an example of historical scholarship on US foreign relations with a similar "internalist" approach, see David F. Schmitz, *The United States and Right-Wing Dictatorships, 1965–1989* (New York: Cambridge University Press, 2006).

might have merited attention, including US assistance to Chile and other Latin American allies, battles over human rights certifications of El Salvador and Argentina, US support for the Solidarity labor movement in Poland, the follow-up process to the Helsinki Final Act, and US policy toward strategically important but repressive regimes in South Korea and the Philippines. Some of these, including Poland and a number of Latin American cases, I have omitted to maintain the diversity of my case studies, having already selected Soviet Jewish emigration and Nicaragua. Moreover, some of these cases have already been well covered by existing scholarship such as Sarah B. Snyder on the Helsinki network, Greg Domber on Poland, and Morris Morley and Chris McGillion on Chile.[38] It will be up to future research to add to our knowledge of the important human rights cases not examined in detail in this book.

The book draws on recently declassified records from the Reagan administration and the National Archives, the archives of numerous NGOs concerned with human rights, twenty-one private manuscript collections of members of Congress, most of which has not previously featured in studies of US human rights policy and some of which I am the first to have accessed. This includes the private manuscript collection of Representative Tom Lantos (D-CA), which contains the archives of the CHRC, the most important new congressional human rights institution of the 1980s. Other key collections used include the papers of members of Congress with a particular interest in human rights issues, such as Dante B. Fascell (D-FL), Thomas 'Tip' O'Neill (D-MA), Jack Kemp (R-NY), and leaders of the Congressional Black Caucus (CBC), as well as the archives of key congressional institutions, such as the US Helsinki Commission and the House Foreign Affairs Committee's Subcommittee on Human Rights. Moreover, the book is based on interviews with key officials from the Reagan administration, members of Congress and their staff, and leaders from the human rights community.[39] Using private manuscript collections and NGO archives not subject to public declassification rules has helped me partly circumvent the limitations imposed by classification of government records.[40] This extensive archival research

---

[38] Domber, *Empowering Revolution*; Morris Morley and Chris McGillion, *Reagan and Pinochet: The Struggle over U.S. Policy toward Chile* (New York: Cambridge University Press, 2015); Snyder, *Human Rights Activism*.

[39] For a list of archives and other sources, see the Bibliography.

[40] Most unpublished records from the House and Senate remain closed for thirty and twenty years, respectively. Both chambers, however, have a fifty-year closure period for investigative files containing personal data about a living person or information sensitive to national security. Declassification is further delayed due to the time needed for processing. This means that although records from the 1980s are increasingly being declassified, many remain unavailable.

has allowed me to write a comprehensive account of the role of human rights in US foreign policy that goes beyond the executive branch to include midlevel actors, most notably several previously neglected members of Congress.

Chapter 1 provides the broader context for human rights concerns in American foreign relations in the 1980s. It summarizes the human rights legacy of the 1970s, examines the role of human rights in the 1980 election, introduces key congressional actors concerned with human rights, and surveys attention to human rights generally along with other expressions of morality. Chapter 2 investigates what happened to US human rights policy in the White House after Reagan replaced Carter. It demonstrates how pressure from Congress led the Reagan administration to revise its initial intention to downplay the role of human rights in foreign policy, opting instead to incorporate human rights into its over-arching foreign policy agenda. Chapter 3 examines the establishment and activities of the hitherto neglected CHRC. The chapter assesses the CHRC's attempt to create a bipartisan human rights policy and presents its limitations and main critics. Chapters 4, 5, and 6 offer in-depth case studies of how shifting coalitions among members of Congress and the administration struggled over the role of human rights in some of the most conspicuous foreign policy issues of the 1980s. Chapter 4 investigates US efforts to encourage Soviet Jewish emigration as a fundamental human right. The chapter demonstrates how a large bipartisan coalition of members of Congress and the administration formed a generally cooperative relationship despite some differences on strategy. Chapter 5 investigates the struggle over US policy toward South African apartheid, focusing in particular on the question of economic sanctions. The chapter demonstrates how a growing coalition of members of Congress spear-headed by the CBC framed apartheid as a human rights issue, ultimately leading to the passage of the Comprehensive Anti-Apartheid Act in 1986. Chapter 6 analyzes the battle over US policy toward Nicaragua, in particular, congressional attempts to restrict the Reagan administration's support for the Nicaraguan Contras. The chapter demonstrates how both the administration and its congressional allies on the one side and the predominantly liberal Democrats on the other side used human rights concerns to justify their policy preferences among a range of other frameworks. The book concludes by comparing the case studies to assess what these allow us to infer about the role of human rights in US foreign policy in the 1980s before pointing to the decade's implications for US human rights policy after the end of the Cold War.

1   After the Breakthrough
Human Rights in American Foreign Relations in the 1980s

During the last decade of the Cold War, human rights concerns were interwoven in the fabric of US foreign policy to an unprecedented degree, fueled by the ongoing contestation between the Reagan administration and members of Congress. The increased salience of human rights concerns and their institutionalization in US foreign policy in the 1970s had forced any new administration to consider its approach to human rights issues as an element in its foreign policy. In the 1980 election, where foreign policy featured more prominently than usual, Ronald Reagan attacked Jimmy Carter's human rights–based foreign policy and appealed to yearnings for a more assertive foreign policy amid perceptions of American decline. The election put a president in the White House who was inclined to dismiss human rights concerns as a core element of US foreign policy and who profoundly changed the composition of Congress. The outcome pitted a Republican president and Senate against a Democratic House that grew increasingly assertive about foreign policy including human rights issues. Throughout the decade, members of Congress used existing and new institutions to draw attention to human rights issues, with liberals predominantly concerned with rightwing dictatorships and conservatives mostly preoccupied with communist countries. These different priorities between institutions, party lines, and ideology, along with strong personal motivations, combined to shape American attention to human rights issues during the 1980s. Finally, human rights concerns became intertwined with other expressions of morality in foreign policy, such as peace movements, opposition to nuclear weapons, and the anti-apartheid movement.

The Breakthrough of Human Rights and Its Legacies

Over the course of a few years in the mid-1970s, human rights went from being a virtually unknown concept on the fringes of foreign policy debates to being a celebrated catchphrase trumpeted by a growing number of NGOs, political activists, members of Congress, and eventually the president.[1] Although ideas about individual freedom and rights had been at the heart of America's political culture since the nation's founding and the United States participated in the codification of universal human rights in the 1940s, it was not until the 1970s that human rights gained a firm foothold in US foreign policy. Although human rights did play a role in US foreign policy in some cases in the 1960s, such as the Johnson administration's policy toward Greece and Southern Rhodesia (now Zimbabwe), the United States was not a frontrunner on international human rights during the 1950s and the 1960s, with other countries taking the lead on human rights at the United Nations.[2]

When President Jimmy Carter declared in his inauguration speech on January 20, 1977, "Our commitment to human rights must be absolute," he became the first US president to make the promotion of human rights a top foreign policy priority.[3] Later that same year, the London-based human rights NGO Amnesty International won the Nobel Peace Prize. The arrival of human rights was evident by the dramatic increase in the use of the term in the American press, with the *New York Times* using the term five times more often in 1977 than in any previous year.[4] The point to which the concept of human rights had arrived in American popular culture by 1977 was further underscored by its inclusion as a subject in the immensely popular Pulitzer Prize–winning comic strip *Doonesbury*, which ran in almost all major American newspapers.[5] Noting these dramatic changes, Samuel Moyn argues that 1977 was the breakthrough year for human rights.[6]

The breakthrough, however, began in Congress. During the second Nixon administration, human rights had become part of a congressional assertiveness on foreign policy that generated substantial conflict between the executive and legislative branches of government.[7] Rising in opposition to the imperial presidency of Richard Nixon and reflecting the breakdown of the Cold War foreign policy consensus over the Vietnam War, members of Congress passed a number of measures to restrict

---

[1] Moyn, *Last Utopia*, 147.

[2] Roland Burke, *Decolonization and the Evolution of International Human Rights* (Philadelphia: University of Pennsylvania Press, 2010); Steven L. B. Jensen, *The Making of International Human Rights: The 1960s, Decolonization, and the Reconstruction of Global Values* (New York: Cambridge University Press, 2016); Sarah B. Snyder, "The Rise of Human Rights During the Johnson Years," in *Beyond the Cold War*, ed. Francis J. Gavin and Mark Atwood Lawrence (Oxford: Oxford University Press, 2014), 237–260.

[3] Jimmy Carter, Inaugural Address, January 20, 1977. Online by Gerhard Peters and John T. Woolley, The American Presidency Project, accessed August 7, 2019, www.presidency .ucsb.edu/node/241475.

[4] Moyn, *Last Utopia*, 4.   [5] Bradley, *The World Reimagined*, 196–197.

[6] Moyn, *Last Utopia*, 129.

[7] Robert David Johnson, *Congress and the Cold War* (New York: Cambridge University Press, 2006), 190–241.

the presidency's prerogatives on foreign policy, including legislation tying elements of US foreign relations to other countries' respect for human rights.[8] Both the Nixon administration and later the Ford administration resisted this congressional intrusion into foreign policy, with Secretary of State Henry Kissinger particularly reluctant to cooperate with Congress on human rights policy. This resistance, however, only provoked members of Congress to push human rights legislation even further.[9] As a result, the executive branch found itself largely on the sidelines, as Congress became the dominant branch of government concerned with human rights issues.

The drivers of this congressional activism on human rights were a few individuals who held hearings and passed legislation, introducing human rights concerns into US foreign policy. Representative Donald M. Fraser (D-MN) initiated the first hearings on international human rights issues in 1973 in his House Foreign Affairs Subcommittee on International Organizations and Social Movements. Over the course of five years, Fraser's subcommittee held a series of hearings, as Congress reduced foreign aid to some countries deemed to be committing gross human rights violations and linked US trade relations to the respect for human rights.[10] In addition to such general legislation, Congress passed several country-specific measures that cut off or reduced assistance to specific countries, including Argentina, Chile, El Salvador, the Philippines, South Korea, and Uruguay.[11] In March 1974, Fraser's subcommittee published a report calling for the United States to take the lead on international human rights and detailing twenty-nine recommendations for integrating human rights concerns in US foreign policymaking.[12]

---

[8] Congressional assertiveness on foreign policy also included a ban on further bombing of Cambodia, as well as the War Powers Resolution of 1973, which limited the president's power to deploy military forces without congressional consent.

[9] Keys, "Congress, Kissinger, and the Origins of Human Rights Diplomacy," 825.

[10] The most important of this legislation was Section 502B of the 1974 Foreign Assistance Act, which restricted security assistance to governments with a consistent pattern of gross human rights violations, and the Harkin Amendment to the 1975 International Development and Food Assistance Act, which extended these restrictions to economic assistance. Forsythe, *Human Rights and U.S. Foreign Policy*, 1–23.

[11] Stephen B. Cohen, "Conditioning U.S. Security Assistance on Human Rights Practices," *American Journal of International Law* 76, no. 2 (1982): 254.

[12] US Congress, *Human Rights in the World Community: A Call for U.S. Leadership* (Washington, DC: US Government Printing Office, 1974). Barbara J. Keys, William Michael Schmidli, and Sarah B. Snyder have all demonstrated the importance of the report, hearings, and legislation, pointing to how it helped institutionalize human rights concerns in US foreign policy and formed the basis for Carter's embrace of human rights. Keys, "Congress, Kissinger, and the Origins of Human Rights Diplomacy"; William Michael Schmidli, "Institutionalizing Human Rights in U.S. Foreign Policy: U.S.–Argentine Relations, 1976–1980," *Diplomatic History* 35, no. 2 (2011): 351–377; Snyder, "'A Call for U.S. Leadership.'"

Under growing congressional pressure, the executive branch accommodated several of these recommendations, including the establishment of a Human Rights Bureau in the State Department in 1976 and the assignment of human rights officers to all its regional bureaus. Congress also mandated that the executive branch deliver annual reports to Congress on the human rights situation in countries receiving US aid.[13]

The members of Congress who introduced human rights concerns into US foreign policy differed in their background, ideology, and motivations. Fraser and other liberal Democrats wanted to stop US support for repressive regimes, such as the Dominican Republic, Chile, and Greece.[14] Fraser came to see hearings on human rights issues as a way to call attention to such issues and possibly develop a more bipartisan approach to human rights grounded on objective measures.[15] Other liberal Democrats, such as Edward (Ted) Kennedy (D-MA), James Abourezk (D-SD), and Alan Cranston (D-CA) in the Senate and Tom Harkin (D-IA) in the House, had similar motives.

Yet members of Congress targeting the Soviet Union and other communist countries also embraced human rights concerns. These anti-communists were generally much less willing than their liberal counterparts to criticize human rights violations by American allies. The most significant proponent of this position was the conservative Democratic Senator Henry M. "Scoop" Jackson (D-WA), who introduced the Jackson–Vanik Amendment, which prohibited the granting of most-favored-nation status and trade credit to communist countries that denied or restricted the right to emigration. Aside from his deep-felt anti-communism and opposition to détente, Jackson believed that his human rights stand against the Soviet Union could help him in a future presidential run by raising support from American Jews and others critical of Soviet emigration restrictions.[16] Moderate figures in both parties, such as Republican Senator Jacob Javits

---

[13] The country reports were later expanded to include all countries, made public, and greatly improved in both scope and details. Judith Innes de Neufville, "Human Rights Reporting as a Policy Tool: An Examination of the State Department Country Reports," *Human Rights Quarterly* 8, no. 4 (1986): 681–682; Rasmus Sinding Søndergaard, "'A Positive Track of Human Rights Policy': Elliott Abrams, the Human Rights Bureau and the Conceptualization of Democracy Promotion," in *The Reagan Administration, the Cold War and the Transition to Democracy Promotion*, ed. William Michael Schmidli and Robert Pee (New York: Palgrave Macmillan, 2019), 31–50.

[14] For an examination of Fraser's motivations, see Keys, *Reclaiming American Virtue*, 77–84.

[15] Snyder, "'A Call for U.S. Leadership,'" 376–378.

[16] Robert Gordon Kaufman, *Henry M. Jackson: A Life in Politics* (Seattle: University of Washington Press, 2000), 266–283. Several members of Jackson's staff, such as Elliott Abrams, Richard Perle, and Paul Wolfowitz, would become leading neoconservatives and go on to occupy senior foreign policy positions, first in the Reagan administration and later the George W. Bush administration.

(R-NY) and the Democratic Representative Dante Fascell (D-FL), also supported anti-communist human rights efforts, while being at least somewhat more restrained in their criticism of American allies.[17]

Despite their different agendas, members of Congress were often able to find common ground on human rights issues. An important reason for this was that conservatives who wanted to cut foreign aid would join liberals in their quests to cut assistance for human rights-violating dictators. In turn, most liberals were willing to support measures against the Soviet Union, despite their principal focus on repressive regimes allied with the United States. Finally, those advocating for human rights were able to take advantage of a broad-based desire to constrain the executive branch and wider opposition to détente.[18]

The legacy of congressional human rights activism in the 1970s tells us three important lessons about congressional involvement with human rights that would continue into the 1980s. First, they testify to the diversity of the motivations behind members of Congress engaged in promoting human rights. Second, they demonstrate the selective adoption of human rights concerns, as members would apply the language of universal human rights to particular agendas of their concern and often stay passive on other issues. Finally, they show the importance of individual members of Congress as foreign policy entrepreneurs who wielded influence beyond their formal powers when they succeeded in forging coalitions behind their human rights positions.[19]

Human rights reached unprecedented heights as a US foreign policy when Carter embraced human rights as the moral language to restore the country's sense of virtue and the guideline for its role in the world in the aftermath of the Vietnam War.[20] Moreover, Carter's human rights based-foreign policy was aimed at resetting America's relations with the world by transcending Cold War contestation and improving relations with specific regions, such as Latin America.[21] In US–Soviet relations,

---

[17] Dante Fascell became a leading figure on human rights issues in the 1980s as chair of the House Foreign Affairs Committee, where he often sided with the Republicans, in particular on policy toward Latin America.

[18] For the liberal critique of right-wing dictatorships and the anti-communist embrace of human rights, see Keys, *Reclaiming American Virtue*, 75–126.

[19] Carter and Scott, *Choosing to Lead*.

[20] Campbell Craig and Fredrik Logevall, *America's Cold War: The Politics of Insecurity* (Cambridge, MA: Harvard University Press, 2009), 292–295.

[21] This aim was illustrated by Carter's unprecedented decision to supplement his inaugural address with a recorded speech addressing the world. Jimmy Carter, United States Foreign Policy Remarks to People of Other Nations on Assuming Office, January 20, 1977. Online by Gerhard Peters and John T. Woolley, The American Presidency Project (accessed August 7, 2019), www.presidency.ucsb.edu/node/242950.

human rights concerns were pursed in combination with détente. In relations with the so-called Third World, a human rights-based policy meant criticism of authoritarian regimes including American allies but also nonintervention.[22] In other words, Carter's human rights-based foreign policy sought to implement the liberal critique of right-wing dictatorships in practice. As Barbara J. Keys points out, Carter's religious beliefs and his interpretation of the civil rights movement made him predisposed to a moralistic foreign policy, but he was slow to adopt human rights language and only did so because he found that it resonated with the public.[23] Although he experienced significant difficulties implementing human rights into foreign policy, Carter played a pivotal role in elevating human rights in the national political debate. Throughout the Carter years, NGOs and members of Congress remained important actors on human rights policy, passing legislation that reduced economic assistance to the Philippines and pushing for sanctions against Uganda due to human rights violations.[24] However, by the end of Carter's presidency, the perceived failure of his foreign policy as well as his presidency overall left American commitment to human rights in the balance.[25]

---

[22] Schmitz and Walker, "Jimmy Carter and the Foreign Policy of Human Rights." For how Carter's emphasis on nonintervention defined his policy toward Nicaragua, see William Michael Schmidli, "'The Most Sophisticated Intervention We Have Seen': The Carter Administration and the Nicaraguan Crisis, 1978–1979," *Diplomacy & Statecraft* 23, no. 1 (2012): 66–86.

[23] Keys, *Reclaiming American Virtue*, 231–241. Influenced by theologian Reinhold Niebuhr's Christian realism, Carter believed the world could not be cleared of injustice but that particular wrongs could be amended – a worldview that fit well with the limited agenda of human rights. As a Southerner supportive of desegregation, Carter also believed that external coercion from the federal government had helped white Southerners to confront their past without losing face – a belief that would inform his approach to promoting human rights abroad.

[24] The most important human rights legislation passed during the Carter years was a section to the International Financial Assistance Act of 1977, which put human rights restrictions on US votes in international financial institutions. Forsythe, *Human Rights and U.S. Foreign Policy*, 11.

[25] The verdict on Carter's human rights policy remains contested among historians, often shaped by ideological perspectives. Most early scholarly assessments were generally critical, accusing Carter's policy of being naive and unsuccessful, whereas historians in the post–Cold War era have been somewhat more positive, giving Carter credit for attempting to move beyond anti-communism. For critical assessments, see Joshua Muravchik, *The Uncertain Crusade: Jimmy Carter and the Dilemmas of Human Rights Policy* (Lanham, MD: Hamilton, 1986); Gaddis Smith, *Morality, Reason, and Power: American Diplomacy in the Carter Years* (New York: Hill & Wang, 1986). For largely positive assessments, see John Dumbrell, *The Carter Presidency: A Re-Evaluation* (Manchester: Manchester University Press, 1995); Mary E. Stuckey, *Jimmy Carter, Human Rights, and the National Agenda* (College Station: Texas A&M University Press, 2008).

Human Rights and the 1980 Election

Although domestic economic problems such as high inflation and unemployment rates dominated the 1980 presidential election, foreign policy, including human rights issues, also received considerable attention.[26] In particular, the ongoing Iran hostage crisis after Iranian students took fifty-two Americans hostage at the American embassy in Tehran on November 4, 1979, drew attention to foreign affairs. This crisis was set in the wider context of the heating up of the Cold War, following the Soviet invasion of Afghanistan in December 1979 and a number of advances by Soviet-supported guerrillas throughout the Third World.[27] Moreover, the United States lost a strong ally in Nicaragua, where the left-wing Sandinistas had taken power after the toppling of Anastasio Somoza in July 1979. Political opponents and several contemporary observers blamed Carter's human rights policy for contributing to these developments by allegedly undermining American allies and demonstrating a weakness that emboldened the Soviets.[28] Combined with the economic crisis, the country's foreign policy woes fed a growing sense among many Americans that American power was in decline.

Each candidate believed that foreign policy was a weakness for his opponent. Beset by economic problems at home, Carter sought to move the focus away from being a referendum on his own record to focus instead on the shortcomings of his opponent. The Carter campaign believed that Reagan's inexperience in international affairs and his reputation as a Cold War hardliner made him vulnerable in the area of foreign policy. During the campaign, Carter repeatedly painted a picture of Reagan as a dangerous warmonger who would cause war with the Soviet Union, framing the election as a choice that would determine "whether we have war or peace."[29] Essentially, the Carter campaign ran a strategy

---

[26] In 1980, the average inflation rate was as high as 13.5 percent, unemployment reached 8 percent, and interest rates soared to 18.5 percent. James T. Patterson, *Restless Giant: The United States from Watergate to Bush v. Gore* (New York: Oxford University Press, 2005), 148.

[27] During 1979, Soviet-supported groups made strong gains in Ethiopia, Angola, and Mozambique and communist Vietnam took over Cambodia.

[28] See, for instance, Jeane J. Kirkpatrick, "Dictatorships and Double Standards," *Commentary* 68, no. 5 (1979): 34–45; Robert W. Tucker, "America in Decline: The Foreign Policy of 'Maturity,'" *Foreign Affairs* 58, no. 3 (1980): 449–484; Norman Podhoretz, "The Present Danger," *Commentary* 69, no. 3 (1980): 27–40.

[29] Edward Walsh, "Carter to Return to 'Peace or War' Issue," *The Washington Post*, September 28, 1980, Nexis Uni; Lou Cannon and Edward Walsh, "War, Peace Dominate Debate War and Peace Theme Dominates Carter-Reagan Debate," *The Washington Post*, October 29, 1980.

designed to frighten the electorate about Reagan rather than seeking to vindicate the president's record.

The Reagan campaign conversely believed that it could exploit the growing perception that Carter was weak on foreign policy and that the international standing of the United States was on the decline. Criticizing Carter's human rights policy figured prominently in this strategy. In 1978, Reagan had described Carter's human rights-based foreign policy as "well-meaning intentions" mixed with a "false sense of guilt" after Vietnam, but by 1980 he struck an even harder line.[30] During the only presidential debate between the two major candidates on October 28, 1980, only a week before the election, Reagan attacked Carter for criticizing the human rights abuses of allies while at the same time seeking détente with the Soviet Union. Reagan lamented that Carter's policy toward allied authoritarian regimes had "in a number of instances, aided a revolutionary overthrow which results in complete totalitarianism."[31] Arguing that Carter's human rights policy had "undercut our friends," Reagan blamed Carter for the fall of American allies such as Somoza in Nicaragua and Mohammad Reza Pahlavi, the Shah of Iran.[32] Along with the Iran hostage crisis and the Soviet invasion of Afghanistan, Reagan's attack on Carter's human rights policy painted a picture of Carter as a weak leader who was unable to withstand communist aggression and Islamic fundamentalism and who failed to support America's allies (Figure 1).

While the Soviet invasion of Afghanistan in 1979 had caused Carter to moderate his foreign policy by stressing a tougher approach to the Cold War, he did not completely abandon his support for human rights concerns in US foreign policy. Carter's human rights policy had focused on détente with the Soviet Union and the promotion of human rights with authoritarian allies in the Third World. The Soviet invasion of Afghanistan effectively destroyed détente, and the overthrow of repressive but US-friendly regimes in Teheran and Managua by forces hostile to the United States demonstrated the risks of criticizing authoritarian allies. Carter responded by hardening his rhetoric toward the Soviet Union, withdrawing from the Strategic Arms Limitations Treaty II (SALT II) negotiations, and boycotting the 1980 Moscow

---

[30] Peterson, *Globalizing Human Rights*, 107.

[31] Quoted in Jimmy Carter, Presidential Debate in Cleveland, October 28, 1980. Online by Gerhard Peters and John T. Woolley, The American Presidency Project, accessed August 7, 2019, www.presidency.ucsb.edu/node/217132.

[32] James Peck, *Ideal Illusions: How the U.S. Government Co-Opted Human Rights* (New York: Metropolitan, 2010), 85.

Figure 1 President Ronald Reagan meets with Jimmy Carter in the
Oval Office of the White House, October 14, 1981.
Bettmann via Getty Images.

Olympics. Yet the Carter administration continued to view human
rights concerns as an important element of US policy toward the Soviet
Union as well as US-friendly regimes, such as Chile, South Korea, and
the Philippines.[33]

Despite Carter's alterations to his human rights policy, the Reagan
campaign maintained that the Carter administration was too soft on the
Soviet Union and too hard on American allies. A Reagan administration,
they claimed, would transform the human rights theme into an instrument to counter Soviet propaganda.[34] Reagan also sought to link America's foreign policy tribulations with domestic economic problems. In his
final statement during the presidential debate, Reagan addressed the
sense of decline by urging the American people to ask themselves, "Are

[33] US Department of State, *Foreign Relations of the United States, 1977–1980, Volume II,
Human Rights and Humanitarian Affairs* (Washington, DC: US Government Printing
Office, 2013), Document 206; Schmitz and Walker, "Jimmy Carter and the Foreign
Policy of Human Rights," 137.
[34] Richard Burt, "Presidential Candidates Stake out Divergent Ground on Foreign
Policy," *The New York Times*, October 19, 1980, 1.

you better off than you were four years ago? Is it easier for you to go and buy things in the stores than it was four years ago? Is there more or less unemployment in the country than there was four years ago? Is America as respected throughout the world as it was? Do you feel that our security is as safe, that we're as strong as we were four years ago?"[35] With Carter's so-called misery index (the combination of inflation and unemployment numbers) peaking at 20.76 in 1980 and the foreign policy embarrassments of Afghanistan and Iran fresh in mind, many Americans decided they could not answer Reagan's questions affirmatively.[36]

The party platforms from the Republican and Democratic National Conventions also testified to the increased attention to human rights. While party platforms do not dictate an administration's foreign policy, they do represent a party's attempt to compromise on a shared set of policy positions. As such, party platforms represent an interesting document attesting to what the different factions of a party can agree on among themselves. Comparing their attention to issues over time offers a glimpse into a party's shifting priorities and positions beyond the scope of the party's presidential candidates. In 1976, both the Republican and Democratic platforms only sparsely mentioned human rights, with three and six mentions, respectively.[37] In both cases, human rights were used to express criticism of détente and the realpolitik of the Nixon administration. In the Republican platform, the appearance of human rights language was also a reflection of the internal power struggle in the party, where a faction supporting Reagan's candidacy used human rights to attack the détente policy associated with President Gerald R. Ford.

In 1980, the Democratic platform hailed the merits of Carter's human rights policy, making no less than thirty-six mentions of human rights, while the Republican platform attacked this policy, making a total of nine

---

[35] Quoted in Jimmy Carter, Presidential Debate in Cleveland, October 28, 1980. Online by Gerhard Peters and John T. Woolley, The American Presidency Project, accessed August 7, 2019, www.presidency.ucsb.edu/node/217132.

[36] United States Misery Index, accessed August 2, 2019, www.miseryindex.us/indexbyyear.aspx. In a move characteristic of his wit, Reagan quipped during the campaign, "A recession is when your neighbor loses his job. A depression is when you lose yours. And recovery is when Jimmy Carter loses his." Ronald Reagan, Remarks at Liberty State Park, Jersey City New Jersey, September 1, 1980. Online by Gerhard Peters and John T. Woolley, The American Presidency Project, accessed August 7, 2019, www.presidency.ucsb.edu/node/285596.

[37] Republican Party Platforms, Republican Party Platform of 1976, August 18, 1976. Online by Gerhard Peters and John T. Woolley, The American Presidency Project, accessed August 7, 2019, www.presidency.ucsb.edu/node/273415. Democratic Party Platforms, 1976 Democratic Party Platform, July 12, 1976. Online by Gerhard Peters and John T. Woolley, The American Presidency Project, accessed August 7, 2019, www.presidency.ucsb.edu/node/273251.

references to human rights.[38] The Democratic platform proclaimed the party's continued commitment to work to "foster the principles set out in the Universal Declaration of Human Rights."[39] The platform stressed the need to be vigilant on human rights violations among allies as well as among enemies. The day after the release of the party platform, Carter defeated Senator Edward Kennedy to win the Democratic nomination for president. In spite of the setbacks to Carter's foreign policy in the preceding years, the 1980 Democratic National Convention thus signaled a continued commitment to Carter's human rights policy within the Democratic Party. The 1980 Republican platform launched a full-scale attack on Carter's human rights policy, arguing that Carter had been too tough on America's allies while failing to crack down on communist human rights offenders, such as the Soviet Union, Vietnam, and Cuba. "The nations of South and Central America," the platform declared, "have been battered by the Carter Administration's economic and diplomatic sanctions linked to its undifferentiated charges of human rights violations."[40] Specifically, the platform lamented Carter's failure to prevent the Sandinista coup against Anastasio Somoza in Nicaragua. The platform promised that a Republican president would rectify Carter's policy on Nicaragua by countering Soviet influence in the country and supporting "a free and independent government" in Nicaragua.[41]

The 1980 election had a higher percentage of newspaper editorials devoted to foreign affairs than had the previous four elections.[42] According to a contemporary study, foreign policy received more newspaper coverage than did domestic and economic issues combined.[43]

---

[38] Republican Party Platforms, Republican Party Platform of 1980, July 15, 1980. Online by Gerhard Peters and John T. Woolley, The American Presidency Project, accessed August 7, 2019, www.presidency.ucsb.edu/node/273420. Democratic Party Platforms, 1980 Democratic Party Platform, August 11, 1980. Online by Gerhard Peters and John T. Woolley, The American Presidency Project, accessed August 7, 2019, www .presidency.ucsb.edu/node/273253.

[39] Democratic Party Platforms, 1980 Democratic Party Platform, August 11, 1980.

[40] Republican Party Platforms, Republican Party Platform of 1980, July 15, 1980.

[41] Ibid.

[42] David S. Myers, "Editorials and Foreign Affairs in Recent Presidential Campaigns," *Journalism Quarterly* 59, no. 4 (1982): 542. The study compared the editorials of ten leading newspapers in the months before the elections of 1964, 1968, 1972, 1976, and 1980.

[43] James Glen Stovall, "Foreign Policy Issue Coverage in the 1980 Presidential Campaign," *Journalism Quarterly* 59, no. 4 (1982): 533–534. The study coded a total of 757 campaign events in forty-nine daily newspapers from September 3 to November 4, 1980. It found that the majority of events concerned the campaign such as comments about the opponents and endorsements. Of the events concerned with policy issues the study found: 118 foreign affairs events (15 percent), sixty-two domestic (8.2 percent), and twenty-six economic (3.4 percent).

Moreover, the study found that four foreign policy issues dominated the coverage: the Iran hostage crisis, the development of stealth aircraft, the SALT II negotiations with the Soviet Union, and the question of war and peace. The Iran hostage crisis, in particular, dominated the news cycle and was the favored topic for newspaper front pages.[44] It also dominated evening news reports, which continually reminded viewers of the number of days the American hostages had been held captive.[45] The coverage was further amplified just before the election, as Election Day fell on the one-year anniversary of the taking of the hostages.

Moreover, contemporary polls and studies indicate that while the economy was the most important issue for voters, foreign policy mattered a great deal to a large part of the electorate. In one study, 56 percent of voters sad the economy was the most important issue, but 32 percent answered foreign policy – a marked increase from a mere 4 percent in the previous election.[46] Foreign policy was decisive for the election because of the large differences between the candidates' foreign policies and the high salience of certain foreign policy issues.[47] First and foremost, it was the Iran hostage crisis that haunted Carter. Initially, the crisis benefitted Carter's popularity as the American people rallied behind their leader, but the continued failure to secure the release of the hostages and Reagan's critique of this turned the issue against Carter.[48] Foreign policy mattered in the 1980 election and international developments worked in Reagan's favor, most clearly illustrated by the release of all hostages the day after Reagan's inauguration, despite hectic efforts by the Carter administration to secure release before stepping down.[49]

Reagan won the election in an unexpected landslide, taking 51 percent of the popular vote against Carter's 41 percent, and the independent

---

[44] Ibid., 540.

[45] Gil Troy, *Morning in America: How Ronald Reagan Invented the 1980s* (Princeton, NJ: Princeton University Press, 2005), 31.

[46] Andrew Busch, *Reagan's Victory: The Presidential Election of 1980 and the Rise of the Right* (Lawrence: University Press of Kansas, 2005), 130.

[47] Stephen Hess and Michael Nelson, "Foreign Policy: Dominance and Decisiveness in Presidential Elections," in *The Election of 1984*, ed. Michael Nelson (Washington, DC: Congressional Quarterly Press, 1985), 143; John H. Aldrich, John L. Sullivan, and Borgida Eugene, "Foreign Affairs and Issue Voting: Do Presidential Candidates 'Waltz before a Blind Audience?'" *The American Political Science Review* 83, no. 1 (1989): 136.

[48] Robert Mason, "The Domestic Politics of War and Peace: Jimmy Carter, Ronald Reagan, and the Election of 1980," in *US Presidential Elections and Foreign Policy* (Lexington: University Press of Kentucky, 2017), 252.

[49] Toward the end of the campaign, the Reagan camp was increasingly worried that Carter would secure the release of the hostages in a so-called October surprise that could provide the incumbent a last-minute popularity boost.

candidate John Anderson picking up close to 7 percent. The victory was even more comfortable measured in electoral votes, where Reagan secured 489 electoral votes against Carter's forty-nine. The Republican Party also took control over the Senate for the first time since 1955 and decreased the Democratic majority in the House by thirty-four seats. In the months leading up to the election, however, a Reagan victory did not appear to be a foregone conclusion. Polls generally indicated a closer race, and only one week before the election a Gallup poll among registered voters even gave Carter 47 percent of the votes and Reagan only 39 percent.[50] Contemporary observers described the election result a massive shift to the right, and Republicans and conservatives were understandably ecstatic about their electoral victory.[51]

However, the landslide was less resounding than it appeared and, despite the contemporary interpretations, Reagan's victory was not an indication of the American electorate enthusiastically embracing conservatism.[52] In the year of conservatism's biggest triumph, only 32 percent of Americans self-identified as conservative.[53] Americans were clearly disgruntled with the malaise of the Carter years and desperate to try something new, but the election result was as much a rejection of Carter as it was an embrace of Reagan.[54] Reagan offered a refreshing optimism and a promise of restoring Americans' confidence in themselves and their country. Still, Reagan's victory came during an election that had the lowest voter turnout since 1924 – only a little above 52 percent, reflecting the general lack of enthusiasm among the population.[55] As Reagan would soon learn, there were limits to how far the American people were willing to "turn right." In a similar vein, Americans might have been ready for a restoration of America's image abroad, but this did not mean they were ready to abandon human rights.

While there were limits to the conservative turn, the 1980 election did signify a rightward move with regards to foreign policy, which had important implication for US human rights policy. Amid concerns over American decline, an increasing number of American's rejected the

---

[50] "Late Upsets Are Rare, but Have Happened," Gallup, October 24–26, 1980, accessed August 2, 2019, www.gallup.com/poll/111451/late-upsets-rare-happened.aspx.
[51] See, for instance, David S. Broder, "A Sharp Right Turn," *The Washington Post*, November 6, 1980, 2; Hedrick Smith, "A Turning Point Seen," *The New York Times*, November 6, 1980, A1.
[52] Troy, *Morning in America*, 49.
[53] Cheryl Hudson and Gareth Davies, eds., *Ronald Reagan and the 1980s: Perceptions, Policies, Legacies* (New York, NY: Palgrave Macmillan, 2008), 45.
[54] Schaller, *Right Turn*, 47; Mason, "The Domestic Politics of War and Peace," 265.
[55] Douglas Brinkley, *The Unfinished Presidency: Jimmy Carter's Journey beyond the White House* (New York: Viking, 1998), 3.

policy of détente for a more interventionist and assertive foreign policy. This trend had been developing throughout the 1970s. The Soviet invasion of Afghanistan in 1979 ended the search for a centrist consensus on national security among Democrats and moderate Republicans that had stretched from the détente of Nixon and Ford to Carter's human rights policy. The breakdown of this search for a consensus in 1979 deepened divisions over foreign policy among Democrats and fostered a new unity in the Republican Party.[56] This breakdown coincided with a resurgence of a foreign policy of conservative internationalism fuelled by the rise of the New Right and the migration of neoconservatives from the Democratic Party to the Republican Party.[57] This shift in party alignments and a general shift toward a more interventionist foreign policy was to have significant implications for the role of human rights concerns in US foreign policy.

Congress and Human Rights in the 1980s

While the 1980 election brought a new approach to human rights into the White House, it also profoundly altered the composition of the legislative branch of government. The election further shifted the internal power balance within Congress from the Senate to the House.[58] The 1978 congressional elections had already turned the Senate more conservative, less active on foreign affairs, and less ideologically consistent.[59] When Republicans won control of the Senate in 1980, in an election that also brought a Republican into the White House, it became apparent that the Senate would be reluctant to criticize the administration too vigorously. While individual Republicans would occasionally defy the administration, the Senate leadership generally backed Reagan's foreign policy. Senate Majority Leader from 1981 to 1985, Howard Baker Jr. (R-TN) went on to serve as Reagan's White House Chief of Staff from 1987 to 1988. His replacement, the conservative Robert Dole (R-KS), also supported Reagan and enjoyed the president's trust, despite having

---

[56] Julian E. Zelizer, "Conservatives, Carter, and the Politics of National Security," in *Rightward Bound: Making America Conservative in the 1970s*, ed. Bruce J. Schulman and Julian E. Zelizer (Cambridge, MA: Harvard University Press, 2008), 265–287.

[57] Henry R. Nau, *Conservative Internationalism: Armed Diplomacy under Jefferson, Polk, Truman, and Reagan* (Princeton, NJ: Princeton University Press, 2013), 2. According to Nau, conservative internationalism seeks to spread freedom, arm diplomacy, and preserve national sovereignty.

[58] Lindsay, *Congress and the Politics of U.S. Foreign Policy*, 57.

[59] Johnson, *Congress and the Cold War*, 242; Lindsay, *Congress and the Politics of U.S. Foreign Policy*, 31.

unsuccessfully challenged him for the Republican nomination.[60] Strongly partisan and influential in the Republican Party, Dole became an immensely powerful presence in the Senate throughout the 1980s. Moreover, prominent liberal Democrats such as Frank Church (D-ID) and George McGovern (D-SD), who had been strong human rights advocates, lost their seats.

The hitherto powerful Senate Foreign Relations Committee lost most of its influence in the 1980s as it suffered from ideological divisions and legislative disarray.[61] It had no subcommittee devoted to human rights and the full committee devoted as little as one staff member to human rights issues. Human rights action in the Senate thus relied on the personal commitment of individuals, without any significant institutional support.[62] From 1981 to 1987, moderate Republicans, who were disinclined to confront a popular Republican president, chaired the Senate Foreign Relations Committee. The first of these, Charles H. Percy (R-IL), demonstrated an interest in human rights issues especially in the Eastern Bloc. His successor, Richard Lugar (R-IN), became an important link between the administration and its critics in Congress, when he became involved with human rights issues in US foreign policy toward the Philippines and South Africa from the mid-1980s onward.[63] When the Democrats regained the Senate majority in 1987, the chairmanship passed to the liberal Claiborne Pell (D-RI), who was in diametric opposition to Reagan in terms of ideology. A strong opponent of the Vietnam War and an idealist committed to world peace, Pell always carried a copy of the UN Charter in his suit pocket, but he was also nonconfrontational by nature and, thus, often moderated his criticism of the administration.[64] Therefore, it mostly befell other liberal Democrats, such as Edward Kennedy and Christopher Dodd (D-CT), to contest Reagan's human rights policy in the Senate.[65] These liberals were met by strong opposition from conservative senators, such as Jesse Helms (R-NC) and Malcolm Wallop (R-WY), who believed the United

---

[60] Johnson, *Congress and the Cold War*, 282. Reagan, for instance, sent Dole as his envoy to the Vatican in 1985 in an attempt to convince the pope to support his Nicaragua policy.

[61] Ibid., 252.   [62] Forsythe, *Human Rights and U.S. Foreign Policy*, 141–142.

[63] John Shaw, *Richard G. Lugar, Statesman of the Senate: Crafting Foreign Policy from Capitol Hill* (Bloomington: Indiana University Press, 2012), 33–35. Unfortunately, the private papers of Richard Lugar are not currently available.

[64] G. Wayne Miller, *An Uncommon Man: The Life & Times of Senator Claiborne Pell* (Lebanon, NH: University Press of New England, 2011), 241–244.

[65] Unfortunately, the papers of Christopher Dodd are currently unavailable and the papers of Edward Kennedy are only open in part, with very little material on the 1980s yet available.

States should reserve human rights criticism for the Soviet Union and other communist countries. On some issues, such as economic sanctions against South Africa, moderate Republicans such as Lugar and Nancy Kassebaum (R-KS) eventually broke the party ranks to side with their liberal colleagues.[66]

With a Republican majority in the Senate, House Democrats formed the natural vanguard of congressional opposition to the Reagan administration, and the Democratic leadership showed great willingness to challenge the president on foreign policy, including on human rights issues.[67] As Speaker of the House from 1977 to 1987, "Tip" O'Neill (D-MA) was at the forefront of this opposition.[68] A liberal Democrat and a critic of American militarism since the early days of the Vietnam War, O'Neill often clashed with Reagan's foreign policy, especially on Central America and human rights issues. The House Majority Leader from 1977 to 1987 and later Speaker of the House from 1987 to 1989, Jim Wright (D-TX) was a less outspoken critic of Reagan's human rights policy, but he challenged the administration on Nicaragua when he took the initiative to mediate in the conflict in 1987.[69] Republican members of the House generally supported Reagan's foreign policy, but given the comfortable Democratic majority, they had limited influence. Throughout Reagan's tenure, Minority Leader Robert H. Michel (R-IL) formally led House Republicans, but on several issues, the increasingly powerful newcomer Newt Gingrich (R-GA) was the GOP's dominant figure in the House. Strongly conservative and willing to use aggressive tactics, Gingrich formed the Conservative Opportunity Society to challenge the Republican establishment and push the party to the right.[70]

Human rights enjoyed a much stronger institutional footing in the House than in the Senate. As its counterpart in the Senate diminished in influence, the House Foreign Affairs Committee took on a more

---

[66] Robert David Johnson, "Congress and the Cold War," *Journal of Cold War Studies* 3, no. 2 (2001): 99.

[67] Lindsay, *Congress and the Politics of U.S. Foreign Policy*, 31, 57, 70.

[68] Robert C. Byrd and Thomas P. O'Neill, Press Release, March 31, 1982, Box 17, Folder 13, Thomas P. O'Neill, Jr. Congressional Papers (CA2009-01), John J. Burns Library, Boston College (hereafter TOP).

[69] Carter and Scott, *Choosing to Lead*, 138–151; Lindsay, *Congress and the Politics of U.S. Foreign Policy*, 72. Jim Wright became the first Speaker of the House to resign because of scandal when he stepped down in 1989 following accusations of financial impropriety.

[70] Julian E. Zelizer, *Arsenal of Democracy: The Politics of National Security from World War II to the War on Terrorism* (New York: Basic, 2010), 314; Meg Jacobs and Julian E. Zelizer, *Conservatives in Power: The Reagan Years, 1981–1989: A Brief History with Documents* (Boston, MA: Bedford/St. Martin's, 2011), 36.

prominent role, with an expanding staff of which several were dedicated to human rights issues.[71] In 1983, Fascell, a long-term human rights advocate, began what would become a ten-year reign as chair of the House Foreign Affairs Committee. Replacing the deceased Clement Zablocki (D-WI), Fascell greatly increased the committee's attention to human rights issues. The Subcommittee on Human Rights continued to be the logical forum for human rights issues in the House. Its chair from 1979 to 1982, Don Bonker (D-WA) was particularly outspoken in his criticism of the Reagan administration's initial attempts to downgrade concerns for human rights. Although his replacement, the more conservative Gus Yatron (D-PA), was less assertive in challenging the administration, Yatron expanded the subcommittee's jurisdiction to include international law in 1985.[72] Unlike the subcommittee's broader examinations of human rights in the 1970s, its hearings in the 1980s were more focused on specific types of human rights violations, such as political killings, religious intolerance, and torture.[73] The activities of the subcommittee and the substantial interest in human rights issues in the full committee also had what political scientist David Forsythe calls a socializing effect, as it led other subcommittees to pay attention to human rights. This effect was evident in the Subcommittee on Africa under the chairmanship of first Stephen Solarz (D-NY) and subsequently Howard Wolpe (D-MI) – both liberal Jewish Democrats with a keen interest in human rights issues in Africa and beyond. It also extended to the Subcommittee on Asia, of which Solarz became the chair in 1981, and the

---

[71] The House Foreign Affairs Committee's staff rose from fifty-four in 1975 to ninety-seven in 1985, while the corresponding numbers for its Senate counterpart remained around sixty during that period. Lindsay, *Congress and the Politics of U.S. Foreign Policy*, 73, Forsythe, *Human Rights and U.S. Foreign Policy*, 143.

[72] Letter, Gus Yatron to Dante Fascell, January 23, 1985, Box HRIO 99th, Folder A-8, House Foreign Affairs Committee Subcommittee on Human Rights. Center for Legislative Archives, National Archives, Washington, DC; United States Congress, House, Committee on International Relations, "Legislative Review of the Committee on International Relations, 104th Congress, 2nd Session," (Washington, DC: US Government Printing Office, 1997), 4; Forsythe, *Human Rights and U.S. Foreign Policy*, 143. Yatron served as subcommittee chairman until 1992.

[73] Clair Apodaca, *Understanding U.S. Human Rights Policy: A Paradoxical Legacy* (New York: Routledge, 2006), 100. See, for instance, Minutes of Meeting, November 17, 1983, Box HRIO 98th 1st, Folder Minutes, House Foreign Affairs Committee Subcommittee on Human Rights. Center for Legislative Archives, National Archives, Washington, DC; Minutes of Meeting, May 2, 1984, Box HRIO 98th 2nd, Folder Minutes, House Foreign Affairs Committee Subcommittee on Human Rights. Center for Legislative Archives, National Archives, Washington, DC; Minutes of Meeting, May 16, 1984, Box HRIO 98th 2nd, Folder Minutes, House Foreign Affairs Committee Subcommittee on Human Rights. Center for Legislative Archives, National Archives, Washington, DC.

Subcommittee on the Western Hemisphere under the chairmanship of the liberal Democrat Michael Barnes (D-MD).[74]

Activity on human rights in the House, however, was not limited to the Foreign Affairs Committee and its subcommittees. In 1983, Representatives John E. Porter (R-IL) and Tom Lantos (D-CA) formed the Congressional Human Rights Caucus (CHRC) to promote bipartisan support for human rights concerns in US foreign policy.[75] Another key human rights institution was the Commission on Security and Cooperation in Europe established in 1976 to monitor compliance with the Helsinki Final Act, and therefore also known as the US Helsinki Commission. While it was formed as a bi-branch agency with members from both the executive and legislative branches of government, the commission was effectively controlled in Congress, with a strong dominance of the House. Having established itself as an influential actor on human rights in East–West relations in the Carter years, the commission continued to play an important role under Reagan. This was in part due to the bipartisan nature of the commission and the fact that it operated on human rights issues that enjoyed broad consensus across the ideological spectrum. As the commission's instigator and chair until 1984, Fascell was particularly dominant on the commission, but representatives and senators from both parties played important roles.[76]

Resembling the ideological positions of the 1970s, liberals, most of whom were Democrats, tended to be particularly concerned with human rights violations in rightwing dictatorships and critical of US support for these countries. Conservatives, most of whom were Republicans, tended to focus more on human rights violations in communist countries and to see conflicts elsewhere through the prism of the Cold War. Between these two positions, there were several members of Congress of a more moderate bend. Belonging to both parties, these members would sometimes support human rights cases triumphed by either liberals or conservatives. Often these members of Congress were crucial for tipping the scale in Congress on more contentious issues. Finally, a small minority of members, mostly among conservative Republicans, preferred that human rights played no role in US foreign policy at all, favoring either isolationism or realpolitik devout of moral principles.

---

[74] Forsythe, *Human Rights and U.S. Foreign Policy*, 143.
[75] For more on the CHRC, see Chapter 3.
[76] Other leading members of the US Helsinki Commission in the 1980s included Rep. Steny Hoyer (D-MD) and Senators Robert Dole (R-KS) and Dennis DeConcini (D-AZ).

The members of Congress who sought to promote human rights concerns in US foreign policy used several measures, spanning formal congressional powers and more informal ways of exerting influence. House Democrats, especially, held numerous hearings to draw attention to human rights issues and to keep oversight of the administration's foreign policy. When they found the administration lacking, they used the "power of the purse" through the appropriations process to constrain the administration's actions. Through the passing of legislation, members of Congress concerned with human rights regulated economic and military assistance, trade relations, and voting in international institutions, and in other ways limited Reagan's room for maneuver in foreign affairs.

Whereas congressional legislation on human rights in the 1970s primarily focused on restrictions on foreign assistance, in the 1980s the focus shifted to defense appropriations measures. In the increasingly polarized political climate, foreign assistance bills became harder to pass and the funding for foreign assistance decreased.[77] On the contrary, defense spending rose significantly under Reagan and thus defense appropriations emerged as a better option for human rights legislation to have a significant impact.[78] Another legislative strategy was the imposition of procedural legislation such as certification requirements, compelling the Reagan administration to certify human rights improvements in countries such as Argentina and El Salvador in order to secure the release of foreign aid. Often, however, members of Congress influenced US human rights policy more indirectly by abetting or restricting the executive branch. As political scientist Stanley Heginbotham notes, "Congressional victory is achieved when restrictive legislation loses, but Congress extracts some policy compromises reflecting congressional concerns."[79] This, for instance, was the case when Reagan imposed moderate economic sanctions against South Africa in 1985 in an attempt to prevent harsher congressional sanctions. Besides, members of Congress adopted an extensive number of nonbinding resolutions on human rights issues around the world. Most often these were not directed against the administration, but rather targeted foreign government, expressing Congress' support for human rights activists or condemnation of a country's human rights violations. Finally, senators used their power to withhold advice and consent on presidential appointments to express

---

[77] Johnson, "Congress and the Cold War," 98.

[78] One of the more famous and consequential examples of restrictions on defense appropriations was the series of Boland Amendments restricting military aid to the Nicaraguan Contras. For more on this, see Chapter 6.

[79] Stanley J. Heginbotham, "Dateline Washington: The Rules of the Games," *Foreign Policy*, no. 53 (1983): 170.

their disapproval of the nomination of Ernest Lefever to head of the Human Rights Bureau.

Members of Congress also relied on a range of more informal powers. They sometimes participated directly in diplomatic relations with foreign countries, to varying degrees of acceptance from the Reagan administration. In 1985, Representative Dick Cheney (R-WY) grumbled that Reagan had to "put up with every member of Congress with a Xerox machine and a credit card running around the world cutting deals with heads of state."[80] By the invitation of the administration, members of Congress participated in the CSCE follow-up meetings at Madrid and Vienna through the US Helsinki Commission, as they had done under the Carter administration.[81] Moreover, members of Congress sought to advance human rights concerns through personal meetings and correspondence with foreign governments. Such interactions increased significantly during the 1980s. As Representative Lee Hamilton (D-IN) noted in 1988, "Visiting heads of government used to come to Washington and visit the President; the Chairman of the World Bank; the Secretary of Defense; the Secretary of State, and go home. Now they insist on coming to Capitol Hill."[82] Members of Congress also participated in fact-finding and consultative delegations abroad. Sometimes they went as far as to conduct their own foreign policy through what political scientist James Lindsay terms "Lone Ranger diplomacy," often attracting considerable criticism.[83] This was the case when certain legislators, such as Speaker Jim Wright (D-TX), held unofficial diplomatic negotiations with the Nicaraguan government without Reagan's approval. More often, however, members of Congress preferred to influence the executive branch rather than going behind its back. Democrats and Republicans alike sought frequent consultations with the administration in their attempt to shape American attention to human rights abroad.

Finally, and possibly most significantly, Congress attempted to influence public and elite opinion by framing foreign policy issues in human rights terms. Similar to their predecessors in the 1970s, members of Congress used congressional hearings, floor speeches, reports, opinion

---

[80] Steven V. Roberts, "Foreign Policy: Lot of Table Thumping Going On," *The New York Times*, May 29, 1985, www.nytimes.com/1985/05/29/us/foreign-policy-lot-of-table-thumping-going-on.html. In a White House meeting with Republican leaders on Nicaragua, Reagan likewise complained, "We've got to get to a point where we can run foreign policy without a committee of 535 telling us what to do."

[81] Snyder, *Human Rights Activism*, 38–52. See also Chapter 4.

[82] Lee H. Hamilton, "Congress and the Presidency in American Foreign Policy," *Presidential Studies Quarterly* 18 (Summer 1988): 508.

[83] Lindsay, *Congress and the Politics of U.S. Foreign Poicy*, 120.

pieces, and media performances to draw attention to human rights issues. Advances in media technology helped expand the reach of those who mastered these platforms. Members of Congress also expanded their engagement in extra-institutional activities, such as protests and orchestrated media events, to shape the political debate and mobilize support for their agendas. The staged arrests in front of the South African embassy by the Free South Africa Movement in 1984 represented a successful example of such an event. As this book demonstrates, when members of Congress successfully managed to frame an issue in human rights terms and benefit from public opinion, they could be powerful opponents to the administration's policy.[84]

American Attention to Human Rights in the 1980s

The 1980s witnessed an unprecedented density of human rights politics as an ever-growing number of actors inside and outside of government invoked human rights concerns for their political agendas. Just as it had been the case in the 1980 election, human rights issues figured prominently in debates over US foreign policy throughout the decade. The range of these debates and the policymakers and NGOs that invoked human rights concerns reflected the widespread appeal of human rights language as well as the degree to which its flexibility made it adaptable for different agendas. Human rights also intersected with other expressions of morality in American foreign relations, such as the nuclear freeze movement, the Central America peace movement, and country-specific movements, such as the anti-apartheid movement and the movement for Soviet Jewry. The following pages survey American attention to human rights in foreign policy beyond the cases studies selected for this book.

While personal experiences were often important motivations for individual American policymakers' advocacy for human rights issues, ideology and party affiliation also strongly shaped attention to human rights. Conservatives, most of whom were Republicans, tended to focus more on human rights violations in communist countries and to see conflicts elsewhere through the prism of the Cold War. Liberals, most of whom were Democrats, tended to be particularly concerned with human rights violations in right-wing dictatorships and critical of US support for these countries. With a conservative Republican administration in the White

---

[84] B. Guy Peters, Jon Pierre, and Desmond S. King, "The Politics of Path Dependency: Political Conflict in Historical Institutionalism," *Journal of Politics* 67, no. 4 (2005): 1284. For more on congressional diplomacy, consultation, and framing, see Lindsay, *Congress and the Politics of U.S. Foreign Policy*, 119–139.

House, Republicans in Congress were generally inclined to support official US foreign policy positions on human rights, which congressional Democrats, on the contrary, were more likely to contest.

The relationship between the Reagan administration and members of Congress concerned with human rights issues was crucial for the role of human rights in US foreign policy during the 1980s. The administration put a high emphasis on human rights concerns in East–West relations, where it generally viewed human rights criticism as a useful component of its foreign policy. Overall, this approach enjoyed bipartisan support from members of Congress. In other regions, such as Central America, the administration mostly sought to downplay human rights concerns, which it viewed as harmful to its agenda of combatting communism. This position led to heated collisions with liberal Democrats in Congress and the peace movement, which opposed US interventionism and saw human rights violations by US-supported regimes as a key cause for instability in the region. Elsewhere, local developments, internal power shifts in the administration, and pressure from members of Congress made the administration increasingly willing to prioritize human rights concerns and support democratic reforms as the decade wore on. In some Latin American countries, such as Argentina, Brazil, and Bolivia, local developments toward democracy made this shift easier as the administration lend its support to a trend favorable to American interests. Yet in other countries, such as Chile, the Philippines, South Korea, and South Africa, changes in US policy occurred as a reaction to deteriorating human rights situations. In all of these cases, members of Congress, especially liberal Democrats sometimes supported by moderate Republicans, added pressure to prioritize human rights concerns. Not all countries with dismal human rights records received equal attention from Americans, however. Several countries, particularly in Africa and Asia, either flew under the radar because they were of lesser importance to the United States or were deemed too important to warrant considerable criticism. Human rights violations in China, for instance, received remarkably little American attention as strategic and economic interests dominated the relatively positive and low-key US–Chinese relations.[85]

American attention to human rights issues abroad spanned a range of human rights abuses, from the most blatant violations of the integrity of the person through physical violence such as killings and torture to the

---

[85] Michael Schaller, "Reagan and the Puzzles of "So-Called Communist China" and Vietnam," in *Reagan and the World: Leadership and National Security, 1981–1989*, ed. Bradley Lynn Coleman and Kyle Longley (Lexington: The University Press of Kentucky, 2017), 191–209.

denial of a number of civil and political rights. Americans expressed their support for human rights activists and dissidents denied their freedom of religion, freedom of speech, freedom of assembly, and the right to due process. They also protested discrimination against ethnic, religious, and racial minorities. Often, these violations were committed by repressive regimes that deprived their population of political participation by denying them the opportunity of representative government through democratic elections. For most Americans, such actions delegitimized these regimes as they conflicted with the most basic American values and principles. Furthermore, this led several Americans to question the United States' relationship with these regimes, as alliances with oppressors conflicted with the image of the United States as a promoter of freedom. By contrast, American attention to human rights abroad rarely concerned economic and social rights, such as food, housing, education, and health. The Reagan administration, members of Congress, as well as most human rights NGOs generally did not pay much attention to these often less visible human rights, but rather focused on individual victims of more discernable assaults rights.[86] Thus, just as American attention to human rights was unevenly distributed between countries and regions, so it was selectively applied to different types of human rights.

Liberal Democrats in Congress interpreted human rights issues through a broader view of US foreign policy in the 1980s that took issue with the Reagan administration's attempt to roll back communism in the Third World through support for anti-communist guerrilla movements and US-friendly dictatorships. Liberal Democrats were also critical of Reagan's hardline approach toward the Soviet Union and opposed the arms race, which they feared might escalate into war. While sharing conservatives' concern with communism, liberals wanted the United States to break with some of its most repressive authoritarian allies and instead encourage liberalization through democratic reforms. Liberal concerns for human rights in the 1980s thus resembled that of liberals in the 1970s, and several members of Congress who had been at the forefront, such as senators Edward Kennedy and Alan Cranston (D-CA), continued to be so during the Reagan era. These veterans were joined by new liberals with a particular interest in human rights issues, such as Representatives Lantos, Barnes, and Solarz. As the Reagan administration developed its conservative human rights policy, liberals increasingly clashed with the administration over the appropriate role for human rights concerns in American foreign relations.

---

[86] Samuel Moyn, *Not Enough: Human Rights in an Unequal World* (Cambridge, MA: Harvard University Press, 2018), 170.

Nowhere was the clash between liberals in Congress and the administration more passionate and intense than over US policy toward Central America. Throughout the decade, the region was marred by civil wars and bloody conflicts as repressive regimes struggled against uprisings often employing the military against their own populations. Guatemala, Nicaragua, El Salvador, and Honduras were particularly hard hit as conflicts in one country often spilled over into another, with the United States and communist bloc countries propping up various regimes and their adversaries. Aside from such Cold War interventions, the region was plagued by poverty, ethnic strife, extreme economic inequality, and military interference in politics, which led to social conflict and instability. The Reagan administration assigned the region high strategic importance, with Jeane Kirkpatrick calling it "the most important place in the world for the United States today."[87] US support for friendly dictators and anti-communist guerillas, most notably the Nicaraguan Contras, aimed at preventing the advance of communism and securing American national interests.[88] Liberal Democrats criticized the administration's support for right-wing dictators and sought to force changes in US policy toward the region.

In the early 1980s, El Salvador was arguably the country in the region that drew the most American attention to human rights issues. Throughout the decade, El Salvador was engulfed in a brutal civil war between its military dictatorship under the leadership of José Napoleón Duarte backed by the United States and leftwing insurgents backed by the Soviet Union, Cuba, and Nicaragua.[89] The Reagan administration viewed El Salvador as a test case for its attempt to stop the expansion of communism in Central America.[90] To that end, the administration pursued

---

[87] Quoted in Walter LaFeber, *Inevitable Revolutions: The United States in Central America* (New York: W.W. Norton, 1993), 271.

[88] The administration did seek to advance democracy and respect for human rights to a limited degree that did not jeopardize the primary purpose of combatting communism. "National Security Decision Directive 124: Central America: Promoting Democracy Economic Improvement, and Peace," February 7, 1984, accessed August 6, 2019, https://fas.org/irp/offdocs/nsdd/nsdd-124.pdf.

[89] With an estimated 75,000 people killed, the civil war caused extensive atrocities, including government-supported death squads targeting civilians. United Nations Commission on the Truth for El Salvador, "From Madness to Hope: The 12-Year War in El Salvador: Report of the Commission on the Truth for El Salvador," UN Document No. S/25500 (1993).

[90] At the administration's first National Security Council meeting, Reagan stated, "We can't afford defeat. El Salvador is the place for a victory." US National Security Council, "NSC 1: Caribbean Basis; Poland," February 6, 1981, www.thereaganfiles.com/1981026-nsc-1.pdf (accessed May 1, 2018). The next meeting's summary conclusion read: "A Victory in El Salvador is essential. It would set a good example for the region." US National Security Council, "NSC 2: Central America," February 11, 1981, www.thereaganfiles.com/19810211-nsc-2.pdf (accessed May 1, 2018).

massive economic and military assistance and support for political and economic reform.[91] Liberal Democrats, such as Barnes and Senators Christopher Dodd and Edward Kennedy, strongly opposed US support for Duarte. In 1981, they managed to impose restrictions on US military assistance to the country, requiring the Reagan administration to certify that El Salvador's human rights situation was improving in order to secure continued assistance.[92] Liberals found support among the Central America peace movement, NGOs, church groups, and the majority of Americans, who grew increasingly uncomfortable with US involvement in the conflict. The certification requirement led the administration to encourage the Salvadorian regime to improve its record to prevent an interruption of aid. In practice, however, such pressure was rendered unconvincing and ineffective as Congress accepted Reagan's certifications that the human rights situation was improving, despite facts to the contrary.[93] El Salvador thus reflected liberal Democrats' dissatisfaction with American support for repressive regimes, but it also demonstrated that most members of Congress were reluctant to push the administration too far, out of fear of undermining US-friendly regimes and the risk of paving the way for communism. Liberals managed to force the administration to address the human rights abuses of an American ally but they failed to force a significant change in US policy. Human rights concerns were hard to ignore, but they were easy to manipulate.

Liberals were equally concerned with US support for repressive regimes further south in Latin America, and here they found the

---

[91] US military assistance to El Salvador totaled nearly a billion dollars in the 1980s. In the preceding years, the Carter administration had cut off military aid to the country over human rights violations in 1977, resumed it again in 1979 after a regime change, before suspending it yet again in 1980 in response to the murder and rape of four American churchwomen. In the Regan administration, hardliners such CIA Director William J. Casey and Secretary of Defense Caspar Weinberger favored firm support for Duarte, while moderates such as Secretary of State George P. Shultz believed the United States had to instigate political reforms and human rights improvements. For Casey's and Weinberger's positions on El Salvador, see, for instance, US National Security Council, "NSC 2: Central America," February 11, 1981, www.thereaganfiles.com/19810211-nsc-2.pdf (accessed May 1, 2018). By the beginning of Reagan's second term, Shultz "was convinced that the U.S. approach was not working." George Pratt Shultz, *Turmoil and Triumph: My Years as Secretary of State* (New York: Maxwell Macmillan International, 1993), 970.

[92] William M. LeoGrande, *Our Own Backyard: The United States in Central America, 1977–1992* (Chapel Hill: University of North Carolina Press, 1998), 122. Congress imposed a similar certification requirement on U.S. foreign assistance to Argentina.

[93] Sikkink, *Mixed Signals*, 169–174; Schmitz, *The United States and Right-Wing Dictatorships, 1965–1989*, 202–216; Renouard, *Human Rights in American Foreign Policy*, 185–190; Hal Brands, *Making the Unipolar Moment: U.S. Foreign Policy and the Rise of the Post-Cold War Order* (Ithaca, NY: Cornell University Press, 2016), 132–137.

administration more susceptible to their views. Although the administration was initially hesitant to criticize allied regimes in South America, it became increasingly willing to support democratic transitions underway in countries such as a Brazil, Argentina, Bolivia, and Uruguay.[94] This change was brought about by the growing influence of moderates inside the administration, combined with pressure from liberal Democrats in Congress and human rights NGOs.[95] While they were quick to point out the inconsistency in the administration's support for democracy in South America and its policy elsewhere, liberals in Congress generally supported this push for democratization. As a consequence, American attention to human rights in most South American countries was relatively noncontentious, with Augusto Pinochet's Chile as the exception confirming the rule.[96]

In other parts of the world, however, the increasing repressiveness of US-backed regimes led congressional liberals to confront the administration. Liberals argued that US support for repressive regimes in countries such as the Philippines, South Korea, South Africa, and Chile was both immoral and counterproductive to American interests.[97] Rather than unconditionally supporting these regimes based on their anti-communism, liberals believed that the United States ought to distance itself from their human rights violations and pressure them to liberalize. In several of these cases, liberal Democrats would eventually receive

---

[94] While the region had its share of human rights violations, developments were generally moving toward more democratic regimes with greater respect for human rights. Brazil held democratic elections in 1982, and in 1985 the military transferred power to civilian rule. In Argentina, the military dictatorship was replaced by constitutional rule with the 1983 elections, and under new President Raúl Alfonsín, the country prosecuted the military leaders for their human rights violations. After a couple of tumultuous years, Bolivia turned from military dictatorship to civilian rule in 1982. Uruguay followed a similar path two years later, replacing the military rule with democracy in elections in 1984. For the significance of Latin America to international human rights, see Patrick William Kelly, *Sovereign Emergencies: Latin America and the Making of Global Human Rights Politics* (New York: Cambridge University Press, 2018).

[95] Importantly, the advances of democracy on the ground, the considerable American influence in the region, and the relatively limited presence of communism also made it the most opportune place to promote democracy. Thomas Carothers, *In the Name of Democracy: U.S. Policy toward Latin America in the Reagan Years* (Berkeley: University of California Press, 1991), 241–244; Brands, *Making the Unipolar Moment*, 142–143.

[96] Sikkink, *Mixed Signals*; Michael Grow, *U.S. Presidents and Latin American Interventions: Pursuing Regime Change in the Cold War* (Lawrence: University Press of Kansas, 2008).

[97] For Chile, see Morley and McGillion, *Reagan and Pinochet*; Morris Morley and Chris McGillion, "Soldiering On: The Reagan Administration and Redemocratisation in Chile, 1983–1986," *Bulletin of Latin American Research* 25, no. 1 (2006): 1–22. For South Korea, see Gregg Brazinsky, *Nation Building in South Korea: Koreans, Americans, and the Making of a Democracy* (Chapel Hill: University of North Carolina Press, 2007). For South Africa, see Chapter 5.

support from more moderate Democrats and moderate Republicans. It was alliances like these that occasionally helped Congress force changes in US foreign policy during the 1980s.

Liberals Democrats became particularly angered by the administration's stubborn support for Ferdinand Marcos's repressive regime in the Philippines. Home to large US air and naval bases and committed to fighting communism, the Philippines was an important strategic ally to the United States. Moreover, Reagan's personal friendship and admiration for Marcos, whom he had known since 1969, made him reluctant to withdraw support for the regime.[98] Liberal Democrats, however, became increasingly determined that the United States ought to push for regime change and a transition to democracy, not least after Marcos was linked to the assassination of his longtime political opponent Benigno "Ninoy" Aquino Jr. in 1983. The event sparked anti-Marcos protest in the Philippines and led some State Department officials to contemplate a strategy to remove Marcos. It also catalyzed Solarz into a very personal campaign to end US support for Marcos. Chair of the House Subcommittee on Asian and Pacific Affairs, Solarz had met Aquino in June 1983 and happened to have met with Marcos in Manila the day before Aquino's assassination.[99] A great admirer of Aquino, Solarz decided to attend Aquino's funeral, where he met with the anti-Marcos opposition. In his memoirs, Solarz recalls how this deeply emotional experience made him determined to help bring democracy to the Philippines.[100] In the following years, his subcommittee held several hearings exposing the corruption and human rights violations of the Marcos regime. In October 1983, Congress passed a resolution calling for an independent investigation of the Aquino assassination and urging free and fair elections in the Philippines.[101] Congress

---

[98] Shultz, *Turmoil and Triumph*, 618; Lou Cannon, *President Reagan: The Role of a Lifetime* (New York: Public Affairs, 2000), 364. Ronald Reagan, Debate Between the President and Former Vice President Walter F. Mondale in Kansas City, Missouri, October 21, 1984. Online by Gerhard Peters and John T. Woolley, The American Presidency Project, accessed August 7, 2019, www.presidency.ucsb.edu/node/217277; National Security Decision Directive 163: US Policy towards the Philippines, February 20, 1985, accessed August 6, 2019, https://fas.org/irp/offdocs/nsdd/nsdd-163.pdf. The NSDD read, "Our goal is not to replace the current leadership of the Philippines, but to preserve the stability of a key ally by working with the Philippine Government."

[99] US Congress, House, Committee on Foreign Affairs, *United States-Philippines Relations and the New Base and Aid Agreement: Hearings before the Subcommittee on Asian and Pacific Affairs of the Committee on Foreign Affairs*, 98th Congress, 1st Session, June 17, 23, and 28, 1983.

[100] Stephen J. Solarz, *Journeys to War & Peace: A Congressional Memoir* (Waltham, MA: Brandeis University Press, 2011), 100–102.

[101] Stanley Karnow, "Reagan and the Philippines: Setting Marcos Adrift," *The New York Times*, March 19, 1989.

also made symbolic cuts in US aid to the Philippines in 1984 and 1985 to demonstrate dissatisfaction with the human rights situation. In reality, however, the cuts were simply a modification from military to economic assistance, since a genuine cut was deemed too risky as it might jeopardize American military bases.[102] By 1986, moderate Republicans such as Lugar and conservative Democrats such as Senator Samuel Nunn (D-GA) joined in calling for the administration to end US support for Marcos.[103] Eventually, Secretary of State George P. Shultz, who had come to see Marcos as a liability, succeeded in persuading Reagan to drop support for Marcos and push for democracy, and by February 1986 the withdrawal of US support contributed to Marcos's downfall.[104]

Liberals were thus uncomfortable with US support for repressive regimes and at times willing to withdraw their support for these over human rights violations. However, their opposition to these regimes was always tempered by concerns about regime changes leading to communist takeovers. Conservatives, on the contrary, were not troubled by this dilemma of balancing concern for human rights issues with fear of communism. Rather, they perceived supporting human rights and fighting communism as essentially the same thing. Much like the Reagan administration, conservatives viewed foreign policy issues almost exclusively through the lens of the Cold War and generally supported the administration's positions. According to conservatives, the United States ought to focus on opposing the influence of communism by taking a strong stance toward Moscow and supporting American allies around the world. This led them to criticize human rights violations in the Soviet Bloc, such as the crackdown on the Solidarity movement in Poland, while downplaying abuses committed by regimes friendly to the United States, such as the Philippines, South Korea, South Africa, and Chile.

---

[102] Memorandum for Members of House Foreign Affairs Committee, April 1, 1985, Box HRIO 99th 1st and 2nd, Folder Country Files: Philippines. House Foreign Affairs Committee Subcommittee on Human Rights. Center for Legislative Archives, National Archives, Washington, DC; Sara Steinmetz, *Democratic Transition and Human Rights: Perspectives on U.S. Foreign Policy* (Albany: State University of New York Press, 1994), 173.

[103] US Department of State, Memorandum, Dole/Lugar/Nunn Action on the Philippines [Nunn letter attached], February 13, 1986, PH03244; The Philippines: U.S. Policy During the Marcos Years, 1961–1986, Digital National Security Archive.

[104] Shultz, *Turmoil and Triumph*, 612–615. National Security Decision Directive 215: Philippines, February 23, 1986, accessed August 6, 2019, https://fas.org/irp/offdocs/nsdd/nsdd-215.pdf. Ronald Reagan, Statement by Principal Deputy Press Secretary Speakes on the Internal Situation in the Philippines, February 24, 1986. Online by Gerhard Peters and John T. Woolley, The American Presidency Project, accessed August 7, 2019, www.presidency.ucsb.edu/node/257946.

While moderate Republicans would sometimes side with liberals in opposing US support for repressive regimes, conservatives were relentless in their commitment to fighting communism by confronting the Soviet Union and supporting anti-communist regimes regardless of their human rights records. The most important proponent of this anti-communist worldview was Senator Helms, who was one of the most entrepreneurial lawmakers in the realm of foreign affairs. In 1977, Helms openly declared his strong support of Jimmy Carter's human rights policy: "Mr. Carter and I belong to different political parties. We may disagree from time to time. But not on human rights."[105] Yet this support was confined strictly to attacking the human rights record of communist countries and conservatives such as Helms vehemently protested what they viewed as Carter's misguided criticism of human rights abuses in American allies. Much more in tune with Reagan's anti-communist human rights policy, Helms strongly supported the administration's attempt to roll back communism in Central America.[106] As chair of the Senate Foreign Relations Committee's subcommittee on the Western Hemisphere, he took a special interest in Latin America and fiercely defended the administration's policy in the region against its liberal critics.

However, Helms was quick to attack the administration whenever it moderated its support to US-friendly regimes. When the administration and a bipartisan coalition in Congress united behind a policy aimed at fostering a democratic transition in Chile in 1986, Helms remained steadfast in his support for Pinochet.[107] Helms also took issue with the administration, whenever it prioritized strategic and economic interests in relations with communist countries at the expense of a more ideological stand. In 1982, he protested the administration's decision to set a ceiling for arms sales to Taiwan to not antagonize China and he criticized the lacking restrictions on US-Chinese trade, despite the country's human rights abuses.[108] Like other anti-communist conservatives, Helms mistrusted the international human rights system. His strong suspicion of the United Nations and any secession of American sovereignty to international institutions, for instance, led him to oppose US

---

[105] Press Release, April 11, 1977, Box 606, Folder 11, The Jesse A. Helms Papers, The Jesse Helms Center Archives, Wingate, NC.

[106] Andrew Stead, "What You Know and Who You Know: Senator Jesse Helms, the Reagan Doctrine and the Nicaraguan Contras," *49th Parallel* 33 (Winter 2014): 55–93.

[107] Shirley Christian, "Helms, in Chile, Denounces U.S. Envoy," *The New York Times*, July 14, 1986, A03.

[108] Jesse Helms, *Here's Where I Stand: A Memoir* (New York: Random House, 2005), 231–233.

ratification of the UN Genocide Convention even after the Reagan administration came to favor it in 1984.[109] Conservatives in Congress, such as Helms, thus both supported the Reagan administration and defended it against its liberal critics, but whenever they found the administration to be too moderate, they were quick to confront.

American attention to human rights concerns was not the only expression of morality in debates over US foreign policy in the 1980s. Americans, concerned with the heightened tensions of the Cold War and US involvement overseas, mobilized large social movements around moral languages. The most prominent of these were the nuclear freeze campaign seeking to pressure the United States and the Soviet Union to freeze testing, production, and deployment of nuclear weapons, and the peace movement opposing US involvement in Central America. Fear of nuclear war rose significantly in both the United States and Western Europe amid the escalating tensions between Moscow and Washington in the late 1970s and early 1980s. Fear of nuclear war led to several protests, including the largest peace rally in American history in New York City on June 12, 1982, with an estimated one million participants.[110] The protest also spawned legislative efforts, with a nuclear freeze resolution passing the House in May 1983 before being rejected by the Senate in June the same year.[111] The nuclear freeze campaign did not make substantial use of human rights language, but rather represented another moral framework for thinking about East–West relations.

The Central America peace movement represented a series of other moral objections to US foreign policy. Throughout the 1980s, more than 1,500 national, regional, and local groups in the United States worked to prevent US intervention in Central America. While an outgrowth of the broader peace movements of the 1960s and 1970s, the Central America peace movement also had a strong religious component with Catholics, Protestants, Quakers, and Jews all playing important roles. Another

---

[109] US Department of State, *Foreign Relations of the United States, 1981–1988, Volume XII, Global Issues II* (Washington, DC: US Government Publishing Office, 2017), Document 72; Memo, Genocide Convention Hearing, March 5, 1985, Box 5, Folder 1, Charles McC Mathias Papers Ms. 150, Special Collections, Milton S. Eisenhower Library, The Johns Hopkins University.

[110] Paul L. Montgomery, "Throngs Fill Manhattan to Protest Nuclear Weapons," *The New York Times*, June 13, 1982, 1.

[111] For more on the nuclear freeze campaign, see William M. Knoblauch, *Nuclear Freeze in a Cold War: The Reagan Administration, Cultural Activism, and the End of the Arms Race, Culture and Politics in the Cold War and Beyond* (Amherst: University of Massachusetts Press, 2017); Angela Santese, "Ronald Reagan, the Nuclear Weapons Freeze Campaign and the Nuclear Scare of the 1980s," *The International History Review* 39, no. 3 (2016): 1–25.

essential aspect of the movement was its extensive transnational network based on personal connections between Americans and their allies in Central America. These different elements of the movement meant that it invoked multiple moral languages, including Christian ideas about social justice such as liberation theology, anti-war sentiments extensively framed around concerns about "another Vietnam," and concern for human rights. While human rights was not the dominant language of the movement, it was part of its vocabulary and the movement often intersected with human rights NGOs and members of Congress concerned with human rights.[112]

The 1980s also witnessed the growth in several country-specific movements framed around moral concerns. The transnational Soviet Jewry movement, advocating for the right of Jews to leave the Soviet Union, became one of the decade's leading human rights movements. The American Jewish community was particularly dominant and Gal Beckerman suggests that the issue even became more important to American Jews than were relations with Israel.[113] The movement had been active since the 1960s but gathered unprecedented levels of support in the 1980s with large demonstrations and significant lobbying of policymakers. While American Jews heavily dominated the movement, it also enjoyed considerable support from non-Jewish Americans. The Soviet Jewry movement repeatedly used human rights language, while also making use of other moral frameworks such as references to the Holocaust. The movement had significant clout in Washington, where it garnered the support of both the Reagan administration and members of Congress from across the ideological spectrum.[114]

The growing transnational movement to end South African apartheid was another major moral issue that mobilized Americans in the 1980s. Although Western Europeans were long at the forefront of the anti-apartheid movement, mobilized American opposition to apartheid grew significantly in the 1980s, spreading from college campuses and churches to the national stage. At its peak, the movement consisted of hundreds of coalitions, committees, and campaigns. Not surprisingly, America's own experience with racial segregation had a significant influence on its

---

[112] For the most comprehensive account of the Central America peace movement, see Christian Smith, *Resisting Reagan: The U.S. Central America Peace Movement* (Chicago, IL: University of Chicago Press, 1996).

[113] Gal Beckerman, *When They Come for Us, We'll Be Gone: The Epic Struggle to Save Soviet Jewry* (Boston, MA: Houghton Mifflin Harcourt, 2010), 7–8.

[114] Stuart Altshuler, *From Exodus to Freedom: A History of the Soviet Jewry Movement* (Lanham, MD: Rowman & Littlefield, 2005). For the Soviet Jewry movement, see Chapter 4.

anti-apartheid movement. The movement relied heavily on activists and tactics from the civil rights movement as well as ideas of Pan-Africanism. Several of its proponents also incorporated human rights language in their critique of the apartheid regime. The movement received legislative support from the Congressional Black Caucus (CBC) and liberal Democrats throughout the years, and by the mid-1980s it eventually gained enough support to force a change in US policy toward the Soviet Union through the imposition of economic sanctions.[115]

Morality-based movements such as the nuclear freeze campaign, the Central America peace movement, the Soviet Jewry movement, and the anti-apartheid movement constituted an important context for the human rights activism of the 1980s. Just like human rights activists, the movements challenged the Reagan administration's foreign policy by mobilizing grassroots and seeking to influence public opinion. They also secured the active support from members of Congress and a range of celebrities, intellectuals, and religious leaders. In doing so, they forced the administration to defend the morality of its foreign policy to the American public. Sometimes these movements would form alliances with members of Congress concerned with human rights, as the case studies in this book demonstrates. Rather than competing with human rights activism, these different expressions of morality supplemented and reinforced American attention to human rights.

Conclusion

In some ways, everything had changed for human rights concerns in US foreign policy from the early days of the human rights breakthrough in the 1970s to the Reagan era. Whereas human rights had been a seldom-cited concept on the fringes of foreign policy debates up until the mid-1970s, less than a decade later it was an established moral language invoked by a substantial number of policymakers across the political spectrum. Human rights were more deeply institutionalized in the foreign policy bureaucracy and, despite its initial resistance, the Reagan administration had crafted a proactive approach to human rights and included human rights concerns in its policies toward several countries. In Congress, human rights concerns were likewise further institutionalized. Fraser's former subcommittee was renamed the Subcommittee on Human Rights and International Organizations to reflect its focus on

---

[115] David Hostetter, *Movement Matters: American Antiapartheid Activism and the Rise of Multicultural Politics* (New York: Routledge, 2006). For the anti-apartheid movement, see Chapter 5.

human rights issues. The US Helsinki Commission expanded its role on human rights concerns in East–West relations. New institutions, such as the CHRC, called attention to human rights issues around the world and sought to mobilize and systematize congressional efforts. Outside of government, an increasing number of evermore-influential NGOs championed human rights, while ethnic and religious groups frequently invoked human rights concerns for their particular agendas. In short, human rights were interwoven into the fabric of American foreign relations to an unprecedented degree.

In other ways, however, much remained the same. Attention to human rights in US foreign policy continued to be intertwined with strategic interests, in particular within the context of the Cold War. While human rights concerns were much more firmly established in American foreign policy, disagreements about their appropriate role continued. Inside the Reagan administration, moderates and hardliners often clashed on the relative importance ascribed to human rights concerns and whether promoting human rights was in America's best interest. Moreover, the executive and legislative branches of government continued to contest their appropriate role. Liberal Democrats in Congress locked heads with the Republican administration in ways that echoed the struggle between the Nixon and Ford administrations and members of Congress in the 1970s. At the same time, some officials in the executive branch and some members of Congress continued to oppose human rights concerns in US foreign policy, although their numbers and influence dwindled. Those members of Congress that championed human rights concerns in US foreign policy continued to do so for very different reasons. Liberals, moderates, and conservatives would pursue different human rights issues at different times for different reasons, sometimes finding common ground and sometimes not. Ideological background, partisanship, and other concerns informed attention to human rights. Often, personal relationships and experiences were decisive as evident in the case of the Philippines, where Reagan's relationship with Marcos and Solarz's relationship with Aquino were crucial for their positions. Thus, while human rights enjoyed popularity as a moral language in the 1980s that would have been almost unimaginable in the early 1970s, the flexibility of human rights as a concept and the varied motivations driving those who invoked them meant that the content of US human rights policy continued to be as contested as ever before.

Ronald Reagan entered the White House highly skeptical of human rights as a foreign policy concern. Yet, within the first year, pressure from members of Congress had led Reagan and his foreign policy advisors to revise their position on human rights. In a direct response to congressional criticism, the administration constructed a conservative human rights policy that integrated human rights concerns into its larger foreign policy vision for combatting communism. While some members of Congress supported the administration's conservative human rights policy or at least parts of it, for several members concerned with human rights the administration's policy was an unintended consequence. Seeking initially to secure human rights as a foreign policy concern, members of Congress soon found themselves locked in a contest with an administration that aggressively sought to define the role of human rights in US foreign policy instead. What at first appeared as a struggle to preserve concern for human rights in US foreign policy evolved into a contest over how, when, and where human rights should inform American foreign relations.

The Reagan Doctrine and Reagan's Foreign Policy Team

Reagan entered office with an ambitious mission to dramatically reform the American government, having urged Americans in his campaign slogan "Let's make America great again."[1] In his inaugural address, Reagan famously promulgated that "government is not the solution to our problem; government is the problem."[2] To save America from its

---

[1] A message repeated by Reagan at his acceptance of the nomination as the Republican candidate. Ronald Reagan, Address Accepting the Presidential Nomination at the Republican National Convention in Detroit, July 17, 1980. Online by Gerhard Peters and John T. Woolley, The American Presidency Project, accessed August 7, 2019, www.presidency.ucsb.edu/node/251302.

[2] Ronald Reagan, Inaugural Address, January 20, 1981. Online by Gerhard Peters and John T. Woolley, The American Presidency Project, accessed August 7, 2019, www.presidency.ucsb.edu/node/246336.

"government problem" and solve its other ills, Reagan prescribed a policy of fiscal conservatism, rugged individualism, and a muscular foreign policy. More than anything else, Reagan sought to revive the nation's morale and vitality.[3] In the realm of foreign policy, Reagan proposed to achieve this revival through a policy of "peace through strength" based on a massive arms buildup, a refusal to negotiate with the Soviet Union, and the use of overt and covert military operations and assistance.[4] This "conservative internationalism," as scholars such as Henry Nau has named it, represented a clear break with détente and substituted the existing strategy of containment with one that aimed to roll back communism, something conservative voices had been advocating since the 1950s.[5] The underlying assumption was that the United States had to establish a position of strength before engaging in negotiations with the Soviet Union. Reagan's muscular foreign policy was likewise a reaction to the almost apologetic nature of Carter's foreign policy and the even more guilt-ridden platform of George McGovern from the 1972 presidential election.[6]

The administration formalized the strategy in National Security Decision Directive 75 (NSDD75) from January 1983, which laid out a three-pronged strategy toward the Soviet Union. First, the United States would seek to "contain and over time reverse Soviet expansionism." Second, it would "promote, within the narrow limits available to us, the process of change in the Soviet Union toward a more pluralistic political and economic system in which the power of the privileged ruling elite is gradually reduced." Third, it would "engage the Soviet Union in negotiations to attempt to reach agreements which protect and enhance US interests."[7] Rather than simply seeking to coexist with the Soviet Union, the United States would seek to change the Soviet system to win the Cold War. By the time the administration compiled NSDD75, it had replaced its initial intent to downgrade human rights with a more proactive approach that made human rights a key component in the struggle with the Soviet Union. Criticism of Soviet human rights violations became an important component of the attempt to change Soviet society and defeat international communism.

The Reagan administration primarily sought to roll back communism in the Third World, where it would support anti-communist forces to

---

[3] Grow, *U.S. Presidents*, 123–124.   [4] Zelizer, *Arsenal of Democracy*, 300–301.
[5] Nau, *Conservative Internationalism*.
[6] For McGovern's foreign policy, see Keys, *Reclaiming American Virtue*, 71–74.
[7] "National Security Decision Directive 75: US Relations with the USSR," January 17, 1983, accessed August 6, 2019, https://fas.org/irp/offdocs/nsdd/nsdd-75.pdf.

diminish communist influence. In April 1985, the conservative colum-
nist Charles Krauthammer dubbed this policy the "Reagan Doctrine."[8]
NSDD75, however, already expressed the essence of the policy. Referring
to Soviet allies in the Third World, NSDD75 stated, "U.S. policy will
include active efforts to encourage democratic movements and forces to
bring about political change inside these countries."[9] Reagan publicly
articulated the Reagan Doctrine in February 1985, when he told
Congress, "We must not break faith with those who are risking their lives –
on every continent, from Afghanistan to Nicaragua – to defy Soviet-
supported aggression."[10] The Reagan Doctrine would prove decisive for
the administration's human rights policy toward the developing world, as
the Cold War allegiance of countries would determine the extent to which
the administration would attack their human rights record.

To achieve the objective of countering Soviet expansionism, Reagan
orchestrated a dramatic increase in the defense budget, which rose from
$171 billion in 1981 to $229 billion in 1985.[11] He argued that such a
buildup was necessary to secure a military superiority over the Soviet
Union, which would allow the United States to negotiate from a position
of strength. Aggressive rhetoric accompanied the arms buildup, with
Reagan predicting in June 1982 that the Soviet Union would soon end
up on the "ash heap of history" before famously labeling the country the
"Evil Empire" in March 1983.[12] Characteristic of his mixture of idealism
and pragmatism, however, Reagan supplemented such harsh rhetorical
attacks with invitations for secret talks with Soviet officials.[13]

Reagan's staunch anti-communism and deep distrust of the Soviet
Union permeated his foreign policy. Convinced that the Soviets were

---

[8] Charles Krauthammer, "The Reagan Doctrine," *Time Magazine*, April 1, 1985.

[9] "National Security Decision Directive 75," 5. See, also Memo, Kenneth Adelman to
William J. Casey, Reagan Doctrine, May 31, 1986, William J. Casey Papers, Box 319,
Folder 14, Hoover Institution Archives.

[10] Ronald Reagan, "Address before a Joint Session of the Congress on the State of the
Union, February 6, 1985," accessed August 1, 2019, www.reaganlibrary.gov/research/
speeches/20685e.

[11] Patterson, *Restless Giant*, 200. Carter had already initiated a significant arms buildup in
the preceding years. Both Carter's and Reagan's arms buildups drew justification from a
report from the so-called Team B commissioned by the CIA in 1976, which concluded
that the United States had underestimated Soviet military power.

[12] Ronald Reagan, Address to Members of the British Parliament, June 8, 1982. Online by
Gerhard Peters and John T. Woolley, The American Presidency Project, accessed
August 7, 2019, www.presidency.ucsb.edu/node/245236. Ronald Reagan, Remarks at
the Annual Convention of the National Association of Evangelicals in Orlando, Florida,
March 8, 1983. Online by Gerhard Peters and John T. Woolley, The American
Presidency Project, accessed August 7, 2019, www.presidency.ucsb.edu/node/262885.

[13] See for instance, National Security Council, *Directive No. 75 on U.S. Relations with the
USSR*, January 17, 1983; Jacobs and Zelizer, *Conservatives in Power*, 152.

seeking military superiority in an attempt to win the Cold War, Reagan was a longtime opponent of détente, which he described as morally corrupt and naive. It had been, Reagan argued, "a one-way street that gives the Soviets what they want with nothing in return," which would ultimately hand Moscow a military advantage.[14] Consequently, Reagan had opposed all major previous peace treaties, including the Strategic Arms Limitation Treaty I and II (SALT I and II), arguing that the United States needed to regain its military superiority before engaging in negotiations with Moscow. Moreover, Reagan did not trust that the conventional doctrine of Mutually Assured Destruction (MAD), which held that the prospect of retaliation prevented a nuclear attack, was a reliable deterrent for Soviet aggression.[15] In this respect, Reagan's perception of the Soviet Union differed in important ways from his predecessor as well as from the Republican establishment, which had supported the détente policy of the Nixon and Ford presidencies.

Reagan's distrust in MAD led him to seek alternative guarantees for national security, which culminated in his proposition for the Strategic Defense Initiative (SDI) in March 1983. SDI proposed the creation of a laser-based shield that would allow the United States and its allies to shoot down incoming missiles, and thereby effectively revoke MAD and bolster American national security without sacrifice from the American people. Some critics of SDI accused it of endangering Cold War relations, while others ridiculed what they viewed as the technological infeasibility of the project, dubbing it "Star Wars."[16] Yet Reagan remained fiercely committed to SDI. This commitment was apparent at the Reykjavik Summit in October 1986, when Reagan walked away from a breakthrough arms deal with the Soviets because he was unwilling to give up on SDI. The historian Chester Pach argues that, unlike other issues, when it came to defense Reagan displayed a remarkable consistency from his time as a candidate and throughout his presidency.[17] Once the opportunity arose in talks with Gorbachev, however, Reagan accepted a dramatic reduction in nuclear arms.

Moreover, Reagan was determined to erase the memory of Vietnam – or rather reshape it – to allow for a resurgent and muscular American foreign policy. Unlike Carter (and McGovern), who had expressed regret about the country's role in Vietnam, Reagan did not believe the United

---

[14] Ronald Reagan, "Tactics for Détente," *Wall Street Journal*, February 13, 1976, 8.

[15] Chester Pach, "Sticking to His Guns: Reagan and National Security," in *The Reagan Presidency: Pragmatic Conservatism and Its Legacies*, ed. W. Elliot Brownlee and Hugh Davis Graham (Lawrence University Press of Kansas, 2003), 89.

[16] Zelizer, *Arsenal of Democracy*, 300.   [17] Pach, "Sticking to His Guns," 107.

States had to apologize for the war. In a speech at a veterans convention in August 1980, the presidential hopeful had labeled the Vietnam War "a noble cause."[18] For the majority of Americans, the lesson of Vietnam was that the United States should avoid intervening in conflicts in Third World countries of limited strategic importance. For Reagan, however, the lesson of Vietnam was that the American government should not fight a war half-heartedly. In his eyes, the war had been lost because American politicians had failed to support the war effort sufficiently. To avoid such situations in the future, Reagan argued, it was imperative that the United States rid itself of the Vietnam syndrome and committed itself to use its power effectively.[19] The United States, he proclaimed, was freedom's "last stand on Earth" and with this came a responsibility to prevail for the sake of all humankind.[20] With such high stakes, there could be no room for weakness or apology.

With a somewhat crude, but helpful, simplification, Reagan's foreign policy team can be divided into two groups. One group of hardliners, often referred to as the "Reaganites," was fiercely committed to the anti-communist agenda and supported strong measures aimed at directly undermining the Soviet Union to weaken its influence around the globe. Consisting of both Cold War warriors and neoconservatives, this group was particularly dominant at the National Security Council and included key officials such as national security advisors (NSA) Richard V. Allen, Robert McFarlane, and John Poindexter, Secretary of State Alexander M. Haig, Secretary of Defense Caspar Weinberger, Central Intelligence Agency (CIA) Director William J. Casey, and UN Ambassador Jeane Kirkpatrick. The group also included senior officials not directly involved with foreign policy issues, such as White House Chief of Staff Don Regan and White House Communications Director Pat Buchanan. The hardliners believed that human rights concerns should be used as a weapon to delegitimize the Soviet Union, but they were reluctant to criticize allied countries. They viewed human rights as a means to win the Cold War, but not an end to be pursued around the world.

In opposition to the hardliners was a more pragmatic group from the moderate wing of the Republican Party. Primarily located in the State Department, this group included Secretary of State George P. Shultz,

---

[18] Ronald Reagan, Address to the Veterans of Foreign Wars Convention in Chicago, August 18, 1980. Online by Gerhard Peters and John T. Woolley, The American Presidency Project, accessed August 7, 2019, www.presidency.ucsb.edu/node/285595.

[19] Pach, "Sticking to His Guns," 96.

[20] Ronald Reagan, Address on Behalf of Senator Barry Goldwater: "A Time for Choosing," October 27, 1964. Online by Gerhard Peters and John T. Woolley, The American Presidency Project, accessed August 7, 2019, www.presidency.ucsb.edu/node/276336.

Assistant Secretary of State for Africa Chester Crocker, and Jack Matlock at the National Security Council. This moderate group was less ideological in its confrontation with communism, and preferred a strategy of strengthening US allies around the world to contain the Soviet Union. Like the hardliners, they were deeply committed to criticizing the Soviet Union for its human rights violations, but they also supported some measure of criticism of American allies, combined with a desire to promote democracy. The two groups would struggle for Reagan's attention on foreign policy issues throughout his tenure, and the turf war between them was a defining feature for the administration's human rights policy. On diplomacy toward the Soviet Union, especially after the rise to power of Mikhail Gorbachev, Reagan increasingly sided with the moderates, to the great frustration of the Cold War warriors. On policy toward Central America and to a lesser extent South Africa, the opposite was mostly the case.[21] Despite being the chief architect of the administration's South Africa policy, Crocker failed to persuade Reagan to moderate this policy in the face of growing congressional opposition, as Reagan decided instead to follow the advice of hardliners to stay firm.

Changes in personnel over time also had important implications for the administration's foreign policy and its approach to human rights. Reagan's first secretary of state, the former general Alexander M. Haig, was the embodiment of a Cold War hardliner. He favored a muscular foreign policy and, for instance, caused a stir by suggesting that a nuclear warning shot in Europe might be a useful way to deter the Soviets. At the time of the assassination attempt against Reagan, Haig upset many in the administration and the American public when he declared that he was now in charge.[22] Ultimately, Haig proved to be too divisive of a character. The former chief of staff in the Nixon White House was unpopular among Democrats in Congress and repeatedly clashed with other Reagan officials, including fellow hardliners such as Weinberger. In July 1982, Haig resigned after less than eighteen months at the position. His replacement with the more moderate Shultz signified an important change in the Reagan foreign policy team. Shultz would become a pivotal figure in the administration's foreign policy, especially in relations with the Soviet Union where he would oversee negotiations to reduce arms and promote human rights and develop strong personal ties with the Soviet leadership.[23]

---

[21] Piero Gleijeses, *Visions of Freedom: Havana, Washington, Pretoria and the Struggle for Southern Africa, 1976–1991* (Chapel Hill: The University of North Carolina Press, 2013), 283–284.

[22] Cannon, *President Reagan*, 165.   [23] Zelizer, *Arsenal of Democracy*, 310.

Secretary of Defense Caspar Weinberger was another fierce Cold War warrior, albeit much more cautious than Haig and determined to avoid unpopular military interventions.[24] The US military interventions in Lebanon and Granada in 1983 made Weinberger cautious about applying military force and led him to develop the so-called Weinberger Doctrine. In this doctrine, he stated that public and congressional support along with clearly defined political and military objectives should be preconditions for the use of force.[25] Shultz, who often clashed with Weinberger, criticized the doctrine for being a too-restrained approach to using military power. On the issue of human rights, Weinberger was highly critical of Carter's human rights policy for abandoning American allies over their human rights records. In a transition team memo before being appointed to Reagan's cabinet, Weinberger argued that the United States had to stop undermining friendly regimes in places such as Iran and Nicaragua before considering the human rights records of the likely successor regimes.[26]

Reagan's decision to appoint his campaign manager William J. Casey as head of the CIA was an unconventional choice. Intelligent, willful, and trusted by Reagan, Casey turned the CIA into a vehicle for his own foreign policy aspirations, enjoying significant autonomy and often clashing with the Departments of State and Defense. In the words of Pulitzer Prize-winning journalist Tim Weiner, Casey believed that if it is secret then it is legal, and he reserved the right to lie and cheat.[27] Casey was even more willing to use military force than either Shultz or Weinberger and certainly did not share the latter's concern for congressional support: "The business of Congress is to stay out of my business", he once asserted.[28] Casey would become particularly significant for US policy in Central America, which would lead to bitter disputes between liberals in Congress and the administration over US support for repressive regimes and guerillas, such the Nicaraguan Contras, despite massive human rights violations.

Reagan also appointed several neoconservatives to prominent foreign policy positions in his administration, several of whom were members of

[24] Ronald J. Granieri, "Beyond Cap the Foil. Caspar Weinberger and the Reagan-Era Defense Buildup," in *Reagan and the World: Leadership and National Security, 1981–1989*, ed. Bradley Lynn Coleman and Kyle Longley (Lexington: The University Press of Kentucky, 2017), 51–79.

[25] Pach, "Sticking to His Guns," 101.

[26] Memo, Caspar Weinberger to William J. Casey, December 5, 1980, William J. Casey Papers, Box 300, Folder 5, Hoover Institution Archives.

[27] Tim Weiner, *Legacy of Ashes: The History of the CIA* (New York: Doubleday, 2007), 376.

[28] Casey, quoted in Johnson, "Congress and the Cold War," 96.

the interest groups the Committee on the Present Danger (CPD) and the lesser known Committee for the Free World (CFW).[29] While the CPD grew out of the so-called Team B, which President Gerald R. Ford had authorized to assess the Soviet Union's military capabilities and intentions, the CFW was established in 1981 by a group of journalists, academics, politicians, artist, and think tank scholars from a dozen Western countries. The two groups shared a significant overlap in membership and were united in their strongly anti-communist worldviews. Focused on national security issues, the CPD argued that the United States needed to increase its military spending to deter Soviet aggression. Concerned with the ideological struggle, the CFW argued that US foreign policy should do more to defend Western democracy against Soviet communism.[30]

The groups provided several individuals for Reagan's foreign policy team, including no fewer than thirty-two members of the CPD, of which Reagan himself was a member. These counted Richard Perle as assistant secretary of defense, Eugene Rostow as head of the Arms Control and Disarmament Agency, Paul Wolfowitz in the State Department, Paul Nitze as top arms negotiator with the Soviet Union, and Richard V. Allen as national security advisor.[31] Another neoconservative and member of the CFW, Elliott Abrams, would become particularly consequential for the administration's approach to human rights. As assistant secretary of state for human rights and humanitarian affairs in Reagan's first term and for inter-American affairs in his second, Abrams was one of the primary architects of the administration's human rights policy. Finally, Reagan appointed Jeane Kirkpatrick, a member of both the CPD and the CFW, as ambassador to the United Nations. Kirkpatrick had attracted widespread attention with her 1979 article "Dictatorships and Double Standards" in the neoconservative journal *Commentary*. Here, Kirkpatrick attacked Carter's human rights policy for neglecting the centrality of the East–West conflict and failing to prioritize the strategic and economic interests of the United States. According to Kirkpatrick, Carter had failed to make a distinction between totalitarian regimes and authoritarian governments. By "totalitarian regimes" Kirkpatrick meant communist

---

[29] Justin Vaïsse, *Neoconservatism: The Biography of a Movement* (Cambridge, MA: Harvard University Press, 2010), 180. According to Vaïsse, neoconservatives can be divided into three ages. The first represented former Cold War liberals who moved to the right over the 1970s and 1980s. The second was Democrats who abandoned Carter for Reagan during 1980, believing Reagan was the candidate best suited for restoring American power. (The third did not begin until 1995.)

[30] Rasmus Sinding Søndergaard, "The Committee for the Free World and the Defense of Democracy," *Journal of Cold War Studies* (in press).

[31] Zelizer, *Arsenal of Democracy*, 304.

regimes for which, she argued, there was no hope of reform. "Authoritarian governments," however, she reasoned, had the potential to develop into democracies. Based on this assertion, Kirkpatrick concluded that authoritarian governments were preferable to totalitarian regimes and, consequently, the United States ought to support friendly authoritarians.[32] The conclusion became known as the Kirkpatrick Doctrine and would be a cornerstone in Reagan's foreign policy. The key implication for human rights was that the United States would criticize human rights violations in communist countries, while largely remaining quiet about violations by allied authoritarian regimes.

In addition to internal power struggles in the administration, members of Congress often interfered to make their mark on the direction of US foreign policy. Democrats and sometimes Republicans in Congress tempered Reagan's foreign policy on several occasions. As much as Reagan sought to rid America of the Vietnam Syndrome, he had to contend with both a Congress and a public highly skeptical of expansive and prolonged military campaigns. Congressional legislation put limits on Reagan's desire to see the Reagan Doctrine implemented, often citing human rights concerns as motivations for restricting economic and military assistance to allies and anti-communist guerrilla groups. Such congressional restrictions and public opinion, along with geopolitical concerns, often led Reagan to rely on covert operations when the administration intervened in Cold War hot spots in the Third World.

Rejecting Human Rights

As evident from the presidential election debates, Reagan entered the White House highly skeptical of human rights as a foreign policy concern. Throughout the campaign, he repeatedly vowed to undo the Carter administration's human rights-based foreign policy. This position was undoubtedly motivated by Reagan's desire to distance himself from Carter, but it also reflected a fundamentally different view of how the United States ought to handle the Cold War. Abrams later said, "I think the Reagan Administration came to office without a conception of human rights policy except the view of the Carter Administration. That conception was viewed as flawed from a pragmatic point of view and leftist from an ideological point of view. [...] As a result of which, the reaction of most of the incoming Administration was: 'This is no good – throw it out!' And this is pretty much what the Administration

---

[32] Kirkpatrick, "Dictatorships and Double Standards." See also, Jeane J. Kirkpatrick, "U.S. Security & Latin America," *Commentary* 71, no. 1 (1981): 29–40.

started with."[33] A human rights-based foreign policy, as practiced by Carter, was both practically and ideologically incompatible with Reagan's conservative internationalism, and the administration's initial reaction was to dismiss human rights concerns altogether.

Early statements by the new administration indicated that human rights had fallen out of favor as a guiding principle for American foreign policy. At his first press conference as Reagan's secretary of state on January 28, 1981, Haig proclaimed that fighting "international terrorism will now take the place of human rights" because terrorism, he argued is the "ultimate abuse of human rights."[34] To Haig and most of the administration hardliners, terrorism was synonymous with communism. The chair of the House Foreign Affairs Subcommittee on Human Rights, Don Bonker (D-WA) retorted that such a statement made no sense and vowed, "any attempt to dismantle or ignore our traditional commitment to human rights will be met with firm resistance in Congress."[35] In reality, Bonker argued, "some totalitarian Communist regimes will be publicly criticized but authoritarian governments of the right will be wined and dined at the White House."[36] Other members of Congress, however, were more supportive of Haig's position. In a meeting with Haig a week before his statement, a ranking member of the House Foreign Affairs Committee, Representative William Broomfield (R-MI), told Haig that he agreed with his assessment that international terrorism would increase in importance at the expense of human rights.[37] In a meeting with Reagan a few days later, Broomfield strongly urged that the United States "get off the human rights kick," a remark Reagan expressed appreciation for.[38]

In the following months, other administration officials continued to issue statements that indicated that human rights would be demoted as a foreign policy concern compared with the Carter administration. Allen declared that the new administration would "not place as much

[33] Quoted in Hauke Hartmann, "US Human Rights Policy under Carter and Reagan, 1977–1981," *Human Rights Quarterly* 23, no. 2 (2001): 424.

[34] Quoted in Peterson, *Globalizing Human Rights*, 108.

[35] Don Bonker, "Human Rights: Will Reagan Learn from Congress?" *The Christian Science Monitor*, February 25, 1981; *Human Rights Watch Records*, Series I: Jeri Laber Files, Box 67, Folder 6, Center for Human Rights Documentation and Research, Rare Book and Manuscript Library, Columbia University Library.

[36] Don Bonker, Statement, April 1, 1981, Box HRIO-96&97, Folder 11, House Foreign Affairs Committee Subcommittee on Human Rights. Center for Legislative Archives, National Archives, Washington, DC.

[37] US Department of State, *Foreign Relations of the United States, 1981–1988, Volume XII, Global Issues II*, Document 40.

[38] Memo for the President's File, January 28, 1981, Richard V. Allen Papers, 1961–1999, Box 45, Folder 2, Hoover Institution Archives.

ideological emphasis on human rights" as had its predecessor.[39] When, at a ceremony for Holocaust victims on April 30, 1981, Reagan proclaimed his commitment to prevent persecution "wherever it takes place in the world," a White House spokesperson felt the need to publicly retract on the president's remarks.[40] Reagan had "not meant to alter his policy of playing down the human rights issue in foreign relations," the spokesperson explained to the press.[41] Clearly, the administration deliberately and consistently expressed its intention to downgrade concern for human rights in US foreign policy.

The new rhetoric on human rights had implications on world affairs even before Reagan's inauguration, as dictators around the globe took note of the new signals coming out of Washington. In the months between Reagan's election victory and his inauguration, human rights abuses soared in several countries.[42] An expelled Haitian journalist explained that the Haitian authorities "thought the international climate was favorable to this sort of thing. They thought human rights was over."[43] In a similar vein, a source informed the US embassy in Buenos Aires in August 1980 that the Argentine minister of interior General Albano Harguindeguy thought Reagan would "applaud the Argentine government tactics in the 'dirty war' and encourage such tactics in Argentina and elsewhere."[44] In South Korea, the media quoted anonymous officials from the country's foreign ministry, who welcomed Reagan's election in the anticipation that this signaled the end to US interference in South Korea's internal affairs in the name of human rights.[45] Evidently, the expectation among several of America's allies was that Reagan's presidency would stop US human rights criticism.

The new view of human rights in the White House also permeated the policies of the Reagan administration. Whereas Carter had made a point to distance the United States from foreign leaders guilty of human rights abuses, Reagan did not shun hosting leaders from countries with dismal

---

[39] American Association for the International Commission of Jurists (AAICJ), *Human Rights and United States Foreign Policy, the First Decade, 1973–1983* (Geneva: International Commission of Jurists, 1984), 33.

[40] Ronald Reagan, Remarks at the First Annual Commemoration of the Days of Remembrance of Victims of the Holocaust, April 30, 1981. Online by Gerhard Peters and John T. Woolley, The American Presidency Project, accessed August 7, 2019, www.presidency.ucsb.edu/node/247160.

[41] Quoted in AAICJ, "Human Rights and United States Foreign Policy," 33.

[42] Sikkink, *Mixed Signals*, 150–151.

[43] Quoted in Jacoby, "The Reagan Turnaround," 1069.

[44] Quoted in Schmidli, *The Fate of Freedom Elsewhere*, 183.

[45] Memorandum, "DCI Meeting with President-Elect's Staff," November 14, 1980, Central Intelligence Agency Electronic Reading Room, Doc. No. CIA-RDP81B00493R0W100090009–5.

Figure 2 Ronald and Nancy Reagan host South Korean President
Chun Doo-hwan and his wife Mrs. Chun, despite protest against the
country's dismal human rights record, February 3, 1981.
Bettmann via Getty Images.

human rights records.[46] On February 2, 1981, less than two weeks after
taking office, Reagan warmly welcomed South Korean President Chun
Doo-hwan to the White House, despite loud protests over the South
Korean regimes' human rights violations (Figure 2).[47] Documents show
that administration officials were concerned with being perceived as
uncritical of such human rights violations but placed more value on the
desire to strengthen security relations with South Korea.[48] The meeting

[46] Carter's attempt to distance the United States from such leaders was by no means
consistent. For instance, Carter hosted the Shah of Iran on November 15, 1977.

[47] See, for instance, Editorial, "Wrong Turns on Human Rights," *The New York Times*,
February 6, 1981, www.nytimes.com/1981/02/06/opinion/wrong-turns-on-human-rights
.html.

[48] Memorandum of Conversation, Subject: Summary of the President's Meeting with
President Chun Doo Hwan of the Republic of Korea, February 2, 1981, 11:20–12:05
PM, Cabinet Room, with Cover Memorandum, Richard V. Allen to President Reagan,
February 6, 1981, Subject: Your Meeting with President Chun of Korea [MDR-Reagan
Library]. Accessed online through the National Security Archive. http://nsarchive
.gwu.edu/NSAEBB/NSAEBB306/. For more on Chun's visit and the role of human
rights in US–Korean relations, see Renouard, *Human Rights in American Foreign Policy*,
193–198.

with Chun was but one of many meetings where Reagan welcomed foreign leaders with abysmal human rights records to the White House. Another example was Argentina's incoming president, General Roberto Eduardo Viola, who in March 1981 became the first Latin American head of state to visit the Reagan White House, despite his role in Argentina's dirty war.[49]

The downgrading of human rights was also apparent in the restructuring of the foreign policy bureaucracy, which included a diminished role for the Human Rights Bureau. The team in charge of the transitioning of the State Department advised that State should no longer delay decisions where human rights concerns conflicted with vital national interests. In a meeting with the leadership of the House Foreign Affairs Committee on January 23, 1981, three days after Reagan's inauguration, Haig asked the for the representatives' assistance in getting rid of the Human Rights Bureau and returning the responsibility for human rights to the various other bureaus. Chairman Clement Zablocki (D-WI) said he was sympathetic to the idea, but warned that he had been defeated when he had tried to shut down his own committee's Subcommittee on Human Rights.[50] While the Human Rights Bureau was never dismantled, the downgraded priority of human rights and the ensuing uncertainty over the bureau's future made it difficult to attract qualified personnel to the bureau.[51] The bureau was, thus, severely weakened during the beginning of Reagan's tenure.

Reagan's disregard for human rights also expressed itself in his nomination of Ernest Lefever for the position as assistant secretary of the State Department's Human Rights Bureau. An outspoken critic of the Carter administration's human rights policy, Lefever was the founder of a right-wing think tank and was poorly regarded in the human rights community. Over the years, Lefever had argued that the United States should dismantle the Human Rights Bureau, put an end to the annual *Country Reports on Human Rights Practices,* and stop promoting human rights abroad.[52] In a letter to the Carter administration in 1977, Lefever had proclaimed, "The consistent and single-marked invocation of the

---

[49] Stephen G. Rabe, *The Killing Zone: The United States Wages Cold War in Latin America* (New York: Oxford University Press, 2012), 158; Schmidli, *The Fate of Freedom Elsewhere,* 183–184.

[50] US Department of State, *Foreign Relations of the United States, 1981–1988, Volume XII, Global Issues II,* Document 40.

[51] Edwin S. Maynard, "The Bureaucracy and Implementation of US Human Rights Policy," *Human Rights Quarterly* 11, no. 2 (1989): 184.

[52] Forsythe, *Human Rights and U.S. Foreign Policy,* 181; Maynard, "The Bureaucracy and Implementation of US Human Rights Policy," 182.

'human rights standard' in making United States foreign policy decisions serves neither our interests nor the cause of freedom."[53] It was, therefore, hardly surprising that Lefever's nomination generated considerable unrest among supporters of an active human rights policy on Capitol Hill and in the NGO sector. The nomination clearly represented an attempt to downgrade the role of human rights in US foreign policy.

In the only comprehensive examination of the nomination of Lefever, Sarah Snyder has demonstrated how opposition to Lefever was driven by substantive differences over policy, doubts about his qualifications, and disapproval of his personal disposition.[54] Focusing on this opposition, Snyder does not account for Lefever's attempt to formulate a policy to implement his views of human rights. A recently declassified memo drafted by Lefever, however, casts light on the human rights policy Lefever intended to pursue. Approved by Haig and circulated internally among officials in the Human Rights Bureau on March 14, 1981, the memo stated, "This administration is determined to pursue a vigorous and human foreign policy." To this effect, the administration would "broaden and deepen the concept of human rights" to go beyond the violations of individuals to include "the imposition of foreign control over other peoples, external subversion, genocide, and terrorism."[55] This broadening and deepening of the concept of human rights was thus not an attempt to supplement the traditional American focus on civil and political rights with the full range of social, economic, and cultural human rights enumerated in the UDHR that the Carter administration had pursued. Rather, the redefinition of human rights was intended to facilitate the labeling of Soviet foreign policies perceived as subversion, expansion, and terrorism as human rights violations. The memo underlined this intention by reciting the logic of the Kirkpatrick Doctrine to argue for a measured response to authoritarian allies and labeling the Soviet Union as the primary human rights violator. Finally, the memo presented four ways to conduct US human rights policy: serving as an example for emulation, supporting allies, raising human rights concerns through quiet diplomacy, and publicly condemning gross violations, which, the memo argued, tended to be committed by the Soviet Union. Lefever relayed this policy in a meeting with leaders of the human rights NGO Helsinki Watch a few days later but, judging from the summary memo of the conversation,

[53] Ernest W. Lefever, *Morality and Foreign Policy: A Symposium on President Carter's Stance* (Washington, DC: Ethics and Public Policy Center, Georgetown University, 1977).
[54] Snyder, "The Defeat of Ernest Lefever's Nomination," 138.
[55] US Department of State, *Foreign Relations of the United States, 1981–1988, Volume XII, Global Issues II*, Document 46.

these did not receive the policy well. Helsinki Watch chairman Robert L. Bernstein, in particular, expressed concern that the Kirkpatrick Doctrine and Haig's statements about terrorism replacing human rights had hurt the public perception of US human rights policy.[56]

The meaning of the nomination was not lost on members of Congress favoring a strong emphasis on human rights in US foreign policy. The confirmation hearing in the Senate Foreign Relations Committee opened with several members of the committee declaring their support for human rights as an essential part of US foreign policy and questioning whether Lefever shared this viewpoint, given his previous statements. The long-serving Democratic Whip of the Senate, liberal Democrat Alan Cranston (D-CA), decried Lefever's track record of attacking human rights, including advocating for close relations with the South African apartheid regime and being blind to human rights violations of right-wing dictatorships.[57] Lefever's opening statement and the subsequent debate did little to convince the skeptics. Citing previous statements by Lefever, Chairman Charles H. Percy (R-IL) and others challenged the nominee's commitment to human rights. Lefever did renounce some of his earlier viewpoints, such as his 1979 statement that the United States should never make foreign assistance contingent on human rights records, and he declared himself a newfound supporter of legislation such as the Jackson–Vanik Amendment.[58] Nevertheless, Lefever insisted that the United States had neither the right nor the power to promote human rights in other sovereign states.

During the Senate confirmation hearing, several human rights NGOs and individuals offered strong statements against the nomination. A significant influence was the Argentinian journalist and former political prisoner Jacobo Timerman, with whom several senators from the committee, including Percy, had met at a dinner hosted by Bernstein the night before.[59] Only a week before the hearing, Timerman had published the book *Prisoner without a Name, Cell without a Number*, in which he described his experiences with imprisonment and torture in Argentina.[60]

---

[56] US Department of State, *Foreign Relations of the United States, 1981–1988, Volume XII, Global Issues II*, Document 48.

[57] US Congress, Senate, Committee on Foreign Relations, *Hearings before the Committee on Foreign Relations on Nomination of Ernest W. Lefever, to Be Assistant Secretary of State for Human Rights and Humanitarian Affairs*, 97th Congress, 1st Session, May 18, 19, and June 4, 5, 1981, 4.

[58] Ibid., 84.

[59] Ibid., 205; Aryeh Neier, *Taking Liberties: Four Decades in the Struggle for Rights* (New York: Public Affairs, 2003), 184.

[60] Jacobo Timerman, *Prisoner without a Name, Cell without a Number* (New York: Knopf, 1981).

The book instantly made headlines, selling out the first two printings before publication and propelling Timerman onto American prime time TV. During the hearing, several senators referred to Timerman's experience as an example of the importance of a strong human rights policy, and Senator Paul Tsongas (D-MA) even cited the book at length to illustrate the horrors of human rights violations.[61] When Timerman's presence in the audience was announced, he received a roaring applause, which led Tsongas to remark, "I am glad he is not eligible to run for the Senate from Massachusetts."[62] Helsinki Watch's executive director, Aryeh Neier, who was present at the hearing, later recalled, "At that moment, I knew Lefever was defeated."[63] Referring to former assistant secretary of the Human Rights Bureau Patricia Derian's advocacy for Timerman during his imprisonment, the moderate Republican Senator Larry Pressler (R-SD) questioned whether Timerman would have been free today if Lefever had been in charge. Lefever brushed aside the question as hypothetical.[64]

As illustrated by such exchanges, the Timerman case became a personal and strongly emotional example of the consequences of Lefever's unwillingness to criticize human rights violations among right-wing allies, such as the military regime in Argentina. "Eventually," according to Neier, "some members of the Senate Foreign Relations Committee came to feel they were choosing between Timerman and Lefever in casting their vote on the latter's confirmation."[65] In the days leading up to the confirmation hearing, Helsinki Watch lobbied most of the senators on the committee to reject Lefever. In one such meeting, the liberal Democrat Claiborne Pell (D-RI) expressed his inclination to let Reagan have his way with the nomination and defended Lefever on some issues. Nonetheless, Pell said that he would read Timerman's book over the weekend. Timerman was Jewish and part of his book dealt with anti-Semitism, a topic of great importance to Pell since he had witnessed the persecution of Jews while traveling through Poland as a young student in 1939.[66] The book apparently influenced Pell, as he was one of the senators who displayed it at the hearing while attacking Lefever. The personal identification many senators felt with the fate of Timerman thus appears to have significantly influenced their view on Lefever's nomination.

---

[61] *Nomination of Ernest W. Lefever*, 96.   [62] Ibid., 288.

[63] Neier, *Taking Liberties*, 185.

[64] *Nomination of Ernest W. Lefever*, 457. For Derian's advocacy for Timerman, see Schmidli, *The Fate of Freedom Elsewhere*, 184–185.

[65] Neier, *Taking Liberties*, 179.   [66] Miller, *An Uncommon Man*, 60–61.

At the end of the confirmation hearing, Lefever failed to convince the skeptics. His testimony left most senators dissatisfied, and in their closing remarks several senators expressed their dissatisfaction by calling Lefever's responses during the hearing evasive, misleading, and even incorrect.[67] Casting his vote against Lefever's nomination, Tsongas stated, "His views on human rights policy are the primary reason for my decision."[68] As a result, the Senate Foreign Relations Committee rejected the nomination with a comfortable thirteen-to-four vote on June 5, 1981. Five of the committee's nine Republican senators joined their eight Democratic colleagues in rejecting the nomination. One of these Republican senators was Nancy Kassebaum (R-KS), who had originally supported the nomination but ended up voting against it. Kassebaum defended her vote by stating that Lefever had become a "lightning rod" for critics of the administration's human rights policy and, therefore, had lost the ability to lead the Human Rights Bureau.[69] Following the rejection, Lefever withdrew his name from consideration for the position.

The opposition to the Reagan administration's downgrading of human rights in general and the Lefever nomination in particular also manifested itself outside Capitol Hill. Some NGOs and private citizens issued press releases and took to the pages of newspapers to express their dissatisfaction. The Ad Hoc Committee of the Human Rights Community, consisting of sixty organizations and individuals from the American human rights community, immediately condemned the nomination of Lefever. According to the committee, the nomination implied "a perversion of internationally recognized human rights values into blind support of authoritarian allies coupled with politically motivated denunciations of perceived United States enemies."[70] The ad hoc committee also wrote the Senate Foreign Relations Committee ahead of the nomination hearing, urging the rejection of Lefever.[71] A *New York Times* editorial on May

---

[67] *Nomination of Ernest W. Lefever*, 499–519.

[68] Paul E. Tsongas, "Statement of Senator Paul E. Tsongas on the Nomination of Dr. Ernest Lefever to Assistant Secretary for Human Rights and Humanitarian Affairs," *Paul Tsongas Digital Archives*, accessed August 9, 2019, https://ptsongasuml.omeka.net/items/show/1651.

[69] US Congress, Committee on Foreign Affairs, *Congress and Foreign Policy – 1981*, Committee Print (Washington, DC: US Government Printing Office, 1982), 13.

[70] Charles Mohr, "Coalition Assails Reagan's Choice for State Dept. Human Rights Job," *The New York Times*, February 25, 1981, www.nytimes.com/1981/02/25/world/coalition-assails-reagan-s-choice-for-state-dept-human-rights-job.html.

[71] Ad Hoc Committee of the Human Rights Community, News Release, May 14, 1981, National Conference on Soviet Jewry Records; I-181A; 290, 11; American Jewish Historical Society, New York (hereafter NCSJR).

24 decried the Reagan administration's "shameful squirming on human rights" and deemed Lefever an "unworthy nominee."[72]

The reaction from the Senate was a surprising rebuttal of the will of the popular incoming president, which would prove illustrative of Congress's commitment to human rights in the coming years. That a committee with a Republican majority had turned down a Republican president's nominee had great symbolic value. It sent a clear signal to the new president that members of Congress were not willing to sell off human rights.[73] It illustrated both the executive and legislative branches' divide over human rights and that bipartisan cooperation on human rights in Congress was possible. The rarity of such a rejection further highlighted its significance. It was extremely unusual for the Senate to reject a presidential nominee, and when this had happened in the past it had normally been a nomination at a much higher level. The nomination of an assistant secretary of state was considered a formality. As argued by Snyder, the defeat of Lefever's nomination was a significant victory for those who wanted to see human rights remain an element of US foreign policy.[74] The result was a great boost to the still-nascent human rights community, as it appeared far more powerful than anybody had anticipated and thereby helped increase its importance.

Public opinion also reflected dissatisfaction with the Reagan administration's failure to prioritize the promotion and protection of human rights as a foreign policy objective. A March 1981 opinion poll asked Americans whether they agreed or disagreed with the Reagan administration's decision of "Giving opposition to international terrorism a higher priority than support for human rights." Fifty percent answered that they disagreed, while forty-three percent said they agreed.[75] It would be wrong, however, to interpret the relatively even split on this question as an indication that the American public was divided over their support for human rights. Polls by Gallup and the Council on Foreign Relations conducted every four years during the Carter and Reagan administrations showed consistent public support for human rights as part of American foreign policy. Asked to rate the importance of US foreign policy goals, the American people consistently expressed support for the goal "promoting and defending human

---

[72] Editorial, "Semantic Antics over Human Rights," May 24, 1981, www.nytimes.com/1981/05/24/opinion/semantic-antics-over-human-rights.html.

[73] Ibid.   [74] Snyder, "The Defeat of Ernest Lefever's Nomination," 137.

[75] Louis Harris & Associates. Harris Survey, March 1981. USHARRIS.042781.R07. Cornell University, Ithaca, NY: Roper Center for Public Opinion Research, iPOLL, accessed August 2, 2019.

rights in other countries." In November 1978, 39 percent answered that this goal was "very important," 40 percent answered "somewhat important," and only 14 percent chose "not important."[76] In October 1982, the corresponding percentages were even more supportive, with 43 percent for "very important," 42 percent for "somewhat important," and only 9 percent "not important."[77] Four years later in October 1986, the numbers remained at 42 percent, 45 percent, and 10 percent, respectively.[78] The American public was clearly committed to American support of human rights as a general concept, when the political and economic costs associated with such support were not addressed. In other words, the support for human rights was widespread, but vague and undefined. Combined with the support for human rights in Congress, such public opinion made it problematic for the Reagan administration to downgrade human rights as a general foreign policy objective.

A Conservative Human Rights Policy

Congressional and public opinion made it clear to the Reagan administration that the failure to seriously address human rights concerns would come at a great political cost. This realization, along with an opportunistic decision to utilize human rights for propaganda purposes in the Cold War, led the Reagan administration to reevaluate its stance on human rights. It became apparent to Reagan's advisors that if the administration was perceived as indifferent to human rights, it could jeopardize popular support for Reagan's general foreign policy.[79] As criticism intensified, the need for at least a superficial human rights policy became ever more apparent and the administration began to contemplate how to integrate a human rights policy into its overall foreign policy strategy.

---

[76] Chicago Council on Foreign Relations. Gallup/CCFR Survey of American Public Opinion and U.S. Foreign Policy 1978, November 1978. USGALLUP.78CFR.R32L. Cornell University, Ithaca, NY: Roper Center for Public Opinion Research, iPOLL, accessed August 2, 2019.

[77] Chicago Council on Foreign Relations. Gallup/CCFR Survey of American Public Opinion and U.S. Foreign Policy 1983, October 1982. USGALLUP.CFR83G.R29B. Cornell University, Ithaca, NY: Roper Center for Public Opinion Research, iPOLL, accessed August 2, 2019.

[78] Chicago Council on Foreign Relations. Gallup/CCFR Survey of American Public Opinion and U.S. Foreign Policy 1986, October 1986. USGALLUP.86CFRP.R21B. Cornell University, Ithaca, NY: Roper Center for Public Opinion Research, iPOLL, accessed August 2, 2019.

[79] Forsythe, *Human Rights and U.S. Foreign Policy*, 139. Snyder reaches the same conclusion. Snyder, "The Defeat of Ernest Lefever's Nomination," 136–161.

Documents from Reagan's NSC show that some voices inside the administration realized early on that the administration needed a strong human rights policy. On February 17, 1981, NSC staffer Carnes Lord warned National Security Advisor Richard V. Allen that there was a widespread perception that the administration had downgraded human rights and urged that the administration take the initiative to correct this view. In the margins, Allen commented, "I agree." Lord went on to recommend that the administration develop a "conceptual coherence in the idea of human rights."[80] To do so, in Lord's opinion, the administration would have to overcome three widespread conceptual failures on human rights. First, it was important to understand that there was no inherent mismatch between anti-terrorism and human rights, since a society under attack by terrorists could never guarantee human rights. Second, it could be necessary to support "regimes whose political systems are less than impeccably democratic" as they might offer the best protection of human rights. Third, a human rights policy should not be a "public lecturing of other nations on their domestic affairs" but rather strive for a less-visible approach.[81] Such perceptions of what a human rights policy ought to look like represented an obvious break with Carter's human rights policy.

A month later, Lord presented Allen with a paper entitled "Human Rights Policy in a Non-Liberal World," in which he further explored the conceptual issues of a human rights policy. In the paper, Lord argued that a human rights policy would have to appeal to the non-Western world and, therefore, should not equate human rights with the promotion of Western-style representative democracy and capitalism. Economic and social aspirations, according to Lord, should not be treated as human rights. Instead, a human rights policy should center on civil rights and the rule of law "defined with enough flexibility that we do not appear to be forcing our Bill of Rights down the throats of other nations."[82] In other words, Lord was advocating for a narrow definition of human rights, with greater flexibility for non-Western regimes to determine which rights they would provide to citizens.

The internal debate about the role of human rights also began to manifest itself in the Reagan administration's rhetoric. On March 31, 1981, Secretary Haig proclaimed in a speech to the transnational elite organization the Trilateral Commission that, "human rights remains a

---

[80] NSC Memo, February 17, 1981, ID#020155, HU, WHORM Subject File, Ronald Reagan Library (hereafter RPL).
[81] Ibid.
[82] NSC memo, March 06, 1981, ID#046147, HU, WHORM Subject File, RPL.

major focus of our foreign policy" because, Haig argued, they were "integral" to American national interests.[83] Such words were in stark contrast to Haig's speech just two months earlier about how international terrorism would replace human rights. However, Haig's speech to the Trilateral Commission only vaguely detailed how human rights remained a major focus in US foreign policy, and the Reagan administration did not turn "Carteresque" overnight. Rather, the speech reflected the emerging calculation in the administration that is was better to reform rather than reject human rights.

The Senate Foreign Relations Committee's rejection of Lefever added to this realization and intensified the administration's quest to develop a robust human rights policy within its overall foreign policy strategy, which could win over critics. With moderate Republicans such as Kassebaum and Charles Mathias (R-MD) voting against Lefever, and the downgrade of human rights concerns he was perceived to represent, the administration's support in the committee was limited to conservatives such as Jesse Helms (R-NC) and Samuel Hayakawa (R-CA) and stalwart Reagan supporters such as Howard Baker Jr. (R-TN). In late July, Charles Fairbanks Jr. from the State Department's Policy Planning Staff circulated a longer draft paper on human rights to a handful of senior officials in the State Department. The paper opened with the words, "Within the Department there is a widespread feeling that we need a more definite human rights policy after the delays caused by Dr. Lefever's nomination process."[84] The paper then stated, "Congress is now troubling us at hearings in a way that we could avoid with a fuller determination of policy... Human rights are now the main area of assault by the Left on the new Administration's foreign policy."[85] The paper expressed concern that if the administration failed to develop a vigorous human rights policy, such problems with Congress would only get worse. Therefore, it declared, "A strong foreign policy will require a strong human rights policy, because the legitimacy of our entire foreign policy at home and before the allies depends heavily on what we do in the human rights area."[86] The paper thus reveals that pressure from members of Congress was a decisive factor behind the Reagan administration's decision to revise its human rights policy.

---

[83] Peterson, *Globalizing Human Rights*, 106–126. For the Trilateral Commission, see Dino Knudsen, *The Trilateral Commission and Global Governance: Informal Elite Diplomacy, 1972–82* (New York: Routledge, 2016).

[84] Memo, Charles Fairbanks to EUR/HA/S/P, July 29, 1981, RAC Box 6, Carnes Lord Files, RPL.

[85] Ibid.   [86] Ibid.

The paper reflected a determination not only to respond to criticism of the administration's human rights policy but to proactively turn human rights into an instrument to advance the administration's ideals and interests. This determination is evident in the twelve basic principles the paper listed as guidelines of a "realistic human rights policy:"

1. Human rights should never be the only factor determining policy.
2. A strong United States and a strong defense were indispensable for a successful human rights policy.
3. The Soviet Union had a profoundly negative impact on human rights, and, therefore, its influence had to be countered.
4. When a government violating human rights was about to be overthrown, the United States should consider the alternative violations of the new regime when deciding its policy.
5. A human rights policy should avoid seeming patronizing.
6. A human rights policy had to apply to both adversaries and allies to be credible.
7. The United States should take the offensive against adversaries violating human rights.
8. The policy should make a distinction between authoritarian and totalitarian regimes, albeit it was noted, the administration should be careful when using this distinction.
9. The United States should acknowledge that a human rights policy was inadequate to change the domestic habits of other states.
10. Quiet diplomacy should always be the first action.
11. Public diplomacy should be used as a supplement to quiet diplomacy.
12. The administration's conception of human rights should be vigorously promoted in public rhetoric in order to shape the debate.[87]

The paper went on to sketch the role of the Human Rights Bureau and outline how the administration ought to deal with the requirements of human rights legislation. Among these was a determination to use the *Country Reports on Human Rights Practices* to shape the debate over human rights by, for instance, redefining social and economic rights as needs rather than actual rights.[88] The need for a strong Human Rights Bureau was repeated in a memo from Director of Policy Planning Paul Wolfowitz and Assistant Secretary for European Affairs Lawrence Eagleburger to Haig in early October, warning that failure to

---

[87] Ibid. The principles are paraphrased from the memo.
[88] Memo, Charles Fairbanks to EUR/HA/S/P, July 29, 1981, RAC Box 6, Carnes Lord Files, RPL.

prioritize the bureau would draw negative attention to the administration's foreign policy.[89]

In late October, the administration leaked a high-level internal State Department memo drafted by Elliott Abrams that called for a renewed commitment to human rights.[90] The memo, partially reprinted in the *New York Times* a week later, repeated many of the arguments of the July report.[91] It recognized the utility of a more active human rights policy, arguing that such an approach would help counter criticism from Congress and other domestic critics, and serve as a useful ideological weapon against the Soviet Union. Although the memo acknowledged that the administration would have to direct some criticism against allies, the focus of the administration's human rights policy was the Communist Bloc. The memo repeated the narrow definition of human rights expressed in Lord's paper. To emphasize this definition of human rights as primarily civil and political rights, the leaked memo suggested that the administration shift to terms such as "individual rights," "civil liberties," and "political rights."[92] The memo marked a new phase in the administration's approach to human rights, moving from rejection to reform. Human rights, too politically costly to ignore, were to be co-opted to serve US foreign policy objectives.

However, the Reagan White House far from enthusiastically endorsed the memo, and the human rights community remained skeptical. Chief of Staff James A. Baker III said on TV that the memo did not constitute "any significant change in policy." In an op-ed in the *New York Times*, Neier noted that the memo alone did not signify a change in human rights policy. Rather, Neier pointed to the Reagan administration's existing failure to abide by congressionally mandated human rights legislation.[93]

---

[89] US Department of State, *Foreign Relations of the United States, 1981–1988, Volume XII, Global Issues II*, Document 53; Barbara Crossette, "Strong U.S. Human Rights Policy Urged in Memo Approved by Haig," *The New York Times*, November 5, 1981, www .nytimes.com/1981/11/05/world/strong-us-human-rights-policy-urged-memo-approved-haig-excerpts-memo-page-a10.html; "Excerpts from State Department Memo on Human Rights," *The New York Times*, November 5, 1981, www.nytimes.com/1981/11/05/world/excerpts-from-state-department-memo-on-human-rights.html.

[90] According to historian Evan McCormick, Abrams confirmed to him in an interview on April 27, 2010, that he was the author of the memorandum. Evan McCormick, "Freedom Tide? Ideology, Politics and the Origins of Democracy Promotion in U.S. Central America Policy, 1980–1984," *Journal of Cold War Studies* 16, no. 4 (2014): 85.

[91] US Department of State, *Foreign Relations of the United States, 1981–1988, Volume XII, Global Issues II*, Document 54; Maynard, "The Bureaucracy and Implementation of US Human Rights Policy," 183.

[92] Crossette, "Strong U.S. Human Rights Policy"; "Excerpts from State Department Memo."

[93] Aryeh Neier, "Of Reagan and Rights," *The New York Times*, November 12, 1981, www.nytimes.com/1981/11/12/opinion/of-reagan-and-rights.html.

The liberal magazine *The New Republic* called the memo "a step in the right direction," but remained skeptical about the administration's sincerity.[94] It would take more than a leaked memo to convince the skeptics that the Reagan administration was suddenly committed to human rights.

On October 30, Reagan appointed Abrams to fill the still-vacant position as assistant secretary for human rights. In his announcement of Abrams, Reagan declared, "In my administration, human rights considerations are important in all aspects of our foreign policy."[95] In a memo to Haig on December 22, Deputy Secretary William P. Clark argued that the Wolfowitz and Eagleburger memo was the key driver for the appointment of Abrams, and it is now clear that Abrams had been involved in shaping the administration's approach to human rights for a while before his appointment.[96] Unlike Lefever, Abrams got an overwhelmingly positive reception on Capitol Hill. A neoconservative and a former special counsel to Senator Henry M. "Scoop" Jackson (D-WA) (1976–1977) and chief of staff for Senator Daniel P. Moynihan (D-NY) (1978–1979), Abrams shared a worldview with some prominent senators.[97] Even liberal Democrats such as Tsongas and Representative Tom Harkin (D-IA) expressed their public support for his nomination, and Abrams's nomination passed the Senate without any major controversies.[98] In December 1981, Harkin, who had testified against Lefever, described Abrams as "light years ahead" of Lefever in his understanding of human rights, arguing that Abrams could "help end the hypocrisy and callousness that has characterized the Administration's non-policy on human rights."[99]

[94] "Human Rights Revisited," *The New Republic*, November 25, 1981; I-181A; 281; 1 NCSJR.

[95] Quoted in US Library of Congress, Congressional Research Service, *Human Rights and US Foreign Policy*, by Vita Bite, IB81125, (1982), 3.

[96] Memo, William P. Clark to Alexander Haig, December 22, 1981, Department of State, Files of the Deputy Secretary of State – William P. Clark, 1981–1982, Lot 82D127, Memos to S, P, T, E, M, C, S/S – 1981).

[97] Union of Councils for Soviet Jews, Congressional Briefing, January 23, 1985; Union of Councils for Soviet Jews Records; I-410, I-410A; 66; 6; American Jewish Historical Society, New York (hereafter UCSJR).

[98] Judith Miller, "A Neoconservative for Human Rights Post," *The New York Times*, October 31, 1981, 7; US Congress, Senate, Committee on Foreign Relations, *Hearing before the Committee on Foreign Relations on Nomination of Elliott Abrams, of the District of Columbia, to Be Assistant Secretary of State for Human Rights and Humanitarian Affairs*, 97th Congress, 1st Session, November 17, 1981.

[99] George Lister to Elliott Abrams, December 10, 1981, George Lister Papers, Benson Latin American Collection, University of Texas Libraries, University of Texas at Austin, accessed August 2, 2019, https://law.utexas.edu/humanrights/lister/assets/pdf/Human%20Rights%20Bureau/listertoabramsdec101981.pdf?id=txu-blac-glp-316.

Moreover, Abrams possessed a refined understanding of the machinery of the State Department and proved skilled at bureaucratic warfare.[100] These qualities would make him a defining figure in the creation of the administration's human rights policy. As a Washington insider, Abrams also understood the need to address congressional and public demands for some form of human rights policy and knew how to manage Congress. He sought to construct a human rights policy that would appeal to neoconservatives and Cold War warriors on Capitol Hill, hoping to create an alliance between like-minded individuals across the two branches of government.[101] As pointed out by Jackson biographer Robert Kaufman, Reagan's human rights policy under Abrams resembled the human rights policy that Jackson had envisioned in the 1970s.[102] Moreover, it harmonized with Reagan's own human rights criticism from the 1976 election and his skepticism of détente and preference for a stronger stance against communism militarily as well as ideologically.

The Reagan administration's perception of human rights deviated from that of the Carter administration in several ways.[103] The prominence of neoconservatives and conservative Cold War warriors within the Reagan administration was an important factor for this. First, where Carter, at least in principle, had subscribed to a relatively broad definition of human rights, which included economic and social rights, Reagan defined human rights more narrowly as civil and political rights.[104] A State Department memo from 1984 declared, "The U.S. Government recognizes two categories of human rights. First, all individuals should be free from violations of the integrity of the person [...] Second, the government recognizes a group of political and civil rights." The memo described economic, social, and cultural rights, as "desirable ends" but not rights.[105] Second, while Carter had focused on human rights violations among allies as well as adversaries, Reagan's human rights policy

---

[100] Maynard, "The Bureaucracy and Implementation of US Human Rights Policy," 184.

[101] For a description of such crosscutting alliances, see Lindsay, *Congress and the Politics of U.S. Foreign Policy*, 7.

[102] Kaufman, *Henry M. Jackson*, 409.

[103] For a comparison, see Hartmann, "US Human Rights Policy under Carter and Reagan"; David Carleton and Michael Stohl, "The Foreign Policy of Human Rights: Rhetoric and Reality from Jimmy Carter to Ronald Reagan," *Human Rights Quarterly* 7, no. 2 (1985): 205–229. See also, "Interview with Elliott Abrams," *U.S. News of the World Report*, September 10, 1984, I-410, I-410A; 22; 1, UCSJR.

[104] US Department of State, *Foreign Relations of the United States, 1977–1980, Volume II, Human Rights and Humanitarian Affairs*, Document 174. The Carter administration listed three categories of fundamental rights: the right to be free from governmental violations of the integrity of the person, the right to fulfill one's vital needs such as shelter, food, health, and education, and civil and political rights.

[105] Memorandum, State Department, September 14, 1984, I-181A; 287, 6, NCSJR.

overwhelmingly targeted the Soviet Union and its allies. As Reagan told *CBS News* in March 1981, "The Soviet Union is the greatest violator today of human rights in all the world."[106] From Reagan's perspective, opposing communism was itself a promotion of human rights. Third, while Carter spoke of human rights inventing America and not the other way around, Reagan perceived human rights as a fundamentally American invention rooted in the US Bill of Rights.[107]

Reagan also personally chose a different approach to practicing human rights policy than that of his predecessor. Where Carter had publicly criticized foreign leaders and governments for their human rights abuses, Reagan preferred to raise human rights concerns behind closed doors through so-called quiet diplomacy. Carter had perceived human rights as a new foreign policy strategy designed to break with the Cold War bipolarity, whereas Reagan made human rights an integral part of superpower contestation. Moreover, as shown, Reagan did not share his predecessor's desire to distance himself from repressive regimes. Dictators who had fallen out of favor under Carter were welcomed into the Reagan White House.[108]

In addition to the appointment of Abrams, the replacement of Haig with Shultz as secretary of state in July 1982 was crucial for the shift in the administration's human rights policy. According to Abrams, "It took two players to achieve any kind of human rights policy in the administration. The first was me, and the second was George Shultz." Abrams recalls, "Alexander Haig wasn't much interested in human rights" and "his thinking on the subject was not clear at all, and his attitude basically negative." Shultz, on the other hand, Abrams remembers, "had a very different and essentially nonideological view of human rights. His thoughts were that of course we're for human rights."[109] Abrams's observations about the two secretaries of state are supported by the attention they give to human rights in their respective memoirs. While

---

[106] "Excerpts from an Interview with Walter Cronkite of CBS News," Reagan Presidential Library, March 3, 1981, accessed August 2, 2019, www.reaganlibrary.gov/research/speeches/30381c.

[107] According to a Reagan administration memo, the United States was the first government "specifically created to preserve human rights." Memorandum, State Department, September 14, 1984, I-181A; 287, 6, NCSJR.

[108] For an early comparison of the human rights policies of Carter and Reagan, see A. Glenn Mower, *Human Rights and American Foreign Policy: The Carter and Reagan Experiences* (New York: Greenwood, 1987).

[109] Interview with Elliott Abrams in: Kenneth W. Thompson, *Foreign Policy in the Reagan Presidency: Nine Intimate Perspectives: Sterling Kernek, Caspar Weinberger, Max M. Kampelman, Dwight Ink, Paul H. Nitze, John C. Whitehead, Elliott Abrams, Paul H. Nitze, Don Oberdorfer* (Lanham, MD: University Press of America, 1993), 106.

Haig hardly uses the term, Shultz discusses his views on human rights multiple times.[110] Shultz was deeply convinced that Soviet improvements on human rights issues and a general opening up of Soviet society was essential for better US–Soviet relations.[111] Moreover, Shultz felt a personal responsibility toward securing the release of Soviet dissidents. Remembering the release of refusenik Ida Nudel, he recalls, "It was a big moment. I can get tears in my eyes today thinking about it. It was such trauma connected with that."[112] Shultz's willingness to prioritize human rights, in particular in relations with the Soviet Union, was thus both a result of his perception of their positive implications for US–Soviet relations and his personal commitment to help dissidents.

The arrival of Shultz drastically improved the working conditions for Abrams at the Human Rights Bureau and contributed to the administration's formulation of a more assertive human rights policy. Enjoying the support of his secretary of state, Abrams emerged as the chief architect of and the key spokesperson for the administration's human rights policy. Under Abrams's stewardship, the administration developed what Abrams himself termed a "conservative human rights policy."[113] Building on the memo leaked to the press in October 1981, this policy adopted a two-track approach to the promotion of human rights. Through the first track, the United States would respond to specific human rights violations in the short term. Through the second track, it would focus on improving the conditions for human rights by promoting the democracy over the long term.[114] In a November 1983 memo to Shultz, Abrams presented this approach as the best way to minimize the potential disadvantages and maximize the potential advantages of a human rights policy. The memo presented the two-track approach as far superior to other alternatives, such as a minimal human rights policy or a policy focused on basic human rights such as torture, since these would both fail to satisfy

---

[110] Shultz, *Turmoil and Triumph*; Alexander Meigs Haig and Clare Boothe Luce, *Caveat: Realism, Reagan, and Foreign Policy* (New York: Macmillan, 1984).

[111] Shultz, *Turmoil and Triumph*, 276–327; US Congress, Senate, Committee on Foreign Relations, *United States-Soviet Relations: Hearings before the Committee on Foreign Relations*, 98th Congress, 1st Session, June 15, 16, 21, 22, and 23, 1983, 3–12; George P. Shultz "Human Rights and the Moral Dimension of U.S. Foreign Policy," February 22, 1984, A1–481B, Department of State Press, Vol. 180, No. 51, Record Group 59, National Archives and Records Administration.

[112] George P. Shultz Interview, December 18, 2002, Reagan Presidential Oral History Project, Miller Center, University of Virginia, Charlottesville, Virginia.

[113] "Interview with Elliott Abrams," *U.S. News of the World Report*, September 10, 1984, I-410, I-410A; 22; 1, UCSJR.

[114] US Department of State, "Country Reports on Human Rights Practices for 1983" (Washington, DC: US Government Printing Office, 1984), 5. Memorandum, State Department, September 14, 1984, I-181A; 287, 6, NCSJR.

the American public and offered little opportunity to take the offensive. On the contrary, the memo argued, the two-track approach had a number of advantages: "This policy correctly understands that specific human rights violations are not an accident; they are symptoms that flow from the underlying political order. Only democracy has proved to be a good guarantee of proper human rights practices. This policy also has the advantage that it takes off part of the pressure to react to human rights violations only in the short term – as in El Salvador – because short-term reaction is not all we are doing. Such a policy thus makes it easier to explain apparent inconsistencies in our short-term human rights responses."[115] According to the memo, the only disadvantage to this policy was the non-democratic nature of some of the United States' allies and the limited knowledge of how to foster their democratization.

Under Abrams, the State Department's *Country Reports on Human Rights Practices* became an essential venue for the official explanation for the administration's human rights policy.[116] Abrams used the introduction to the reports to clarify the administration's priorities on human rights, merging human rights with democracy promotion to legitimize the administration's foreign policy at home and abroad.[117] The first introduction redefined human rights by stating that the United States recognized two categories of human rights: freedom from government violations of the integrity of the person, and a list of civil and political liberties. Economic and social rights, despite their equal standing with civil and political rights in international human rights law, were relegated to lesser importance and described merely as aspirations.[118] This redefinition was impressed on all embassies as early as August 1981.[119] By contrast, the Carter administration's country reports had used three categories of human rights, which in addition to the two categories employed by the Reagan administration included "the right to the fulfillment of vital needs such as food, shelter, healthcare, and education."[120] Although the Carter administration would often afford limited attention to such economic and social issues in its actual policy, the Reagan administration's downgrade of economic and social rights represented

---

[115] US Department of State, *Foreign Relations of the United States, 1981–1988, Volume XII, Global Issues II*, Document 66.

[116] Forsythe, *Human Rights and U.S. Foreign Policy*, 127.

[117] Søndergaard, "'A Positive Track of Human Rights Policy'," 31–50.

[118] US Department of State, *Country Reports on Human Rights Practices for 1981* (Washington, DC: US Government Printing Office, 1982), 2.

[119] US Department of State, *Foreign Relations of the United States, 1981–1988, Volume XII, Global Issues II*, Document 51.

[120] US Department of State, *Country Reports on Human Rights Practices for 1979* (Washington, DC: US Government Printing Office, 1980), 2.

a significant rhetorical break with the previous official US government definition of human rights.

Moreover, the introductions argued for the superiority of democratic systems as protectors of human rights, presenting the promotion of democracy as the best way to secure human rights. In the 1982 edition, for instance, Abrams declared, "the Administration believes that we should treat not only the symptoms but the disease – that we should not only respond to human rights violations but also should work to establish democratic systems in which human rights violations are less likely to occur."[121] The country reports thus argued for a direct positive link between democratic governance and respect for human rights and reasoned that the United States should actively promote democracy as a core component of its human rights policy. Similarly, the reports proclaimed the existence of positive links between democracy and economic development and peace.[122]

As the administration used the country reports to redefine the definition of human rights and legitimize a human rights policy aimed at promoting democracy, human rights NGOs and critics of the administration became increasingly distrustful of the reports. However, because the administration valued the reports as an important part of its attempt to shape the debate on human rights and because they had to live up to congressional scrutiny, the overall quality of the reporting steadily improved.[123] Consequently, the country reports were both increasingly politicized and greatly expanded and improved. This meant that the country reports that had been introduced by Congress as a measure to force Henry Kissinger to address human rights concerns in the 1970s became a serious source of information on human rights abuses by the early 1980s, comprising more than a thousand pages on the human rights situation around the world. As noted by political scientist David Forsythe, there was a noticeable discrepancy between the improved human rights reporting of the Reagan administration and its emphasis on human rights in its foreign policy.[124] Still, the reports represented an ongoing institutionalization of human rights concerns in debates over foreign policy and helped strengthen the position of the Human Rights Bureau responsible for them. The annual submission of the reports was followed by congressional hearings, at which members of Congress and

---

[121] US Department of State, *Country Reports on Human Rights Practices for 1982* (Washington, DC: US Government Printing Office, 1983), 9.

[122] Søndergaard, "'A Positive Track of Human Rights Policy,'" 47–48.

[123] For an example of an exception to the rule, see the examination of the highly politicized reporting on Nicaragua in Chapter 6.

[124] Forsythe, *Human Rights and U.S. Foreign Policy*, 127, 162.

representatives from human rights NGOs discussed the country report with the assistant secretary for human rights.[125] The country reports and hearings drew considerable attention from the press and human rights NGOs, which closely monitored the administration's focus on specific rights and countries.[126] The reports, and the debates surrounding them, thus helped draw attention to human rights and underscored their legitimacy as a foreign policy issue.

Abrams threw himself eagerly into the debates over the country reports and the administration's broader human rights policy, appearing frequently before Congress and in the media to debate the merits of the administration's position. One of his many media appearances debating the administration's human rights policy was an interview with the US government-funded broadcasting organization Radio Free Europe/Radio Liberty in October 1984. In that interview, Abrams acknowledged that human rights criticism might damage relations with a country in the short run but argued that it would improve relations in the long run, as the people of the country in question would appreciate such American intervention. Abrams also acquiesced that he preferred the term "individual rights" to "human rights," but accepted that the latter had become the established term. Abrams clarified that when the Reagan administration referred to human rights, what it meant was "civil and political rights."[127] Through such public engagements, Abrams and other members of the administration engaged its critics and sought to take the offensive in the contestation over the role of human rights concerns in US foreign policy.

The intertwining of human rights and democracy in opposition to communism became a defining feature of the administration's human rights policy. Reagan clearly articulated this constellation in his famous speech before the British Parliament at Westminster on June 8, 1982. The Soviet Union, Reagan asserted, "runs against the tide of history by denying human freedom and human dignity to its citizens." To counter the Soviet Union, Reagan maintained, the West had to "take actions to assist the campaign for democracy" in order to secure "the march of freedom

---

[125] State, *Country Reports on Human Rights Practices for 1983*, Appendix A, 1470.

[126] See, for instance, *Summary of Hearing: Human Rights and International Organizations Subcommittee Hearings, Amnesty International USA, Memorandum, February 23, 1982*, Amnesty International of the USA, Inc.: National Office Records, Box II.2.11, Folder 19; Rare Book and Manuscript Library, Columbia University Library (hereafter AIUSA). "New Report Card on Human Rights," *CQ Weekly* (February 16, 1985): 314. http://library.cqpress.com/cqweekly/WR099404254.

[127] "Interview with Elliott Abrams," *Radio Free Europe/Radio Liberty*, October 5, 1984, I-181A; 281, 1, NCSJR. When pressed to select the human right he found most important, Abrams answered freedom of religion, arguing, "Respect for this shows respect for the individual's commitment to a higher obligation than the state."

and democracy which will leave Marxism-Leninism on the ash heap of history." Invoking the UDHR, Reagan argued, "We must be staunch in our conviction that freedom is not the sole prerogative of a lucky few, but the inalienable and universal right of all human beings. So states the United Nations Universal Declaration of Human Rights, which, among other things, guarantees free elections."[128] For Reagan, fighting communism and promoting democracy was two sides of the same coin. Democracy was the best guarantee for the respect of human rights, whereas communism was the direct opposite. In his work on American democracy promotion in the twentieth century, political scientist Tony Smith has argued that the Reagan administration was unparalleled in its "commitment to the promotion of democracy worldwide" since the presidency of Woodrow Wilson.[129] Moreover, Reagan's anti-statism and firm belief in the free-market economy deeply influenced the administration's policy toward human rights and democracy promotion. Reagan and Shultz were convinced that there was a synergetic relationship between democracy and the free market, in the sense that an open economy would lead to democracy.[130] Reagan's skepticism of government stood in contrast to the neoconservatives' more positive belief in the utility of state power. Yet their shared commitment to free markets and strong anti-communism meant that differing views on state power could be largely ignored.

This merging of human rights with democracy promotion guided by anti-communism permeated most aspects of the administration's foreign policy. The administration redirected foreign assistance from multilateral programs to bilateral programs to increase the opportunity to align it with national security concerns in the struggle against communism. It also orchestrated a redirection from economic assistance to military assistance to the same effect. It then directed foreign assistance to countries threatened by communism or allies strategically located in the Soviet periphery.[131] Another example was refugee policy, where the administration gave preference to refugees fleeing communism in Indochina, the Soviet Union, and Eastern Europe. The historian Carl Bon Tempo has argued, "For Reagan and his advisors, refugees from communism were living examples of the Soviet Union's and communism's failures."[132] The administration's support for Soviet Jewish emigration, examined in

---

[128] Ronald Reagan, Address to Members of the British Parliament, June 8, 1982.

[129] Tony Smith, *America's Mission: The United States and the Worldwide Struggle for Democracy in the Twentieth Century* (Princeton, NJ: Princeton University Press, 1994), 268.

[130] Ibid., 291–295.   [131] Apodaca, *Understanding U.S. Human Rights Policy*, 90–91.

[132] Carl J. Bon Tempo, *Americans at the Gate: The United States and Refugees During the Cold War* (Princeton, NJ: Princeton University Press, 2008), 188.

Figure 3 Ronald Reagan meets with the Soviet dissident and human rights activist Andrei Sakharov – one of the refugees from communism whom Reagan viewed as a testament to the failure of the Soviet Union, November 14, 1988.
Diana Walker/The LIFE Images Collection via Getty Images.

Chapter 4, was perhaps the most conspicuous example of such emigration policy (Figure 3).

The administration's desire to turn its human rights policy into an offensive weapon in the struggle with communism also influenced the establishment of the National Endowment for Democracy (NED) in 1983. The NED was set up as a federally funded private organization, tasked with promoting democracy globally through the distribution of grants to civil society groups.[133] As Abrams pointed out in a memo to

---

[133] The NED resembled a similar initiative previously envisioned by congressional human rights pioneers Dante Fascell (D-FL) and Donald Fraser (D-MN). For the establishment of the NED and its early activities, see Robert Pee, *Democracy Promotion, National Security and Strategy: Foreign Policy under the Reagan Administration* (London: Routledge, 2015). For the NED's role in promoting democracy in Guatemala and Chile in the 1980s, see Evan D. McCormick, "Breaking with Statism? U.S. Democracy Promotion in Latin America, 1984–1988*," *Diplomatic History* 42, no. 5 (2017): 745–771. For the NED's efforts to promote democracy in the Soviet Union in the years prior to its collapse, see Kate Geoghegan, "A Policy in Tension: The National Endowment for Democracy and the U.S. Response to the Collapse of the Soviet Union," *Diplomatic History* 42, no. 5 (2018): 772–801.

Shultz in November 1983, the NED was, in essence, the institutional manifestation of the administration's two-track policy of combining human rights criticism in the short term with the promotion of democracy over the long term.[134] A few months earlier, the Human Rights Bureau had drafted a proposal for the program, delineating its objectives and a preliminary budget.[135] Yet the formation of the NED is also another example of how members of Congress shaped the administration's approach to human rights and democracy. Following Reagan's call to promote democracy in his Westminster speech in June 1982, the administration proposed to establish a Project Democracy that would have been run from the United States Information Agency (USIA) and effectively controlled by the NSC, with a primary focus on the Soviet Union. Members of Congress, however, rejected this constellation, with many Democrats, in particular, favoring an NGO structure with much less government control and a wider campaign, to include friendly dictatorships.[136] The result became an institution much less under the administration's control than it would have liked but which, as historian Robert Pee has argued, essentially promoted US-style procedural democracy with no serious socio-economic reform and generally supported low-intensity democracies in the Third World focused on elites and aimed to defuse popular movements.[137] Political scientist Nicholas Guilhot has observed, "the emergence of various democracy promotion programs [during the Reagan era] was a direct consequence of the neoconservative human rights doctrine or, better, the substitute for a human rights policy."[138]

The administration also took a critical approach to international law and the United Nations (UN), which it believed lacked legitimacy due to the dominance of non-democratic countries and anti-American sentiments. In accordance with the Kirkpatrick Doctrine, the administration continuously sided with American allies despite their blatant human rights violations, for instance voting against motions to condemn Chile for the use of torture.[139] As Richard Schifter, the US representative to the UN Commission on Human Rights from 1983 to 1985, recalls, "The

---

[134] US Department of State, *Foreign Relations of the United States, 1981–1988, Volume XII, Global Issues II*, Document 66.

[135] Memorandum, State Department, "Briefing on the Democracy Initiative," May 11, 1983, Human Rights Collection, 60, 46, 4, Andrei Sakharov Archives, 1852–2002 (MS Russ 79), Houghton Library, Harvard University.

[136] Pee, *Democracy Promotion, National Security and Strategy*, 117-22.   [137] Ibid., 192.

[138] Nicolas Guilhot, *The Democracy Makers: Human Rights & International Order* (New York: Columbia University Press, 2005), 79.

[139] Sikkink, *Mixed Signals*, 152.

Administration did not believe that the UN was able to play a significant role in advancing the human rights cause. The problem we thought was that a majority of the UN membership and the Commission did not respect human rights."[140] The prevalent anti-Americanism among several of the member states from the developing world further strengthened the administration's skepticism of the UN. After the US military intervention in Grenada in 1983, a journalist confronted Reagan with a UN resolution deploring the invasion, to which Reagan responded, "It didn't upset my breakfast at all."[141] Not only did the administration not think highly of the United Nations, it was not afraid to show it. Another case in point was the administration's decision to leave the United Nations Educational, Scientific, and Cultural Organization (UNESCO) in December 1984 because it believed the body was pro-Soviet and anti-American. The administration took a similar approach to international law and institutions, such as the International Court of Justice (ICJ). Faced with international criticism for its mining of Nicaraguan harbors in 1984, the administration decided to boycott the ICJ and vetoed a UN Security Council resolution condemning attacks on Nicaragua.[142]

Conclusion

In a remarkable turn of events, the Reagan administration changed its approach to human rights from rejection to reform, constructing a conservative human rights policy that fit its overarching foreign policy strategy. Jacoby spoke of a "Reagan turnaround on human rights."[143] Scholars have since offered different accounts of the timing and the factors behind this shift in policy. In her examination of the Senate Foreign Relations Committee's rejection of Lefever, Sarah Snyder argues that the event led the administration to reevaluate its approach to human rights. Snyder places considerable importance on the support for human rights among members of Congress and the general public.[144] Focusing on the administration's broader foreign policy, political scientist Beth

---

[140] Author's interview with Richard Schifter, May 30, 2016. See also Michael Novak and Richard Schifter, *A Conversation with Michael Novak and Richard Schifter: Human Rights and the United Nations, Held on April 3, 1981* (Washington, DC: American Enterprise Institute for Public Policy Research, 1981). Schifter would become head of the Human Right Bureau in 1985.

[141] Quoted in Brian Loveman, *No Higher Law: American Foreign Policy and the Western Hemisphere since 1776* (Chapel Hill: University of North Carolina Press, 2010), 324.

[142] US Congress, Committee on Foreign Affairs, *Congress and Foreign Policy – 1984*, Committee Print (Washington, DC: US Government Printing Office, 1985), 32.

[143] Jacoby, "The Reagan Turnaround."

[144] Snyder, "The Defeat of Ernest Lefever's Nomination," 151–152.

A. Fischer argues that Reagan dramatically changed his approach to the Soviet Union in January 1984 as a result of heightened fears of a nuclear war in the aftermath of the NATO exercise Able Archer in November 1983.[145] Historian Joe Renouard locates a shift in Reagan's approach to human rights in his second term, noting that the administration became much more active on "the humanitarian front," increasing its efforts to promote democracy and its willingness to criticize allies. The most important factors for this change, Renouard argues, were a stronger defense posture, Reagan's reelection, and changes in the foreign policy team.[146] In her examination of US human rights policy in Latin America, political scientist Kathryn Sikkink similarly claims that Reagan's policy can be divided into two phases: "a first phase of active implementation of the Kirkpatrick Doctrine, and a second phase that included increasing emphasis on the promotion of democracy." Sikkink, however, notes that the first phase continued throughout Reagan's tenure in Central American and particularly in Nicaragua.[147]

This chapter has demonstrated a gradual change in the Reagan administration's approach to human rights during 1981, leading to the development of a conservative human rights policy in the coming years. Similar to Snyder's work, the chapter points to the importance of the rejection of Lefever in June 1981. The Lefever incident underscored the cost of abandoning human rights and pushed the administration to reevaluate its position. Aryeh Neier later recalled about the rejection of Lefever, "In retrospect, that struggle was far more significant that I realized. It was, I now believe, the turning point in establishing the human rights cause as a factor in U.S. foreign policy."[148] By the summer of 1981, the idea that the administration needed a more definite human rights policy was gaining momentum in the State Department. However, this chapter also demonstrates that while the rejection of Lefever was a crucial moment, the seeds for a more assertive human rights policy were present in internal debates in the NSC as early as February 1981. Abrams was a key architect for the new policy, merging human rights and democracy promotion under the overall strategy of defeating communism. The replacement of Haig with Shultz in July 1982 greatly boosted the creation of a policy that actively sought to shape the role of human rights concerns in American foreign relations. The administration's turnaround on human rights was, thus, a gradual development

---

[145] Fischer, *The Reagan Reversal*, 147–148.
[146] Renouard, *Human Rights in American Foreign Policy*, 198–199.
[147] Sikkink, *Mixed Signals*, 149.   [148] Neier, *Taking Liberties*, 189.

driven by multiple factors both inside and outside the administration during Reagan's first term.

Members of Congress concerned with human rights played a vital role in the Reagan turnaround on human rights. Seeking initially to secure human rights as a foreign policy concern, members of Congress soon found themselves locked in a contest with an administration that aggressively sought to shape US human rights policy instead. What at first looked like a struggle to keep human rights concerns on the agenda then turned into a contestation over how, when, and where the United States ought to promote human rights. To most of these members of Congress, this situation represented an unintended consequence of their initial opposition to the administration's rejection of human rights. Throughout the 1980s, the contestation between members of Congress and the administration over the appropriate role for human rights concerns in American foreign relations would become the defining factor shaping US human rights policy. The three case study chapters examine this contestation in detail, but first, the book turns to the most significant new addition to the congressional human rights landscape in the 1980s.

3 The Congressional Human Rights Caucus and the Limits of Bipartisanship

"How did these two get together?" a passerby remarked about Representatives Henry Hyde (R-IL) and Ronald Dellums (D-CA) standing shoulder to shoulder when the Congressional Human Rights Caucus (CHRC) was having its photo taken on the steps of the Capitol building in the late 1980s.[1] The remark was understandable because Hyde and Dellums could hardly have been any further apart on the issues, foreign or domestic. A conservative Republican, Hyde was a staunch defender of Reagan's foreign policy, including the contentious Iran–Contra affair. A democratic socialist belonging to the left wing of the Democratic Party, Dellums, on the contrary, castigated virtually every aspect of Reagan's foreign policy. Yet the two could agree that the United States should defend human rights in broad terms and occasionally joined forces in the CHRC, for instance by signing a letter to the Soviet government on behalf of the Soviet dissident Andrei Sakharov.[2] As CHRC staff director from 1987 to 1995 Alexandra Arriaga recalls, "Human rights and the caucus could be used to bring together people who otherwise did not agree on most issues."[3] If only for a while and with significant limitations, the CHRC united members of Congress as different as Hyde and Dellums behind a common commitment to protect and promote human rights.

The CHRC first saw the light of day in January 1983, when two junior members of Congress, John E. Porter (R-IL) and Tom Lantos (D-CA), launched it as a new forum for human rights on Capitol Hill. By the end of the decade, it had significantly expanded congressional human rights activism.[4] The first caucus dedicated to human rights issues, the CHRC

---

[1] Author's interview with Alexandra Arriaga, June 8, 2018.
[2] Letter, CHRC to Konstantin Chernenko, March 5, 1984, Box 107, Folder 8, Tom Lantos Papers, BANC MSS 2008/121, The Bancroft Library, University of California, Berkeley (hereafter TLP).
[3] Author's interview with Alexandra Arriaga, June 8, 2018.
[4] "Dear Colleague" Letter, January 24, 1983, box 141, MS-341, The Tony Hall Papers Collection, Special Collections and Archives, University Libraries, Wright State University, Dayton, Ohio.

sought to "encourage broad bipartisan attention to human rights abuses."[5] Congressional caucuses are formed by members of Congress who unite in the pursuit of common legislative objectives. They share certain characteristics but vary greatly in membership, interests, activities, and strategies, spanning from large ideological coaltions such as the Conservative Opportunity Society to racial groups such as the Congressional Black Caucus (CBC) to specific interest caucuses such as the Congressional Travel and Tourism Caucus.[6] As a caucus, the CHRC operated outside the formalized structures of parties and committees but had the ability to influence the policy process through a range of activities aimed at setting the political agenda. Over the years, the CHRC expanded and systematized congressional human rights activism, spawned several spin-off initiatives, and provided human rights activists and NGOs with a new access point in Congress. Consistently one of the largest caucuses with hundreds of members, but essentially run by its two founders, the CHRC illustrated how dedicated foreign policy entrepreneurs could set the congressional agenda on human rights. The CHRC also exemplified the mixed motivations that drove American attention to human rights and underlined the importance of personal encounters with victims and lived experience. Nevertheless, the CHRC's history has not previously been the focus of sustained scholarly attention.[7]

A bipartisan venture, the CHRC demonstrated the broad appeal of certain human rights issues among members of Congress, underscoring the degree to which human rights had arrived as a moral language that would have been unthinkable a decade earlier. However, it also revealed the limitations of a bipartisan consensus on human rights. The CHRC largely limited its focus to noncontroversial issues, and the flexible nature

---

[5] CHRC Brochure 1985, Box 102, Folder 21, TLP.

[6] Susan Webb Hammond, *Congressional Caucuses in National Policy Making* (Baltimore, MD: Johns Hopkins University Press, 1998), 20, 55. The number of foreign policy caucuses rose dramatically from three during Eisenhower's presidency to nearly one hundred during Reagan's presidency. This development was partially fuelled by a comprehensive decentralization of Congress in the 1970s, combined with a growing willingness of a new generation of members of Congress to challenge party leadership. Lindsay, *Congress and the Politics of U.S. Foreign Policy*, 68.

[7] Elsewhere, I have demonstrated how the issue of Soviet Jewish emigration was crucial for the consolidation of the CHRC. Rasmus Sinding Søndergaard, "The Congressional Human Rights Caucus and the Plight of the Refuseniks," in *The Cold War at Home and Abroad: Domestic Politics and U.S. Foreign Policy since 1945*, ed. Andrew L. Johns and Mitchell B. Lerner (Lexington: University Press of Kentucky, 2018), 224–246. The only other article dedicated to the CHRC examines motivations for membership in the period 2001–2005, James M. McCormick and Neil J. Mitchell, "Commitments, Transnational Interests, and Congress," *Political Research Quarterly* 60, no. 4 (2007): 579–592. There are also a few scattered remarks on the CHRC in Hammond, *Congressional Caucuses in National Policy Making*.

of caucuses meant that most members selectively supported human rights issues of their choosing. Consequently, despite its bipartisanship, the CHRC often reproduced the preferences of liberals and conservatives. Moreover, reflecting Western attention to human rights more broadly, the CHRC virtually ignored economic, social, and cultural rights. Probably because of this focus and approach, the CHRC did not have any serious enemies. In the few instances when members of Congress took issue with the CHRC, their criticism was directed at particular issues, not against its broader agenda.

The initiative for the CHRC originated in a weeklong fact-finding trip to the Soviet Union in September 1982 organized by the Union of Councils for Soviet Jews (UCSJ). On this trip, Porter met with more than forty Jewish families who had been denied permission to emigrate, so-called refuseniks, despite attempts by Soviet authorities to break up the meetings. Porter subsequently recalled how the injustices suffered by these families left a strong impression on him.[8] Toward the end of the trip, Porter and his wife Kathryn Porter, who was traveling with him, experienced the harassment of the Soviet authorities firsthand, when the female members of their delegation were strip-searched in the airport.[9] The experience shocked the couple, who concluded that if they, a member of Congress and his wife, could be treated like that, it would be much worse for others.[10] The encounter with the Jewish families and the harassment in the Soviet airport motivated Porter to do something to help alleviate the struggle of those being denied the right to emigrate.[11] On the plane back to the United States, Porter told his wife, "We have caucuses for everything, but we do not have one for human rights."[12] Upon his return, he asked one of his staffers, Elizabeth Schrayer, then a twenty-one-year-old recent college graduate, to examine how to create a congressional caucus for human rights.[13]

A moderate Republican, Porter was elected to Congress from Illinois's tenth district, covering the affluent northern suburbs of Chicago. Porter won the seat in a special election in 1980 to fill a vacancy left by Democrat Abner Mikva (D-IL), having narrowly lost the election to

---

[8] US Congress, Senate, Committee on Foreign Relations, *Hearing before the Committee on Foreign Relations, United States Senate on the Promotion and Protection of Human Rights in Eastern Europe and the Soviet Union*, 98th Congress, 1st Session, November 9, 1983, 149.

[9] 146 *Congressional Record*, 106th Congress, 2nd Session, H10242-H10254 (October 18, 2000).

[10] Gayle Worland, "Congressional Maverick," *Illinois Issues* (July/August 1997): 19–20.

[11] Author's interview with Alexandra Arriaga, June 8, 2018.

[12] Author's interview with Rep. John E. Porter, October 17, 2018. Unfortunately, Porter's private papers are not available for research.

[13] Author's interview with Elizabeth Schrayer, January 22, 2015.

Mikva in 1978. Before arriving in Congress, Porter had served as a member of the Illinois General Assembly from 1973 to 1979 and worked as a lawyer in the private sector. With his father serving as a judge, Porter grew up in a family dedicated to public service and he recalls how it was in his father's courtroom that he first gained great respect for the majesty of the law and the dignity it provided for the individual.[14] In Congress, Porter obtained a seat on the powerful Appropriations Committee, which regulates government spending. As a fiscal conservative, Porter was deeply concerned with balancing the federal budget, but on social issues, he was a moderate, in favor of gun control and abortion and strongly committed to environmental protection.[15] In his own words, Porter's district was "the most globalist-thinking, well-educated, and bipartisan district you can imagine," which reflected itself in his internationalist outlook on foreign policy.[16]

To gain the widest possible backing for his idea, Porter decided to look for another representative with a complementary political profile to serve as cochair of the caucus. The ideal candidate would have to be a Democrat, engaged with human rights issues, and preferably a member of the House Foreign Affairs Committee. Based on these criteria, he decided to reach out to Lantos, a liberal Democrat from California. As a member of the House Foreign Affairs Committee and its Subcommittee on Human Rights, Lantos was already involved with human rights issues. More importantly, Lantos's personal history made him deeply committed to the protection of human rights and a strong supporter of Soviet Jewry.

Born to Jewish parents in Budapest, Hungary, in 1928, Lantos was sixteen years old when Nazi Germany occupied Hungary in 1944. On two occasions, he managed to escape from forced labor camps and he eventually survived through the help of the Swedish diplomat Raoul Wallenberg, who saved thousands of Hungarian Jews in safe houses throughout Budapest. Lantos would later devote himself to honor the legacy of Wallenberg, who disappeared after the end of World War II, never to be found. Having escaped the forced labor camps, Lantos joined the Hungarian underground resistance against the Nazis. In August 1947, he immigrated to the United States to study, earning a PhD in economics from the University of California at Berkeley in 1953. In the following years, he worked as a professor, business consultant, and media analyst before becoming a senior foreign policy advisor to members of Congress. In 1980, he beat the incumbent Republican candidate to win a

---

[14] Author's interview with Rep. John E. Porter, October 17, 2018.
[15] Worland, "Congressional Maverick," 16–21.
[16] Author's interview with Rep. John E. Porter, October 17, 2018.

seat in the House of Representatives from California's eleventh district, covering southwestern San Francisco and San Mateo County.[17]

Lantos's personal experience as the only Holocaust survivor to serve in the US Congress gave him a unique moral authority. Having lost most of his family in the Holocaust and experiencing the atrocities of the Nazis firsthand, he had a very personal commitment to preventing human rights violations. Lantos was particularly determined to prevent discrimination against minorities such as Soviet Jews and he visited refuseniks in the Soviet Union several times, including as the leader of a congressional delegation in 1983.[18] His personal experience in the United States also made him a lifelong American patriot, frequently expressing his strong gratitude to the United States and describing himself as "an American by choice."[19] These two experiences combined to make him a strong supporter of an interventionist US foreign policy to prevent human rights abuses. As he expressed it when voting in favor of the resolution that authorized the use of military force against Iraq in 2002, "If the costs of war are great, the costs of inaction and appeasement are greater still."[20] He continued by making a historical analogy between the appeasement of Adolf Hitler in 1938 and the failure to confront Saddam Hussein. Unlike that of most of his colleagues, Lantos's worldview was decisively shaped by the lesson of Munich not the dangers of interventionism represented by Vietnam. The United States, according to Lantos, although not infallible, was a force for good and had a moral responsibility to intervene to prevent atrocities abroad.

As Porter and Lantos sought to recruit members to their new caucus, they took great care to emphasize its bipartisan nature. According to Elizabeth Schrayer, "the strategy was to get people from both ideological wings on board to convince other members of Congress that it was 'safe' to join."[21] The early membership of ideological outliers such as the liberal Democrat Barney Frank (D-MA) and the conservative Republican Henry Hyde helped achieve this goal. This conscious effort

---

[17] David M. Herszenhorn, "Tom Lantos, 80, Is Dead; Longtime Congressman," *The New York Times*, February 12, 2008, D6. For a tribute to Tom Lantos's career, see Anna-Mária Bíró and Katrina Lantos-Swett, eds. *The Noble Banner of Human Rights: Essays in Memory of Tom Lantos* (Leiden: Brill Nijhoff, 2018).

[18] US Congress, House, Commission on Security and Cooperation in Europe, *Soviet Jewry Hearing and Markup before the Subcommittee on Human Rights and International Organizations of the Committee on Foreign Affairs and the Commission on Security and Cooperation in Europe*, 98th Congress, 1st Session, June 23 and 28, 1983, 6.

[19] Herszenhorn, "Tom Lantos, 80, Is Dead."

[20] 148 *Congressional Record*, 107th Congress, 2nd Session, H7195 (October 8, 2002). Lantos would later become an opponent of the war in Iraq.

[21] Author's interview with Elizabeth Schrayer, January 22, 2015.

to bridge ideological and partisan divides helped grow the CHRC's membership at an impressive pace. By June 1985, two and a half years after the CHRC's founding, it counted 142 representatives.[22] Eventually, membership also extended to the House leadership, and by 1988 the CHRC counted the chairs of ten full committees among its ranks.[23]

Despite the wide membership, the CHRC effectively remained a project of its two founders. As cochairs, Porter and Lantos drove the caucus agenda with an executive committee of other very active members operating below them, while a large group of regular members mostly played a more passive role. This uneven division of labor was typical for most caucuses and continued well into the 2000s when McCormick and Mitchell concluded about the CHRC that, "a few individuals bear most of the costs of sustaining the internal operation of the caucus."[24] Lantos became particularly central to the operation of the CHRC. "Tom Lantos played a big role in the early days," Schrayer recalls. "John Porter was the initiator, but Lantos was the major driving force of the caucus."[25] As late as 2007, the year before his death, several representatives and staffers described Lantos as vital for the operation of the CHRC.[26] The wives of the two cochairs also played important roles, with Lantos's wife Annette Lantos working as an unpaid assistant to the CHRC. She, for instance, scheduled meetings with newly elected members of Congress, inviting them to participate in the CHRC, often with positive effect.[27] Essentially, the CHRC was the institutional manifestation of the aspirations of two dedicated members of Congress, who used it to pursue their legislative objectives on human rights.

While the CHRC gave Lantos and Porter a platform from which to call attention to human rights issues, it also had a positive impact on their careers. The CHRC established them as leaders in Congress, which helped pave the way for them to other leadership positions and to shape their legacies.[28] When Porter's congressional colleagues paid tribute to his service in Congress upon his retirement in 2000, his leadership on human rights through the CHRC was repeatedly cited as one of his most

---

[22] *CHRC Newsletter*, June 1985, Box 102, Folder 19, TLP.

[23] *The Congressional Human Rights Foundation Statement of Purpose* (description of CHRC), 1988, Box 113, Folder 19, TLP.

[24] McCormick and Mitchell, "Commitments," 588.

[25] Author's interview with Elizabeth Schrayer, January 22, 2015.

[26] McCormick and Mitchell, "Commitments, Transnational Interests, and Congress," 588.

[27] Memo, Alex Arriaga to Laura Glickson, August 18, 1995, Box 114, Folder 22, TLP.

[28] Hammond, *Congressional Caucuses in National Policy Making*, 158.

significant legacies.[29] The impact of the CHRC on Lantos's career was even greater. In 1993, he became the chair of the Subcommittee on Human Rights and in 2007 the chair of the Foreign Affairs Committee. In addition, several human rights institutions, programs, and awards have been established in his name, including the Tom Lantos Foundation for Human Rights & Justice, the Tom Lantos Human Rights Prize, and the Tom Lantos Institute in his native Hungary.

The CHRC generally enjoyed a constructive relationship with existing human rights institutions in Congress, and Lantos and Porter secured the support of both the Subcommittee on Human Rights and the US Helsinki Commission before launching the CHRC.[30] An important reason for the constructive relationship was that, as a caucus, the CHRC complemented rather than competed with the existing institutions. Not part of the formalized structures of parties and committees, caucuses seek to advance the common goals of their members by, for instance, distributing information and advocating for policy concerns. Yet they do not encroach on the main territory of committees, such as passing legislation and holding hearings, for which they have no formal authority. Rather, caucuses like the CHRC often assist committees, for instance by cosponsoring events when their agendas overlapped.[31] Lantos recalled how the Subcommittee on Human Rights recognized the value of the CHRC and "on certain issues, will work with us."[32]

The bipartisanship of the CHRC and its tendency to avoid controversial issues also minimized the risk of confrontations. Chief of staff at the US Helsinki Commission at the time, R. Spencer Oliver, recalls that "the two groups were in-sync on all policy issues."[33] Another important factor that helped to secure good relations was the significant overlap in membership between the CHRC leadership and the other institutions. A snapshot from 1985 illustrates this point. Lantos served on the Subcommittee on Human Rights and Porter served on the US Helsinki Commission, while two CHRC Executive Committee members, Dante Fascell (D-FL) and Gus Yatron (D-PA), chaired the House Foreign

---

[29] 146 *Congressional Record*, 106th Congress, 2nd Session, H10242–H10254 (October 18, 2000).

[30] "Dear Colleague" Letter, February 23, 1983, Box 141, MS-341, The Tony Hall Papers Collection, Special Collections and Archives, University Libraries, Wright State University, Dayton, Ohio.

[31] In the years leading up to the establishment of the CHRC, the number of caucuses grew substantially as members of Congress sought to respond to a mixture of demands that made their work increasingly complex and demanding. Hammond, *Congressional Caucuses in National Policy Making*, 11–19, 67.

[32] Tom Lantos quoted in ibid., 158.

[33] Author's interview with R. Spencer Oliver, July 8, 2014.

Affairs Committee and the Subcommittee on Human Rights, respectively. The CHRC was, thus, closely interwoven into the existing congressional human rights infrastructure and counted the leaders of the key committees and commissions among its members.

Initially, the CHRC operated out of the offices of its founders, who also assigned staffers to carry out its work, but eventually it was formalized with a more permanent setup. Under the original setup, staffers from Porter and Lantos's offices would work part-time at the CHRC when their schedules permitted it. In November 1984, these staffers debated the merits of institutionalizing the caucus by providing it with its own office and staff partly financed through higher membership fees. At first, Porter and his staffer Nancy Kohn opposed the idea, arguing that it was an unnecessary change and expressing concern that an increase in membership fees would decrease membership. Lantos staffer Rick Nelson disagreed, arguing that an institutionalization offered significant benefits. First, he maintained, the caucus would become more efficient if it did not have to rely on borrowed staffers from the offices of Porter and Lantos, which he believed imposed a time constraint on its work. Second, he argued, such a change would allow the caucus to become more visible and provide a better service to its members, which meant that it would not necessarily lose many members over an increased membership fee.[34] Ultimately, Lantos and Porter decided to follow through on the institutionalization by providing the CHRC its own staff in the fall of 1985 and a separate office in the spring the following year financed through increased membership fees.[35] The new office space was not luxurious, however. As Arriaga recalls, "The first office when I arrived was in annex two, where we would set up in Tom Lantos's storage room. We then swapped into a real office."[36] Contrary to the concerns of Porter and Kohn, membership continued to increase under the CHRC's new setup. The decision to institutionalize also proved decisive in the long run as it separated the CHRC's lifespan from the congressional tenures of its founders and thereby helped secure its longevity.

---

[34] Memo, "The Institutionalization of the Human Rights Caucus," November 30, 1984, Box 102, Folder 18 TLP.

[35] *CHRC Summary of Activities 1985*, Box 111, Folder 34, TLP. CHRC Newsletter, April 1, 1986, Box 102, Folder 19, TLP. Letter, Tom Lantos to Committee on House Administration, January 7, 1986, Box 112, Folder 18, TLP. As of January 1, 1986, membership fees were set at $10,000 for cochairs, $1,000 for executive members, and $250 for regular members. McCormick and Mitchell, "Commitments, Transnational Interests, and Congress," 580. In 1995, a reform of congressional rules changed the status of caucuses, revoking most of their privileges, including their ability to charge membership fees and hire staff.

[36] Author's interview with Alexandra Arriaga, June 8, 2018.

Expanding Human Rights Activism on Capitol Hill

According to a 1985 CHRC brochure, "One of the principal aims of the Congressional Human Rights Caucus is to increase congressional awareness of human rights violations and to encourage congressional action in support of the observance of human rights."[37] As such, the aim of the CHRC was two-fold: to inform members of Congress about human rights violations, and to mobilize them against these violations. Consequently, the CHRC put significant emphasis on disseminating information about human rights issues to put these on the political agenda. A regularly published newsletter circulated to caucus members provided information on pending legislation, petitions, and letters pertaining to human rights, along with relevant committee hearings and CHRC activities and services. The newsletters also presented profiles of caucus members, highlighting their work on human rights. For instance, one of the first newsletters from November 1983 praised Yatron for his leadership as chair of the Subcommittee on Human Rights.[38] As such, the newsletter served three key functions: raising awareness, mobilizing action, and commending achievements. Another method was the so-called "Dear Colleague" letters that members of Congress circulate internally on Capitol Hill to encourage support or opposition to legislation, collect signatures for letters, and inform about events, rule changes, and more.[39]

The CHRC also arranged numerous events, spanning from briefings, seminars, and roundtables to more imaginative ones, such as art displays and film screenings in Congress. Not part of the formal committee structure, caucus briefings and seminars lacked the legislative gravitas of hearings, but their less-formal nature had other advantages. Because they were not on the congressional record, they could allow for more frank discussions. The CHRC, for instance, took advantage of this by hosting seminars with assistant secretaries of state to discuss the State Department's *Country Reports on Human Rights Practices*.[40] Furthermore, the CHRC's caucus status allowed it to host events that formal congressional institutions could not. "For instance," Arriaga explains, "when the Dalai Lama visited the United States and, because of political reasons,

---

[37] CHRC Brochure 1985, Box 102, Folder 21, TLP.

[38] *CHRC Newsletter*, November 1983, Box 111, Folder 34, TLP.

[39] US Library of Congress, Congressional Research Service, *"Dear Colleague" Letters in the House of Representatives: Past Practices and Issues for Congress* (2017).

[40] See, for instance, seminars with Elliott Abrams and Richard Schifter. *CHRC Newsletter*, March 12, 1985, Box 102, Folder 19, TLP; *CHRC Annual Report* 1986, Box 111, Folder 34, TLP.

Figure 4 Representatives Tom Lantos and John E. Porter host the
Dalai Lama at the Congressional Human Rights Caucus,
September 1987.
International Campaign for Tibet.

Congress could not host him officially, the caucus could provide a semi-
official setting, where he could meet with members of Congress without
it being an official event" (Figure 4).[41] At other times, the CHRC
cohosted events with other institutions and members of Congress concerned with specific human rights issues. In 1985, for instance, the
CHRC sponsored a seminar on the possibilities for reform in South
Africa with one of the leading congressional opponents of South African
apartheid, Representative William Gray (D-PA).[42]

The less traditional events such as art displays and film screenings were
arguably the CHRC's most important contribution to the congressional
human rights calendar. These events told the stories of individual victims
of human rights abuses to members of Congress in other formats than the
usual reports and memos. In doing so, they put faces and names to
human rights issues, making it easier for members of Congress to identify
with the people the CHRC was trying to help.[43] In July 1983, the CHRC

---

[41] Author's interview with Alexandra Arriaga, June 8, 2018. *CHRC Newsletter*, October
1987, Box 102, Folder 19, TLP; Rene Sanchez, "Dalai Lama Urges Tibetan Freedom,"
The Washington Post, September 22, 1987, Nexis Uni.
[42] *CHRC Summary of Activities 1985*, Box 111, Folder 34, TLP.
[43] Mark Bradley has demonstrated how visual culture such as art, films, and paintings was
significant in shaping the global human rights imagination of the 1940s. Bradley, *The
World Reimagined*, 157.

sponsored an exhibition of "Unofficial Soviet Art" in the rotunda of the Cannon House Office Building with the artwork of imprisoned or exiled Soviet artists. The artwork exposed passersby to a broad range of paintings, spanning anything from realism to abstraction, but the exhibition drew attention to the persecution of artists in the Soviet Union. One of the artists, Mihail Chemiakin, was there in person to share his experience of being imprisoned in a Moscow mental hospital, where he reported to have been tied to a table as colored lights flashed at his eyes.[44] Other art exhibits sponsored by the CHRC drew attention to human rights issues in Cypress, Brazil, Guatemala, and Albania.[45] Among the CHRC's film screenings was the US premiere of a documentary on the torture of children in South African prisons in September 1988. The screening served to draw attention to a resolution concerned the issue introduced by Senator Barbara Mikulski (D-MD).[46]

CHRC events also opened Congress to human rights issues and activists who otherwise received little attention. Arriaga recalls how the indigenous Hmong people living in China and Southeast Asia were such an example. "They were maybe not so high on the agenda, but they could reach out to the caucus and the caucus would meet with them and help them draw attention to their cause."[47] In other words, the CHRC was more accessible than were committees such as the Subcommittee on Human Rights, which was preoccupied with the legislative process and tended to focus on more established issues. The broad membership of the CHRC also meant that it had members with a broad range of interest. So while certain issues, such as Soviet Jewry, received a disproportionate amount of its attention, members of the CHRC also worked on less visible issues such as the Macuxi and Yanomamo peoples in Brazil and the Penan in Malaysia.[48] It thus both expanded the quantity and diversity of human rights events in Congress.

To capture the attention of a broader audience and increase the pressure for action on human rights issues, the CHRC held press conferences, often in collaboration with human rights activists and dissidents. A typical example was a press conference held January 3, 1985, with

[44] Ann Jo Lewis, "Deep in the Art of Russia," *The Washington Post*, July 13, 1983, Nexis Uni.

[45] *CHRC Annual Report 1989*, Box 116, Folder 29, TLP. *CHRC Events of 1992*, December 1992, Box 113, Folder 5, LTP. *CHRC Annual Report 1992*, Box 116, Folder 29, TLP.

[46] Invitation, "Censorship in South Africa: The Children's Story Gets Out," September 14, 1988, Box 110, Folder 4, TLP.

[47] Author's interview with Alexandra Arriaga, June 8, 2018. See, also CHRC Correspondence May–October 1991, Box 114, Folder 20, TLP.

[48] *CHRC Newsletter*, June 1988, Box 102, Folder 19, TLP. CHRC Annual Report 1989, Box 116, Folder 29, TLP.

Avital Sharansky, the wife of famed Soviet dissident and refusenik Natan Sharansky. The press conference took place days before a meeting between Secretary of State George P. Shultz and Soviet Foreign Minister Andrei Gromyko and garnered considerable press coverage.[49] In characteristic fashion for the CHRC's work, the meeting was followed by letters to the Soviet General Secretary Konstantin Chernenko, requesting Sharansky's release, and a letter to Shultz, urging him to raise Sharansky in his meeting with Gromyko.[50] The State Department subsequently responded favorably to the letter, assuring CHRC cochair John Porter that Shultz had raised Sharansky at the meeting.[51] While Sharansky was not released at the time, his mother and brother were allowed to visit him for the first time; an improvement that Avital Sharansky gave the CHRC considerable credit for. "The letter sent by members of Congress to President Chernenko played a major role in the positive developments that have followed the Geneva discussions," she wrote Lantos in the aftermath.[52]

As a caucus, the CHRC provided a range of legislative services to its members that made it easier for them to engage in human rights activism. These services included technical assistance in promoting human rights legislation, human rights reference center services, congressional liaison services, congressional internship programs, a human rights news line, and meetings with high-level dignitaries and experts. According to political scientist Susan Hammond, such legislative services that help members of Congress acquire information and reduce the costs of their work are among the key drivers for caucus membership.[53] One of the more innovative services of the CHRC was the launch of a "computer tracking system," which maintained a record of all congressional activity on human rights. Using this tracking system, legislators could gain systematic information about any specific human rights issue Congress had acted on, as well as access a list of their own human rights activities.[54] By 1986, this system contained information on nearly two thousand human rights cases from more than forty countries.[55] The entries on each human rights case would detail background information, the

---

[49] CHRC Press Release and Letter, January 3, 1985, Box 107, Folder 11, TLP.
[50] Letter, CHRC to Konstantin Chernenko, January 3, 1985, Box 107, Folder 10, TLP. Letter, CHRC to George P. Shultz, January 3, 1985, Box 107, Folder 11, TLP.
[51] Letter, W. Tapley Bennett Jr. to John E. Porter, January 15, 1985, Box 107, Folder 10, TLP.
[52] Letter, Avital Shcharansky to Tom Lantos, January 17, 1985, Box 107, Folder 11, TLP.
[53] Hammond, *Congressional Caucuses in National Policy Making*, 52–53.
[54] *CHRC Newsletter*, April 30, 1984, Box 102, Folder 19, TLP.
[55] *CHRC Newsletter*, April 1, 1986, Box 102, Folder 19, TLP.

contact details of victims, and congressional legislation and statements. The first of its kind, this system became Congress's collective memory of human rights issues, providing an in-house resource that helped members of Congress to identify an issue and coordinate action on it. The system also kept track of the activities of individual members of Congress on any human rights issue, allowing the caucus to generate detailed human rights profiles. In April 1986, it started an annual practice of sending all members of Congress their individual profile.[56] In this way, the CHRC helped members of Congress to keep track of their own actions and made it easy for them to inform their constituents on their support for popular human rights issues.

Writing to foreign leaders on behalf of victims of human rights violations was a major part of the CHRC's work and from 1985 onward it arranged annual letter writing campaigns. In October 1985, CHRC staff prepared more than 150 letters on specific human rights cases to heads of states in the Soviet Union, Poland, Romania, East Germany, Iran, South Africa, Gabon, Nigeria, Somalia, Chile, Cuba, El Salvador, Guatemala, Taiwan, China, South Korea, and the Philippines. The letters covered a broad range of issues but focused primarily on discrimination against minorities and dissidents, political prisoners, the use of torture, and individuals denied emigration.[57] In the CHRC newsletter for August 1986, Lantos expressed his belief in the importance of such letters, "This is the ultimate power of the Congressional Human Rights Caucus. By focusing congressional attention directly on the most serious human rights violations, we emphasize the tremendous bipartisan support for human rights in the Congress."[58] The CHRC continuously dedicated substantial resources to such letters and repeatedly stated its belief that it was an effective weapon for bringing justice to victims of human rights abuses.[59]

Members of the CHRC also corresponded with foreign dissidents and occasionally met in person with these, when possible. Through such exchanges, members of Congress learned about the lives and grievances of the people they were trying to help. Conversely, individuals stuck in hopeless situations were reassured that they were not forgotten and that their cause was on the agenda of American policymakers. This sometimes led to strong personal connections that both sides would characterize as friendships. In a typical example, former refusenik Yakov

[56] *CHRC Newsletter*, April 1, 1986, Box 102, Folder 19, TLP.
[57] *CHRC Newsletter*, November 1, 1985, Box 102, Folder 19, TLP.
[58] *CHRC Newsletter*, August 1, 1986, Box 102, Folder 19, TLP.
[59] See, for instance, *CHRC Newsletter*, Spring 1993, Box 102, Folder 19, TLP.

Galperin wrote to Lantos in July 1987 two months after leaving the Soviet Union, "I want to bow before you on behalf of many people who have escaped the tenuous clutches of the KGB."[60] On September 16, 1987, Porter and the refusenik Zachar Zunshine, whose release Porter had helped secure, were among the audience as Reagan delivered a speech commemorating the 200th anniversary of the Constitution of the United States. "We had tears streaming down our faces," Porter recalls, describing the moment as heartwarming.[61] Such personal connections and the emotional bonds they created were important motivators for congressional human rights activism, and the CHRC encouraged them whenever possible.

Although the CHRC could not participate directly in the legislative process, it did seek to influence legislation. Its dissemination of information about human rights issues and its efforts to mobilize congressional human rights activism were often directed at desired policy changes. When its members introduced resolutions and bills as individuals, the CHRC sought to increase their chances of success through its newsletters, "Dear colleague" letters, and events to build support. In a nutshell, the CHRC worked as a lobbying group for the interests of its members and as such operated as a voice for a greater emphasis on human rights in congressional legislation on foreign policy.

The CHRC also initiated several spin-off initiatives and sponsored several outreach programs, the majority of which focused on human rights issues in the Soviet Union. In June 1983, Porter, Lantos, and Senators Charles Grassley (R-IA) and Dennis DeConcini (D-AZ) cosponsored the formation of the International Parliamentary Group for Human Rights in the Soviet Union (IPG) with the UCSJ.[62] The IPG aimed to coordinate the efforts of Western parliamentarians on behalf of human rights issues in the Soviet Union. At the launch of the IPG, Porter declared that by "joining together, Western European and American parliamentarians will work to maximize the pressures on the Soviet Union to end human rights violations." Lantos echoed the need for a coordinated effort, stating, "We have to speak in one voice stretching from Norway to New Zealand."[63] The IPG set up headquarters in

---

[60] Letter, Yakov Galperin to Tom Lantos, July 30, 1987, Box 106, Folder 8, TLP.

[61] Author's interview with Rep. John E. Porter, October 17, 2018. Zachar Zunshine had been one of the refuseniks adopted by Porter's wife, Kathryn Porter, through the Committee of 21. *CHRC Newsletter*, March 6, 1987, Box 111, Folder 20, TLP.

[62] *CHRC Newsletter*, November 1983, Box 111, Folder 34, TLP.

[63] "New Human Rights Group Formed," *Jewish Telegraph Agency*, June 14, 1983, www.jta .org/1983/06/30/archive/new-human-rights-group-formed.

Washington, DC, and London and appointed UCSJ executive director Paul Meek as its daily leader.[64]

Two years after its formation, the IPG was comprised of more than 700 parliamentarians from the United States, Canada, and most Western European countries and had formed standing human rights committees in a number of national parliaments.[65] It coordinated legislative efforts, arranged trips to the Soviet Union, and sought to increase public awareness of human rights issues.[66] It was particularly active in coordinating Western positions at international conferences within the framework of the Helsinki Accords such as, for instance, the CSCE Ottawa Human Rights Expert Meeting in 1985.[67] The same year, the chair of its advisory group, the American lawyer Rita Hauser, testified on the implementation of the Helsinki Accords before the US Helsinki Commission.[68] Ahead of the opening of the CSCE Vienna Review Meeting in November 1986, the IPG sent Shultz a list of recommendations for how best to emphasize human rights at the meeting.[69] IPG recommendations tended to correlate with the policies of the Reagan administration. In a response to an IPG report sent to Reagan ahead of his 1987 summit with Mikhail Gorbachev, the administration assured that "the areas of concern outlined in the IPG's report were dealt with fully during the summit."[70] To some degree, the IPG represented an international extension of the CHRC with a focus limited to the Soviet Union.

Lantos and Porter also established the Congressional Human Rights Foundation (CHRF) in 1985 as "a bipartisan, nonprofit educational organization, which actively addresses political, ethnic, religious, racial, and other human rights violations around the world."[71] According to former CHRF president David L. Phillips, the foundation was created as

---

[64] Ibid. Meek had accompanied Porter on the September 1982 trip to the Soviet Union that gave him the idea for the CHRC.

[65] IPG News, April 24, 1985, I-181A, box 301, Folder 6, NCSJR.

[66] Report, *IPG Call to Conscience*, December 3, 1987, ID #548208, HU, WHORM: Subject File, RPL.

[67] CSCE Human Rights Expert Meeting Ottawa, IPG Report, June 1985, Box 130, Folder 12, Jack Kemp Papers, Manuscript Division, Library of Congress, Washington, DC (hereafter JKP).

[68] US Congress, House, Commission on Security and Cooperation in Europe, *Implementation of the Helsinki Accords Hearing before the Commission on Security and Cooperation in Europe,* 99th Congress, 1st Session, October 3, 1985.

[69] Letter, IPG to George P. Shultz, October 1, 1986, Box 110, Folder 17, TLP.

[70] Letter, John Evans to Charles Grassley, January 19, 1988, ID#548208, HU, WHORM Subject File, Ronald Reagan Library.

[71] Congressional Human Rights Foundation, Statement of Purpose, Box 113, Folder 21, TLP.

a "private sector initiative operating parallel to the CHRC."[72] The CHRF dedicated itself to working with US government agencies and NGOs to "assure that human rights are fully considered in the development of United States foreign policy."[73] To this end, the CHRF raised money for activities such as international conferences, fact-finding missions, and cultural events, as well as offered strategic planning for human rights NGOs. The close relationship to the CHRC was evident from the composition of the CHRF's board, which included CHRC members such as Lantos, Porter, Fascell, and Peter Rodino (D-NJ). However, in 1992 the CHRC and the CHRF cut all ties amid concerns about the perception of ethical issues due to the links between the two entities. According to Arriaga, "We just wanted to make sure that there was no confusion and no ethical issues. For instance, if it could be argued that donating to the foundation could give special privilege to access a member of Congress that would be a problem."[74] At the request of Lantos and Porter, the CHRF subsequently changed its name to the Parliamentary Human Rights Foundation to prevent future misunderstandings.[75]

Another initiative stemming from the CHRC was the Congressional Spouses Committee of 21 (Committee of 21). Launched in 1985, the Committee of 21 consisted of twenty-one spouses of members of Congress, who each adopted a high-profile refusenik to draw attention to their struggle.[76] The idea for the initiative came from refuseniks, who told Annette Lantos during a visit to Moscow that they feared the West would forget about them.[77] The members of the Committee of 21 sought to prevent this by taking advantage of their status as both spouses of prominent politicians and ordinary private citizens. The former gave them access to media coverage and meetings with Soviet officials, while the latter allowed them to speak freely without concern about reelection or restrictions associated with representing the US government. As Annette Lantos explained in a 1986-article in the *New York Times*, "Every time we go [to the Soviet Union], we name these people to the authorities. We don't let them forget."[78] The Committee of 21 also

---

[72] Author's interview with David L. Phillips, July 30, 2015.

[73] Congressional Human Rights Foundation, Statement of Purpose, Box 113, Folder 21, TLP.

[74] Author's interview with Alexandra Arriaga, June 8, 2018.

[75] Letter, Tom Lantos and John E. Porter to David Phillips, December 2, 1993, Box 113, Folder 21, TLP; Memo, Alex Arriaga to Laura Glickson, August 18, 1995, Box 114, Folder 22, TLP.

[76] *CHRC Summary of Activities 1985*, Box 111, Folder 34, TLP.

[77] *CHRC Newsletter*, June 1985, Box 102, Folder 19, TLP.

[78] "Wives' Group: 'Not Just John Q. Citizens,'" *The New York Times*, February 21, 1986, www.nytimes.com/1986/02/21/us/wives-group-not-just-john-q-citizens.html.

organized a school outreach program, through which its members visited high schools in their spouses' home districts and encouraged school children to adopt refusenik children of their own age.[79] The impact of such activities on the situation of the refuseniks in question was likely limited. To the spouses who participated, however, it appears to have been a rewarding and meaningful experience and helped raise the salience of the issue in the districts of members of Congress. Although impossible to prove, it cannot be ruled out that this could have had a positive impact not just on constituents' support for refuseniks but also for their support for the members of Congress in question.

The Committee of 21 resembled other CHRC-initiated adoption programs that all contributed to bringing members of Congress into contact with human rights victims. These various programs targeted individuals, "who are persecuted or incarcerated for their beliefs, color, sex, ethnic origin, language or religion and who have not used or advocated violence."[80] The programs included the Religious Prisoners Adoption Program, the Prisoners of Conscience Outreach, the Soviet Christian Adoption Program, Soviet Prisoners of Conscience, and Divided Spouses Adoption. The CHRC also launched the Congressional Interns for Soviet Jewry in July 1986, with more than one hundred participating interns, encouraging them to take action on behalf of Soviet Jews denied emigration.[81] One other similar group, not directly linked to the CHRC, was the Congressional Friends of Human Rights Monitors (CFHRM) established by Representative Tony Hall (D-OH) and Senator Daniel P. Moynihan (D-NY) in 1983.[82] Prompted by the human rights NGO Helsinki Watch, the CFHRM sought to lend congressional support to human rights monitors around the world by writing letters on their behalf.[83] Together, these programs dramatically expanded the number of legislators, staff, and interns involved in human rights activism and established personal connections between these and persecuted individuals.

This expansion of congressional human rights activism and the establishment of personal connections were some of the CHRC's key achievements. At the time of the CHRC's establishment, the committee

---

[79] *CHRC Newsletter*, December 1, 1986, Box 111, Folder 34, TLP.

[80] *CHRC Annual Report 1989*, Box 116, Folder 29, TLP.

[81] *CHRC Newsletter*, August 1, 1986, Box 102, Folder 19, TLP.

[82] Congressional Friends of Human Rights Monitors to Mikhail Gorbachev, April 1, 1986, Box 142, MS-341, The Tony Hall Papers Collection, Special Collections and Archives, University Libraries, Wright State University, Dayton, Ohio.

[83] Memo, Peter Galbraith to Claiborne Pell, June 14, 1983, Records of the United States Senate, Record Group 46; Galbraith Files, Box 56, Center for Legislative Archives, National Archives, Washington, DC.

positions in Congress dealing with human rights issues was limited to
nine seats on the Subcommittee on Human Rights and twelve on the US
Helsinki Commission. The CHRC and its spin-off initiatives offered
members of Congress without one of these seats another outlet through
which to become involved with human rights issues. In addition, the
CHRC, to a higher degree than the formal committees, emphasized
personal connections with persecuted individuals. Lacking the ability to
hold official hearings and pass legislation on broader issues, the CHRC
was limited to speaking out against human rights violations. This
approach offered members of Congress a way to engage human rights
issues in a manageable and selective fashion by supporting individuals of
their choosing.

This activist approach was advanced further over the years, as the
CHRC developed a mutually beneficial relationship with human rights
NGOs and other groups, which provided the CHRC with essential information, expertise, and legitimacy that made its work both easier and
better. Information from NGOs, for instance, was crucial for the CHRC's
identification of cases for its letter-writing campaigns, and various NGOs
cosponsored and supported the CHRC's spin-off groups.[84] In this way,
NGOs lowered the operating costs of the CHRC and helped it compensate for its limited resources and staff. In turn, the CHRC offered NGOs
an access point to reach members of Congress and a megaphone for their
message inside and outside of Capitol Hill.[85]

The number and size of human rights NGOs grew dramatically
during the late 1970s and the 1980s and several of these increasingly
sought to influence policymakers.[86] While access to the executive
branch naturally was high on the agenda of anyone seeking to influence
US foreign policy, this was often difficult to obtain. Moreover, NGOs
concerned with human rights issues outside the Eastern Bloc found the
Reagan administration less receptive of their viewpoints than the Carter
administration had been. As a result, several NGOs increased their
focus on Congress during the 1980s where they quickly found a sympathetic ally in the CHRC.[87]

---

[84] *CHRC Newsletter*, September 9, 1985, Box 102, Folder 19, TLP; *CHRC Newsletter*, November 1, 1985, Box 102, Folder 19, TLP.

[85] Eventually, the collaboration would also lead to a revolving door between personnel in the CHRC and NGOs. McCormick and Mitchell, "Commitments, Transnational Interests, and Congress," 588–589.

[86] Kenneth Cmiel, "The Emergence of Human Rights Politics in the United States," *Journal of American History* 86, no. 3 (1999): 1242–1243; Sikkink, *Mixed Signals*, 20.

[87] Zachary Steven Ramirez, "International Human Rights Activism in the United States During the Cold War" (PhD dissertation, University of California, Berkeley, 2013), 230.

The CHRC hosted a number of events to facilitate contact between members of Congress and NGOs and encourage collaboration between these. In February 1985, for instance, the CHRC sponsored a briefing for congressional staffers to become acquainted with human rights NGOs. At the seminar, representatives of Amnesty International USA (AIUSA), Helsinki Watch, America's Watch, and the US Helsinki Commission explained to staffers how individual members of Congress could help fight for human rights around the world and detailed the types of assistance NGOs could provide to congressional offices.[88] The CHRC also sponsored a more specialized seminar with AIUSA on the use of torture against political prisoners in repressive regimes.[89] A reception in December 1988 included more than twenty-five representatives from NGOs.[90]

The CHRC enjoyed a particularly close relationship with AIUSA.[91] AIUSA's program for influencing the US government in 1986 explicitly listed the CHRC as a target for its efforts to lobby policymakers, and over the following years the two organizations collaborated on several initiatives.[92] In March 1986, Lantos introduced a bill in collaboration with AIUSA, commemorating the NGO's 25th anniversary and calling on Americans to support its work.[93] Ahead of the 40th anniversary of the Universal Declaration of Human Rights in 1988, the CHRC helped AIUSA collect signatures of members of Congress for an appeal to the United Nations, urging all countries to live up to the declaration.[94] The CHRC and AIUSA also co-hosted several events on Capitol Hill, including briefings on AIUSA's activities in 1986 and the human rights situation in South Africa in 1989.[95] In the 1991, the collaborative efforts of the CHRC, AISUA, and the Lawyers Committee for Human Rights secured passage of the Torture Victim Protection Act.[96]

[88] *CHRC Newsletter*, February 1, 1985, Box 102, Folder 19, TLP.

[89] *CHRC Summary of Activities 1985*, Box 111, Folder 34, TLP.

[90] Memo, CHRC Reception, Alex Arriaga to Tom Lantos, December 5, 1988, Box 113, Folder 3, TLP; CHRC "Dear Colleague" Letter, October 11, 1989, Box 113, Folder 4, TLP.

[91] Report for the May 1985 Planning Meeting, Washington, DC, Office, Box VII 3.324, Folder 13; AIUSA. See also Ramirez, "International Human Rights Activism in the United States during the Cold War," 230.

[92] AIUSA Program vis-à-vis the US Government, March 14, 1986, Box VII 3.324, Folder 13; AIUSA.

[93] Letter, 'Pat' to Jack Healy, Lantos Bill on Amnesty International, March 6, 1986, Box II.3.39, Folder 1; AIUSA.

[94] *CHRC Newsletter*, June 1988, Box 102, Folder 19, TLP.

[95] *CHRC Newsletter* April 1, 1986, Box 102, Folder 19, TLP; "Dear Colleague" Letter, Invitation to CHRC Briefing on October 12, 1989, Box 113, Folder 4, TLP.

[96] Ramirez, "International Human Rights Activism in the United States during the Cold War," 234.

The CHRC also worked closely with interest groups focused on specific human rights issues or specific regions. Due to its significant emphasis on Soviet Jewry, the CHRC collaborated extensively with American Jewish groups focused on the Soviet Union, such as the National Conference on Soviet Jewry (NCSJ) and the UCSJ, which had arranged the trip that led to the CHRC's formation. In June 1983, the Chicago branch of the NCSJ declared in a news release, "The Congressional Human Rights Caucus is critically important now for marshaling attention to this issue [Soviet Jewry]," and executive director of the UCSJ Paul Meek added, "There is nothing else like it in Congress."[97] Over the years, the NCSJ, the UCSJ, and other American Jewish groups briefed the CHRC about discrimination against Soviet Jews on numerous occasions and facilitated contact between members of Congress and refuseniks in particular.[98]

The case of refusenik Alexander Lerner offers an illustrative example of the nexus between the CHRC, NGOs, and persecuted individuals. An internationally known authority in the field of cybernetics, Lerner had first applied to leave the Soviet Union for Israel in 1971. After the Soviet authorities rejected his request to emigrate, Lerner was dismissed from his job, expelled from the Communist Party, and subjected to surveillance and harassment from the KGB (Committee for State Security). Lerner was among the refuseniks Porter met on his September 1982 trip to the Soviet Union. Porter and the CHRC, therefore, naturally joined the ongoing campaign to pressure the Soviet Union to allow Lerner to leave. Porter maintained frequent correspondence with Lerner, taking an interest in his life, congratulating him on his son's marriage, and informing him of efforts undertaken to assist his cause, such as the formation of the CHRC and the IPG.[99] In his correspondence with Lerner, Porter was continuously supported by the NCSJ, which sent him updates on Lerner's situation and reminders of Lerner's birthday with an encouragement to write Soviet officials on his behalf and insert statements in the Congressional Record.[100] Porter complied with these requests, writing Soviet Foreign Minister Gromyko, referring

---

[97] Chicago Conference on Soviet Jewry: *News*, June 13, 1983, I-181A; 292; 6, NCSJR.

[98] On August 9, 1988, for instance, the UCSJ briefed the CHRC on anti-Semitism in the Soviet Union based on a fact-finding mission. Statement of the UCSJ to the CHRC, August 9, 1988, I-410A, box 66, folder 14, UCSJ.

[99] Letter, John E. Porter to Aleksandr Lerner, January 6, 1984, Box 103, Folder 11, TLP; Letter, John E. Porter to Aleksandr Lerner, June 4, 1984, Box 103, Folder 11, TLP.

[100] Letter, NCSJ to John E. Porter, September 4, 1984, Box 103, Folder 11, TLP.

to how the 210 members of the CHRC shared his concern for Lerner's situation.[101] Amid growing pressure from Western governments and NGOs, Lerner was finally allowed to immigrate to Israel in January 1988 as one of the last remaining refuseniks in the Soviet Union.

Lacking any legislative powers, the CHRC was limited to speaking out against human rights violations by seeking to stigmatize repressive regimes through "naming and shaming." A tactic employed by human rights NGOs, media, and governments alike, naming and shaming seeks to attract public attention to human rights violations in an attempt to increase the costs for offenders and thereby act as a deterrence of repressive behavior.[102] Human rights NGOs such as Amnesty International, for instance, employed naming and shaming in their efforts on behalf of prisoners of conscience and their campaign against torture.[103] While this tactic is sometimes dismissed as cheap talk without any implications, there is some evidence to support that under the right circumstances naming and shaming have an impact on governments' human rights records.[104]

The tactic was well suited for the CHRC's focus on advocating for the release of political prisoners and ending discrimination against minorities. A CHRC newsletter argued, "The most powerful weapon to aid the unjustly oppressed is the glare of public scrutiny. In many cases, world attention is the principal reason repressive governments have moderated their behavior."[105] Another CHRC newsletter from 1986 noted, "A letter or a phone call from a congressional office may mean the difference between torture and due process."[106] Porter recalls how he and other members of the CHRC "would get the name of someone in a Soviet prison and call the prison warden to let them know that we were watching."[107] In this way, the CHRC sought to reduce the suffering of people in hopeless situations abroad. When successful, this

---

[101] Letter, John E. Porter to Andrei Gromyko, September 14, 1984, Box 103, Folder 11, TLP.

[102] Emilie M. Burton-Hafner, "Sticks and Stones: Naming and Shaming the Human Rights Enforcement Problem," *International Organization* 62 (Fall 2008): 689.

[103] Stephen Hopgood, *Keepers of the Flame: Understanding Amnesty International* (Ithaca, NY: Cornell University Press, 2006); Keys, "Anti-Torture Politics," 201–221.

[104] Amanda M. Murdie and David R. Davis, "Shaming and Blaming: Using Events Data to Assess the Impact of Human Rights INGOs," *International Studies Quarterly* 56, no. 1 (2012): 1–16. Murdie and Davis find that shaming combined with the presence of international human rights NGOs in the targeted country and pressure by third-party countries, individuals, and organizations best secure improvements in human rights practices.

[105] *CHRC Newsletter*, November 1983, Box 111, Folder 34, TLP.

[106] *CHRC Newsletter*, April 1, 1986, Box 102, Folder 19, TLP.

[107] Author's interview with Rep. John E. Porter, October 17, 2018.

was hugely significant to the individual in question, and ultimately lives could sometimes be saved.

Naming and shaming, however, also had clear limitations. There was a risk of backfiring if targeted regimes developed counter-narratives that sought to delegitimize the criticism directed against them. The CHRC experienced this when Soviet officials accused it of inappropriate interference in internal affairs and labeled its activities as part of an anti-Soviet Zionist campaign.[108] After the CHRC hosted the Dalai Lama, the Chinese government likewise condemned Congress for meddling in internal affairs.[109] Another risk was that countries might offer concessions on particular rights under scrutiny but secretly ramp up other human rights violations not afforded the same spotlight. International attention without leverage might even serve to worsen the situation of the people in question if the regime responded by increasing repression.[110]

Moreover, while naming and shaming could be useful to address violations of individuals' rights, it was much less useful for addressing underlying structures of human rights problems such as, for instance, poverty or complex issues preventing peaceful solutions to conflicts. The reliance on naming and shaming also made the CHRC less likely to champion economic, social, and cultural rights. A government's failure to guarantee its citizens' right to education, health care, and housing was less visible and dramatic than its failure to guarantee them a fair trial, the right to vote, or bodily integrity and, thus, harder to shame. Hence, the CHRC's reliance on naming and shaming reinforced its focus on civil and political rights and neglect of economic, social, and cultural rights.

A Bipartisan Human Rights Policy?

Comprising close to half of the representatives in the House by the late 1980s and spanning wide ideological divides, the CHRC offers an interesting case through which to examine the contours of American commitment to human rights. Strongly dedicated to fostering a bipartisan consensus, the CHRC provides insight into the types of human rights and the specific cases members of Congress could agree, or not agree, to get behind. Moreover, to the extent that the composition of Congress

---

[108] Cable, Response to U.S. Congressmen on Jewish Emigration, June 21, 1983, Box 111, Folder 33, TLP.

[109] Edward A. Gargan, "Chinese Report Protest by Lamas to Free Tibet," *The New York Times*, October 1, 1987, A8; Porter, Remarks at Tibet Rally, March 10, 1988, Box 102, Folder 35, TLP.

[110] Burton-Hafner, "Sticks and Stones," 689–716.

represents the American public by reflecting the views of the electorate, the CHRC was the most representative institution for American attention to human rights. The CHRC thus offers a unique opportunity to study what a minimal American consensus on human rights looked like.

The CHRC grounded its work in the Universal Declaration of Human Rights (UDHR) from 1948, declaring its commitment to advance the universally recognized human rights in this founding document of international human rights. Letters and statements by the CHRC addressed to foreign governments violating human rights frequently invoked the UDHR, pointing to how these governments failed to honor their commitment to a document they had signed. The CHRC thus used the UDHR to emphasize the universality of human rights, seeking to protect itself from accusations of American encroachment on the domestic politics of other countries. When relevant, the CHRC also made references to other international human rights documents, such as the International Covenant on Civil and Political Rights (ICCPR), the International Convention on the Elimination of All Forms of Racial Discrimination, and the Helsinki Final Act.[111]

At the same time, the CHRC repeatedly referred to human rights as part of the American experience, citing the American Declaration of Independence and the Bill of Rights as foundational for its activities.[112] In a 1985 brochure, it declared, "Human Rights are America's legacy to the world," and stated that the CHRC was dedicated to maintaining that legacy.[113] According to its 1994 annual report, CHRC strove to "focus bipartisan attention on the most fundamental American values: the sanctity of the individual and the inalienable rights on which the Founders created our country."[114] Such statements underlined the strong identification with the particular American rights tradition, and while there are important overlaps between the rights expressed in the American documents and those included in the UDHR, there are also significant differences. Most notably, whereas the UDHR includes an extensive list of civil, political, economic, social, and cultural rights, the American human rights documents focus exclusively on civil and political rights.[115]

---

[111] For the use of the Helsinki Final Act as leverage in US human rights diplomacy toward the Soviet Union, see Snyder, *Human Rights Activism and the End of the Cold War*.

[112] See, for instance, *CHRC Annual Report 1989*, Box 116, Folder 29, TLP.

[113] CHRC Brochure 1985, Box 102, Folder 21, TLP.

[114] *CHRC Annual Report 1994*, Box 102, Folder 20, TLP.

[115] United Nations General Assembly, *Universal Declaration of Human Rights*, December 10, 1948, accessed August 13, 2019, https://www.un.org/en/universal-declaration-human-rights/, United States, *Declaration of Independence* (1776), United States, *The Constitution of the United States* (1789).

In other words, the UDHR represents a much more expansive list of human rights than do the American documents. The CHRC, nonetheless, referred to these almost interchangeably without reflecting on their differences in scope and the resulting implications for the conception of human rights. In doing so, the CHRC embodied a core paradox in US human rights policy, namely the notions that human rights are at the same time both universal and inherently American, rooted in beliefs in American exceptionalism.[116]

Moreover, the CHRC put a strong emphasis on the sanctity of the individual, taking inspiration from both religion and social justice movements. A CHRC newsletter from 1983 opened with a quote paraphrasing the Talmud, "Whoever saves a single soul, is as if he had saved a whole world."[117] A brochure from 1985 invoked the spirit of the civil rights leader Dr. Martin Luther King Jr.: "The Human Rights Caucus is motivated by the belief that human rights are indivisible – that the denial of fundamental freedoms and human rights anywhere is a threat to free men and women everywhere."[118] The emphasis, in these quotes, on the connection between the life and freedom of any individual and humanity at large and the sense of global solidarity with those denied their basic human rights was a core tenet of the CHRC's mission.

To forge a bipartisan human rights policy in practice, the CHRC had to overcome divisive factors, such as partisanship, ideology, religion, and personal experiences, that shaped American attention to human rights. Despite broad-based support for human rights in the abstract, several specific human rights issues remained highly contested and members of Congress often disagreed vehemently about the appropriate role of

---

[116] For a broad engagement with American Exceptionalism and human rights, see Michael Ignatieff, ed., *American Exceptionalism and Human Rights* (Princeton, NJ: Princeton University Press, 2005). For an argument that the United States is not exceptional when it comes to human rights, see David P. Forsythe and Patrice C. McMahon, *American Exceptionalism Reconsidered: US Foreign Policy, Human Rights, and World Order* (New York: Routledge, 2017).

[117] *CHRC Newsletter*, November 1983, Box 111, Folder 34, TLP. "And whoever saves a life of Israel, it is considered as if he saved an entire world." Mishnah Sanhedrin 4:5; Yerushalmi Talmud 4:9, Babylonian Talmud Sanhedrin 37a. A similar phrase can be found in the Quran.

[118] CHRC Brochure 1985, Box 102, Folder 21, TLP. "Injustice anywhere is a threat to justice everywhere." Martin Luther King Jr., "Letter from Birmingham Jail," *The Atlantic Monthly* 212, no. 2 (1963): 78–88. The quote is also reminiscent of a phrase in Jimmy Carter's inaugural address: "Because we are free we can never be indifferent to the fate of freedom elsewhere." Jimmy Carter, United States Foreign Policy Remarks to People of Other Nations on Assuming Office, January 20, 1977. Online by Gerhard Peters and John T. Woolley, The American Presidency Project, accessed August 7, 2019, www.presidency.ucsb.edu/node/242950.

human rights concerns in US foreign policy.[119] Generally, liberals and conservatives differed on the relative emphasis that human rights should play in relations with the Soviet Bloc and American allies. To overcome divisive factors, the CHRC employed tactics designed to minimize the risk of conflict among its members and external criticism.

First, Lantos and Porter stressed their intentions to find common ground from the outset. In their first letter introducing the new CHRC to members of Congress, they argued, "While all of us may disagree over some issues, we can agree on the basic principles of human rights that our nation has cherished since its birth."[120] The CHRC sought to form a bipartisan consensus around the most basic human rights – not an expansive definition. It sought to leave aside disagreements and focus on the issues with a broad convergence of support. Schrayer recalls, "The caucus was consciously limiting itself to issues with broad bipartisan support and was careful to select issues that would not polarize."[121] By extension, the CHRC also refrained from actively confronting the administration on contentious issues. In short, the CHRC was cautious and nonconfrontational in the issues it addressed.

Second, the CHRC adapted its actions on any given issue based on how timely, prominent, and controversial the issue was to its members and the public. If an issue had already received considerable attention and enjoyed strong bipartisan support, the CHRC would stage press conferences, demonstrations, and other activities that sought to mobilize members of Congress to act. If an issue was less familiar to members of Congress or was deemed controversial, the CHRC would instead limit itself to distribute information and host events geared toward staffers, such as briefings and roundtables that did not require the participation of members of Congress.[122] In a nutshell, the CHRC focused its more active mobilization on safe issues with broad appeal and took a cautious approach to issues that could divide its members.

Third, the CHRC allowed its members considerable flexibility on what issues they wanted to support and how much time they would dedicate to these issues. As a caucus, the CHRC had no leverage to demand

---

[119] For public support for human rights in the abstract, see Chicago Council on Foreign Relations. Gallup/CCFR Survey of American Public Opinion and U.S. Foreign Policy 1986, October 1986. USGALLUP.86CFRP.R21B. Cornell University, Ithaca, NY: Roper Center for Public Opinion Research, iPOLL, accessed August 5, 2019.

[120] "Dear Colleague" Letter, February 23, 1983, Box 141, MS-341, The Tony Hall Papers Collection, Special Collections and Archives, University Libraries, Wright State University, Dayton, Ohio.

[121] Author's interview with Elizabeth Schrayer, January 22, 2015.

[122] Memo, Alex Arriaga to Laura Glickson, August 18, 1995, Box 114, Folder 22, TLP.

consistency from its members. Rather, its members were free to disregard any issue or action they did not agree with. Arriaga recalls, "The caucus's letterhead would always include the names of all members, but on some issues only some members would sign. We of course always tried to get everyone to sign."[123] This meant that most of its members split down the liberal–conservative divide in their chosen focus.[124] Moreover, the CHRC allowed its members the opportunity to dedicate sustained attention to issues of particular concern to them and remain passive on other issues. Reflecting the special interests of its members, the CHRC set up ad hoc committees in 1984, which would meet regularly to discuss issues with government officials, private organizations, and diplomatic personnel to facilitate joint action. Some of these committees focused on regions, such as Latin America, Africa, Eastern Europe, and Asia, while another addressed the issue of torture.[125] The composition and focus of these ad hoc committees changed over time to accommodate the interest of CHRC members. By 1989, the groups included country-specific ones on Peru, Tibet, Romania, El Salvador, and Somalia and thematic ones concerned with refugees and cultural genocide.[126] In 1994, it added a group on anti-Semitism.[127] This flexibility to devote time to issues of particular interest without any demand for consistency made membership both expedient and politically safe.

Joining the CHRC allowed members of Congress to demonstrate support for human rights in the abstract, which was very popular among the American public, without having to associate themselves with particular issues that risked offending their constituents. The cautiousness of the CHRC, both in the issues it adopted and the actions it undertook and with the flexibility it allowed its members, help explain why members would join the CHRC. This supplements a political science study that argues policy motivations of members and the subsidizing role of human rights NGOs account for motivations to join the CHRC.[128]

Although it covered a broad range of human rights issues, the CHRC focused predominantly on civil and political rights of persecuted

---

[123] Author's interview with Alexandra Arriaga, June 8, 2018.
[124] Katrina Lantos Swett, "An Indispensable Catalyst. Congress, Human Rights and American Foreign Policy" (PhD dissertation, University of Southern Denmark, 2007).
[125] *CHRC Newsletter*, July 24, 1984, Box 102, Folder 19, TLP.
[126] *CHRC Annual Report 1989*, Box 116, Folder 29, TLP.
[127] Memo, Alex Arriaga to Laura Glickson, August 18, 1995, Box 114, Folder 22, TLP.
[128] McCormick and Mitchell, "Commitments, Transnational Interests, and Congress," 588.

individuals as well as the protection from bodily harm (the integrity of the person), while largely ignoring economic, social, and cultural rights. This was reflected in the CHRC's failure to invoke the International Covenant on Economic, Social, and Cultural Rights (ICESCR). Although the United States only signed and failed to ratify the ICESCR, it did come into effect in 1976 and was part of the international human rights body that the CHRC claimed to be championing. In this regard, the CHRC was not unique among American, or indeed Western, human rights advocates. During the 1970s, virtually all governments and human rights NGOs in Western democracies abandoned attempts to address economic inequality through an emphasis on economic and social rights in favor of a more modest human rights agenda of shaming repressive governments.[129] Even Carter, who rhetorically placed an unprecedented emphasis on economic and social rights, effectively afforded them less attention in practice. The Reagan administration explicitly elevated civil and political rights above economic and social rights, which it described as mere aspirations.[130] The CHRC's emphasis thus simply reflected the dominant trend of its time.[131]

Focused on government persecution of individuals and minorities, the CHRC, in particular, spoke out for victims of religious, ethnic, racial, and political persecution.[132] Initially, its focus was predominantly confined to dissidents and religious and ethnic minorities in a handful of countries, such as the Baha'í in Iran; Jews and Christians in the Soviet Union; and political dissidents in Cuba. According to Schrayer, "The two main issues adopted early on were Soviet Jewry and Baha'í," while Arriaga recalls, "Initially, the focus was on Soviet Jewry, Cuba, and Soviet Pentecostals."[133] The CHRC's computer database reflected this disproportionate focus on Soviet Jewry, in particular.[134] Similarly, the various adoption programs initiated by the CHRC and its spin-offs

---

[129] Moyn, *Not Enough*, 187–198.

[130] Elliott Abrams, off-the-record remarks at the Carnegie Endowment, January 19, 1982, Box II.2.11, Folder 19; AIUSA. See also Søndergaard, "'A Positive Track of Human Rights Policy.'"

[131] Economic, social, and cultural rights since experienced a resurgence within the framework of the United Nations in the post-Cold War era. See, for example, the declaration from the World Conference on Human Rights in Vienna in 1993, the United Nations Millennium Development Goals in 2000 and the United Nations Sustainable Development Goals in 2015.

[132] See, for instance, *CHRC Newsletter*, November 1, 1985, Box 102, Folder 19, TLP.

[133] Author's interview with Elizabeth Schrayer, January 22, 2015. Author's interview with Alexandra Arriaga, June 8, 2018.

[134] *CHRC Newsletter*, April 1986, Box 102, Folder 19, TLP. For more on the CHRC's advocacy for refuseniks, see Søndergaard, "The Congressional Human Rights Caucus and the Plight of the Refuseniks."

targeted people persecuted or incarcerated for their beliefs, color, sex, ethnic origin, language, or religion.

Geographically, the CHRC focused primarily on the Eastern Bloc throughout the 1980s, although it also addressed abuses elsewhere, including by American allies such as Chile, South Korea, the Philippines, and even Great Britain.[135] Yet it largely avoided the thorniest issues, such as US policy toward Central America, although the human rights situation in countries such as Guatemala, El Salvador, and Nicaragua captured the attention of policymakers, NGOs, and millions of Americans.[136] The CHRC only addressed Nicaragua in the summer of 1988 after the Sandinista regime and the US-backed Contras had signed a cease-fire agreement and even then it steered clear of the contested issue of US aid for the Contras and directed its attention to political prisoners kept by the Sandinistas.[137]

South African apartheid represents an illustrative case of the CHRC's cautious approach to potentially controversial issues. The significant divergence between the Reagan administration's policy of "constructive engagement" with the South African government and the growing congressional and public pressure for a tougher approach made it a divisive issue in the mid-1980s. Although several of its members strongly opposed apartheid, the CHRC was initially reluctant to forcefully address human rights violations in South Africa and refrained from taking a position on US policy. Only after Congress voted in favor of economic sanctions against South Africa in 1985, backed by considerable public support, did the CHRC more actively condemn apartheid and support a tougher US policy.[138] Even then, most of CHRC activities on South Africa protested individual cases rather than delivering a more comprehensive critique of apartheid. The CHRC became particularly involved in advocating for clemency to six black South Africans, known as the Sharpeville Six, who had been sentenced to death for the alleged murder of the deputy mayor of the township Sharpeville.[139] When the CHRC addressed

---

[135] The CHRC's activism on Great Britain concerned a group of Irish prisoners known as the Birmingham Six, whose freedom it helped secure, and criticism of Great Britain's policing practices in Northern Ireland. *CHRC Annual Report 1992*, Box 116, Folder 29, TLP.

[136] David Bassano, *Fight and Flight: The Central America Human Rights Movement in the United States in the 1980s* (Newcastle upon Tyne: Cambridge Scholars Publishing, 2016).

[137] CHRC, Invitation to Briefing on Political Prisoners in Nicaragua, July 20, Box 113, Folder 3, TLP. Letter, CHRC to President Ortega, October 28, 1988, Box 109, Folder 16, TLP.

[138] *CHRC Annual Report 1987*, Box 111, Folder 34, TLP.

[139] See, for instance, CHRC Press Release, March 16, 1988, Box 110, Folder 4, TLP.

economic sanctions in 1989, it did so through a debate to discuss the positive and negative consequences of these with the participation of representatives of the South African business sector and human rights monitors.[140] Through such events, the CHRC drew attention to issues without taking positions that risked alienating its members.

In the late 1980s and early 1990s, the CHRC gradually broadened its scope both in terms of countries and types of rights addressed. In 1992 and 1993, members of the CHRC protested human rights violations in 111 countries, covering issues including trafficking, torture, "disappearances," ethnic genocide, violations against women, rights of indigenous peoples, internally displaced persons, anti-Semitism and Nazi war crimes, religious intolerance, human rights monitors, and human rights training of military personnel.[141] The common denominator for these cases continued to be the focus on state oppression of minorities and individuals. Some of these issues were the focus on extensive campaigns with broad caucus backing, while only a few dedicated members championed other, less prominent issues.

One of the issues that received broad bipartisan attention was China's suppression of Tibet and violations against human rights activists and dissidents. In addition to the CHRC being the first American government institution to host the Dalai Lama in 1987, members of the CHRC introduced legislation in 1989 that linked the observance of Tibetan human rights to US policy toward China.[142] The CHRC also strongly condemned the crackdown on pro-democracy protesters in Tiananmen Square in 1989 and hosted survivors at a briefing in Congress.[143] In 1993, the House passed a resolution, introduced by Lantos, opposing Beijing's candidacy to host the 2000 Olympics because of Chinese human rights violations, including repression of Tibet.[144] When the Olympics were awarded to Sydney contemporary observers argued the human rights campaign against Beijing's candidacy had had a significant impact on the outcome.[145]

In the late 1980s and early 1990s, the CHRC also took a sustained interest in the rights of indigenous people and environmental protection

---

[140] *CHRC Annual Report 1989*, Box 116, Folder 29, TLP.
[141] *CHRC Annual Report 1994*, Box 102, Folder 20, TLP.
[142] *CHRC Annual Report 1989*, Box 116, Folder 29, TLP.
[143] *CHRC Newsletter*, December 1989, Box 102, Folder 19, TLP.
[144] *Congressional Record*, 103rd Congress, 1st Session, H5096 (July 26, 1993), Box 100, Folder 10, TLP; Barbara J. Keys, "Harnessing Human Rights to the Olympic Games: Human Rights Watch and the 1993 'Stop Beijing' Campaign," *Journal of Contemporary History* 53, no. 2 (2016): 432.
[145] Alan Riding, "Olympics; 2000 Olympics Go to Sydney in Surprise Setback for China," *The New York Times*, September 24, 1993, A01.

in countries such as Brazil, Ecuador, the Philippines, Kenya, Malaysia, Guyana, and Honduras. It met with indigenous people and environmental activists on multiple occasions and in 1989 it hosted a briefing with representatives of the Coordinating Body of the Indigenous Organizations of the Amazon Basin, who represented over one million people.[146] Addressing the destructive impact of international development projects, the CHRC wrote the Brazilian government in 1988 on behalf of Kaiapo Indians, protesting the building of dams on tribal land that would destroy forests and force them to relocate.[147] Members of the CHRC also protested deforestation and government repression against tribal people in Malaysia, fighting to stop logging on their ancestral lands.[148] In March 1990, Porter delivered the keynote at a conference in the United Kingdom, linking the rights of indigenous people and environmental policy.[149] The CHRC thus demonstrated a sustained concern for the rights of indigenous people and environmental protection. Curiously enough, it rarely framed the issue in terms of economic, social, and cultural rights despite that fact that both indigenous people themselves and the United Nations frequently did so.[150] Although the CHRC gradually narrowed the gap between its practice and its rhetoric of supporting international human rights everywhere, it never embraced economic, social, and cultural rights.

While the scope of issues the CHRC engaged was shaped by its quest for bipartisanship, the personal motivations and interests of Porter and Lantos directed its priorities, as to a lesser extent did those of other active members. The CHRC's early focus on Soviet Jews and Baha'í, for instance, clearly reflected the personal motivations of Porter and Lantos. Lantos's background as a Jewish Hungarian Holocaust survivor reflected itself in a particularly strong commitment to protecting Jews and other religious minorities. It also made him a strong supporter of Israel, as well as a proponent of Hungarian minorities in Eastern Europe.[151] In addition to his encounter with Soviet Jews in 1982, Porter's interactions with politically active minorities in his district shaped his activism. His relations with the Baha'í community in his home district, where he

---

[146] *CHRC Annual Report 1989*, Box 116, Folder 29, TLP.
[147] *CHRC Newsletter*, October 1988, Box 102, Folder 19, TLP.
[148] *CHRC Annual Report 1989*, Box 116, Folder 29, TLP. *CHRC Annual Report 1992*, Box 116, Folder 29, TLP.
[149] *CHRF Activities 1990*, Box 113, Folder 22, TLP.
[150] Patrick Thornberry, *Indigenous Peoples and Human Rights* (Manchester: Manchester University Press, 2002), 182–198.
[151] Lantos, for instance, spoke at a rally of American-Hungarians demonstrating the treatment of Hungarian minorities in Romania. *CHRC Newsletter*, June 1984, Box 102, Folder 19, TLP.

occasionally attended services, made him take a special interest in stopping the persecution of the Baha'í in Iran.[152] Porter recalls that he had been aware of the Baha'í since he was a kid because the religious group was constructing one of its main temples in the neighborhood where he grew up.[153] Porter's district also had a significant Jewish population of about 20 to 25 percent. Porter's human rights activism demonstrates the importance of mobilized interest groups, directing the attention of legislators to particular issues.

Despite substantial disagreements over human rights among liberals and conservatives and the different perceptions of individual members of Congress, there were few outright critics of the CHRC in the 1980s.[154] Its bipartisanship and cautious nature meant it did not generate serious enemies. Moreover, its wide range of activities and determination to find commonalities with anyone meant that almost any member of Congress supported at least some of its efforts. As the CHRC noted in its annual report from 1987, "During 1987, all 435 members of Congress participated in some congressional activities in support of human rights around the globe."[155] The most dominant line of criticism against the CHRC, according to Porter, was that "we did not to focus on internal human rights issues in the United States but solely on external human rights abuses. Some thought we should focus on all of these, including in the United States."[156] Focusing on domestic human rights issues, of course, could have opened up a can of worms with members of Congress, who would take issue with their states or districts being the target of criticism. By providing a smorgasbord of international human rights issues for members to sign on to, while steering clear of the most controversial cases, the CHRC largely avoided making enemies.

The only major crisis of the CHRC was a significant scandal related to the Gulf War in 1990–1991. On October 10, 1989, a fifteen-year-old Kuwaiti girl, identifying herself as "nurse Nayirah," testified before the CHRC in a briefing on Iraqi human rights abuses in Kuwait. In her testimony, she detailed how she had personally witnessed Iraqi soldiers

---

[152] Seth Mydans, "Bahais Seek the Glare of Publicity," *The New York Times*, April 27, 1984, A16.

[153] Author's interview with Rep. John E. Porter, October 17, 2018.

[154] Neither the Tom Lantos papers nor the contemporary news coverage contain any sustained criticism of the CHRC and its agenda during the 1980s. My interviews have backed up this observation.

[155] *CHRC Annual Report 1987*, Box 111, Folder 34, TLP.

[156] Author's interview with Rep. John E. Porter, October 17, 2018.

kill fifteen infants by removing them from their incubators.[157] The allegations received extensive press coverage both in the United States and abroad and President George H. W. Bush referred to the Nayirah testimony on a number of occasions to build support for US military intervention.[158] However, in 1992, it was revealed that the woman was the daughter of the Kuwaiti ambassador to the United States and that her testimony was fictitious and orchestrated by the public relations firm Hill and Knowlton on behalf of the Kuwaiti-sponsored campaign Citizens for a Free Kuwait.[159] Confronted with the false testimony, Lantos, who favored war against Iraq, admitted that he knew the true identity of the witness but argued that he had had no reason to doubt her credibility.[160] Widely reported on by the press, the incident damaged the reputation of the CHRC and led to a *New York Times* editorial criticizing the relationship between caucuses and companion nonprofit foundations that attract funds from private donors. For instance, the CHRF, which had then only recently cut ties with the CHRC, received a donation from Citizens for a Free Kuwait shortly after the Iraqi invasion of Kuwait.[161] Nevertheless, the CHRC recovered and the incident did not affect CHRC membership, which stood at 250 in 1993.[162]

Aside from the blowback from the Nayirah scandal, the CHRC received isolated cases of criticism directed at particular initiatives but never at the broader agenda of the CHRC. A scholar at the Hoover Institution, William Radcliff, wrote Porter to protest the attendance of the 1992 Nobel Laureate and Guatemalan human rights activist Rigoberta Menchú at the CHRC's tenth anniversary event in 1993, calling her a fraud and accusing her of aiding Sandinista repression of Miskitos Indians in Nicaragua.[163] Even the members of Congress most critical

---

[157] Congressional Human Rights Caucus, *Human Rights Violations in Kuwait*, C-SPAN, 1990, accessed August 5, 2019, www.c-span.org/video/?14441-1/human-rights-violations-kuwait. Lantos explained her identity was kept secret her to protect family members in Kuwait.

[158] George Bush, The President's News Conference, October 9, 1990. Online by Gerhard Peters and John T. Woolley, The American Presidency Project, accessed August 7, 2019, www.presidency.ucsb.edu/node/264967.

[159] John R. MacArthur, "Remember Nayirah, Witness for Kuwait?" *The New York Times*, January 6, 1992, A15; Hurst Hannum et al., *International Human Rights: Problems of Law, Policy, and Practice* (New York: Wolters Kluwer, 2018), 581–584.

[160] Clifford Krauss, "Congressman Says Girl Was Credible," *The New York Times*, January 12, 1992, www.nytimes.com/1992/01/12/world/congressman-says-girl-was-credible.html. Porter was unaware of the true identity of Nayirah, so the blowback from the incident only hit Lantos.

[161] Editorial, "Deception on Capitol Hill," *The New York Times*, January 15, 1992, A20.

[162] *CHRC Annual Report 1994*, Box 102, Folder 20, TLP.

[163] Letter, William Radcliff to John E. Porter, April 20, 1993, Box 98, Folder 21, TLP.

of international human rights treaties, such as Jesse Helms (R-NC), were generally supportive of the CHRC. Helms, for instance, found common ground with the CHRC on issues in the Soviet Union and Chinese repression of Tibet.[164]

Only as some conservatives called for the United States to scale down its international engagement and prioritize domestic issues in the mid-1990s did the CHRC experience more substantial opposition to parts of its agenda. When Republicans won control of the House in the 1994 elections, ending forty years of Democratic majority, they enacted an expansive reform agenda under the leadership of the new Speaker of the House Newt Gingrich (R-GA). Outlined in the Contract with America, signed by several Republicans shortly before the elections, the reforms addressed domestic issues such as taxes, welfare, and crime, but they also reflected a growing skepticism with US commitments abroad, exemplified by cuts in funding for United Nations peacekeeping operations. Arriaga recalls, "When Newt Gingrich changed Congress there were some international human rights issues that were not seen as politically advantageous by some members of Congress. Not for all members, but for some."[165]

Of even greater consequence to the CHRC, Republicans also sought to abolish the existing caucus system as part of a reform overhaul of Congress. The abolition of caucuses was presented as a budget-saving measure, but critics also referred to the problematic relationships between some caucuses and external groups and affiliated foundations.[166] With the revelation of the Nayirah scandal a few years earlier, the CHRC was certainly one of the caucuses critics had in mind. Most Democrats, however, opposed the reform, arguing that caucuses served important functions to members of Congress.[167] The CHRC also received strong support from its allies in the human rights community.[168] The outcome became a reformulation of the caucus system. Caucuses,

---

[164] Helms, for example, co-signed a letter with the CHRC to the Chinese government in support of the Dalai Lama in 1987. *CHRC Newsletter*, October 1987, Box 102, Folder 19, TLP. According to Arriaga, "There were no members of Congress that was directly against human rights as such in the 1980s. Jesse Helms was very supportive of human rights, for instance on the issue of Tibet." Author's interview with Alexandra Arriaga, June 8, 2018.

[165] Author's interview with Alexandra Arriaga, June 8, 2018.

[166] Robert Singh, "The Rise and Fall of Legislative Service Organisations in the United States Congress," *The Journal of Legislative Studies* 2, no. 2 (1996): 89.

[167] For the congressional debate over caucus reform, see 141 *Congressional Record*, 104th Congress, 1st Session, 468–483 (January 4, 1995).

[168] See, for instance, this op-ed by the UCSJ. Pamela B. Cohen and Micah H. Naftalin, "Congress Should Save Human Rights Caucus," *The New York Times*, December 6, 1994, A22.

which until then had been known as Legislative Service Organizations, were dismantled and replaced by Congressional Membership Organizations (CMOs), which operated under much stricter regulations and were not allowed separate staff and offices.[169] Contrary to the belief of contemporary observers, however, the reforms did not lead to a decrease in the number of caucuses, which continued to expand as CMOs.[170] The CHRC also continued to flourish under the new rules, maintaining a membership of 150 to 200 members of Congress since 1995.[171]

The continued popularity of the CHRC was manifested in September 2008 when the CHRC became the only caucus ever to be elevated to the status of a permanent commission under the name the Tom Lantos Human Rights Commission (TLHRC) following the death of Lantos. Underscoring the bipartisan support for the CHRC, the House approved with unanimous consent the establishment of the commission.[172] Continuing the agenda of its predecessor, the mission of the TLHR is "to promote, defend and advocate internationally recognized human rights norms as enshrined in the Universal Declaration of Human Rights, and other relevant human rights instruments, in a nonpartisan manner, both within and outside of Congress."[173] For the first ten years of its existence, the TLHRC relied on volunteers and temporary fellows for most of its work but in March 2018, Congress directed funds to the commission for the first time.[174] The CHRC had opened up its membership to senators in 2006, but when the TLHRC was established it once again became limited to representatives.[175] In September 2014, however, Senator Mark Kirk (R-IL), a former chief of staff for Porter, and Senator Chris Coons (D-DE) formed a separate Senate Human Rights Caucus in the spirit of

---

[169] "A CMO is an informal organization of Members who share official resources to jointly carry out activities ... [It has] no separate corporate or legal identity apart from the Members who comprise it ... [It] is not an employing authority, and no staff may be appointed by, or in the name of a CMO. A CMO may not be assigned separate office space." Cited in US Library of Congress, Congressional Research Service, *Congressional Member Organizations: Their Purpose and Activities, History, and Formation*, by Robert Jay Dilger and Jessica C. Gerrity, R40683, (2013), 21.

[170] Hammond, *Congressional Caucuses in National Policy Making*, 209–212.

[171] McCormick and Mitchell, "Commitments, Transnational Interests, and Congress," 580.

[172] "History," Tom Lantos Human Rights Commission, accessed August 5, 2019, https://humanrightscommission.house.gov/about/history.

[173] "Mission," Tom Lantos Human Rights Commission, accessed August 5, 2019, https://humanrightscommission.house.gov/about/mandate.

[174] "House Approves Funding for Lantos Human Rights Panel," Roll Call, accessed August 5, 2019, www.rollcall.com/news/politics/house-approves-funding-lantos-human-rights-panel.

[175] McCormick and Mitchell, "Commitments, Transnational Interests, and Congress," 591.

the CHRC.[176] This continued institution building underlines the lasting contribution of the CHRC to human rights concerns in Congress.

Conclusion

The CHRC and its spin-off initiatives expanded and systematized congressional human rights activism while forging new links between members of Congress and human rights activists and NGOs. Operating outside the formalized committee structure, the CHRC both supported existing human rights institutions on Capitol Hill and supplemented these through less traditional events that put a human face on human rights issues. Its lack of legislative powers led the CHRC to rely heavily on naming and shaming foreign governments in its efforts to aid persecuted individuals. More than any other human rights initiative, the CHRC illustrated how individual members of Congress could set the congressional agenda, operating as foreign policy entrepreneurs. The stories of Porter and Lantos also testify to how personal encounters with victims and the personal background of members of Congress were often crucial drivers for their involvement with human rights.

The large and diverse membership of the CHRC and the ever-expanding scope of its activities demonstrated the broad-based bipartisan support for human rights issues in Congress during the 1980s. Yet the CHRC's cautious tactics, its unwillingness to address controversial issues, and the selective case-by-case support of many of its members also underscored the limitations of the bipartisan consensus. The CHRC could muster considerable bipartisan support for its key issues, such as dissidents and minorities, but it often failed to address more controversial issues. While it directed its criticism against the Soviet Bloc as well as American allies during the Cold War, it was often more cautious in the latter case. The most glaring omission, however, was the failure to seriously address economic, social, and cultural rights – although it reflected a larger trend in Western attention to human rights in this regard. These same limitations, however, were what secured the CHRC's popularity in Congress, where it generated very little criticism and fewer enemies. Offending few and finding commonalities with most, the CHRC grew its membership and survived congressional reforms to eventually gain the status of a permanent commission, making a lasting contribution to congressional human rights activism.

---

[176] "On the Hill: Senate Establishes Human Rights Caucus," accessed August 5, 2019, https://thehumanist.com/voices/on_the_hill/on-the-hill-senate-establishes-human-rights-caucus.

4   The Right to Leave
Soviet Jewish Emigration

On May 13, 1986, a Soviet author received a ten-minute standing ovation from hundreds of excited members of the US Congress. At the same occasion, he received a Congressional Gold Medal and later that day he spent forty minutes talking to Ronald Reagan in the White House (Figure 5).[1] This was Natan Sharansky, a thirty-eight-year-old Soviet human rights activist who had become the symbol of Soviet Jews struggling to leave the Soviet Union after his arrest in 1977. For years, human rights groups, members of Congress, and the Reagan administration had tried to secure his release. When he finally arrived on Capitol Hill as a free man, members of Congress showered him with praise, calling him "a giant of a man," "one of the most courageous men of our time," and "a major symbol for human rights."[2] Representative Robert Dornan (R-CA) recalls how he and Sharansky broke a remembrance bracelet that Dornan had been wearing for eight years in honor of Sharansky. Seeing the bracelet broken into a "V," Dornan proclaimed, "V for victory." But Sharansky responded, "No a V for visa," highlighting the need to keep fighting for the release of the Jews still trapped in the Soviet Union.[3]

Sharansky's sudden release on February 11, 1986, marked a dramatic highpoint for the movement for Soviet Jewry at a time when it had enjoyed limited success. In the preceding years, the plight of Soviet Jews seeking to emigrate from the Soviet Union had risen to become a vital part of East–West relations. Along with other human rights issues, Soviet Jewish emigration had become a major impediment to improvement in US–Soviet relations and, as such, a vital element of Cold War diplomacy alongside issues of arms reduction, regional conflicts, and economic

---

[1] Beckerman, *When They Come for Us*, 505; Ronald Reagan and Douglas Brinkley, *The Reagan Diaries* (New York: Harper Collins, 2007), 411. In his diary, Reagan described the meeting as "fascinating."

[2] 131 *Congressional Record*, 99th Congress, 2nd Session, 10443, 10444, 10556 (May 13, 1986). Representatives Robert Dornan (R-CA), James Courter (R-NJ), and Chester Atkins (D-MA) respectively gave the three statements cited.

[3] 131 *Congressional Record*, 99th Congress, 2nd Session, 10443 (May 13, 1986).

Figure 5 Representatives Christopher Smith, Alfonse D'Amato, Don
Ritter, Steny Hoyer, and John E. Porter present Natan Sharansky with a
Congressional Gold Medal, May 13, 1986.
Terry Ashe/The LIFE Images Collection via Getty Images.

cooperation. The issue attracted extensive attention from human rights
groups, American Jews, and members of Congress in the United States.
Journalist Gal Beckerman has suggested that among American Jews the
cause arguably became even more prominent than relations with Israel.[4]
To human rights advocates inside and outside of government, the issue
represented one of the least divisive human rights cases, uniting people
from across the political spectrum.

Historical research on human rights in US–Soviet relations in the
1980s has revolved around the summits between Reagan and Mikhail
Gorbachev and the multilateral meetings in Belgrade, Madrid, and
Vienna under the Conference on Security and Cooperation in Europe
(CSCE) following the signing of the Helsinki Final Act in 1975.[5] Other

---

[4] Beckerman, *When They Come for Us*, 7–8.
[5] Christian Philip Peterson, "'Confronting' Moscow: The Reagan Administration, Human
Rights, and the Final Act," *Historian* 74, no. 1 (2012); Peterson, *Globalizing Human
Rights*. The summits are also covered in several memoirs: A. L. Adamishin and Richard
Schifter, *Human Rights, Perestroika, and the End of the Cold War* (Washington, DC: United
States Institute of Peace, 2009); Jack F. Matlock, *Reagan and Gorbachev: How the Cold
War Ended* (New York: Random House, 2004); Shultz, *Turmoil and Triumph*. For the

scholars have examined the role of Soviet Jewry in American politics, such as Fred A. Lazin's account of the struggle between Israel and the American Jewish groups over the destination of Soviet Jewish emigration.[6] While Congress played a role in these narratives, none of them focus primarily on congressional advocacy for Soviet Jewry. This chapter does exactly that as it examines how members of Congress framed the issue of Soviet Jewish emigration as a human rights issue in an attempt to elevate its priority in US foreign policy and put pressure on the Soviet Union.

In broad terms, American positions on Soviet Jewry in the 1980s were characterized by consensus. Most liberals and conservatives, Democrats and Republicans, and legislators and administration officials could agree on supporting the right of Soviet Jews to emigrate. Most Americans also agreed that Soviet Jewry and other human rights issues should play a role in American policy toward the Soviet Union, on a superficial level at least.[7] However, beyond this general consensus there was plenty of room for disagreement: How much emphasis should the United States put on human rights and Jewish emigration compared to other issues, such as arms control, trade, and a general improvement of East–West relations? Should the United States pursue collaboration in other fields independently of the status of Jewish emigration or should progress in one field be linked to progress in another? Should the Jackson–Vanik Amendment be upheld, waived, or reformed? Should the United States rely on public criticism or quiet diplomacy to influence the Soviet Union? Should the focus be on securing the release of high-profile refuseniks or increasing general emigration numbers?

To be sure, Soviet Jewish emigration was only one of several human rights issues in US–Soviet relations situated within a larger context of human rights contestation between East and West. The persecution of

CSCE, see Daniel C. Thomas, *The Helsinki Effect: International Norms, Human Rights, and the Demise of Communism* (Princeton, NJ: Princeton University Press, 2001); Sarah B. Snyder, "The Foundation for Vienna: A Reassessment of the CSCE in the Mid-1980s," *Cold War History* 10, no. 4 (2010): 493–512; Sarah B. Snyder, "The CSCE and the Atlantic Alliance: Forging a New Consensus in Madrid," *Journal of Transatlantic Studies* 8, no. 1 (2010): 56–68; Snyder, *Human Rights Activism*.

[6] Fred A. Lazin, *The Struggle for Soviet Jewry in American Politics: Israel Versus the American Jewish Establishment* (Lanham, MD: Lexington, 2005). See also, Beckerman, *When They Come for Us*; Altshuler, *From Exodus to Freedom*.

[7] For public opinion on the importance of emphasizing human rights in US–Soviet relations, see Time/Yankelovich, Skelly & White Poll, March 1983. USYANK.838614. R28A2. Cornell University, Ithaca, NY: Roper Center for Public Opinion Research, iPOLL, accessed August 5, 2019; Gallup/Newsweek Poll, September 1987. USGALNEW.87220.R20H. Cornell University, Ithaca, NY: Roper Center for Public Opinion Research, iPOLL, accessed August 5, 2019.

political dissidents and other religious and ethnic minorities, such as Christian Pentecostals, also became important elements of Cold War diplomacy. Yet, arguably, no other issue received as much attention from American policymakers and the American public as the case of Soviet Jewish emigration. As the former Soviet ambassador to the United States Anatoly Dobrynin recalled in his memoirs, "Probably no other single question did more to sour the atmosphere of détente than the question of Jewish emigration."[8] The issue had become increasingly salient in US foreign policy during the 1970s due to sustained lobbying from the American Jewish community and the passage of the Jackson–Vanik Amendment to the Trade Act of 1974, which denied granting most-favored nation status to communist countries that restricted emigration.[9] For Soviet Jews seeking to emigrate, the immediate effect of Jackson–Vanik was distinctly negative, as the number of Jews allowed to leave fell dramatically in the years after its passage.[10] Amid the CSCE review meeting in Belgrade in 1978–1979 and Soviet concerns to secure agreement on the SALT II treaty, emigration numbers rose again, reaching a record high of 51,320 in 1979. The improvement was short lived, however, as East–West relations worsened dramatically after the Soviet invasion of Afghanistan in December 1979. In the following years, emigration numbers for Soviet Jews hovered around one thousand annually, culminating in an historic low of only 896 in 1984.[11]

The Reagan Administration and Soviet Jewry

Reagan's conservative internationalism of "peace through strength" dominated the administration's policy toward the Soviet Union. A reestablishment of US military superiority through a massive arms buildup would precede negotiations with Moscow. Moreover, rather than simply containing the Soviet Union, the administration would pursue a rollback of communism in the Third World through the Reagan Doctrine. However, the administration would not limit itself to fighting communism abroad; it also aimed to transform the Soviet Union itself. The NSDD75 from January 1983 clearly outlined this ambition, declaring it US policy to counter Soviet expansionism, press for internal

---

[8] Anatoly Dobrynin, *In Confidence: Moscow's Ambassador to America's Six Cold War Presidents (1962–1986)* (New York: Random House, 1995), 334.

[9] Keys, *Reclaiming American Virtue*, 109–113.   [10] Vaïsse, *Neoconservatism*, 114–118.

[11] US Congress, House, Commission on Security and Cooperation in Europe, *Implementation of the Helsinki Accords: Hearing before the Commission on Security and Cooperation in Europe, Glasnost: The Soviet Policy of "Openness,"* 100th Congress, 1st Session, March 4, 1987, 82.

Soviet reform, and engage in negotiations on the principle of strict reciprocity in agreements.[12]

After the Reagan administration had reevaluated its stance on human rights by the summer of 1981, human rights came to occupy a central role in policy toward the Soviet Union. Early on, the administration appeared most interested in using human rights for propaganda purposes. A State Department memo circulated by Haig to senior officials in October 1981 stated that emphasizing human rights issues provided the best opportunity to signal the fundamental difference between the United States and the Soviet Union, and as such was crucial to resisting the Soviets around the world. "Our human rights policy is at the center of our response," the memo continued, "and its audience is not only at home but in Western Europe and Japan, and among electorates elsewhere."[13] The administration thus viewed human rights criticism of the Soviet Union as a way to both please domestic critics and take the moral high ground on the international scene. As the administration developed its policy on human rights and democracy, it became more genuinely interested in promoting domestic reform in the Soviet Union, as expressed in NSDD75. Reagan and his top officials came to believe that a liberalization of the Soviet Union, including greater respect for human rights, was necessary for serious long-term improvements in superpower relations.[14]

Soviet Jewry emerged as the dominant human rights issue in US–Soviet relations, aided in part by Reagan's personal commitment to the issue. Richard Schifter recalls that both Reagan and Secretary of State George P. Shultz insisted that Soviet Jewry was the first issue on the agenda in human rights dialogues with the Soviet Union.[15] Reagan's religiosity and fierce anti-communism made him particularly concerned with religious minorities in the Soviet Union, such as Soviet Jews and Christian Pentecostals.[16] As Gal Beckerman points out, "The individual refusenik struggling against a repressive Communist regime fit perfectly into Reagan's narrative."[17] Reagan's diary shows that the president harbored strong sympathy and admiration for the plight of Soviet Jews,

---

[12] "National Security Decision Directive 75."

[13] US Department of State, *Foreign Relations of the United States, 1981–1988, Volume XII, Global Issues II*, Document 54.

[14] Peterson, "'Confronting' Moscow," 68.

[15] Adamishin and Schifter, *Human Rights, Perestroika*, 58, 138; Altshuler, *From Exodus to Freedom*, 174. Stuart Altshuler observes that Shultz was "the Soviet Jewry movement's leading advocate within the administration."

[16] US Department of State, *Foreign Relations of the United States, 1981–1988, Volume III, Soviet Union, January 1981–January 1983*, x.

[17] Beckerman, *When They Come for Us*, 419.

including refuseniks such as Sharansky. After a meeting with Sharansky's wife, Avital, on May 28, 1981, Reagan wrote in his diary about the Soviets "D—n those inhuman monsters [...] I promised I'd do everything I could to obtain his release & I will."[18] Despite his preference for quiet diplomacy, Reagan was not afraid to declare his public support for Soviet Jewry and met with prominent Soviet Jews. In February 1983, Reagan stated that the "issue of Soviet Jewry is of high priority to the administration."[19] Shultz shared Reagan's sympathy for Soviet dissidents and refuseniks and was deeply convinced that Soviet improvements on such issues were essential for better US–Soviet relations.[20] In addition to being agreeable to Reagan and Shultz's personal views, support for Soviet Jewry was generally good domestic politics, as the cause enjoyed broad support from across the political spectrum.

Despite Reagan's sympathy for Soviet Jews, his sincere interest in promoting Soviet reform, and the good politics of criticizing Soviet human rights abuses, there were limits to the issue's salience on the administration's agenda. There was never any doubt that Reagan's top priorities in dealing with the Soviets were security issues, such as arms control and regional conflicts.[21] Consequently, the administration was reluctant to make human rights improvements such as Jewish emigration a precondition for cooperation in other fields. In April 1981, Reagan lifted Carter's grains embargo, and over the next years he allowed the lifting of some economic sanctions, negotiated on Confidence Building Measures, and signed agreements in a range of areas from environmental protection to space travel without obtaining concrete human rights improvements.[22] While Reagan would have liked to see human rights improvements in the Soviet Union, he was not ready to let the issue delay progress in other areas, and he rejected a firm linkage between arms control and Jewish emigration.[23] According to Jack Matlock, Reagan did not see linkage as a rigid quid pro quo but rather as a principle that improvements in one area could not get too far ahead of improvements in others.[24] In his memoirs, Shultz recalls that he believed linkage had too often become a trap that the Soviets had exploited to press the United

---

[18] Peterson, *Globalizing Human Rights*, 110; Reagan and Brinkley, *The Reagan Diaries*, 21.
[19] Quoted in Lazin, *The Struggle for Soviet Jewry*, 183.
[20] Shultz, *Turmoil and Triumph*, 276–277; US Congress, Senate, Committee on Foreign Relations, *United States-Soviet Relations*, 3–12; George P. Shultz, "Human Rights and the Moral Dimension of U.S. Foreign Policy," February 22, 1984, A1–481B, Department of State Press, Vol. 180, No. 51, Record Group 59, National Archives and Records Administration.
[21] Matlock, *Reagan and Gorbachev*, 153.   [22] Peterson, *Globalizing Human Rights*, 120.
[23] Peterson, "'Confronting' Moscow," 72; Lazin, *The Struggle for Soviet Jewry*, 212.
[24] Matlock, *Reagan and Gorbachev*, 152.

States for economic and strategic concessions in return for improvements on human rights and Soviet Jewish emigration.[25] An undated policy paper on human rights and communist countries prepared in the Human Rights Bureau stated that while linking human rights with bilateral relations had sometimes been successful, "Linkage can only be effective if it is used and timed carefully."[26] The administration was, thus, willing to attempt to link progress on human rights issues such as Jewish emigration with other issues, but ultimately Reagan would not allow linkage to destabilize constructive relations.

Reagan's approach to human rights in US–Soviet relations was thus simultaneously both ideological and pragmatic, encompassing virulent rhetorical attacks on the Soviet Union and a preference for handling specific human rights cases through private diplomacy. Reagan was especially uncompromising in his attacks on the Soviet Union during his first term, famously labeling the Soviet Union the "Evil Empire," until fear of nuclear war toned down his rhetorical aggressiveness in late 1983.[27] Yet, from the beginning, Reagan accompanied such public rhetoric with a decidedly pragmatic approach of quiet diplomacy, where Reagan wrote polite letters to Soviet leaders urging the release of Soviet Jews such as Sharansky, promising to keep his request a secret.[28] In his memoirs, Shultz maintains that Reagan was firmly committed to human rights. Yet, according to Shultz, Reagan understood that "politicians even in your [Gorbachev] circumstances have to worry about how they look and don't want to be pushed around in public [...] I simply want people to be allowed to get out, and if you let them go I won't crow about it."[29] Again, while Reagan wanted to see improvements on human rights, he believed that pushing Gorbachev too hard on the issue could be counterproductive. The administration sincerely believed quiet diplomacy was the most effective approach, which it continuously argued before Congress.

A discussion at the White House on July 18, 1983, following a trip by Ambassador Walter Stoessel to Western Europe to discuss Soviet human rights violations and Jewish emigration illustrates the administration's thinking on tactics.[30] During the debriefing on Western European views,

---

[25] Shultz, *Turmoil and Triumph*, 488.

[26] US Department of State, *Foreign Relations of the United States, 1981–1988, Volume XII, Global Issues II*, Document 58.

[27] Ronald Reagan, Remarks at the Annual Convention of the National Association of Evangelicals in Orlando, Florida, March 8, 1983.

[28] Peterson, *Globalizing Human Rights*, 115–116; Reagan and Brinkley, *The Reagan Diaries*, 15.

[29] Shultz, *Turmoil and Triumph*, 1095.

[30] George P. Shultz had decided to send Stoessel to Western Europe in July 1983 to apprise European leaders of American views on how to handle the worsening human rights

Reagan interjected, "sometimes it is useful to address human rights cases publicly, but in certain circumstances it can be counterproductive." Stoessel responded that the Europeans believed that a mixture of public pressure and private diplomacy could be effective and professed, "publicity has helped in resolving some of the family reunification cases." Reagan responded, "The Nixon Administration's endorsement of quiet diplomacy on human rights issues seemed to contribute to increased Soviet Jewish emigration." Elliott Abrams, who had accompanied Stoessel on the mission, argued, "Usually it is best for the relevant private groups and organizations to persevere and keep public pressure on the Soviets and for the government to deal with these issues privately."[31] The exchange illustrates Reagan's preference for Nixon-style quiet diplomacy (not without irony, given Reagan's fierce criticism of Nixon's détente policy). However, at the same time, it demonstrates that the administration was aware of the benefits of some public pressure from outside the executive branch. NGOs and members of Congress addressing human rights issues in the Soviet Union provided exactly such pressure, while allowing the administration the opportunity to prioritize quiet diplomacy.

With no bilateral meetings between the two superpowers at the highest level between 1979 and 1985, international forums such as the CSCE and the United Nations became the most important venues for US–Soviet negotiations on human rights and other issues. On the campaign trail in 1980, Reagan had been a fierce critic of US participation in the CSCE and he entered office highly skeptical of its value. The administration's initial intention to downplay human rights in its foreign policy and its insistence on building up the American military before engaging in negotiations with the Soviet Union initially resulted in a low priority for the CSCE process. However, as the administration revised its human rights policy and realized the benefits of engaging the Soviet Union on human rights, it came to value the CSCE as an important part of its strategy of seeking human rights concessions along with

---

situation in the Soviet Union, including the stagnation of Jewish emigration, and to seek fuller European involvement on the issue. Memo, Charles Hill to William P. Clark May 27, 1983, ID#146421, HU, WHORM: Subject File, RPL.

[31] "Memorandum of the President's Meeting with Ambassador Stoessel: Report on Presidential Mission to Europe on Soviet Human Rights Performance," July 18, 1983, 017R, Box 10; European and Soviet Affairs Directorate, NSC, RPL. See also Richard Schifter before the US Helsinki Commission in June 1985. US Congress, House, Commission on Security and Cooperation in Europe, *Implementation of the Helsinki Accords: Hearing before the Commission on Security and Cooperation in Europe, the Ottawa Human Rights Experts Meeting and the Future of the Helsinki Process*, 99th Congress, 1st Session, June 25, 1985, 36, 152.

strengthening national security interests.[32] In fact, it largely continued the Carter administration's commitment to the process, illustrated by Reagan's decision to retain the Carter-appointed Max Kampelman as the head of the US delegation at the CSCE meeting in Madrid. Kampelman's ideological affinity with neoconservatives such as Jeane Kirkpatrick may also have played a role.[33]

By the time Reagan and Gorbachev began their summits in 1985, human rights were an established part of the Reagan administration's four-part agenda for negotiations, along with arms control, regional conflicts, and bilateral relationships in trade and cultural exchanges.[34] This agenda would remain the guiding framework for the administration's negotiations with the Soviet Union throughout Reagan's tenure. As historian Christian Peterson has demonstrated, Reagan gradually became more willing to support Soviet dissidents in public from the fall of 1986. According to Peterson, this change reflected Reagan's decreased concern with potential negative effects of such criticism as well as a reaction to growing congressional pressure to deliver progress on Soviet Jewry.[35]

Members of Congress and Soviet Jewish Emigration in the Early 1980s

Members of Congress played prominent roles in American policy on Soviet Jewry, taking advantage of the position Congress had carved out for itself in the 1970s through institutions such as the US Helsinki Commission and legislation such as the Jackson–Vanik Amendment. Together with concerned NGOs, members of Congress lobbied the Reagan administration to put greater emphasis on Jewish emigration in multilateral negotiations with the Soviets, such as the CSCE and later on in bilateral summit meetings. In addition, they engaged the Soviet Union directly, criticizing discrimination of Jews, pushing for the release of individual refuseniks, and urging emigration reform. Congressional efforts on behalf of Soviet Jewry often received the support of the vast majority of Congress, and some resolutions even passed unanimously, reflecting the issue's broad appeal across ideological and partisan lines.

Most congressional efforts on Soviet Jewry germinated in the US Helsinki Commission and the House Foreign Affairs Committee's

---

[32] Peterson has labeled this policy "dynamic detente." Peterson, "'Confronting' Moscow," 69.

[33] Snyder, *Human Rights Activism*, 135–138. Kampelman would since go on to become Reagan's chief negotiator on arms talks with the Soviets.

[34] Peterson, "'Confronting' Moscow," 59, 69.

[35] Peterson, *Globalizing Human Rights*, 144–147.

subcommittees on Europe and Human Rights. As chair of the US Helsinki Commission from 1976 to 1984 and chair of the House Foreign Affairs Committee from 1983 to 1993, Dante Fascell (D-FL) was a leading foreign policy entrepreneur on Soviet Jewry. A long-term human rights advocate, Fascell was also strongly committed to forging a bipartisan foreign policy.[36] While this desire for bipartisanship sometimes led him to break ranks with his more liberal party colleagues and side with the Reagan administration on Latin America, for instance, on the issue of Soviet Jewry he helped unite liberals and conservatives. Reflecting on his human rights advocacy years later, Fascell recalled taking particular pride in helping refuseniks, because he was convinced American support for human rights issues in the Eastern Bloc helped to disintegrate the Soviet Union.[37] Members of Congress also formed new groups in the 1980s that dealt specifically with Soviet Jewry, including the bipartisan Congressional Human Rights Caucus (CHRC) established by Representatives John E. Porter (R-IL) and Tom Lantos (D-CA) in 1983. Some of these groups were started through the initiative of American Jewish NGOs, such as the Congressional Coalition for Soviet Jews created by the National Conference on Soviet Jewry (NCSJ), to coordinate congressional advocacy more effectively.[38]

The bipartisan support for Soviet Jewish emigration in Congress was also evident in the broad ideological range of other members of Congress that took leadership positions on the issue. Conservative Republicans such as senators Robert Dole (R-KS) and Alfonse D'Amato (R-NY), who both served as cochairs of the US Helsinki Commission, played active roles in the struggle for Soviet Jewry. To such conservative Republicans, the issue of Soviet Jewry was closely connected to a desire to confront the Soviet Union. In a report to Speaker "Tip" O'Neill (D-MA) following a trip to the Soviet Union in 1983, conservative Republican Jack Kemp (R-NY), for instance, argued that the individual stories of the refuseniks were a testament to the terror and oppression of the Soviet state.[39] To anti-communist conservatives, fighting communism

---

[36] Richard Pearson, "Florida Congressman Dante B. Fascell Dies," *The Washington Post*, November 30, 1998, B6.

[37] Eric Pace, "Rep. Dante B. Fascell, 81; Headed Foreign Affairs Panel," *The New York Times*, November 30, 1998, www.nytimes.com/1998/11/30/us/rep-dante-b-fascell-81-headed-foreign-affairs-panel.html.

[38] "Dear Colleague" Letter, November 30, 1984, Series IV, Box POL-009, Folder 10 Caucuses – CCSJ, Peter W. Rodino, Jr. Archives, Rodino Law Library, Seton Hall University School of Law (hereafter PRP). Groups such as the Congressional Coalition for Soviet Jews were bipartisan and generally enjoyed large and broad membership in Congress.

[39] Jack Kemp, Report: "The Soviet Question," July 14, 1983, Box 130, Folder 5, JKP.

was synonymous with promoting human rights, and this perception, in addition to personal sympathies, motivated their support for Soviet Jewish emigration.

Although liberal Democrats felt differently about the relationship between anti-communism and human rights in other parts of the world, they were equally critical of the Soviet Union and supportive of Soviet Jewish emigration. One of the foremost American Jewish organizations concerned with Soviet Jewish emigration, the Union of Councils for Soviet Jews (UCSJ) described the liberal Democrat Senator Claiborne Pell (D-RI) as "the single most important member of the Senate for our issue."[40] Perhaps not surprisingly, Jewish members of Congress, most of whom were liberal Democrats, were also very active on the issue. Aside from Lantos, these included Representatives Stephen Solarz (D-NY), Henry Waxman (D-CA) and Barbara Boxer (D-CA), who the UCSJ in 1987 called "our strongest congressional advocate."[41] Solarz first visited refuseniks in the Soviet Union in 1980 and in his memoirs he recalls, "I strongly identified with their cause."[42] The issue also received active support from more-moderate figures in foreign policy leadership positions, such as chair of the Senate Foreign Relations Committee from 1981 to 1985 Charles H. Percy (R-IL), chair of the House Foreign Affairs Committee 1985 to 1994 Steny Hoyer (D-MD), and cochair of the US Helsinki Commission 1986 to 1994 Senator Dennis DeConcini (D-AZ). The issue of Soviet Jewry thus united a broad spectrum of members of Congress, including some who often found themselves fiercely opposing each other on US human rights policy elsewhere.

The broad consensus among American policymakers that Jewish emigration was a human rights issue meant that there was no real debate about whether the issue was a legitimate human rights concern. This is not to say that there were no competing interests and priorities, such as security concerns, but advocates for Soviet Jewish emigration did not have to justify using the human rights framework. The extent to which policymakers used the terms "Jewish emigration" and "human rights" interchangeably illustrates this point. When Reagan and others referred to human rights in the Soviet Union, it was well understood that this included Jewish emigration.[43] The administration and human rights advocates in Congress shared the perception that the denial of Jewish

---

[40] Letter, Pam to Micah, June 12, 1987, I-410, I-410A; 66; 8, UCSJR.
[41] Report on California Congressional Activity, July 1987, I-410, I-410A; 66; 8, UCSJR.
[42] Solarz, *Journeys to War & Peace*, 63.
[43] See, for instance, Bernard Weinraub, "President Links Rights in Soviet to Summit Success," *The New York Times*, October 8, 1986, A6.

emigration was a human rights violation. The plight of a religious minority oppressed by the Cold War enemy represented a clear moral case for conservatives and liberals alike. Therefore, the case of Soviet Jewry did not lead to significant clashes over what US human rights policy ought to achieve. Rather, disagreements centered on the best strategy to obtain the desired goals, leading to a relatively cooperative relationship among the administration and members of Congress.

As evident from Chapter 3, human rights NGOs played an important role in congressional human rights activism in the 1980s. On the issue of Soviet Jewry, American Jewish groups such as the UCSJ and the NCSJ were particularly influential. Both organizations functioned as umbrella organizations for a host of national and local Jewish groups across the United States seeking to coordinate efforts on behalf of Soviet Jews. The UCSJ covered most of the United States, with local councils in most major cities.[44] At its peak, the NCSJ included about fifty national organizations, including B'nai B'rith, the American Jewish Committee, and the Student Struggle for Soviet Jewry.[45] The UCSJ and the NCSJ and similar American Jewish NGOs lobbied intensively among policymakers and the public for the cause of Soviet Jews. The extent to which these groups focused their energy on Congress is evident from their meticulous monitoring of performance of members of Congress performance on Soviet Jewry and their elaborate guides for how to lobby Congress. The NCSJ guide "Working with the Congress" from December 1984, for instance, listed five key areas in which members of Congress played an important role on Soviet Jewry: lobbying the administration, holding hearings and passing resolutions, intervening with the Soviet officials, visiting Soviet Jews, and addressing local communities in the United States.[46] An internal UCSJ memo from June 1987 kept a detailed list of which members of Congress "received Jewish money," how they had been active on Soviet Jewry, and who needed to be pressured to do more.[47] The American Jewish NGOs thus viewed members of Congress as important allies, but members of Congress also found the NGOs helpful. In addition to their influence on constituents, the NGOs' main asset to members of Congress and the Reagan administration was the

---

[44] American Jewish Historical Society, *Guide to the Records of Union of Councils for Soviet Jews*, Undated, 1948, 1954, 1963-1965, 1967–2000, accessed August 5, 2019, http://findingaids.cjh.org/?pID=161195.

[45] American Jewish Historical Society, *Guide to the Records of National Conference on Soviet Jewry*, Undated, 1949, 1954, 1956, 1958-1993, accessed August 5, 2019, http://digifindingaids.cjh.org/?pID=338009.

[46] NCSJ Working with the Congress, December 1984; I-181A; 293, 4; NCSJR.

[47] For the UCSJ, see Altshuler, *From Exodus to Freedom*, 52–53, 67.

information they possessed because of their contact with the Soviet Jewry movement behind the Iron Curtain.

Other NGOs with a broader human rights focus also contributed to the struggle for Soviet Jewry, but they were far less significant to the cause than were the Jewish NGOs. As the civil society counterpart to the US Helsinki Commission, Helsinki Watch played a particularly prominent role on human rights issues within the CSCE process.[48] However, according to its executive director at the time, Helsinki Watch focused mainly on dissidents who were persecuted for reasons other than because they were Jewish or wanted to migrate to Israel, since this group of dissidents already attracted a lot of support.[49] The bipartisan watchdog organization Freedom House also monitored compliance with the Helsinki Accords, but its archives reveal little involvement with Soviet Jewish emigration.[50]

Members of Congress, NGOs, and the Reagan administration all wished to see a rise in Soviet Jewish emigration and improvements to the human rights situation in the Soviet Union, and generally cooperated toward achieving these goals. Yet differences existed over the relative weight the United States should put on Soviet Jewish emigration and other human rights issues in East–West relations as well as the best strategic approach to obtaining Soviet concessions. As commander-in-chief, Reagan often prioritized national security interests at the expense of Jewish emigration. NGOs and their allies in Congress generally preferred a stronger emphasis on human rights issues and actively sought to push the administration in that direction. Disagreements over strategy centered on two main issues. First, the question of whether progress on Jewish emigration should be linked to progress on other issues, such as arms reductions and trade. Second, the question of reliance on quiet diplomacy behind closed doors versus public diplomacy through naming and shaming of the Soviet Union for its failure to comply with international human rights.

Some members of Congress believed the United States should pursue a strict linkage between progress on Soviet Jewish emigration and improved US–Soviet relations. Proponents of this strategy argued that progress on Soviet Jewish emigration should be a prerequisite for progress on other issues, such as arms control and trade. Such a linkage was the very essence of the Jackson–Vanik Amendment, which denied

---

[48] Author's interview with Jeri Laber, November 6, 2015. "Our staff worked closely with the Helsinki Commission staff, sharing information freely."
[49] Author's interview with Aryeh Neier, October 15, 2015.
[50] Bon Tempo, "From the Center-Right," 229–231.

most-favored nation status to communist countries that restricted emigration. Linkage was also a fundamental principle of the Helsinki Accords, which linked progress on security, trade, and human rights. Members of Congress differed on the degree to which they believed linkage should be implicit or explicit and how rigidly it should be pursued. Overall, however, congressional support for linkage in the early 1980s was limited.[51] Yet once members of Congress began to sense a better opportunity to influence Soviet behavior, support for linkage increased. Some members of Congress, such as Kemp and Moynihan (D-NY), took a different approach, urging Reagan in 1985, "to call upon the Soviet Union to enter into discussions dealing solely with the free emigration of the large number of Jews who seek to leave the Soviet Union" detached from any other issues.[52]

In some ways, the strategy of linkage pursued by human rights advocates in the 1980s resembled the Nixon administration's attempt to link nuclear and economic cooperation with the Soviet Union and China with collaboration on restraining revolutions in the developing world.[53] The difference, of course, was that, unlike Nixon, human rights advocates in the 1980s sought to link Soviet domestic issues to international diplomacy. A related issue was how many Jews the Soviet Union should allow to emigrate to obtain improved relations with the United States. In other words, what was the exchange rate between Soviet Jews and arms reductions and trade deals? Some members of Congress argued for specific numbers like a restoration of the 1979 level of fifty thousand émigrés a year, while others believed that free emigration should be the criterion.[54]

The question of whether to rely on quiet or public diplomacy was the other main issue of contention between human rights advocates in Congress and the administration. Congressional human rights advocates from both parties and NGOs criticized Reagan's reliance on quiet diplomacy as being too limited and demanded that the administration speak publicly about the plight of Soviet Jews and other Soviet human

[51] US Congress, Committee on Foreign Affairs, *Congress and Foreign Policy–1983*, Committee Print (Washington, DC: US Government Printing Office, 1984), 78.

[52] Letter, Jack Kemp and Daniel P. Moynihan to Reagan, March 8, 1985, Box 131, Folder 6, JKP.

[53] US Department of State, *Foreign Relations of the United States, 1969–1976, Volume I, Foundations of Foreign Policy, 1969–1972* (Washington, DC: US Government Printing Office, 2003), Document 10, Document 118.

[54] The call for free emigration grew over the 1980s as the number of Jews allowed to leave increased. See, for instance, US Commission on Security and Cooperation in Europe, "Chairman Deconcini Opposes Waiver of Jackson–Vanik," *CSCE Digest* (August 1989): 1. Yet others made the case for extending emigration requests beyond Jews to include other ethnic and religious minorities seeking emigration.

rights violations.[55] Favoring a tactic of naming and shaming human rights violators, the bipartisan CHRC was among the congressional voices that most clearly called for the administration to raise its public criticism of the Soviet Union.[56] From their position on the sidelines of Cold War diplomacy, members of Congress had more freedom to take a principled stand on Soviet Jewry than did officials in the executive branch, who had to balance the issue against national security concerns. Outspoken members of Congress used their position in the legislative branch as a pulpit to pressure the administration to give greater priority to the cause of Soviet Jewry. While such congressional pressure challenged the administration to publicly condemn the Soviets for denying Jews the right to emigrate, it also supplemented the administration's quiet diplomacy by offering the public diplomacy it would rather not do itself. Over time, however, the administration became more outspoken in its support for Soviet Jewry.[57]

The CSCE process offered members of Congress a unique opportunity to advance the cause of Soviet Jewish emigration. Through the US Helsinki Commission, members of Congress had played an influential role in the Carter administration's CSCE policy, both at the first CSCE follow-up meeting in Belgrade from 1977 to 1978 and the second that began in Madrid in 1980. This practice continued under Reagan, once the administration adopted a constructive approach to the CSCE. During the negotiations in Madrid, Max Kampelman consulted closely with members of Congress on the US Helsinki Commission as well as with NGOs, which, unlike at the meeting in Belgrade, had been allowed to attend.[58] As pointed out by Sarah B. Snyder, the US Helsinki Commission held a unique position at the CSCE review meetings, operating as an intermediary between State Department officials and unofficial groups.[59] From this position, the members of Congress on the US Helsinki Commission took a firm stance on human rights issues, criticizing the State Department for not doing enough to secure a strong role for human rights in US policy at Madrid. "The Commission believes strongly that human *rights* should be a prominent concern," a US Helsinki Commission memo

---

[55] See, for instance, comments by Senators Mel Levine (D-CA) and Henry Heinz (R-PA) in discussions with Elliott Abrams. US Congress, House, Commission on Security and Cooperation in Europe, *Soviet Jewry Hearing and Markup*, 10–11, 19–20; Peterson, "'Confronting' Moscow," 65.

[56] Søndergaard, "The Congressional Human Rights Caucus and the Plight of the Refuseniks," 234.

[57] Peterson, "'Confronting' Moscow," 74–76, Peterson, *Globalizing Human Rights*, 144–147.

[58] Snyder, *Human Rights Activism*, 116–118.   [59] Ibid., 51.

from 1980 read. "The tactic of naming specific names and countries when discussing human rights violations was an agreed allied tactic at Belgrade, and should continue to be so at Madrid."[60]

Negotiations at Madrid, however, were complicated by increasing East–West tensions following the Soviet invasion of Afghanistan in December 1979 and Reagan's rhetorical attack on the Soviet Union.[61] After almost three years of discussions, the meeting ended in September 1983 without any significant results on human rights or other issues. Nevertheless, the meeting did provide the United States with a forum to criticize Soviet noncompliance with the Helsinki Final Act, including denying Jews the right to emigrate. In addition to members of the US Helsinki Commission, other prominent members of Congress, such as Dole, also attended and spoke of the importance that Congress placed on human rights in East–West relations.[62] Such congressional advocacy occurred alongside a strong presence of human rights NGOs. Helsinki Watch even established a small office in Madrid from which it reviewed the implementation of Helsinki Accords from 1980 to 1983.[63] A US Helsinki Commission report from November 1983 noted that "the Madrid Meeting produced a more thorough and candid review of implementation than was achieved at Belgrade," and that the Soviets reacted to human rights criticism in a "more relaxed and resigned manner."[64]

Ultimately, the US Helsinki Commission was quite successful in pressing its views on the executive branch.[65] Internal documents from the Reagan administration, such as a 1981 memo from Haig to Reagan, demonstrate that the administration sought to secure the release of Soviet Jews in part to satisfy congressional concerns.[66] A 1985 report by the United States General Accounting Office found that commissioners and staffers from the US Helsinki Commission had played a leading

---

[60] CSCE Madrid Review Meeting memo, January 18, 1980, 96th Congress, Records of the Commission on Security and Cooperation in Europe, Record Group 519; Box 3, Center for Legislative Archives, National Archives, Washington, DC.

[61] Moreover, the meeting ended just days after the Soviet Union shot down the Korean commercial airliner KAL007, killing all 269 passengers, including sixty-one Americans, one of whom was a member of Congress.

[62] Travel Report: Congressional Delegation to Europe and the USSR, November 14–26, 1982, 97th Congress, Records of the Commission on Security and Cooperation in Europe, Record Group 519; Box 14, Center for Legislative Archives, National Archives, Washington, DC.

[63] Author's interview with Aryeh Neier, October 15, 2015.

[64] Report by the Commission on Security and Cooperation in Europe, *The Madrid CSCE Review Meeting*, November 1983, Box 128, Folder 1, JKP.

[65] Peterson, *Globalizing Human Rights*, 123.

[66] US Department of State, *Foreign Relations of the United States, 1981–1988, Volume XII, Global Issues II*, Document 55.

role in the preparation and conduct of American participation in the CSCE process. Through such efforts, the report concluded, the US Helsinki Commission had managed to make human rights the center-piece of US policy at the CSCE. Furthermore, interviews conducted for the report revealed that officials in the executive and legislative branches and NGO leaders all held the US Helsinki Commission in high regard.[67]

Members of Congress also conducted oversight of the compliance with the Helsinki Accords during and in between meetings. The US Helsinki Commission functioned as the natural focus for this activity, with rele-vant subcommittees and caucuses also contributing to the effort. In the spring of 1980, the US Helsinki Commission held three hearings dedi-cated to reviewing Soviet and Eastern European compliance with the Helsinki Accords in preparation for the CSCE Madrid follow-up meet-ing. Testimonies by William Korey from the American Jewish NGO B'nai B'rith and the former refusenik Lev Ulanovsky painted a bleak picture of the treatment of Soviet Jewry.[68] Ulanovsky reported how Soviet Jews who applied for permission to emigrate risked being the victims of all possible forms of harassment from the Soviet authorities, ranging from losing their jobs to arrests and beatings.[69] Through such testimonies in open hearings before Congress, the US Helsinki Commis-sion helped give voice to victims of Soviet human rights abuses and put the issue on the national agenda. This congressional oversight continued throughout the 1980s as legislators used the CSCE follow-up meetings to draw attention to Soviet human rights violations and to issue calls for a stronger American stance on the issue.

In June 1983, a few months before the conclusion of the Madrid follow-up meeting, the US Helsinki Commission along with the House Foreign Affairs Subcommittee on Human Rights held another hearing devoted to Soviet Jewry. The hearing examined the low Jewish emigra-tion numbers and the rise of anti-Semitism in the Soviet Union through testimonies from the president of the UCSJ Lynn Singer, former chair-man of the NCSJ Theodore Mann, the refusenik Igor Tufeld, and the Reagan administration. Testifying on behalf of the administration, Abrams assured Congress that the administration raised the issue of Jewish emigration with the Soviets at "every appropriate opportunity,"

---

[67] The report's findings were generally supported by scholarly literature: Margaret E. Galey, "Congress, Foreign Policy and Human Rights Ten Years after Helsinki," *Human Rights Quarterly* 7, no. 3 (1985): 355–372.

[68] US Congress, House, Commission on Security and Cooperation in Europe, *Hearing before the Commission on Security and Cooperation in Europe on Basket III: Implementation of the Helsinki Accords*, 96th Congress, 2nd Session, April 29, 1980, 2–15.

[69] Ibid., 4.

both at the CSCE and in bilateral talks.[70] The debate that followed the Abrams's testimony, however, indicated that the majority of representatives present remained unconvinced about the administration's policy on Jewish emigration. Noting the deteriorating conditions for Jews in the Soviet Union, Fascell asked whether the administration was considering any new initiatives in its relations with the Soviet Union. Abrams responded that the administration's basic position was to make sure that Soviet repression of Soviet Jewry hurt the Soviet Union's trade interest and its international image. Lantos questioned Abrams's statement because Reagan had lifted Carter's grains embargo against the Soviet Union without securing concessions on human rights. According to Lantos, this action illustrated a failure to make human rights violations costly to the Soviet Union. Abrams pushed back by arguing that the grains embargo did not give the United States any leverage over the Soviet Union.[71]

Members of Congress were clearly concerned about the administration's apparent willingness to collaborate with the Soviet Union without securing improvements on human rights issues, such as Jewish emigration. Seeking to accommodate such sentiments, Abrams maintained that the administration would "negotiate with the Soviets about their human rights behavior when they seek various things from us in economic and political terms. That is we do not have a separate human rights agenda."[72] Despite Abrams's explanation, most representatives remained unconvinced about the administration's commitment to pursue linkage of Jewish emigration and other issues. Representative Christopher Smith (R-NJ) suggested that the linkage between human rights and trade should be expanded to include other human rights in addition to Jewish emigration.[73] Other representatives, such as Edward Markey (D-MA) and Mel Levine (D-CA) questioned Reagan's hostile rhetoric toward the Soviet Union, suggesting it only made things worse for Jews seeking to emigrate. Abrams dismissed such concerns, arguing that while the drop in Jewish emigration was connected to the worsened East–West relations, this worsening of relations was a result of the Soviet invasion of Afghanistan and crackdown in Poland rather than American policies.[74]

The passage of resolutions offered members of Congress another avenue to voice their dissatisfaction with the Soviet Union's human rights record. During the 1980s, Congress passed an ever-increasing number of resolutions, calling on both American and Soviet authorities to allow free Jewish

---

[70] US Congress, House, Commission on Security and Cooperation in Europe, *Soviet Jewry Hearing and Markup*, 10.
[71] Ibid., 15.   [72] Ibid., 17.   [73] Ibid., 21.   [74] Ibid, 22–25.

emigration and respect basic human rights.[75] Some of these were general resolutions like H.J.Res.373, which declared it the sense of Congress that the Soviet Union should respect the rights of its citizens to practice their religion and to emigrate, and that these matters should be among the issues raised at the thirty-eighth meeting of the United Nations Commission on Human Rights at Geneva in February 1982.[76] Others called on the Soviet Union to allow specific Soviet Jews to emigrate.[77] Sponsored by liberals and conservatives alike, the resolutions generally passed with resounding bipartisan majorities. Reagan signed several of them and thereby reaffirmed the joint position of Congress and the executive branch.[78]

Naming certain days in support of human rights and dissidents in the Soviet Union represented another way that members of Congress sought to increase the salience of human rights issues. In 1983, Congress designated May 21, 1983, as "Andrei Sakharov Day" after the famed human rights activist, who at the time was placed in internal exile on the Soviet Union and declared August 1, 1983, as "Helsinki Human Rights Day."[79] Yet another way was to pass resolutions declaring support for the so-called Solidarity Sundays held annually in New York City since 1972 by American Jews and their allies.[80] Although both the Reagan administration and refuseniks argued that the Soviets paid attention to such resolutions, it is difficult to provide evidence of their impact overseas.[81] Nonetheless, they helped increase American attention to Soviet human rights violations and provided succor for Soviet dissidents.

Writing letters to the Reagan administration and the Soviet authorities constituted another frequent avenue for congressional human rights activism. Letters to the administration were generally complimentary of its policy, while encouraging a stronger emphasis on human rights and Soviet Jewish emigration.[82] Letters to the Soviet Union listed a range of concerns

---

[75] For a summary of congressional resolutions on Soviet Jewry, see Galey, "Congress, Foreign Policy and Human Rights Ten Years after Helsinki," 352–355.

[76] H.J.Res.373 – 97th Congress (1981–1982) (became law on March 22, 1982).

[77] See, for instance, H.J.Res.230 – 97th Congress (1981–1982).

[78] Peterson, *Globalizing Human Rights*, 117.

[79] S.J.Res.51 – 98th Congress (1983-1984). S.J.Res.96 – 98th Congress (1983–1984).

[80] H.Res.450 – 98th Congress (1983-1984). S.Res.367 – 98th Congress (1983–1984). By the 1980s, these Solidarity Sundays drew attendances of more than 100,000.

[81] US Congress, House, Commission on Security and Cooperation in Europe, *Soviet Jewry Hearing and Markup*, 28.

[82] See, for instance, Letter, Stephen Solarz to George P. Shultz, September 24, 1982, Box 1058, Stephen Solarz Papers, Robert D. Farber University Archives and Special Collections, Brandeis University (unprocessed collection); Letter, Members of Congress to Ronald Reagan, April 13, 1984, Box 131, Folder 6, JKP. Members of Congress urged, "The issues of immigration and human rights should remain high on the agenda in all relevant forums."

about discrimination of Soviet Jews, but overwhelmingly focused on the low emigration numbers. Often, members of Congress received letters from NGOs, which they would then forward to the Soviet Union.[83] Members of Congress thus functioned as mouthpieces for concerned NGOs, lending their voice to the movement for Soviet Jewry. After its establishment in 1983, the CHRC became particularly active in advocacy on behalf of individual Soviet Jews, launching letter writing campaigns and introducing programs in which Americans would adopt refuseniks, with whom they kept in regular contact.[84] The Soviets rarely replied to such advocacy, but in June 1983, the Soviet Anti-Zionist Committee responded to the CHRC's advocacy by accusing it of a "Zionist psychological war against the Soviet Union."[85] Presumably not the response the CHRC hoped for, but it goes to show that the Soviets were not completely oblivious to the congressional human rights advocacy.

Members of Congress also took part in delegations to the Soviet Union. Some of these delegations were official parliamentary exchanges between members of Congress and members of the Soviet parliament, while others were smaller, informal delegations often organized in cooperation with American Jewish NGOs. The NSCJ, for instance, provided senators William Cohen (R-ME) and Joseph Biden (D-DE) with lists of refuseniks and a general briefing ahead of their visit to Moscow to discuss arms control in February 1983. Upon his return, Cohen delivered an account of his trip to the NSCJ, including on his meetings with refuseniks.[86] Official parliamentary exchanges had begun in 1975, and in July 1983 House Majority Whip Thomas Foley (D-WA) led the third US delegation to the Soviet Union on a trip that also included a stop at the CSCE Madrid Meeting.[87] At this parliamentary exchange, as with previous ones, members of Congress appealed directly to their Soviet counterparts to release refuseniks and prisoners of conscience.[88] Just like when the United States raised human rights concerns at Madrid, however, the Soviets refused to address the issue. According

---

[83] See, for instance, Senator Pell's letter to the Soviet Union on behalf of the NCSJ. Claiborne Pell to Mr. E Avrusin, September 13, 1982, Box 3, Folder 94, The Senatorial Papers of Claiborne Pell: Congresses, Mss. Gr. 71.3, University of Rhode Island Library, Special Collections and University Archives.

[84] *CHRC Summary of Activities 1985*, Box 111, Folder 34, TLP.

[85] "Response to US Congressmen on Jewish Emigration," June 28, 1983, Box 111, Folder 33, TLP.

[86] NCSJ Legislative Update 1984; I-181A; 293, 2, NCSJR.

[87] Thomas Foley to Jack Kemp, June 28, 1983, Box 130, Folder 4, JKP.

[88] Representative Jack Kemp, for example, presented Soviet authorities with a list of refuseniks urging a reconsideration of their cases. "Notes of official meeting in Moscow," Undated, Box 130, Folder 5, JKP.

to a report on the trip, several members of the Soviet parliament demonstratively removed their headphones when Representative Henry Waxman criticized Soviet human rights violations.[89]

Congressional advocacy for Soviet Jewry and human rights in the Soviet Union in general resonated with the American public, who supported pressuring the Soviets on human rights. A March 1983 opinion poll indicated that Americans were strongly in favor of making human rights issues a topic for discussion in the relationship with the Soviet Union. In the poll, 54 percent of Americans answered that they believed the United States should place "a great deal of emphasis" or "some emphasis" on "stepped-up crackdown on human rights and dissenters in the Soviet Union." By contrast, only 18 percent believed "not much emphasis" should be put on the issue.[90] In a different opinion poll in November 1987, public support for including human rights in US policy toward the Soviet Union was even higher. Asked about the importance of "Getting the Soviets to improve human rights in their own country," 48 percent answered "very important," 32 percent "somewhat important," and only 20 percent "not too important."[91] Although the polls are not directly comparable, they do indicate growing public support for raising human rights issues with the Soviets. This increase in support might be the result of several factors, such as increased awareness of human rights issues, diminished fear of nuclear war, perceptions that the Soviets had become more susceptible to American concerns, and so forth.

The multitude of efforts undertaken by Congress kept the pressure on the Reagan administration as well as the Soviet Union. Although congressional criticism did not have a detectable impact on the Soviet Union in the first half of the 1980s, as emigration figures remained low and discrimination against Soviet Jews continued, it did help to keep the issue on the agenda of US–Soviet diplomacy. As Representative Peter Rodino (D-NJ) argued following the conclusion of the Madrid meeting, even if ignored by the Soviets, criticizing human rights violations through the CSCE process kept "world attention" on Soviet abuses, hurting their prestige.[92] Furthermore, Congress provided legitimacy and attention to

---

[89] Jack Kemp, "The Soviet Question," July 14, 1983, Box 130, Folder 5, JKP.

[90] Time/Yankelovich, Skelly & White Poll, March 1983. USYANK.838614.R28A2. Cornell University, Ithaca, NY: Roper Center for Public Opinion Research, iPOLL, accessed August 5, 2019. The rest of the respondents answered either "not familiar" with the issue or "not sure."

[91] ABC News/Washington Post Poll, November 1987. USABCWP.274.R06A. Cornell University, Ithaca, NY: Roper Center for Public Opinion Research, iPOLL, accessed August 5, 2019.

[92] Speech, Peter Rodino, November 8, 1983, Box B.PPR-021, Folder 25, PRP.

the cause of Soviet Jewry. Congressional hearings offered American Jewish NGOs, dissidents, and human rights activists a forum in which to present their concerns. Statements and resolutions by members of Congress helped to draw public attention to the plight of Soviet Jewry and, according to the refuseniks, offered hope in a hopeless situation.[93] The primary contribution of early congressional advocacy for Soviet Jewry was, thus, to keep the issue on the agenda and sustain the energy of the movement as Moscow continued to ignore calls for Jewish emigration.

Soviet Jews as Bargaining Chips

By 1985, changes inside the Soviet Union indicated that US–Soviet relations might be entering a new phase. In March 1985, Mikhail Gorbachev became the fourth general secretary of the Soviet Union in less than two and a half years. In a series of rapid leadership changes, Yuri Andropov had replaced the deceased Leonid Brezhnev in November 1982, only to pass away fifteen months later and be replaced by Konstantin Chernenko, who lasted an even shorter time, dying in March 1985 after only thirteen months at the helm. Significantly younger and more open to Western ideas than were his predecessors, Gorbachev personalized a new beginning in East–West relations. Gorbachev was determined to reinvigorate the ailing Soviet economy and minimize a widening military gap, and to achieve these goals he knew he had to halt the expensive arms race and promote collaboration on trade and technology with the West. Gorbachev realized that such collaboration required an improvement in East–West relations, which could only be obtained by addressing Western concerns about human rights. American human rights advocates within and outside government saw this situation as an opportunity to push for concessions on Jewish emigration. Moderates in the Reagan administration, such as Shultz and Vice President George H. W. Bush as well as several political commentators, were impressed with Gorbachev and perceived him as a new breed of Soviet leader, with whom the United States might be able to do business. Neoconservatives and hardliners in the administration, such as Caspar Weinberger, however, remained deeply skeptical.[94]

---

[93] See, for instance, the following letters: UCSJ to Tom Lantos, June 24, 1987, Box 106, Folder 4, TLP; Alexander Yampolsky to John E. Porter, November 9, 1989, Box 113, Folder 4, TLP.

[94] Beckerman, *When They Come for Us*, 450; Shultz, *Turmoil and Triumph*, 532–533; Archie Brown, "Gorbachev, Perestroika, and the End of the Cold War," in *Reagan and the World: Leadership and National Security, 1981–1989*, ed. Bradley Lynn Coleman and Kyle Longley (Lexington: The University Press of Kentucky, 2017), 111–126.

At first, Gorbachev's rise to power did not seem to indicate significant changes for Jews in the Soviet Union. Emigration numbers remained as low as ever during the first year after Gorbachev assumed power. It was not until late 1986 when Gorbachev launched his reform agenda of glasnost and perestroika that a potential relaxation on emigration seemed possible, and even then emigration numbers remained low.[95] Neverthe-less, it became increasingly clear that human rights violations in general, and the issue of Jewish emigration in particular, was the major impedi-ment to the improvement in US–Soviet relations that both Gorbachev and Reagan sought.

The CSCE Ottawa Human Rights Expert Meeting held from May 7 to June 14, 1985, did little to solve East–West disagreement over human rights. The Ottawa meeting had been called for in the concluding docu-ment in Madrid and brought together politicians and experts on human rights to discuss the implementation of human rights provisions of the Helsinki Accords. Disagreement extended to the agenda and even the proceedings of the meeting but eventually, the delegations agreed on a compromise consisting of two sessions open to the press and the public. The first session was dedicated to reviewing implementation, while the second focused on human rights recommendations and the drafting of a concluding document. Ultimately, the participating states' failure to agree on a concluding document led to a frustrating end to the meeting. Returning from the meeting CHRC cochair Porter expressed disappoint-ment over the Soviet delegation and declared, "If we find the human rights basket empty, then the Soviet Union ought to expect to find the political and economic benefits baskets empty as well."[96]

Although Ottawa did not result in any Soviet concessions on human rights, the meeting did provide Western human rights advocates with another opportunity to confront the Soviets over the status on Jewish emigration. As the International Parliamentary Group for Human Rights in the Soviet Union (IPG) concluded after Ottawa, the value of the CSCE process as a forum to hold the Soviet Union accountable in the court of world public opinion remained unquestionable.[97] The dialogue at Ottawa failed to deliver, but it was a dialogue, nonetheless. The

---

[95] Glasnost (openness) entailed reform of the political structure, lessening the influence of the Communist Party and a greater openness to criticism of the government. Perestroika (restructuring) restructured the economy, decentralizing economic control and encouraging self-financed enterprises in an attempt to bring the Soviet economy on par with capitalist countries.

[96] *CHRC Newsletter*, September 9, 1985, Box 102, Folder 19, TLP.

[97] CSCE Human Rights Expert Meeting Ottawa. IPG Report, June 1985, Box 130, Folder 12, JKP.

Soviets, for instance, tried to reverse the logic of linkage by telling Assistant Secretary for Human Rights Richard Schifter that until the West treated the Soviet Union better, Moscow would not change its position on Jewish emigration.[98] Such exchanges helped position Jewish emigration as an important component of the dialogue on the improvement of East–West relations. The very existence of an expert meeting on human rights within the CSCE context helped to solidify human rights as a legitimate topic for discussion.[99] The US Helsinki Commission used the occasion to subsequently host a hearing on the outcome of Ottawa and keep the pressure on the administration to continue to raise human rights with the Soviets.[100]

Later that year in November, Reagan and Gorbachev met in Geneva in the first face-to-face meeting between an American president and a Soviet general secretary in more than six years. The summit failed to produce any major agreements and was not perceived as a significant step forward at the time. However, the summit laid the foundation for future breakthroughs as the two leaders left the summit with a better understanding of each other and an agreement to continue talks in Washington and Moscow in the following years. For human rights advocates in Congress and American Jewish NGOs, the resumption of US–Soviet bilateral summits offered a new opportunity to press for progress on Jewish emigration. In the months leading up to the summit, they lobbied heavily for a strong American stance on human rights at Geneva and continued to call for the release of refuseniks. The Democratic leadership in the House issued a strong statement on human rights urging the Reagan administration to make the Soviet Union understand that its human rights record affected US–Soviet relations. Other House Democrats followed up by demanding that the Soviet Union allow the refuseniks such as Sharansky and Ida Nudel to emigrate and open up for free emigration for others who wanted to leave.[101] Numerous members of Congress wrote Reagan on Soviet Jewry issues ahead of Geneva.

---

[98] US Congress, House, Committee on Foreign Affairs, *Religious Persecution in the Soviet Union.* Part I – *Soviet Jewry. Hearing before the Subcommittees on Europe and the Middle East and on Human Rights and International Organizations of the Committee on Foreign Affairs,* 99th Congress, 1st Session, September 11, 1985, 11.

[99] Sarah B. Snyder has similarly argued for the overlooked importance of the CSCE expert meetings at Ottawa and elsewhere between 1984 and 1986. Snyder, "The Foundation for Vienna," 503–504.

[100] US Congress, House, Commission on Security and Cooperation in Europe, *Implementation of the Helsinki Accords: The Ottawa Human Rights Experts Meeting.*

[101] House Democratic Leadership Statement on Geneva, November 1985, Box 2480, Folder 21, Dante B. Fascell Congressional Papers, Special Collections, University of Miami Libraries, Coral Gables, Florida.

Waxman forwarded Reagan more than three thousand cards from concerned citizens organized by the UCSJ expressing approval of the decision to raise the issue of Soviet Jewish emigration at Geneva.[102] Others, such as Lantos, sent Reagan lists of refuseniks, urging him to bring up their cases with Gorbachev.[103] Even the CBC, which normally focused its human rights advocacy on Africa and the Caribbean, asked Reagan to raise the issue of Soviet Jewry, citing the need to uphold the Helsinki Accords.[104] Geneva mobilized the full breadth of congressional human rights advocacy.

The amount of congressional travel to the Soviet Union also increased during 1985 as congressional and public interest in Soviet Jewry and human rights continued to increase. In 1985, more than sixty senators and representatives visited the Soviet Union, meeting with refuseniks and Soviet officials.[105] The NCSJ played an important supporting role for such trips, briefing members of Congress about Soviet Jewry before departure.[106] In August and September 1985, a congressional delegation met personally with Gorbachev, informing the Soviet leader that continued human rights violations hindered improved US–Soviet relations. Following the trip, participants organized a letter to Reagan signed by all one hundred senators, urging him to focus on human rights at the Geneva Summit.[107]

Shortly before the summit, human rights advocates gained the first symbolic victory, when Gorbachev permitted human rights activist Yelena Bonner to travel to the United States for medical treatment. Bonner, the wife of the famed nuclear physicist and 1975 Nobel Peace Prize winner Andrei Sakharov, was placed in internal exile along with her husband in the remote city of Gorky. Sakharov had been in Gorky since 1980 for his criticism of the Soviet war in Afghanistan, and Bonner had joined him on a five-year sentence in 1984, accused of "anti-Soviet agitation and propaganda." Although not Jewish themselves, Sakharov

---

[102] Letter, Henry Waxman to Ronald Reagan, November 18, 1985, ID #352732, FO006–09, WHORM: Subject File, RPL.

[103] Letter, Tom Lantos to Ronald Reagan, November 15, 1985, ID #360720, FO006–09, WHORM: Subject File, RPL.

[104] Letter, Louis Stokes to Ronald Reagan, November 20, 1985, ID #352595, FO006–09, WHORM: Subject File, RPL. See also Presidential Log of Selected House Mail, November 8, 1985, Series III, Box 51 Geneva Meeting, Jack F. Matlock Jr. Files, RPL.

[105] Letter, NCSJ Washington Office to NCSJ Leadership and Activists, December 1985, I-181A; 293, 4, NCSJR.

[106] Newsletter, NCSJ Congressional Update (several versions), May 11, June 8, July 10, August 7, 1987, I-181A; 283, 2, NCSJR.

[107] Robert Byrd to Bill Lowery, Letter, November 5, 1985, Box 103, Folder 19, TLP.

and Bonner's agitation for human rights had included support for Soviet Jews since the early 1970s and the American movement for Soviet Jewry consequently showed a strong interest in their situation. Most major American newspapers viewed the gesture to Bonner as a pre-Geneva maneuver aimed at generating American goodwill before the negotiations. Several editorials interpreted it as an encouraging sign.[108] Soviet documents indicate that this assessment was correct as an excerpt from the minutes of a Politburo session on August 29, 1985, showed that Bonner's case was discussed in the framework of its potential impact on Western perceptions of the Soviet Union ahead of the Geneva Summit.[109]

Reagan did push Gorbachev on human rights issues, including Jewish emigration, at Geneva. He explained to Gorbachev that congressional and public opinion meant that improvements on human rights, including Jewish emigration, were required to improve US–Soviet relations. As Reagan's NSC staffer at the time, Jack Matlock, recalls, "without improvement on human rights, Congress would not have approved many of the cooperative agreements the Soviets wanted, particularly in respect to trade."[110] Reagan explained to Gorbachev that if Gorbachev would allow Soviet Jews and members of divided families to leave the Soviet Union, it would be much easier for Reagan to attain congressional approval for cooperation on other issues, such as trade, that Gorbachev sought.[111] When Gorbachev denied that there was a problem and argued that countries should refrain from meddling with other countries domestic affairs, Reagan pushed the issue further and referred to Soviet obligations under the Helsinki Final Act.[112] Reagan continued to list specific human rights cases and noted how they affected congressional opinion until Gorbachev lost his temper and accused Reagan of using Congress as a pretext for gaining concessions on human rights. Although Reagan failed to convince Gorbachev about the power of Congress to obstruct US–Soviet relations, it is clear from such exchanges that Reagan sought to use congressional human rights advocacy as leverage against Gorbachev.[113]

---

[108] Memo, US Editorial Comment on Reagan–Gorbachev Meeting, November 1, 1985, Series III, Box 51 Geneva Meeting, Jack F. Matlock Jr. Files, RPL.

[109] Excerpt from *Minutes of the Politburo Session*, August 29, 1985, National Security Archive, accessed October 20, 2015, http://nsarchive.gwu.edu/NSAEBB/NSAEBB172/Doc12.pdf.

[110] Author's interview with Jack Matlock, December 24, 2015. Richard Schifter emphasized the same point. Author's interview with Richard Schifter, May 30, 2016.

[111] Matlock, *Reagan and Gorbachev*, 161, 218. Reagan repeated this argument at Reykjavik.

[112] US Department of State, *Foreign Relations of the United States, 1981–1988, Volume XII, Global Issues II*, Document 80.

[113] Christian Peterson has made a similar argument. Peterson, "'Confronting' Moscow," 74.

Despite the limited concrete progress at Geneva, both leaders expressed satisfaction about their meeting and optimism for the future. Although Gorbachev failed to persuade Reagan to pursue ratification of SALT II and to abandon SDI, he returned to Moscow optimistic about having achieved a joint statement declaring that a "nuclear war cannot be won and must never be fought." Reagan boasted that he had stood his ground on SDI and confronted the Soviet Union on human rights.[114] Still, the summit did not produce any perceptible progress on human rights. Gorbachev agreed to review individual cases, but he was not willing to accept the protection of human rights as a legitimate subject for international attention.[115] On Capitol Hill, reactions to the Geneva Summit were more mixed. Speaker O'Neill and the Republican Senator Richard Lugar (R-IN) expressed relief that the world appeared safer with the two leaders talking. Human rights leaders Fascell and Lantos were more critical, expressing their disappointment over the failure to make progress on arms control and human rights at the summit.[116] Contemporary observers likewise expressed mixed feelings about the prospects of progress on Jewish emigration, but the Geneva Summit did help put the issue front and center in the public debate.[117]

Although the main objective for members of Congress was a general increase in emigration, much of their advocacy for Soviet Jewry centered on individual high-profile refuseniks. These Soviet Jews had become leaders of the Jewish emigration movement through their struggle to leave the Soviet Union. From prison cells, labor camps, or under de facto house arrest, these individuals became icons for a transnational human rights movement. Their cause found support among other, non-Jewish Soviet dissidents who also protested the repressive Soviet regime and advocated for the respect for human rights. By the mid-1980s, many of these refuseniks, such as Ida Nudel, Josef Begun, and Vladimir Slepak had become household names in the West, winning them the active support of celebrities such as actor Jane Fonda.[118] Perhaps the most famous of these was Natan Sharansky, who had first applied to leave the Soviet Union in 1973. After being denied to leave, Sharansky became

---

[114] "To the Geneva Summit," The National Security Archive, accessed August 5, 2019, http://nsarchive.gwu.edu/NSAEBB/NSAEBB172/.

[115] Matlock, *Reagan and Gorbachev*, 166.

[116] Miami Herald, "Members of Congress React," November 22, 1985, Box 2480, Folder 21, Dante B. Fascell Congressional Papers, Special Collections, University of Miami Libraries, Coral Gables, Florida.

[117] Lazin, *The Struggle for Soviet Jewry*, 215; Beckerman, *When They Come for Us*, 478.

[118] Letter, Jane Fonda to Mikhail Gorbachev, April 24, 1985, Box 265, Alan Cranston Papers, BANC MSS 88/214 c, The Bancroft Library, University of California, Berkeley (hereafter ACP).

increasingly more engaged in the refusenik movement and in 1977 he was arrested for his criticism of the Soviet regime and accused of being an American spy. From his imprisonment in a Siberian labor camp, Sharansky became a powerful symbol of the struggle for Jewish emigration. Sharansky, however, was far from the only one.

Members of Congress and NGOs collaborated with the leaders of the refusenik movement to the extent that their situation in the Soviet Union made it possible. Sometimes internal exile, prison sentences, or Soviet censorship of international mail prevented contact between the refuseniks and their Western allies. However, even from a prison cell (or especially from there), a refusenik could become a powerful icon for the plight of Soviet Jewry. Refuseniks and dissidents who had successfully emigrated, as well as family members of the ones still detained in the Soviet Union, often performed important roles in congressional advocacy. Avital Sharanksy, for instance, played a leading role in calling for her husband's release.[119]

Natan Sharansky was suddenly released from prison and allowed to leave for Israel on February 11, 1986, as part of a spy exchange that also included the release of dissident Yuri Orlov. Sharansky's immigration to Israel became an international media event, and the Jewish emigration movement celebrated it as a much-needed victory. The release gave renewed energy to a movement that had not had many victories to celebrate in the preceding years. In a comment on the Senate floor, Senate Minority Leader Robert Byrd (D-WV) described the release as "a reward for millions in one man's freedom."[120] "Shcharansky seemed the hardest," Annette Lantos of the Congressional Spouses Committee of 21 told the press after the release. She expressed optimism about the group's other adopted refuseniks, "If he can go free, maybe our whole group can be released."[121]

As it turned out, the release of Sharansky marked the beginning of several releases of high-profile refuseniks. In the following months, most high-profile refuseniks were allowed to emigrate, including almost every refusenik adopted by the Committee of 21.[122] Congressional human rights advocates in the US Helsinki Commission and the CHRC who had been deeply involved in these cases celebrated the breakthrough, but at the same time advocated the need to continue the fight for the large numbers of unknown refuseniks and other Jews still trapped in the Soviet

---

[119] CHRC Press Release and Letter, January 3, 1985, Box 107, Folder 11, TLP.
[120] 132 *Congressional Record*, 99th Congress, 2nd Session, 2134 (February 18, 1986).
[121] Special to the *New York Times*, "Wives' Group."
[122] *CHRC Newsletter*, March 6, 1986, Box 111, Folder 20, TLP.

Union. Speaking at the annual prayer vigil on Capitol Hill in June, Porter cautioned that the release of Sharansky should not lead to complacency, but rather prompt him and his colleagues to "re-double our efforts."[123]

By the mid-1980s, well-known refuseniks had become bargaining chips in Soviet–US relations. High-profile human rights activists represented a commodity that Moscow sought to trade for Western cooperation in other fields. At the same time, their imprisonment in the Soviet Union hurt the international image of the Soviet Union. Two days before the release of Sharansky, the *New York Times* wrote that if rumors of Sharansky's release were true, "it will be in part because the Kremlin hopes to relieve itself of an international symbol of the plight of human rights activists here."[124] The release of Sharansky and other notable refuseniks indicated that the Soviets were aware of the positive publicity such concessions generated and willing to use human rights concessions in negotiations with the West.[125]

In October 1986, Reagan and Gorbachev met again to revive the negotiations of nuclear arms reductions, this time in Reykjavik, Iceland. Just as in Geneva, the Reykjavik Summit ultimately failed to produce an agreement on arms control, as Reagan insisted on continuing SDI, but it represented a significant breakthrough on human rights. Reagan used the summit to try to tie arms reduction to human rights and Jewish emigration, presenting Gorbachev with a list of 1,200 Soviet Jews awaiting permission to emigrate, and for the first time, Gorbachev acknowledged human rights as a legitimate discussion topic.[126] According to Shultz, "Reagan and Gorbachev agreed that human rights would become a regular and recognized part of our agenda," but the failure to agree on arms control meant that the summit failed to produce a public statement.[127]

Before the summit, the Reagan administration held frequent meetings with congressional human rights advocates and NGOs, which according

---

[123] *John E. Porter Newsletter*, February 11, 1986, Box 110, Folder 10, TLP.

[124] Serge Schmemann, "What It Means for Moscow and the Refuseniks," *The New York Times*, February 6, 1986, www.nytimes.com/1986/02/09/weekinreview/what-it-means-for-moscow-and-the-refuseniks.html.

[125] It is possible that the emphasis put on refuseniks by the West was counterproductive to their cause as it increased their value to the Soviets. While it is hard to make definitive conclusions on this, the eventual release of virtually all refuseniks on the lists presented to the Soviets and the low emigration numbers before the Soviets came to see the refuseniks as bargaining chips, however, appears to suggest otherwise.

[126] Renouard, *Human Rights in American Foreign Policy*, 240; Memo, Shultz to Reagan, "Reykjavik," October 2, 1986, accessed July 7, 2016, http://nsarchive.gwu.edu/NSAEBB/NSAEBB203/Document04.pdf.

[127] Shultz, *Turmoil and Triumph*, 776.

to Shultz "directly participated in the formulation of our negotiation position."[128] In the days ahead of the summit, Reagan met with leaders of the American Jewish community, including the president of the NCSJ, Morris Abram, to reassure his commitment to Soviet Jewish emigration. An internal White House memo for the meeting expressed concern that Reagan was losing the support of the Soviet Jewry movement and that this could have "very serious political consequences."[129] Back in 1982, strategists in the White House staff had expressed similar concerns about the political consequences of dropping support from the Jewish community and identified foreign policy issues, such as support for Israel and Soviet Jewish emigration, as vital to change this.[130] The administration was sensitive to the domestic political consequences of failing to champion the cause of Soviet Jewry.

The day following the meeting with the American Jewish leaders, at a press conference with Yuri Orlov, Reagan emphasized his commitment to raising human rights in Reykjavik. "I'll make it amply clear to Mr. Gorbachev," Reagan declared, "that unless there is real Soviet movement on human rights, we will not have the kind of political atmosphere necessary to make lasting progress on other issues."[131] Reagan hereby explicitly linked progress on human rights to progress on other issues at future summit meetings. Moreover, he sought to use the domestic political climate to press for Soviet concessions on human rights. The statement thus demonstrates how human rights advocacy by members of Congress and NGOs served as leverage in Reagan's public diplomacy with the Soviet Union. Moreover, the statement is a clear example of how Reagan became more willing to express his public support for Soviet human rights activists from late 1986 onward. As Christian Peterson argues, this change might reflect Reagan's decreased concerned about the negative impact that such human rights criticism might have on general US–Soviet relations.[132] Other factors, such as Gorbachev's reforms, the lessoned fear of nuclear war, and growing US military superiority, might also have played a role. Finally, is appears likely that sustained domestic pressure from Congress and NGOs contributed to as

---

[128] Peterson, *Globalizing Human Rights*, 156.

[129] Memo, Mari Maseng and Rodney McDaniel to Frederick J. Ryan, Oval Office Meeting with Leaders of the Soviet Jewry Movement, October 6, 1986, ID #440961, CO165, WHORM: Subject File, RPL.

[130] Memo, Elizabeth Dole to Edwin Meese III et al., Jewish Strategy, March 25, 1982, ID #097164, HU013-60, WHORM: Subject File, RPL.

[131] Press Release, Remarks by the President in Meeting with Human Rights Leaders, October 7, 1986, Series I, Box 47, Anthony "Tony" R. Dolan Files, RPL. Weinraub, "President Links Rights in Soviet to Summit Success."

[132] Peterson, "'Confronting' Moscow," 74.

the pressure on Reagan to take a tougher stance on human rights, as expressed by the White House memo cited. The example lends credence to the theoretical claim by Margaret E. Keck and Kathryn Sikkink of the ability of "nontraditional international actors to mobilize information strategically" to help persuade and pressure traditional state actors.[133]

It appeared that Soviet calculus on human rights was changing. In the aftermath of Reykjavik, the Soviet Union made another human rights concession by ending Andrei Sakharov's internal exile in Gorky.[134] According to Jack Matlock, Reykjavik led Gorbachev to realize that a normalization of relations with the United States required improvements on all issues, including human rights.[135] Memos from the Soviet Politburo appear to support Matlock's assessment. In internal debates in November 1986, Gorbachev argued that the Soviet Union had to improve its stance on human rights and that allowing dissidents to leave was a costless way to achieve this.[136] It appeared that the Western insistence on human rights improvements was beginning to have an impact on Gorbachev and that the persistent congressional pressure on Reagan to bring up human rights was paying off.[137]

Nevertheless, the encouraging signs of Gorbachev's willingness to address human rights issues and the release of high-profile dissidents were not matched in progress on the total number of Jews allowed to emigrate from the Soviet Union. During 1986, only 914 Jews were allowed to leave the Soviet Union, with thousands still waiting in vain.[138] Concerned members of Congress and NGOs continued to stress this fact as often as they could. Again, the CSCE process offered an opportune moment to draw attention to the issue as the next follow-up meeting began in Vienna in November 1986. A month before the opening of the Vienna meeting, the CHRC sent Shultz a letter that warned against being fooled into believing that Soviet performance on Jewish emigration had improved. The letter also contained a set of IPG recommendations for

---

[133] Margaret E. Keck and Kathryn Sikkink, *Activists beyond Borders: Advocacy Networks in International Politics* (Ithaca, NY: Cornell University Press, 1998), 2.

[134] Philip Taubman, "Soviet Offers East–West Rights Talks in Moscow," *The New York Times*, November 6, 1986, www.nytimes.com/1986/11/06/world /soviet-offers-east-west-rights-talks-in-moscow.html; Beckerman, *When They Come for Us*, 498–499.

[135] Jack F. Matlock, *Autopsy on an Empire: The American Ambassador's Account of the Collapse of the Soviet Union* (New York: Random House, 1995), 97.

[136] See Snyder, *Human Rights Activism*, 172.

[137] As Sarah B. Snyder has pointed out, Reykjavik was significant for this change, but it was just one event in a pattern of international pressure on Gorbachev, which included pressure from other Western leaders, such as Britain's Margaret Thatcher. Ibid., 172–173.

[138] Lazin, *The Struggle for Soviet Jewry*, 309 (table 303).

the follow-up meeting urging that progress on security or economy be matched by progress on human rights.[139] The staunchest advocates for Jewish emigration in Congress were getting complacent because of the release of few prominent individuals.

Vienna, Washington, and Moscow: The Challenge of Progress

The period spanning the duration of the Vienna Meeting from November 1986 to January 1989 witnessed significant Soviet human rights improvements and eventually delivered the progress on Jewish emigration that members of Congress and NGOs had so long advocated for. The negotiations at Vienna were instrumental for this progress but it also came about through bilateral US–Soviet meetings in Washington in 1987 and Moscow in 1988. Moreover, American and Soviet officials intensified their dialogue on human rights, meeting as frequently as every six weeks in the first half of 1988 to discuss human rights issues.[140] The progress was incremental, however, and officials in the Reagan administration, members of Congress, and NGOs disagreed considerably on whether or not to trust the Soviets and how best to respond to the new winds blowing from Moscow. How to respond to progress thus became as much of a challenge as how to handle stagnation had been in the early 1980s. Eventually, Soviet human rights improvements also led to a reevaluation of the centerpiece legislation of the Jackson–Vanik Amendment.

The Vienna Meeting opened with a bombshell when Soviet Foreign Minister Eduard Shevardnadze announced the Soviet Union's desire to host a human rights conference in Moscow as part of the CSCE process.[141] In the Reagan administration, hardliners in the NSC opposed the conference on any grounds. In a September 1987 memo to National Security Adviser Frank Carlucci, Special Assistant for National Security Affairs Peter W. Rodman argued that the Soviets might agree to extensive American demands for human rights improvement so secure support for the conference. Yet, he contended, the Soviets would do so only because it would be worth it to them by conferring extraordinary legitimacy to the Soviet system.[142] Moderates in the State Department, such as

---

[139] CHRC to George P. Shultz, Letter, October 1, 1986, Box 110, Folder 17, TLP.

[140] Adamishin and Schifter, *Human Rights, Perestroika*, 144–150.

[141] Appointed as Foreign Minister by Gorbachev in 1985, Shevardnadze played a leading role in implementing perestroika and established a close working relationship on human rights issues with his Western counterparts.

[142] US Department of State, *Foreign Relations of the United States, 1981–1988, Volume XII, Global Issues II*, Document 97.

Shultz and Schifter, as well as Max Kampelman, while initially skeptical, came to favor support for the conference in exchange for considerable human rights improvements.[143]

Among members of Congress and NGOs, the Soviet proposal was likewise met with considerable skepticism. In a meeting with Senator Alan Cranston (D-CA) in August 1987, Andrei Sakharov argued that the West should exploit the Soviets' desire for a conference to extract human rights concessions, before ultimately rejecting the proposal.[144] In a November 1987 memo to Reagan, the newly appointed National Security Advisor Colin Powell summarized the American approach and demands, "We have tried to use the Soviet desire for such a conference as leverage to extract human rights improvements from Moscow. We have told the Soviets that we could only consider their proposal seriously if they greatly improved their human rights record [...] These included the freeing and total rehabilitation of all political and religious prisoners, a significant rise in immigration, resolution of all divided family cases, continued cessation of radio jamming, and credible guarantees that human rights improvements would continue in the future."[145] Ultimately, the Kremlin's desire to host a human rights conference became a gold mine for human rights advocates, who managed to secure numerous concessions from the Soviets in turn for Western support for a conference.[146] The Moscow human rights conference eventually took place in September 1991, a few months before the collapse of the Soviet Union.

The Moscow human rights conference, however, was only one of several initiatives to emerge out of the Vienna meeting and bilateral meetings. In January 1987, the Soviet leadership introduced a new emigration law that allowed people with first-degree relatives abroad to apply for family reunification. In 1987, the Soviets also ceased jamming Western radio broadcasting, first the British Broadcasting Corporation (BBC) in January and the Voice of America in May. A further sign of change occurred in a meeting between Shultz and the Soviet foreign minister Eduard Shevardnadze in Moscow in April 1987, when Shevardnadze accepted human rights as a legitimate discussion topic in US–Soviet relations.[147] Subsequently, Shevardnadze began changing the Soviet approach to human rights, creating an office on human rights in the Soviet Ministry of Foreign Affairs with the explicit aim to bring the

---

[143] Ibid., Document 99, Document 106.
[144] Memo, Joy to Alan/Gerry, Sakharov meeting, August 26, 1987, Box 274, ACP.
[145] Memo, Colin Powell to Ronald Reagan, November 1987, 005R, B4 (8717), Nelson C. Ledsky Files, RPL.
[146] Snyder, *Human Rights Activism*, 208–209.
[147] Matlock, *Reagan and Gorbachev*, 259.

Soviet Union into compliance with its Helsinki obligations.[148] In the *Country Reports on Human Rights Practices* for 1987, the State Department concluded that the Soviets had demonstrated progress through greater tolerance for demonstrations, the continued release of political prisoners, and an increase in Jewish emigration.[149]

As the Soviet Union continued to make concessions, human rights activists responded by making new demands for further improvements, making sure that the pressure to reform remained high. Sarah B. Snyder has demonstrated that the transnational Helsinki network of human rights activists contributed significantly to change the Soviet approach to human rights, especially at Vienna.[150] Members of Congress likewise played an important role in this change, working closely with the Helsinki network and American Jewish NGOs to keep Jewish emigration on the agenda. Days before the next US–Soviet summit in Washington, DC, in December 1987, Sharansky testified before Congress along with other newly released refusenik leaders, such as Ida Nudel and Vladimir Slepak. The refuseniks agreed that their release had been an attempt by Gorbachev to placate Western critics in the hope of obtaining progress on the economic cooperation that he so badly needed. Noting that the United States found itself in a good bargaining position with the Soviet Union, the refuseniks raised their demands and called for Gorbachev to allow free Jewish emigration to Israel.[151] The IPG shared this assessment of Gorbachev's intentions. In a report sent to Reagan before the Washington Summit, they applauded Soviet reforms but argued that Gorbachev was motivated by a desire to improve world opinion and not by a genuine concern for human rights.[152] A bipartisan group of members of Congress expressed similar sentiments in a joint letter to Gorbachev and Reagan, praising reforms but urging further progress on emigration.[153]

[148] US Department of State, *Foreign Relations of the United States, 1981–1988, Volume XII, Global Issues II*, Document 85; Matlock, *Reagan and Gorbachev*, 265.

[149] US Department of State, *Country Report on Human Rights Practices for 1987* (Washington, DC: US Government Printing Office, 1988), 1045–1055.

[150] Snyder, *Human Rights Activism*, 174–185.

[151] US Congress, House, Commission on Security and Cooperation in Europe, *Implementation of the Helsinki Accords: Hearing before the Commission on Security and Cooperation in Europe, Soviet Jewry Struggle*, 100th Congress, 1st Session, December 4, 1987. NCSJ Congressional Update, February 1, 1988, Box 24, Max Green Files, RPL. Months before, Sharanksy had delivered a similar message to Shultz: Memo and Talking Points, Frank Carlucci to Ronald Reagan, September 21, 1987, ID #506980, CO165, WHORM: Subject File, RPL.

[152] Report, Charles Grassley to Ronald Reagan, December 3, 1987, ID#548208, HU, WHORM: Subject File, RPL.

[153] Letter, Congress to Ronald Reagan and Mikhail Gorbachev, December 4, 1987, Box 109, Folder 19, TLP.

The CHRC was one of the congressional voices most skeptical of Soviet reforms. In June 1987, Porter noted that the progress on Jewish emigration was modest, with 2,030 Jews allowed to leave the Soviet Union in the first five months of 1987.[154] A few months later, he stressed that the Soviet emigration process remained "a frustrating struggle against a mindless bureaucracy," and he pointed out that approximately 11,000 refuseniks had been denied emigration, while as many as 375,000 Jews were interested in leaving but had not yet applied for a visa.[155] In August, the CHRC circulated a report on Capitol Hill that interpreted the recent rise in emigration as "house cleaning" before the Soviets shut the door, pointing out that the released persons almost exclusively consisted of known refuseniks from American lists. The report expressed concern that the vast majority of Jews still in the Soviet Union would be forgotten after the release of high-profile refuseniks and the establishment of improved US–Soviet relations. The report also attested to the continued discrimination against Jews in the Soviet Union.[156]

The actions of the Reagan administration indicated that it was susceptible to congressional concerns. A few days before the Washington Summit, Reagan followed the advice of a congressional resolution and met with spouses of refuseniks still in the Soviet Union. Reagan also met with Natan Sharansky and told him that he was not opposed to the massive demonstration that the Soviet Jewry movement was contemplating in Washington ahead of the summit.[157] Reagan subsequently told Gorbachev about the meeting, to emphasize his commitment to the cause of Soviet Jewry.[158] Reagan had paid attention to congressional advocacy and had become markedly less concerned with the potential backlash to challenging the Soviet Union on human rights issues.

The day before the summit, as many as 250,000 American Jews and supporters, including Speaker Jim Wright (D-TX) and Senate Majority Leader Dole, gathered in Washington to put maximum pressure on

---

[154] Porter Extended Remarks to the Congressional Record, July 8, 1987, Box 102, Folder 35, TLP.

[155] Report by John E. Porter, October 28, 1987, Box 106, Folder 1, TLP.

[156] Letter with Report, CHRC to Peter Rodino, August 12, 1987, Box POL-010, Folder 1, PRP; Søndergaard, "The Congressional Human Rights Caucus and the Plight of the Refuseniks," 237–239.

[157] Anatoly Shcharansky, *The Case for Democracy: The Power of Freedom to Overcome Tyranny and Terror* (New York: Public Affairs, 2004), 139–140.

[158] Peterson, *Globalizing Human Rights*, 149. For another example of Reagan's receptiveness to congressional calls to meet with Soviet dissidents, see Memo, Frederick Ryan to Colin Powell, January 27, 1988, ID #523781, CO165, WHORM: Subject File, RPL.

Gorbachev and Reagan to address Jewish emigration.[159] Outspoken on Soviet human rights violations, Wright had raised human rights issues in meetings with Soviet leaders during a visit to Moscow earlier that year.[160] The demonstration generally struck a positive tone that acknowledged the achieved progress on emigration but also demanded that progress continue.[161] The demonstration reflected the general mood in the American public, which was overwhelmingly in favor of making human rights a key issue at the Washington Summit. In a Gallup Poll from September 1987, 78 percent of Americans declared that they believed it was "very important" to discuss human rights at the summit; only 5 percent chose the option "not so important."[162] Another poll conducted in November 1987 found that human rights was second only to reducing nuclear weapons when Americans were asked which issues were the most important in America's policy toward the Soviet Union. Forty-five percent chose "reducing nuclear weapons" and 31 percent chose "human rights," with "making Western Europe safe" and "situations like Afghanistan" ranking much lower.[163] That human rights came in second on such a list underlines the importance that Americans ascribed to the issue.

In contrast to the previous summits at Geneva and Reykjavik, the Washington Summit concluded in a comprehensive agreement on arms control in the form of the historic Intermediate-Range Nuclear Forces (INF) Treaty, which reduced both countries' nuclear arsenals. Although Reagan did raise the issue of Jewish emigration, the summit itself did not produce any significant progress on human rights. Still, the State Department concluded, "our discussion has become systematized. We talk about everything: names, lists of cases, Soviet laws."[164] According to Matlock, the Soviets even arranged their discussion agenda to include human rights in a similar way as the United States did.[165]

The year 1988 provided further improvements on human rights, as the issue featured more prominently in US–Soviet relations than ever

[159] NCSJ Congressional Update, February 1, 1988, Box 24, Max Green Files, RPL.
[160] J. Brooks Flippen, *Speaker Jim Wright: Power, Scandal, and the Birth of Modern Politics* (Austin: University of Texas Press, 2018), 361.
[161] Beckerman, *When They Come for Us*, 527.
[162] Newsweek. Gallup/Newsweek Poll, September 1987. USGALNEW.87220.R20H. Cornell University, Ithaca, NY: Roper Center for Public Opinion Research, iPOLL, accessed August 5, 2019.
[163] ABC News/Washington Post Poll, November 1987. USABCWP.274.R07. Cornell University, Ithaca, NY: Roper Center for Public Opinion Research, iPOLL, accessed August 5, 2019.
[164] Quoted in Renouard, *Human Rights in American Foreign Policy*, 244.
[165] Matlock, *Reagan and Gorbachev*, 268.

before.[166] In January, the Soviet Union ended its opposition to engage human rights groups by inviting Helsinki Watch and other human rights groups to Moscow to meet with Soviet officials. In a congressional hearing in May on US policy toward the Soviet Union, Richard Schifter expressed cautious optimism, noting that the changes on Jewish emigration had been "more than cosmetic but less than fundamental."[167] Schifter repeated this sentiment in a memo to Shultz a few days later, noting that the Soviets had been processing new applications in larger numbers and with few restrictions since February.[168] Unlike earlier the Soviets now showed a willingness to discuss individual cases of refuseniks with the West.

The expectations of the human rights community were therefore high going into Reagan and Gorbachev's fourth and final summit in Moscow in May 1988. The month before, Shultz had met with Gorbachev to prepare for the meeting, and in his memoirs Shultz recalls leaving Moscow feeling impressed with Gorbachev's willingness to criticize the Soviet Union and discuss human rights.[169] A few weeks before the summit, Reagan hosted the leading human rights NGOs and former refuseniks in the White House, giving them assurances that the administration would deliver progress on human rights at the summit.[170] In the days before the summit, Reagan also put more emphasis on human rights in his public speeches than he had previously done.[171] On May 27, during a highly symbolic stopover in Helsinki on route to his summit meeting with Gorbachev, Reagan proclaimed, "There is no true international security without respect for human rights."[172] Reagan's rhetoric was accompanied by continued pressure from Congress. In a letter to Gorbachev a few days earlier, congressional human rights advocates increased their demands, including a benchmark of 50,000 Jewish exit visas per year.[173]

---

[166] Adamishin and Schifter, *Human Rights, Perestroika*, 144.

[167] US Congress, House, Committee on Foreign Affairs, *U.S. Human Rights Policy toward the Soviet Union: Pre-Summit Assessment and Update: Hearings and Markup before the Committee on Foreign Affairs and Its Subcommittee on Human Rights and International Organizations*, 100th Congress, 2nd Session, May 4, 11, and 18, 1988, 151.

[168] US Department of State, *Foreign Relations of the United States, 1981–1988, Volume XII, Global Issues II*, Document 108.

[169] Shultz, *Turmoil and Triumph*, 1098. During the summit, Reagan delivered resounding praise for human freedom in front of students of the Moscow State University.

[170] Memo, Meeting with Leaders of Human Rights Leaders Organizations, May 17, 1988, ID #562398SS, CO165, WHORM: Subject File, RPL.

[171] Matlock, *Reagan and Gorbachev*, 290; Cannon, *President Reagan*, 706–707.

[172] US Commission on Security and Cooperation in Europe, "President Reagan in Helsinki," *CSCE Digest* (May 1988): 3.

[173] Letter, Alan Cranston to Mikhail Gorbachev, May 24, 1988, Box 265, ACP.

Although the Moscow Summit did not result in a breakthrough agreement like the INF Treaty in Washington the year before, it delivered extensive progress on human rights. Pushing hard on human rights during meetings and delivering a list of specific human rights cases, Reagan secured significant concessions from Gorbachev, including an increase in Jewish emigration and a liberalization of the restrictions on Jewish life in the Soviet Union.[174] Furthermore, the president sent a strong signal of his intention to prioritize human rights by meeting with some one hundred refuseniks during his first day in Moscow.[175] The final agreement secured the institutionalization of US–Soviet human rights forums established the year before as a fixed component of relations. It also stipulated regular meetings to discuss human rights violations in both countries and declared that private citizens and NGOs played an important role in US–Soviet relations.[176]

After the conclusion of the Moscow Summit, US–Soviet negotiations focused increasingly on the ongoing CSCE Vienna follow-up meeting. Emboldened by the Soviet willingness to discuss human rights, members of Congress upped their demands for Soviet Jewish emigration. In November 1988, the chair of the House Foreign Affairs Committee and vice-chair of the US delegation at Vienna, Steny Hoyer, suggested the United States demand "a zero option for human rights," meaning zero political prisoners, zero refuseniks, and zero discrimination in the Soviet Union.[177] Seeing an opportunity to add to his legacy, Reagan became deeply committed to closing the meeting before the end of his term in January 1989.[178] Reagan reached that goal just in time as the Vienna meeting concluded on January 19, 1989, the day before he left office. The concluding document held significant advances on human rights, expressing respect for emigration and religious freedom as well as a more prominent role for NGOs and private citizens in East–West relations. Vienna also resulted in three future conferences on the human dimension in Paris, Copenhagen, and Moscow over the subsequent three years. The Soviet Union secured Western support for hosting such a conference in Moscow after agreeing to a number of human rights concessions, including the release of several political prisoners and

[174] US Department of State, *Foreign Relations of the United States, 1981–1988, Volume XII, Global Issues II*, Document 109; Cannon, *President Reagan*, 703.
[175] Lazin, *The Struggle for Soviet Jewry*, 230; Matlock, *Reagan and Gorbachev*, 300–301.
[176] Peterson, *Globalizing Human Rights*, 155.
[177] US Commission on Security and Cooperation in Europe, "Statement by Representative Steny H. Hoyer," *CSCE Digest* (November 11, 1988): 4.
[178] Adamishin and Schifter, *Human Rights, Perestroika*, 161–162.

continued rising emigration numbers. As Sarah B. Snyder has shown, the Vienna meeting was a turning point for Soviet and Eastern European compliance with the Helsinki Accords.[179] Members of Congress noticed this change at the time. In a report from a US Helsinki Commission delegation trip to the Soviet Union in November 1988, DeConcini noted he had visited the Soviet Union in 1978, 1983 and 1985 and "the change in attitude of Soviet officials on this past trip was startling."[180] Unlike in the past when the Soviets had argued that human rights were "internal concerns" or simply rejected that human rights abuses took place, according to DeConcini, Soviet officials were now willing to discuss human rights and even admitted the need for reform.

The improvements in East–West relations and the gradual rise in Soviet Jewish emigration also reopened the debate over the Jackson–Vanik Amendment. The political support for the Jackson–Vanik Amendment had been broad based and consistent throughout the 1980s from the Reagan administration, the majority of Congress, and most American Jewish groups and human rights NGOs.[181] Still, the period of historically low emigration during the first half of the 1980s had led a minority of politicians, journalists, and even some Jewish leaders to question the merits of Jackson–Vanik. Some even proposed a suspension, to signify an act of good faith that might lead the Soviets to soften their stance on Jewish emigration.[182] In the summer of 1982, old enemies of the Jackson–Vanik Amendment, Richard Nixon and Henry Kissinger, both publicly stated their opposition to such linkage of trade and emigration, arguing that quiet diplomacy had proven more effective.[183] In a June 1983 hearing, supporters of Jackson–Vanik, however, questioned Moscow's inclination to show such good faith and pointed out that by giving up Jackson–Vanik the United States would

---

[179] Snyder, *Human Rights Activism*, 248.

[180] Report, US Commission on Security and Cooperation in Europe Congressional Delegation Trip to the Soviet Union November 12 to November 20, 1988 (undated), I-410, I-410A; 91; 12, UCSJR.

[181] Jimmy Carter had considered suspending Jackson–Vanik in 1979 as a reaction to the improved Jewish emigration numbers but backed away from the idea as he did not find sufficient support for it on Capitol Hill or among the American Jewish community. Robert B. Cullen, "Soviet Jewry," *Foreign Affairs* 65, no. 2 (1986): 261.

[182] Geoffrey P. Levin, "Before Soviet Jewry's Happy Ending: The Cold War and America's Long Debate over Jackson–Vanik, 1976–1989," *Shofar* 33, no. 3 (2015): 71–75; Lazin, *The Struggle for Soviet Jewry*, 181.

[183] "Rejects Assertion Jackson–Vanik Law Harmed Soviet Jewish Immigration," *Jewish Advocate*, June 2, 1983. NCSJ Statement, 1984, Box 15, MS-341, The Tony Hall Papers Collection, Special Collections and Archives, University Libraries, Wright State University, Dayton, Ohio.

lose its best weapon in the struggle for Jewish emigration.[184] Testifying at the hearing, Elliott Abrams stated that the administration had reached the same conclusion and consequently opposed significant changes to the legislation and generally did not want to use a potential repeal in negotiations with the Soviets.[185]

However, as signs of reform and progress started to flow from the Kremlin following the election of Gorbachev, the voices calling for a waiver of Jackson–Vanik began to gain traction. The release of prominent human rights advocates and refuseniks in 1986, including Natan Sharansky and Yuri Orlov in particular, reinvigorated the debate. In April 1986, Dole suggested that a waiver could function, as "an encouragement and incentive to the Soviets to take another look at their human rights policies."[186] An editorial in the liberal magazine *The Nation* in May argued that Jackson–Vanik had been a mistake from the beginning and that it had ruined the satisfactory level of Jewish emigration under détente. Describing the celebrations surrounding Sharansky's triumphant visit to the United States, the editorial observed, "In the heated atmosphere of superpower conflict, it is hard to see the difference between the hero of the struggle for Jewish emigration from the Soviet Union and the captain of ideological battalions in the Cold War."[187] More significantly, the NSCJ also changed its position to favor an adjustment. In a statement circulated to the press, the NCSJ recommended that under the "appropriate circumstances" a modification of trade restrictions in nonstrategic items could occur.[188]

In Congress, however, the leading advocates for a firm stance on Soviet Jewish emigration continued to favor the Jackson–Vanik Amendment. In a hearing before the US Helsinki Commission in April 1986, cochairman D'Amato even raised the question of whether the United States should consider expanding Jackson–Vanik to include other human rights issues than emigration.[189] Proponents of Jackson–Vanik also

---

[184] US Congress, House, Commission on Security and Cooperation in Europe, *Soviet Jewry Hearing and Markup*, 93.

[185] Ibid., 24–25.

[186] Clyde H. Farnsworth, "Dole Proposes Suspension of Law Restricting Soviet Trade," *The New York Times*, April 25, 1986, www.nytimes.com/1986/04/25/world/dole-proposes-suspension-of-law-restricting-soviet-trade.html.

[187] Editorial, *The Nation* 242, no. 20 (May 24, 1986): 714.

[188] Bernard Gwertzman, "U.S. Jewish Group Shifts on Soviet," *The New York Times*, May 25, 1986, 15.

[189] US Congress, House, Commission on Security and Cooperation in Europe, *Implementation of the Helsinki Accords: Hearing before the Commission on Security and Cooperation in Europe: Soviet and East European Emigration Policies*, 99th Congress, 2nd Session, April 22, 1986, 54.

rightfully pointed out that the vast majority of Soviet Jews wishing to leave were still in the Soviet Union and that sufficient reform of Soviet emigration practices had not yet taken place. Congressional opinion, naturally, was paramount on this issue, as the decision to repeal or maintain Jackson–Vanik ultimately rested with Congress. While the president could waive the amendment by providing "evidence of Soviet improvements," at the end of the day it was up to members of Congress to determine whether the evidence presented was sufficient.

As emigration numbers increased somewhat in 1987 before rising significantly the following years, the majority consensus on the Jackson–Vanik Amendment began to erode. Some members of Congress voiced their support for waiving or modifying Jackson–Vanik if the Reagan administration could secure assurance that emigration numbers would continue to rise.[190] Even the amendment's cosponsor, the liberal Democrat and then former-Representative Charles Vanik (D-OH), had pondered waiving Jackson–Vanik in May 1987 if emigration numbers continued to rise.[191] In 1988, Congress held several hearings to discuss a possible waiver but ultimately decided not to act.[192] The administration continued to assure Congress of its commitment to Jackson–Vanik under the current circumstances.[193] Yet, by the end of 1988, Schifter recalls, officials in the administration also began contemplating a waiver, "After 1988 I thought it would make good sense to find them in compliance with Jackson–Vanik."[194] On a trip to Moscow in November 1988, Schifter had been positively surprised by the Soviets' willingness to resolve 120 cases of refuseniks before Reagan left office.[195]

As the calls for a waiver or a revision of the Jackson–Vanik Amendment grew louder in 1989, the amendment's most committed supporters in Congress and the UCSJ continued to insist that the Soviet Union had to implement lasting emigration reforms first.[196] In a House hearing in June 1989, US Helsinki Commission chair DeConcini maintained that the conditions necessary to waive Jackson–Vanik had not yet been met and

---

[190] US Library of Congress, Congressional Research Service, *Emigration and Human Rights in the USSR: Is There a New Approach?* (1988), Box 110, Folder 11, TLP.

[191] Robert S. Greenberger, "U.S. Looks to Jewish Leaders for Cues on Prodding Soviets over Emigration," *Wall Street Journal*, May 18, 1987, 22.

[192] US Congress, Committee on Foreign Affairs, *Congress and Foreign Policy – 1988*, Committee Print (Washington, DC: US Government Printing Office, 1989), 28.

[193] Letter, Dennis DeConcini to Ronald Reagan, May 2, 1988, ID#568107, HU, WHORM: Subject File, RPL.

[194] Author's interview with Richard Schifter, May 30, 2016.

[195] Adamishin and Schifter, *Human Rights, Perestroika*, 169–172.

[196] Altshuler, *From Exodus to Freedom*, 95.

cautioned, "Without the guarantee of real legal reform, emigration policy remains an arbitrary exercise to be carried out at the whim of the Kremlin leadership."[197] That same month, however, the NCSJ announced in its conclusions to a yearlong examination of the issue that it would support a waiver if Reagan received "appropriate assurances" of continued Soviet immigration reform.[198] This endorsement from part of the American Jewish community and the continued increase in Jewish emigration tipped congressional opinion in favor of a waiver. On June 15, 1989, Moynihan and Thomas Downey (D-NY) introduced a resolution, echoing the sentiments of the NCSJ's support for a waiver.[199] The following day, UCSJ president Pam Cohen complained about the falling congressional support for Jackson–Vanik in a memo to Sharansky, "DeConcini, Hoyer, Gramm, and most of the conservatives are supporting our position, as will probably Schumer, Bradley, Frank, Berman. That is to say, our supporters are committed, though not many."[200] Soviet improvements had narrowed down congressional support for Jackson–Vanik to a dwindling coalition of US Helsinki Commission leaders, hardline anti-communists, and liberal Jews. Eventually, Reagan's successor, George H. W. Bush, temporarily waived parts of Jackson–Vanik in December 1990, but it was not formally waived until 2004.[201]

As members of Congress debated the merits of Jackson–Vanik in 1989, the world continued to change at an unmitigated pace. On November 9, 1989, the biggest change of them all occurred. The Berlin Wall, the very symbol of the separation of East and West, suddenly came down at the hands of ordinary Germans citizens. A few weeks later, Bush and Gorbachev used their first summit to declare the Cold War over. The State Department's annual *Country Reports on Human Rights Practices* reported that although there was still considerable room for improvement, 1989 "witnessed a remarkable opening up of the political process and improvements in human rights practices" in the Soviet Union.[202] That same year, a staggering 71,196 Jews left the Soviet Union, more than the total for the

---

[197] Europe, "Chairman Deconcini Opposes Waiver of Jackson–Vanik," 1.
[198] US Congress, Committee on Foreign Affairs, *Congress and Foreign Policy – 1988*, 18.
[199] 135 Congressional Record, 101st Congress, 1st Session, 12180 (June 15, 1989).
[200] Quoted in Altshuler, *From Exodus to Freedom*, 99.
[201] George Bush, Remarks on the Waiver of the Jackson–Vanik Amendment and on Economic Assistance to the Soviet Union, December 12, 1990. Online by Gerhard Peters and John T. Woolley, The American Presidency Project, accessed August 7, 2019, www.presidency.ucsb.edu/node/265352. "U.S. Acts to Ease Trade with East Bloc," in *CQ Almanac 1990*, CQ Almanac Online Edition (Washington, DC: Congressional Quarterly, 1991).
[202] US Department of State, *Country Reports on Human Rights Practices for 1989* (Washington, DC: US Government Printing Office, 1990), 1274.

decade up until then.[203] The following years, Jewish emigration continued to increase dramatically, with more than 570,000 leaving between 1990 and 1993. Loosened emigration practices combined with rising anti-Semitism and the instability of Soviet society, as the Soviet Union came apart, spurred a mass emigration of Jews who had not previously sought to leave. The majority left for Israel, with the United States as the second-most popular destination. For members in Congress, the main challenge changed from helping Jews to get out of the Soviet Union to helping them get into the United States. In a scenario completely unthinkable only a few years before, the United States now struggled to take in all the Soviet Jews who wanted to immigrate.

The large number of Soviet Jews who wanted to come to the United States put the country's immigration system under significant pressure. By mid-1989, the system was already breaking down. Despite advocating for increased Soviet Jewish emigration for years, the United States proved neither willing nor able to accept the number of people knocking on its door as the Cold War ended. Until 1980, all people leaving the Soviet Union had been eligible to enter the United States. This policy changed with the passage of the Refugee Act of 1980, but almost all Soviet Jewish émigrés were still accepted through an application process going through Rome.[204] By October 1989, the United States restricted its acceptance so that only Jewish refugees with close relatives in the United States or other links were given special preference.

Conclusion

Several members of Congress across the ideological spectrum were strong advocates for Soviet Jewish emigration throughout the 1980s and they consistently framed the issue of Soviet Jewish emigration as a human rights issue. Using both legislative actions such as resolutions and nonlegislative actions, such as hearings and speeches, members of Congress kept the issue on the political agenda. Members of Congress also pushed the issue in frequent consultations with the Reagan administration and contributed directly to US diplomacy at the CSCE review meetings, where the US Helsinki Commission participated by invitation of the administration. In addition, dedicated members of Congress engaged the Soviets directly to encourage human rights improvements and increases in Jewish emigration. This engagement took the form of

---

[203] Lazin, *The Struggle for Soviet Jewry*, 309.
[204] For more on the Refugee Act of 1980, see Bon Tempo, *Americans at the Gate*, 167–196; Forsythe, *Human Rights and U.S. Foreign Policy*, 11–12.

extensive correspondence as well as direct meetings with Gorbachev and other officials during congressional delegations to the Soviet Union and Gorbachev's visit to the United States.[205] Finally, members of Congress collaborated closely with American Jewish groups and human rights NGOs, for whom they served as a medium to influence policy. These groups found sympathetic allies among members of Congress, who often proved more accessible than the administration, yet still capable of influencing the political agenda.

Unlike certain other more contentious foreign policy issues in the 1980s, members of Congress and the Reagan administration agreed that Soviet Jewish emigration constituted a human rights issue. Liberals and conservatives in the two branches of government shared the perception that the plight of Soviet Jews was a human rights issue that ought to shape US foreign policy toward the Soviet Union. Members of Congress aimed at strengthening the administration's emphasis on human rights by encouraging it to ramp up its public criticism of the Soviet Union and pursue a linkage between progress on Jewish emigration and other issues. At the same time, they did not challenge that the United States had legitimate security interests in its relations with Moscow, and that these also deserved consideration.

The basic agreement between the executive and legislative branches on the goals of US policy toward the Soviet Union makes it difficult to measure the impact of members of Congress. However, it is evident that congressional activism helped raise the salience of the plight of Soviet Jewry and helped secure the issue a prominent position on the agenda of East–West diplomacy. Arguably, this contribution was especially crucial during the first half of the 1980s, when the prospects of meaningful progress looked bleak. Members of Congress and their NGO allies never succeeded in forcing a rigid linkage policy, but their pressure increased the political costs of failing to deliver on Jewish emigration, something to which the administration was sensitive according to internal memos. To put it differently, strong congressional support for Soviet Jewish emigration provided the administration significant political backing to raise the issue in negotiations with Gorbachev. The administration did become more willing to link progress on human rights and Jewish emigration to progress in other areas during the summits with Gorbachev. While it is difficult to isolate the impact of Congress from other factors, it is apparent that congressional advocacy increased the pressure on Reagan to

---

[205] Members of Congress held several meetings with Gorbachev during the Washington Summit. Memo, Fritz Ermarth and Bob Linhard to Paul Schott Stevens, November 23, 1987, Box 22, Coordination Office, NSC: Records, RPL.

push Gorbachev on Jewish emigration.[206] Along the same lines, members of Congress also did not manage to change Reagan's preference for quiet diplomacy, but Reagan did become more outspoken in his public criticism of Soviet human rights violations over the years. Christian Peterson has argued that congressional and public opinion made the administration more willing to publicly criticize the Soviet Union than it initially preferred.[207] While this observation appears plausible, there is little empirical evidence to push the claim further than to conclude that members of Congress kept the issue on the agenda and increased the political costs, adding pressure on Reagan to deliver results. However, there is evidence that congressional activism provided Reagan with additional leverage in negotiations with Gorbachev. Reagan actively used congressional concern for Soviet Jewish emigration to emphasize the strong American views on the issue. Congressional activism helped him make the case that it was not just propaganda aimed at hurting the Soviet Union and that progress on Jewish emigration was essential to improve US–Soviet relations and secure progress on other areas.

The activism of members of Congress thus had a largely constructive impact on US foreign policy by adding another weapon to the administration's arsenal rather than challenging it. The US Helsinki Commission was particularly important, providing the administration with expertise and information that helped to strengthen its position in negotiations. The positive impact of members of Congress becomes even more apparent if one sees progress on Jewish emigration as a bridge to improvements on arms control and overall US–Soviet relations. In the short term, congressional criticism hurt US–Soviet relations, as it upset the Soviets and complicated improvements in superpower relations. In the long term, however, progress on Jewish emigration and other human rights issues contributed to an overall improvement in bilateral relations between the two countries.[208] Of course, members of Congress must share credit for this development with Reagan and Gorbachev, but there is no denying that dedicated members of Congress were paramount in

---

[206] Memo, Shultz to Reagan, "Reykjavik," October 2, 1986, accessed July 7, 2016, http://nsarchive.gwu.edu/NSAEBB/NSAEBB203/Document04.pdf. Memo for Shultz, "The President's Trip to Reykjavik, Iceland, October 9–12, 1986 – Issues Checklist for the Secretary," October 7, 1986, accessed July 7, 2016, http://nsarchive.gwu.edu/NSAEBB/NSAEBB203/Document07.pdf.

[207] Peterson, *Globalizing Human Rights*, 122–123; Peterson, "'Confronting' Moscow," 58.

[208] In her examination of US–Chinese relations during the Cold War, Meredith Oyen has made a similar argument about how lower-stakes migration issues helped superpowers take small steps on a path to improved relations. Meredith Oyen, *The Diplomacy of Migration: Transnational Lives and the Making of U.S.–Chinese Relations in the Cold War* (Ithaca, NY: Cornell University Press, 2016).

putting human rights and Jewish emigration at the forefront of the diplomatic agenda.

Finally, the issue of Soviet Jewish emigration significantly strengthened the role of human rights in US foreign policy. The issue helped consolidate existing institutions concerned with human rights, such as the US Helsinki Commission, as it provided them with a popular issue to address, which helped justify their raison d'etre. In addition, it inspired the establishment of new institutions dealing with human rights, such as the CHRC, and institutions more narrowly devoted to Soviet Jewry, such as the Congressional Coalition for Soviet Jews. The issue of Soviet Jewry was vital to the longevity of the CHRC, as it drove its expansion more than any other issue throughout the 1980s.[209] Thus, the issue of Soviet Jewry, arguably more than any other issue in the 1980s, helped institutionalize human rights concerns in Congress and the wider infrastructure of American foreign policymaking.

---

[209] Søndergaard, "The Congressional Human Rights Caucus and the Plight of the Refuseniks," 240.

5   "A Universal Human Rights Issue"
South African Apartheid

The imposition of economic sanctions on South Africa through the passage of the Comprehensive Anti-Apartheid Act of 1986 (CAAA) on October 2, 1986, marked a watershed moment in US–South African relations and US human rights policy. Not only did members of Congress radically alter US policy from a focus on geopolitical and economic interests to a concern for human rights, but they also asserted Congress's foreign policy powers at the expense of the executive branch. The significance of the act was further highlighted by the fact that a Republican-controlled Senate overrode Ronald Reagan's veto to force the passage of the law. Only once before in the twentieth century had Congress overridden a presidential veto on foreign policy.[1] An even more remarkable aspect was that it marked the first time in history that a minority group in Congress, namely African Americans, successfully imposed its will on foreign policy on a sitting president.[2]

Along with a growing number of civil society groups, a few primarily African American members of Congress, organized in the Congressional Black Caucus (CBC), had protested South Africa's apartheid regime of institutionalized racial segregation for years, with limited success.[3] Since the early 1970s, they had called for American divestment and economic sanctions against South Africa. The election of Reagan in 1980 and his reelection in 1984 made economic sanctions appear even more unlikely. The Reagan administration pursued a policy of "constructive engagement"

---

[1] The other veto override led to the passing of the War Powers Act in 1973.

[2] Alvin B. Tillery, "Foreign Policy Activism and Power in the House of Representatives: Black Members of Congress and South Africa, 1968–1986," *Studies in American Political Development* 20, no. 1 (2006): 88.

[3] For the organizational history of the CBC, see Robert Singh, *The Congressional Black Caucus: Racial Politics in the U.S. Congress*, Contemporary American Politics (Thousand Oaks, CA: Sage, 1998). For the CBC's foreign policy views, see Raymond W. Copson, *The Congressional Black Caucus and Foreign Policy* (New York: Novinka, 2003). For a broader account of African Americans in Congress, see Carol M. Swain, *Black Faces, Black Interests: The Representation of African Americans in Congress* (Lanham, MD: University Press of America, 2006).

toward South Africa, which offered firm US support to the white minority regime in Pretoria and rejected any form of sanctions. Nevertheless, at the behest of the CBC in 1986, Congress passed the CAAA, imposing comprehensive economic sanctions against South Africa and effectively derailing constructive engagement.

Why, then, did Congress successfully impose economic sanctions in 1986 after more than fifteen years of futile efforts by the CBC to do just that? What had changed? Why had an overwhelming majority of Americans inside and outside of Congress come to support economic sanctions? Inevitably, several factors contributed to change the American attitude toward sanctions. Most notably, the situation inside South Africa deteriorated dramatically from 1984, with escalating violence and repression from the South African government. International media coverage of these events increased awareness of apartheid and shaped public opinion against it. The anti-apartheid movement in the United States gained momentum during the 1980s as protests spread from college campuses to the national stage, inspired by the growing transnational anti-apartheid movement.[4] Lessened Cold War tensions, as the relationship between Moscow and Washington improved from 1985 onward, also made it increasingly possible to view apartheid within a framework of decolonization rather than Cold War contestation.[5] The American experience with racial segregation and the legacies of Pan-Africanism and the civil rights movement also shaped American opposition to apartheid.[6] The role of human rights in American opposition to apartheid, however, has only received limited attention.[7] This chapter traces how members of Congress, especially in the CBC, framed

---

[4] For the American anti-apartheid movement, ranging from political activism to political culture, see Hostetter, *Movement Matters*. For the British anti-apartheid movement, see Roger Fieldhouse, *Anti-Apartheid: A History of the Movement in Britain: A Study in Pressure Group Politics* (London: Merlin, 2005). For a transnational history centered on Sweden and Britain, see Håkan Thörn, *Anti-Apartheid and the Emergence of a Global Civil Society* (Basingstoke: Palgrave Macmillan, 2006). For a theoretical approach to international opposition to apartheid, see Audie Klotz, *Norms in International Relations: The Struggle against Apartheid* (Ithaca, NY: Cornell University Press, 1995).

[5] For opposition to apartheid within the context of decolonization in the 1950s and 1960s, see Ryan M. Irwin, *Gordian Knot: Apartheid and the Unmaking of the Liberal World Order* (Oxford: Oxford University Press, 2012). For an excellent examination of the relations between the United States, Cuba, and South Africa during the late Cold War, see Gleijeses, *Visions of Freedom*.

[6] For an argument that Pan-Africanism has been of lesser importance to African American views on Africa than domestic politics, see Tillery, "Foreign Policy Activism"; Alvin B. Tillery, *Between Homeland and Motherland: Africa, U.S. Foreign Policy, and Black Leadership in America* (Ithaca, NY: Cornell University Press, 2011).

[7] Even Robert Massie's monumental account of US–South African relations hardly mentions human rights concerns. Robert Massie, *Loosing the Bonds: The United States*

apartheid as a human rights issue in their attempt to challenge the Reagan administration's South Africa policy. It demonstrates that human rights constituted an important framework in the American debate over economic sanctions.

The Reagan Administration and Constructive Engagement

If the election of Jimmy Carter in 1976 had brought optimism to the anti-apartheid movement, the election of Reagan four years later had the opposite effect. Reagan's break with Carter's foreign policy and human rights also extended to South Africa. Reagan's determination to send communism to the "ash heap of history" and oppose communism in the Third World led him to seek even closer relations between Washington and Pretoria. The South African government's strong stance against communism and the ties between black South African groups, such as the African National Congress (ANC), and the Soviet Union weighed much heavier in Reagan's deliberation than did the racial segregation of the apartheid regime.[8] Furthermore, according to the logic of the Kirkpatrick Doctrine, the United States could hope to persuade South Africa to reform, but any push to reform should be tempered with an awareness of the risk of losing the country to communist totalitarianism.[9]

Arguably, no single individual had a larger impact on the Reagan administration's South Africa policy than did Assistant Secretary of State for African Affairs Chester Crocker. Serving the entire duration of Reagan's presidency, Crocker became the chief architect of the Reagan administration's policy toward South Africa. Similar to how Kirkpatrick landed her job as US ambassador to the United Nations in part based on her 1979 article in *Commentary*, Crocker landed his position partly due to a 1980 article in *Foreign Affairs*. This article, titled "South Africa: Strategy for Change," laid out the foundation of what would become the administration's South Africa policy. Crocker argued that it should be

---

and South Africa in the Apartheid Years (New York: Doubleday, 1997). For the most extensive treatment of human rights in US foreign policy toward South Africa, see Alex Thomson, *U.S. Foreign Policy Towards Apartheid South Africa, 1948-1994: Conflict of Interests* (Basingstoke: Palgrave Macmillan, 2008). For the role of human rights in Jimmy Carter's South Africa policy, see Simon Stevens, "'From the Viewpoint of a Southern Governor': The Carter Administration and Apartheid, 1977–81," *Diplomatic History* 36, no. 5 (2012): 843–880. For South African history as a struggle for human rights, see Saul Dubow, *South Africa's Struggle for Human Rights: The History of Rights in South Africa* (Athens: Ohio University Press, 2012).

[8] H. W. Brands, *Reagan: The Life* (New York: Doubleday, 2015), 532.
[9] Kirkpatrick, "Dictatorships and Double Standards."

a basic American objective to support change in South Africa, but that such change should be pursued through constructive engagement, not through economic pressures.[10]

Crocker, however, met considerable opposition from hardliners within the Republican Party who believed he was too critical of the South African regime. This perception was partly caused by Crocker's past, when he had been highly critical of South Africa, for instance, participating in boycotts of South African lecturers during his years as a student of African history in the 1960s. His views, however, increasingly moved toward the center and by 1970, he landed a job at the National Security Council working for Henry Kissinger.[11] Still, conservative Republicans, such as Senator Jesse Helms (R-NC), who led the charge against Crocker in his Senate confirmation hearing, believed that Crocker was still too critical of Pretoria. Only after Majority Leader Howard Baker Jr. (R-TN) intervened to quell the opposition did the Senate Foreign Relations Committee confirm Crocker's nomination on June 9, 1981.[12]

The mixed support for Crocker's nomination from Republicans in Congress also found expression in the divisions over the policy of constructive engagement within the administration. Crocker and Secretary of State George P. Shultz formed the leadership of the mainstream pragmatic wing of the administration committed to constructive engagement. They found staunch opposition among so-called hardliners, such as Defense Secretary Caspar Weinberger, UN Ambassador Jeane Kirkpatrick, Robert McFarlane and John Poindexter at the NSC, Don Regan and Pat Buchanan at the White House, and CIA director William J. Casey. The hardliners generally opposed any form of criticism of Pretoria, because South Africa was an important ally in the struggle against communism. According to Shultz's memoirs, Casey was the leader of the group and actively used the CIA to undermine his and Crocker's policy.[13] As on many foreign policy issues, Reagan did not fall squarely in either camp. Crocker recalls, "The turf wars were very real, and ultimately we won most of the big battles and the president would not allow these other people to change the policy."[14] Despite such

---

[10] Chester A. Crocker, *High Noon in Southern Africa: Making Peace in a Rough Neighborhood* (New York: W. W. Norton, 1992), 323–351.

[11] Massie, *Loosing the Bonds*, 482.

[12] "Few Reagan Nominees Meet Serious Trouble," in *CQ Almanac 1981*, 37th edn., 17-A-32-A. (Washington, DC: Congressional Quarterly, 1982).

[13] Shultz, *Turmoil and Triumph*, 1116.

[14] Author's interview with Chester Crocker, June 9, 2016. The main battle on economic sanctions in 1986, however, would prove to be the exception. Gleijeses, *Visions of Freedom*; Crocker, *High Noon*, 316–329.

disagreements between moderates in the State Department and more hawkish individuals in other parts of the administration, the Reagan team managed to display united support for the policy of constructive engagement under the leadership of Crocker.

The objective of constructive engagement was to promote peaceful change in southern Africa through engaging with the South African regime and reassuring it of American support.[15] This policy rested on the assumption that the United States could convince the South African government of its interest in the gradual reform of apartheid. In a May 1981 memo to then-Secretary of State Alexander Haig, Crocker argued that "the possibility may exist for a more positive and reciprocal relationship between the two countries based upon shared strategic concerns in southern Africa, our recognition that the government of Pieter W. Botha represents a unique opportunity for domestic change, and a willingness of the Reagan administration to deal realistically with South Africa."[16] Crocker believed that the South African government, under the leadership of Prime Minister Botha, was willing to undertake meaningful reforms that would eventually end apartheid. In terms of tactics, constructive engagement relied on quiet diplomacy, or "friendly persuasion," as Crocker labeled it, as the preferred approach to push for South African reforms. The intention was to tone down the harsh rhetoric of the Carter administration by downplaying racial injustice and opposing economic sanctions. Instead, Crocker called for a "tone of empathy" with the South African government, which he described as pragmatic and flexible "modernizers."[17]

In talks with South African Foreign Minister Pik Botha and Defense Minister Magnus Malan, Crocker went to great lengths to reassure the South African government of the new administration's commitment to improved US–South African relations. Crocker promised Botha and Malan that the Reagan administration would have "more backbone in face of pressure than the previous one."[18] Crocker even went as far as to

---

[15] Smith, *America's Mission: The United States and the Worldwide Struggle for Democracy in the Twentieth Century*, 274–275. Tony Smith has pointed out that constructive engagement was generally in line with the American tradition of democracy promotion through the engagement of local elites.

[16] Quoted in Pauline Baker, "The United States and South Africa: Persuasion and Coercion," in *Honey and Vinegar: Incentives, Sanctions and Foreign Policy*, eds. Richard N. Hass and Meghan O'Sullivan (Washington, DC: Brookings Institute, 2000), 96.

[17] Chester A. Crocker, "South Africa: Strategy for Change," *Foreign Affairs* 59, no. 2 (1980): 337.

[18] Department of State, "Memo of Crocker–Botha and Malan Talks," April 15–16, 1981, Pretoria, South Africa, Box 68, Folder 'CBC Meeting June 3, 1981,' William H. Gray III Congressional Records, Schomburg Center for Research in Black Culture, Manuscripts, Archives and Rare Books Division, The New York Public Library (hereafter WHG).

tell the South Africans that while the United States would like to see successful reforms in South Africa, it was not a condition for improved relations between Washington and Pretoria.[19] The administration's early commitment to promoting domestic reforms in South Africa was thus moderate at best, and constructive relations with Pretoria were the primary objective.

While the Reagan administration wanted to see domestic reforms in South Africa, the primary objective of the policy of constructive engagement, Crocker recalls in his memoirs, was to resolve regional conflicts to foster a "regional climate conducive to compromise and accommodation."[20] Crocker was convinced that regional security would have to predate domestic South African reform – not the other way around.[21] Crocker particularly hoped that better relations between Washington and Pretoria could secure South African cooperation on American objectives in Namibia and Angola.[22] South Africa, as part of the British Empire, oversaw the administration of Namibia from the time it had dispelled German colonial forces in 1915. Since Angola's independence in 1975, Cuba had deployed forces in the country to support the leftist People's Movement for Liberation of Angola against US-backed South African interventions. Cuban forces also supported the Namibian independence movement. Crocker's plan was to link Namibia's independence from South Africa to the removal of Cuban forces from Angola, two issues that US policy had hitherto treated largely separately. Conservatives in the administration were highly concerned with removing the Cubans from Angola, but had little interest in Namibia. The international community, however, was primarily focused on the South African occupation of Namibia. In 1978, the UN Security Council adopted Resolution 435 calling for a ceasefire and UN-supervised elections in Namibia. After Zimbabwe gained independence in 1980, Namibia was "hot" and "the next issue" on the international political agenda for Africa, Crocker recalls.[23]

In May 1981, the *Washington Post* published an article based on leaked documents from the State Department obtained by the lobbying group TransAfrica. The article confirmed that the Reagan administration was hoping to use improved relations with Pretoria in exchange for cooperation on a solution for Namibia.[24] The documents made it clear that the

---

[19] Department of State, "Memo of Crocker–Botha and Malan Talks," April 15–16, 1981, Pretoria, South Africa, Box 68, Folder 'CBC Meeting June 3, 1981,' WHG.
[20] Crocker, *High Noon*, 75.   [21] Ibid., 77.
[22] Baker, "The United States and South Africa," 96.   [23] Crocker, *High Noon*, 74.
[24] Joe Ritchie, "U.S. Details Terms for Closer South African Ties," *The Washington Post*, May 29, 1981, A21.

administration intended to let Pretoria know that it saw the continuation of the "Namibia problem" as a primary obstacle to improved US–South African relations.[25] In an internal memo to Haig, Crocker argued that a settlement of Namibia could "contribute to the leverage we need to produce a withdrawal of Soviet/Cuban military forces from Angola."[26] Solving the dual Namibia–Angola issue, not ending apartheid, was Crocker's primary objective with constructive engagement.

Reagan publicly justified the policy of constructive engagement by referring to the strategic importance of maintaining good relations with South Africa in the struggle to counter Soviet expansion in southern Africa. In early March 1981, Reagan told an interviewer that South Africa was a loyal ally that deserved American support and reasoned, "If we're going to sit down at a table and negotiate with the Russians, surely we can keep the door open and continue negotiations with a friendly nation like South Africa."[27] In contrast to its substantial criticism of human rights violations in the Eastern Bloc, the administration rarely framed apartheid as a human rights issue, although it did become slightly more willing to do so as criticism of constructive engagement intensified. Interestingly, the administration's preferred invocation of human rights regarding South Africa was a concern for the economic rights of black South Africans. The administration would counter calls for sanctions by arguing that black South Africans would be the ones to suffer the most from a weakened economy.[28] Hereby, the administration essentially sought to use concern for economic rights as an argument against the concerns for civil and political rights raised by proponents of sanctions. Given the administration's general position that US human rights policy should focus on "civil rights and the rule of law" and

[25] "CBC Memorandum on Foreign Affairs," June 3, 1981, Box 68, Folder 'CBC Meeting June 3, 1981,' WHG.

[26] Chester Crocker, "Your Meeting with South African Foreign Minister Botha," Memo from Crocker to Haig, May 14, 1981, Department of State, Box 68, Folder 'CBC Meeting June 3, 1981,' WHG.

[27] Joseph Lelyveld, "Reagan's Views on South Africa Praised by Botha," *The New York Times*, March 5, 1981, 15. "Excerpts from the transcript of the interview by Walter Cronkite," enclosed in correspondence from constituent to Senator Claiborne, March 5, 1981, Box 3, Folder '93, Countries: South Africa,' The Senatorial Papers of Claiborne Pell: Congresses, Mss. Gr. 71.3, University of Rhode Island Library, Special Collections and University Archives.

[28] Ronald Reagan, "Remarks of the President on Signing Executive Order regarding South Africa," September 9, 1985, SA01894, South Africa: The Making of U.S. Policy, 1962–1989, Digital National Security Archive. Ronald Reagan, Remarks to Members of the World Affairs Council and the Foreign Policy Association, July 22, 1986. Online by Gerhard Peters and John T. Woolley, The American Presidency Project, accessed August 7, 2019, www.presidency.ucsb.edu/node/259098.

downplay economic and social rights as mere aspirations, its priority on South Africa casts serious doubts about the sincerity of its commitment to human rights.[29]

The Reagan administration took several actions to support South Africa during its first term, some more symbolic than substantial. Most importantly, the administration shielded South Africa in international forums. At the UN, Jeane Kirkpatrick protected apartheid by vetoing four UN Security Council resolutions imposing bans on trade with South Africa. The CBC leveled harsh criticism against these decisions, arguing in one case that the veto "epitomizes the administration's support for fascist regimes around the world."[30] In November 1982, the administration announced its support of a South African loan application of $1.1 billion to the International Monetary Fund (IMF). The CBC sought to block the loan by proposing legislation that would prohibit the United States from supporting IMF loans to countries that violated human rights. Members of Congress also sent a letter to Treasury Secretary Don Regan expressing their disapproval.[31] The chair of the House Subcommittee on Africa, Howard Wolpe (D-MI), announced plans for special hearings on the issue.[32] The UN General Assembly likewise sent a strong signal of disapproval as it voted overwhelmingly against granting the loan. Nonetheless, the IMF approved the loan shortly after.[33]

On the more symbolic level, the Reagan administration abstained from distancing itself from the South African regime on numerous occasions. In March 1981, the administration allowed a group of high-ranking South African military officials, including the chief of the South African military intelligence, Pieter W. van der Westhuizen, entry into the United States, where they met with government officials, including Kirkpatrick.[34] When the visit became public knowledge, the State Department brushed it off as a mistake and argued that Kirkpatrick was unaware of van der Westhuizen's role in South Africa. The CBC again sought to challenge the administration by unsuccessfully

---

[29] NSC memo, March 06, 1981, ID#046147, HU, WHORM: Subject File, RPL.

[30] Congressional Black Caucus Newsletter, "Caucus Levels Sharp Criticism of Reagan Administration's UN Veto," September 1, 1981, Box 15, Folder 8, TransAfrica Collection, Manuscript Division, Moorland-Spingarn Research Center, Howard University.

[31] Thomas Downey, Mike Lowry, and others to Donald Regan, October 19, 1982, Box HRIO-96&97, Folder 10, House Foreign Affairs Committee Subcommittee on Human Rights. Center for Legislative Archives, National Archives, Washington, DC.

[32] Richard M. Weintraub, "Members of Congress Fight IMF Loan to South Africa," *The Washington Post*, November 2, 1982, Nexis Uni.

[33] Massie, *Loosing the Bonds*, 497.   [34] Ibid., 486.

calling for Kirkpatrick to step down.[35] Two months later on May 15, 1981, Reagan and Haig hosted South African foreign minister Pik Botha in Washington. CBC member Representative John Conyers (D-MI) decried the meeting as "another overt signal from the Reagan administration that it does not plan to follow through with the human rights policies that were falteringly begun by the Carter administration."[36] Similarly, in July that year, the South African national rugby team, a symbol of the white regime and an object of hate for most South African blacks, played in the United States. Subsequently, in September, Representative William Gray (D-PA) unsuccessfully attempted to pass a resolution to ban the team from playing in the United States.[37] Through such actions, from significant statements in international forums to more symbolic acts, the administration helped strengthen the South African regime's grasp of power.

Early Congressional Challenges to Constructive Engagement

The seeds for congressional activism against apartheid in the Reagan years were planted in the 1970s as a growing number of African American representatives took an interest in US foreign policy toward Africa. Landmark events included the appointment of Representative Charles Diggs (D-MI) as chair of the House Foreign Affairs Committee's Subcommittee on Africa in 1969, and the establishment of the CBC by fourteen African American representatives in 1971.[38] In the coming years, the CBC provided legislative support for the nascent anti-apartheid movement, introducing numerous sanction bills against South Africa.[39] In 1971, members of the CBC met with African American workers from a Polaroid plant in Boston, which produced cameras used by the South African government for taking the ID pictures for the

---

[35] Copson, *The Congressional Black Caucus and Foreign Policy*, 28; CBC, "South Africa Military Visit," CBC letter to Secretary Haig, March 16, 1981, Box 68, Folder 'Braintrust,' WHG.

[36] 127 *Congressional Record*, 97th Congress, 1st Session, 9735 (May 14, 1981).

[37] William H. Gray, "Dear Colleague," September 21, 1981, Box HRIO-96&97, Folder 10, House Foreign Affairs Committee Subcommittee on Human Rights. Center for Legislative Archives, National Archives, Washington, DC.
    H.Con.Res.183 – A Concurrent Resolution Expressing the Sense of the Congress That the National Rugby Team of South Africa Should Not Play in the United States, H.R. Res. 183, 97th Congress (1981).

[38] Francis Njubi Nesbitt, *Race for Sanctions: African Americans against Apartheid, 1946-1994*, Blacks in the Diaspora (Bloomington: Indiana University Press, 2004); Massie, *Loosing the Bonds*, 157–426; Singh, *The Congressional Black Caucus*, 51–72.

[39] Tillery, "Foreign Policy Activism," 89.

"reference books" that blacks were required to carry to restrict their mobility. The workers wanted their employer to cut ties to the South African government and the CBC raised the issue in a meeting with President Richard Nixon, where they urged him to discourage American firms from further investment in South Africa.[40] Ultimately, nothing came of the meeting, but CBC member Ronald Dellums (D-CA) later recalled that the Polaroid workers helped the CBC "define our mission in those early years" as legislators for the anti-apartheid movement.[41]

Failing to gain traction for its legislative efforts, the CBC intensified its collaboration with anti-apartheid activists. This led to the establishment of the Black Forum on Foreign Policy in 1975 as a "study group" of intellectuals and activists, seeking to press the US government to further "black interests abroad."[42] In 1977, the CBC and the National Association for the Advancement of Colored People (NAACP) established TransAfrica to lobby the US government. Such alliances with activists and civil rights groups in the Africa American community came naturally to the CBC, as several of its founding members had been leaders in the civil rights movement. The CBC's opposition to apartheid was clearly informed by the civil rights movement's interest in Africa in the 1960s, such as Dr. Martin Luther King Jr.'s call for sanctions against South Africa 1962.[43] The CBC also built on notions of Pan-Africanism stretching back to the 1920s and the legacy of African American political and intellectual leaders, such as Marcus Garvey and W. E. B. Du Bois.[44]

In the early months of the Reagan presidency, there was little indication that the administration's South Africa policy would face serious public criticism. Most politicians and newspapers abstained from criticizing constructive engagement, waiting to see whether Crocker's plan would have the desired effect. Public opinion was also largely supportive. According to an opinion poll from March 1981, 58 percent of Americans agreed with the Reagan administration's decision of "working closely with the government of South Africa, despite

---

[40] Nesbitt, *Race for Sanctions*, 91.

[41] Ronald V. Dellums and H. Lee Halterman, *Lying Down with the Lions: A Public Life from the Streets of Oakland to the Halls of Power* (Boston, MA: Beacon, 2000), 123.

[42] US Congress, House, Committee on House Administration and Office of History and Preservation, *Black Americans in Congress, 1870–2007* (Washington, DC: US Government Printing Office, 2008), 388.

[43] For Martin Luther King Jr.'s use of human rights language, see Thomas F. Jackson, *From Civil Rights to Human Rights: Martin Luther King, Jr., and the Struggle for Economic Justice* (Philadelphia: University of Pennsylvania Press, 2007).

[44] Klotz, *Norms in International Relations*, 94–98.

differences with them on racial policy."[45] The only criticism came from a vocal minority of anti-apartheid activists, including leaders of the African American community, and NGOs, such as TransAfrica and the American Committee on Africa (ACOA).[46] In Congress, outspoken opposition to apartheid was mostly confined to the CBC, while the majority of Democrats and moderate Republicans argued that constructive engagement should be given a chance.[47] By the end of 1982, however, faith in constructive engagement began to erode and the policy came under fire from both the left and the right. On the one hand, liberals argued that the policy had failed to promote domestic reform in South Africa and was tacitly encouraging regional destabilization by Pretoria. On the other hand, conservatives attacked Crocker for being too pragmatic with leftist regimes in the region, such as Zimbabwe and Mozambique, fearing that this would antagonize South Africa.[48]

As a caucus, the CBC was a loosely organized group, but its members strove to act as a unified bloc whenever possible. Consisting exclusively of Democrats, several of whom were leftwing liberals, the CBC took an adversarial position to Reagan's conservatism, including on foreign policy. CBC members agreed on favoring the imposition of economic sanctions as a measure to push for the abolition of apartheid, but they disagreed on how comprehensive the sanctions should be.[49] A skilled coalition builder, William Gray was a leading figure among the moderate wing of the CBC.[50] The third-generation Baptist pastor and community activist was strongly engaged in US policy toward Africa, lobbying for more foreign aid to the continent and a leader in securing famine aid to Ethiopia in 1984. An activist-turned-politician from Berkeley and a self-proclaimed democratic socialist, Dellums represented the more radical wing of the CBC. While Gray was a master of working the legislative system, Dellums was skillful at mobilizing grassroots movements and comfortable engaging in protests.[51]

---

[45] Louis Harris & Associates. Harris Survey, March 1981. USHARRIS.042781.R05. Cornell University, Ithaca, NY: Roper Center for Public Opinion Research, iPOLL, accessed August 6, 2019.

[46] Baker, "The United States and South Africa," 101. For a history of the ACOA and TransAfrica, see Hostetter, *Movement Matters*, ACOA 13–41, TransAfrica 65–93.

[47] Massie, *Loosing the Bonds*, 497.

[48] Baker, "The United States and South Africa," 101.

[49] For a table of CBC leaders 1971–1994, see Singh, *The Congressional Black Caucus*, 65.

[50] Ibid., 131.

[51] Ibid., 126. Former president of the Congressional Human Rights Foundation David L. Philips recalls, "Ron Dellums was a leader on this issue [economic sanctions against South Africa]." Author's interview with David L. Philips, July 30, 2015. Chester Crocker likewise recalls Gray and Dellums as leaders of the "anti-apartheid lobby group within Congress." Transcript, Chester Crocker Oral History Interview, June 5, 2006, 152, by

CBC members accused the Reagan administration's South Africa policy of being racist and failing to live up to American commitments to human rights. At a CBC press conference on the administration's policy in March 1981, Congressional Delegate Walter E. Fauntroy (D-DC) declared, "We cannot help but conclude that there seems to be racist motivations underlying these fundamental changes."[52] The CBC also criticized the administration for not speaking out against human rights violations in South Africa in the same manner as in the Soviet Union. The CBC pointed to how racial segregation represented extensive violations of black South Africans' civil, political, and economic rights. It listed violations of internationally recognized human rights, such as the right to vote, the freedom of movement, the freedom of assembly, and the right to a fair legal process. The CBC's main point of human rights criticism, however, was the South African government's physical violence against black South Africans, ranging from beatings to killings. In a newsletter from 1984, the CBC described how South Africa had a "legal regime in which the use of torture to extract confessions can go unchecked" and continued to list two cases of police killing the detainees Tembuyise Simon Mndawe and Pares Molefi Malatje.[53]

Throughout the 1980s, the American anti-apartheid movement would become the most widespread and successful foreign policy dissent movement of the decade.[54] As more people started to question the policy of constructive engagement, the movement stepped up its efforts to force a change in US policy toward South Africa. Since the US–South African relationship was first and foremost of an economic nature, measures directed at South Africa's economy were an obvious choice. In 1983, American banks had a total of $343 million in outstanding loans to the South African government and $4.6 billion to the private sector. Together, Americans owned stocks worth up to $7.6 billion in South African companies. American companies had $2.3 billion invested in South Africa and employed 120,000 South Africans.[55] Thus, reducing US economic relations with South Africa offered considerable

Charles Stuart Kennedy, the Association for Diplomatic Studies and Training Foreign Affairs Oral History Project, accessed August 8, 2019, www.adst.org/OH%20TOCs/Crocker,%20Chester%20Arthur.toc.pdf

[52] CBC, "Congressional Black Caucus Attacks Strong Racist Overtones of Reagan administration Foreign Policy Shifts," Press Advisory, March 25, 1981, Box 68, Folder 'CBC March 25, 1981,' WHG.

[53] CBC Newsletter, 'Point of View,' Spring 1984, Box 67, Folder 'Other CBC Special Projects,' WHG.

[54] Hostetter, Movement Matters, 2.

[55] US Congress, Committee on Foreign Affairs, Congress and Foreign Policy – 1985–1986, Committee Print (Washington, DC: US Government Printing Office, 1988), 16. For a

opportunities to hurt the South African economy and thereby the apartheid regime.

Members of Congress, NGOs, and anti-apartheid activists pursued a range of measures to undermine the economy of apartheid, ranging from ethical principles over divestment to sanctions. The least comprehensive of these was the so-called Sullivan Principles. Introduced in 1977 by Reverend Leon Sullivan, an African American board member of General Motors, these principles devised a set of voluntary guidelines for American companies operating in South Africa.[56] By 1983, more than half of the American companies operating in South Africa had signed up for them. Despite some delays and difficulties with implementation, proponents of the Sullivan Principles had managed to establish these as the standard by which American investors judged corporate behavior.[57] For companies, adopting the Sullivan Principles functioned as insurance against divestments by their shareholders and investors and offered a less costly alternative to withdrawing from South Africa altogether. In a period of six years from 1977 to 1983, the Sullivan Principles went from being considered radical to being seen as a moderate alternative to tougher measures, such as divestment and sanctions. Proponents of the Sullivan Principles argued that American companies helped to reform South African society through their adoption of ethical standards.

Even the Reagan administration declared its support for the Sullivan Principles, although it resisted congressional legislation on the issue. Thus, in the summer of 1981, when Representative Stephen Solarz (D-NY) attempted to pass a law to make the Sullivan Principles mandatory for all US companies operating in South Africa, the administration voiced its strong opposition.[58] A State Department report sent to the House Foreign Affairs Committee argued that the strength of the Sullivan Principles lay in their voluntary nature.[59] Indicative of the limited support for sanctions in Congress during the early years of the administration, Solarz's bill failed to make it through the House and the Sullivan Principles remained voluntary. Solarz, however, would continue to play a leading role in congressional opposition to apartheid throughout the

---

table showing US–South African economic relations during the Cold War, see Thomson, *U.S. Foreign Policy Towards Apartheid*, 11.
[56] Massie, *Loosing the Bonds*, 408.   [57] Ibid., 524–527.
[58] Solarz, *Journeys to War & Peace*, 82. Solarz had become convinced of the widespread support for the Sullivan Principles among South African blacks on a visit to South Africa in July 1980. Transcript of Press Conference in South Africa, July 11, 1980, Box 1353, Stephen Solarz Papers, Robert D. Farber, University Archives and Special Collections, Brandeis University.
[59] Memo, Allen J. Lenz to Ronald K. Peterson, June 30, 1981, ID #031500, CO141, WHORM: Subject File, RPL.

1980s, as a strong critic of the administration's foreign policy.[60] Other opponents of apartheid, however, believed that applying the Sullivan Principles was insufficient. The goal should not be to force American companies in South Africa to adopt ethical practices but rather to make these companies withdraw from the country altogether. Members of Congress, such as Dellums, argued that American companies could not end apartheid by employing South African blacks, and in order to put effective pressure on the South African government, American companies had to leave.[61] The exiled South African executive director of the ACOA, Jennifer Davis, echoed this criticism in a May 1983 article titled "Face It: The Sullivan Principles Haven't Worked."[62]

Increasingly, anti-apartheid advocates called for divestment from South Africa, urging various forms of American economic withdrawal from South Africa. Proponents of divestment advocated the withdrawal of American companies, the termination of investment in companies failing to live up to the Sullivan Principles and the divestment of American assets in South Africa. The goal was to undermine the South African economy by draining the country of foreign investment. While the Reagan administration was supportive of the Sullivan Principles as a voluntary measure, it outright rejected divestment. Both the moderates and the hardliners argued that divestment was counterproductive to US objectives. Even as pressure for sanctions was building in 1985, Shultz, as the leading representative of the moderate wing, continued to oppose divestment, with the argument that American companies were major forces of positive change in South Africa and tht divestment would hurt such influence.[63] Reagan's representative to the UN Human Rights Commission, Alan Keyes, delivered the same message before the UN. Keyes, himself an African American, declared that while the United States abhorred apartheid and its denial of "fundamental human rights to South Africa's black population," it did not support disengagement from South Africa.[64]

With the Reagan administration firmly opposed to divestment and insufficient support for the issue in Congress, activists in the early

---

[60] Lindsay, *Congress and the Politics*, 41; Carter and Scott, *Choosing to Lead*, 123. Carter and Scott emphasize Solarz as a successful foreign policy entrepreneur.

[61] Dellums and Halterman, *Lying Down*, 124.

[62] Jennifer Davis, "Face It: The Sullivan Principles Haven't Worked," American Committee on Africa, May 21, 1983, African Action Archive.

[63] George P. Shultz, "Toward an American Consensus on Southern Africa," Address before the National Press Club, April 16, 1985, SA01794, South Africa: The Making of U.S. Policy, 1962–1989, Digital National Security Archive.

[64] Alan Keyes, "We Will Not Abandon the People of South Africa...," Statement before the UN Human Rights Commission, Geneva, February 15, 1984, SA01576, South Africa: The Making of U.S. Policy, 1962–1989, Digital National Security Archive.

1980s intensified their lobbying of state legislators and city officials. A strategy pursued by activists since the 1970s but without much success. In June 1982, after years of lobbying by the Connecticut Anti-Apartheid Committee, Connecticut became the first state to pass a law that divested state pension funds from all companies that did not score well under the Sullivan Principles. The law attracted nationwide attention and by the end of 1982, Michigan, Massachusetts, and the cities of Philadelphia, Wilmington, and Grand Rapids had followed suit.[65] National anti-apartheid groups such as the ACOA traveled from state to state to testify in favor of divestment before state legislators and to lend their support to local divestment groups.[66] Their efforts paid off. During the 1980s, a total of twenty-three states and eighty cities across the United States used economic measures to protest apartheid.[67] Nevertheless, state-level divestment and economic sanctions were not satisfactory substitutes for national sanctions, and by the early 1980s, the combined effect of state-level sanctions remained limited. Therefore, congressional sanctions on the federal level were still the primary objective for most of the anti-apartheid movement.

Having been almost alone in its support for economic sanctions during the 97th Congress (1981–1982), the CBC found the 98th Congress (1983–1984) more amendable to its views. As violence increased in South Africa and the repressiveness of the regime became increasingly undeniable, apartheid gained greater salience in the American political debate. In September 1983, South Africa adopted a new constitution. Prime Minister Botha presented it as democratic reform, but rather than being celebrated as such, the new constitution sparked lengthy and vigorous protest. The new constitution created racially segregated parliaments for Coloreds and Indians and promised to improve the standard of living for blacks. Through such a move, Botha hoped to counter domestic and international criticism of apartheid and strengthen his position of power. The new constitution also terminated the post of prime minister and allowed Botha to continue his reign in the capacity of state president.[68] Botha, however, did not get the reaction he had hoped. Black South Africans took to the streets in large numbers to express their frustration over the constitution's failure to give them political rights. The South African government responded quickly and without mercy, with the greatest crackdown ever seen in

---

[65] Massie, *Loosing the Bonds*, 535.
[66] American Committee on Africa, "ACOA Action News," Spring 1982, No. 12, Box 21, Folder 'Disinvestment Bills,' WHG.
[67] Smith, *Foreign Attachments*, 80.   [68] Massie, *Loosing the Bonds*, 550.

South Africa.[69] Extensive media coverage of the brutal government repression, including television images of horrendous violence against protesters, fueled outrage in the United States and made the American public increasingly uncomfortable with US support for the regime. Consequently, debate over constructive engagement intensified and calls for sanctions grew louder.[70]

Despite the growing support for sanctions among the public and members of Congress, the Republican-controlled Senate continued to support Reagan's constructive engagement. Conservative senators such as Helms and Malcolm Wallop (R-WY), especially, fervently opposed any punitive measures against South Africa. As a result, few bills critical of South Africa made it through both chambers of Congress. One of the few exceptions occurred on November 18, 1983, when Congress passed a CBC-sponsored amendment prohibiting US support for IMF loans to South Africa like the one the Reagan administration had voted in favor of a year before. Testifying before the Subcommittee on International Trade, Investment, and Monetary Policy in the House, CBC chairman Julian Dixon (D-CA) argued that South Africa deserved to be singled out for US disapproval over its human rights violations against its black population.[71] At the end of the year, the CBC hailed the passage of the amendment as "a major victory for the CBC's efforts to restrain United States economic support of South Africa."[72]

On October 28, 1983, the House had passed another CBC-sponsored amendment introduced by Gray that banned all new investment in South Africa by American companies or individuals.[73] The bill passed with the support of several prominent Democrats, including former presidential candidate George McGovern, and Reverend Jesse Jackson, who all wrote Gray to notify him of their support and offer

---

[69] Baker, "The United States and South Africa," 102.

[70] Richard Goldstone, "Ambiguity and America: South Africa and US Foreign Policy," *Social Research* 72, no. 4 (2005): 817; Baker, "The United States and South Africa," 104–105; Pauline Baker, "Getting It Right. U.S. Policy in South Africa," in *Implementing U.S. Human Rights Policy: Agendas, Policies, and Practices*, ed. Debra Liang-Fenton (Washington, DC: Institute of Peace, 2004), 97.

[71] US Congress, House, Committee on Banking, Finance, and Urban Affairs, *To Increase the U.S. Quota in the International Monetary Fund and Related Matters: Hearings before the Subcommittee on International Trade, Investment, and Monetary Policy of the Committee on Banking, Finance, and Urban Affairs*, 98th Congress, 1st Session, April 7, 26–28, and May 3, 1983, 637–638.

[72] CBC, "1983 Legislative Achievements," Box 67, Folder 'Other CBC Special Projects,' WHG.

[73] Warren Brown, "Export Bill Approved by House: Riders Bars S. Africa Investment," *The Washington Post*, October 28, 1983, Box 17, Folder 'South Africa Investments,' WHG.

their assistance.[74] From the streets of Washington, DC, the Gray Amendment received the support of half a million people brought together by the New Coalition for Conscience on the twentieth anniversary of the 1963 civil rights movement's "March on Washington." Although the march focused overwhelmingly on domestic issues, the New Coalition for Conscience included the Gray Amendment on a list of legislation it supported in the spirit of helping to bring Martin Luther King Jr.'s dream to life.[75] Nevertheless, despite the support of national figures and half a million demonstrators, the Gray Amendment suffered the same faith as most congressional legislation on South Africa that year: after it had passed the House, it was defeated in the Republican-controlled Senate.

The same month, the House also passed a proposal by Solarz that would prohibit the importation of the South African gold coins, Krugerrands, or any other South African gold into the United States, as well as ban most bank loans to South Africa.[76] At the time, Americans had bought Krugerrands worth $600 million.[77] To Solarz, human rights concerns were front and center of his desire to restrict economic ties with South Africa. In a letter to the *New York Post* in June 1983, responding to criticism from the conservative commentator Pat Buchanan, Solarz argued, "While it is true we have not acted against human rights violators everywhere, that fact hardly countenances our policy of acting against human rights abuses nowhere. If we believe human rights to be important considerations in our foreign policy, it would seem to be particularly inappropriate to carry on business as usual with the apartheid regime."[78] Solarz's bill received the support of six Democratic presidential candidates, including Walter Mondale, who would go on to win the Democratic nomination.[79] Yet, just as with the Gray Amendment, the Solarz Amendment failed to make it through the Senate. According to Senator Robert Byrd (D-WV), Senate Republicans turned down the proposal at

---

[74] Letters, September 26 & 28, 1983, Series II, Box LEG-151, Folder '1, Foreign Policy: South Africa 1983–1986,' PRP.

[75] CBC, "Dear Colleague," September 29, 1983, Box 17, Folder 'CDI,' WHG.

[76] Warren Brown, "Export Bill Approved by House: Riders Bars S. Africa Investment," *The Washington Post,* October 28, 1983, Box 17, Folder 'South Africa Investments,' WHG.

[77] US Congress, Committee on Foreign Affairs, *Congress and Foreign Policy – 1985–1986,* 16.

[78] Letter, Stephen Solarz to *The New York Post,* June 16, 1983, Box 1080, Stephen Solarz Papers, Robert D. Farber University Archives and Special Collections, Brandeis University.

[79] Letter, Walter Mondale to Stephen Solarz, September 26, 1983, Box 1353, Stephen Solarz Papers, Robert D. Farber University Archives and Special Collections, Brandeis University.

the request of the White House.[80] Sanctions against apartheid remained a highly partisan matter, as a consensus was building among Democrats for some form of a legislative measure while Republicans continued to stand by the administration.

As the 98th Congress reconvened for its second session in 1984, sanctions against South Africa dominated the debates over the extension of the Export Administration Act of 1984. Gray pushed hard for a new version of his amendment to ban all new investment in South Africa, which had died in the Senate the year before. The amendment made it into a conference committee between the House and the Senate, but there it met staunch opposition from Republican senators. Ultimately, the conference committee accepted a compromise proposed by Solarz and Senator Henry Heinz (R-PA), which prohibited new bank loans to the South African government and required American companies to submit reports on their compliance with the Sullivan Principles to the secretary of state. The compromise was much weaker than Gray's original amendment, and Gray complained that it only achieved 10 percent of the sanctions in the House version.[81] TransAfrica declared itself shocked over the dilution of the Gray Amendment, noting that the bank loan prohibition was purely symbolic, as the South African government could circumvent it by going through private banks.[82]

The CBC and other congressional opponents of apartheid also adopted informal strategies to influence US policy toward South Africa in collaboration with the wider anti-apartheid movement. These strategies included several efforts to raise awareness of the horrors of apartheid in order to increase pressure on the Reagan administration. The collaboration between the CBC and TransAfrica proved particularly influential, as the two groups coordinated activities and shared information.[83] In May 1981, for instance, TransAfrica provided the CBC with the leaked State Department documents mentioned earlier.[84] In the summer of 1983, the CBC joined a nationwide cultural boycott of South

[80] US Congress, Committee on Foreign Affairs, *Congress and Foreign Policy – 1984*, Committee Print (Washington, DC: US Government Printing Office, 1985), 123.

[81] "Conferees Accept Heinz-Solarz Language on South Africa Sanctions," October 2, 1984, Box 17, Folder 'CDI,' WHG.

[82] Randall Robinson to Conferees, Letter, October 3, 1984, Box 24, Folder 'Foreign Affairs South Africa TransAfrica,' WHG.

[83] TransAfrica also actively opposed the Reagan administration's policy in Nicaragua. TransAfrica Issue Brief, "Washington's War with Nicaragua," October 1983, Box 31, Folder 19, TransAfrica Collection, Manuscript Division, Moorland-Spingarn Research Center, Howard University.

[84] Memorandum from Gray to CBC, June 3, 1981, Box 68, Folder 'CBC Meeting June 3, 1981,' WHG.

Africa launched by TransAfrica and Artists and Athletes against Apartheid. The boycott aimed at getting artists and athletes to refuse to perform in South Africa until the country abolished apartheid as a way to increase the international isolation of the regime.[85] It thus entered into a tradition of cultural boycotts of South Africa that has been occurring sporadically since the 1940s and would gain international prominence with the 1985 campaign by musicians against performing at the South African casino Sun City.[86] In 1984, TransAfrica joined CBC members Gray, Fauntroy, Dixon, Parren Mitchell (D-MD), and Charles Rangel (D-NY) in a coordinated lobbying effort in favor of the Gray Amendment to the Export Administration Act of 1984, mentioned above.[87] An important factor for the close-knit relationship was the personal relationship between CBC members and TransAfrica's long-serving executive director, activist lawyer Randall Robinson, who was a former staffer for both Diggs and William Clay (D-MO).[88] The combined efforts of TransAfrica and the CBC helped to emphasize a bond between the suffering of African Americans and black South Africans, encouraging a new form of Pan-Africanism.[89]

Although the predominant focus of congressional human rights activism on apartheid was on changing US–South Africa policy through legislation, members of Congress also advocated directly on behalf of individual South Africans. As with the advocacy for Soviet Jewry, members of Congress passed resolutions and wrote letters to the South African government, urging the release of political prisoners, such as ANC leader Nelson Mandela, and the respect for the human rights of black South Africans.[90] In September 1984, for instance, congressional

---

[85] Julian C. Dixon to CBC, "Re: Endorsement of Nationwide Boycott of South Africa," June 30, 1983, Box 67, Folder 'Other CBC Special Projects,' WHG.

[86] Mahmood Monshipouri, *Information Politics, Protests, and Human Rights in the Digital Age* (New York: Cambridge University Press, 2016), 112. The most notable exception to this boycott was American artist Paul Simon's controversial decision to record part of his 1986 *Graceland* album with black musicians in South Africa. For more on Sun City and *Graceland*, see Hostetter, 95–111.

[87] TransAfrica News Release, July 24, 1984, Box 17, Folder 'CBI,' WHG.

[88] Nesbitt, *Race for Sanctions*, 104. For Robinson's account, see his memoirs, Randall Robinson, *Defending the Spirit: A Black Life in America* (New York: Dutton, 1998).

[89] Hostetter, *Movement Matters*, 65–67.

[90] George W. Crockett, "Dear Colleague," February 8, 1984, Box 105, Folder 21, TLP. Walter E. Fauntroy, news release, September 23, 1985, Box 97, Folder 51, Walter E. Fauntroy Papers, Special Collections Research Center, Gelman Library, The George Washington University, Washington, DC (hereafter WFP); Dante Fascell, "Dear Colleague," August 15, 1986, Series II, Box LEG-151, Folder '1 Foreign Policy: South Africa 1983–1986,' PRP; Ronald V. Dellums, "Dear Colleague," August 25, 1988, Box 22, Folder 36, Ronald V. Dellums Congressional Papers, African American Museum & Library at Oakland, Oakland Public Library.

human rights activists intervened on behalf of six black South Africans, known as the Sharpeville Six, who has been sentenced to death for the alleged murder of the deputy mayor of the township Sharpeville. The case led to widespread international condemnation of South Africa, including two resolutions by the UN Security Council. The CHRC, which otherwise played a limited role with South Africa, became strongly involved in advocating clemency for the convicted. The CHRC spearheaded a lobbying campaign that included letters to Botha and world leaders such as British Prime Minister Margaret Thatcher.[91] The case ended with Botha commuting the sentences into prison sentences, which paved the way for the release of all six after the fall of apartheid. Another prominent case concerned the Reverend T. Simon Farisani. Arrested on several occasions, including in November 1986, Amnesty International considered Farisani a prisoner of conscience.[92] Several members of Congress became deeply involved in advocating for the release of Farisani, who had testified on the human rights situation in South Africa before the House Subcommittee on Human Rights in August 1984.[93] Members of Congress passed resolutions urging the release of Farisani and wrote directly to Botha, eventually securing his release in January 1987.[94] Finally, members of Congress functioned as intermediaries between American citizens opposed to apartheid and the Reagan administration. In July 1983, for instance, Gray sent Reagan a petition with four thousand signatures urging Reagan to end US support for apartheid, by the request of the Universal Negro Improvement Association.[95]

The Birth of the Free South Africa Movement

On November 6, 1984, following escalating unrest and violence in South Africa, Reagan won reelection in a landslide victory. The hardliners in

---

[91] Congressional Human Rights Caucus, Press Release, March 16, 1988, Box 110 Folder 4, TLP.

    John Conyers, "Dear Colleague," June 24, 1988, Box 110, Folder 4, TLP.

[92] Amnesty International USA, Press Release, December 10, 1986, Box 368, Folder 12; AIUSA.

[93] US Congress, House, Committee on Foreign Affairs, *The Human Rights Situation in South Africa, Zaire, the Horn of Africa, and Uganda: Hearings before the Subcommittee on Human Rights and International Organizations and the Subcommittee on Africa of the Committee on Foreign Affairs*, 98th Congress, 2nd Session, June 21, August 9, 1984.

[94] Letter, Ron Wyden to Pieter W. Botha, January 12, 1987, Box 368, Folder 12; AIUSA.

    Steve Gunderson, "Dear Colleague," January 21, 1987, Box 368, Folder 12; AIUSA.

[95] Letter, William H. Gray to Ronald Reagan, July 7, 1983, ID #154309, CO141, WHORM: Subject File, RPL.

the administration interpreted the result as a broad mandate for a bold foreign policy and called for an even more supportive policy toward Pretoria. According to a South African newspaper, the regime in Pretoria was "plainly delighted" with the result.[96] While Pretoria was delighted about Reagan's reelection, the anti-apartheid movement in the United States was dismayed. Randall Robinson felt that the situation called for radical action. On November 21, he visited the South African embassy in Washington, DC, with Fauntroy, member of the US Civil Rights Commission Mary Frances Berry, and noted civil rights activist and law professor Eleanor H. Norton. Here, they presented the South African ambassador with a demand for the release of detained leaders from a South African anti-apartheid group and, in the spirit of the civil rights sit-ins, refused to leave before their demands were met. As a result, the ambassador called the police to have them removed. Robinson, Fauntroy, and Berry refused and consequently spent the night in jail.[97] After his release, Fauntroy described the demonstration as an act of "moral witness."[98] The arrests of such esteemed protesters generated widespread national attention.[99] However, the incident was just the beginning of members of Congress and anti-apartheid activists employing the tactics of the civil rights movement to their foreign policy entrepreneurship on apartheid.

A few days later, Robinson, Fauntroy, and Berry announced the launch of a new campaign aimed at ending apartheid, which they called the Free South Africa Movement (FSAM).[100] In the subsequent days, more arrests followed as people flocked to the embassy to protest. "Everybody wants to get arrested," Fauntroy told the press.[101] A former leader in the civil rights movement, Fauntroy was no stranger to civil disobedience and organized protest. Other members of Congress among the first arrestees included Fauntroy's fellow CBC members Dellums, Conyers, and Charles Hayes (D-IL). Dellums recalled that when Fauntroy called to ask him to participate his response was, "It's a good

---

[96] "Disinvestment Is Still a Threat to SA's Euphoria over Reagan," *Cape Times*, November 10, 1984.

[97] Kenneth Bredemeier and Michel Marriott, "Fauntroy Arrested in Embassy; Delegate, 2 Others Protest S. African Acts," *The Washington Post*, November 22, 1984, Nexis Uni. Norton was not arrested, as she had stepped out to address the media at the time of the arrest. For a description of the sit-in at the embassy, see Hostetter, 65–66.

[98] Quoted in Massie, *Loosing the Bonds*, 559.

[99] Bredemeier and Marriott, "Fauntroy Arrested in Embassy."

[100] Courtland Milloy, "Blacks Form 'Free S. Africa Movement'," *The Washington Post*, November 24, 1984, Nexis Uni.

[101] Michel Marriott and Karlyn Barker, "1960s Tactics Revived for Embassy Sit-Ins," *The Washington Post*, November 29, 1984, Nexis Uni.

day to go to jail. Where do you want me to be and what time?"[102] So many people signed up for the protests that FSAM had to limit the number of protesters to be arrested to three per day, while several others protested outside the embassy. In organizing FSAM and recruiting volunteers to be arrested, Fauntroy relied on the same network that had been used to mobilize the New Coalition for Conscience's "March on Washington" in 1983.[103] FSAM also orchestrated satellite demonstrations in front of South African consulates in other American cities. By July 1985, some 2,900 people had been arrested in front of the South African embassy, including 21 representatives and 2 senator, and 4,000 had been arrested elsewhere in the country in similar protests.[104]

FSAM provided new visibility to American opposition to apartheid and linked anti-apartheid sentiments to economic sanctions.[105] The range and status of demonstrators and arrestees helped expand people's knowledge of the anti-apartheid movement and legitimize civil disobedience as an acceptable form of protest. Apart from members of Congress, protesters comprised of union leaders, college students, musicians, professors, mayors, movie stars, and religious leaders. Among the most notable ones were musicians Stevie Wonder and Harry Belafonte, former presidential candidate Jesse Jackson, Jimmy Carter's daughter Amy, Martin Luther King's children and widow Coretta Scott King, prominent civil rights activists such as Rosa Parks, and several young members of the Kennedy family.[106] The participation of such well-known figures secured FSAM extensive media coverage and added renewed vigor and attention to the struggle against apartheid. Equally important, FSAM unified activists and legislators behind the cause to impose economic sanctions, with TransAfrica and CBC providing the crucial link.

Due in large part to the impact of FSAM, shortly after the 1984 election, the Reagan administration faced the toughest pressure for sanctions to date. In a memo to Solarz in November 1984, one of his staffers summarized the impact of the FSAM demonstrations: "Seriously, the anger expressed by these demonstrations at South Africa indicates to me that we may be entering another era on this issue. The

---

[102] Dellums and Halterman, *Lying Down*, 128.
[103] Walter E. Fauntroy, "Dear Supporter," November 29, 1984, Box 388, Folder 42, WFP.
[104] US Congress, Committee on Foreign Affairs, *Congress and Foreign Policy – 1985–1986*, 15. In June 1985, a group of rabbis staged a similar protest in front of the Soviet Jewish embassy. Letter, Members of Congress to Edwin Meese III, June 11, 1985, I-410, I-410A; 42; 44, UCSJR.
[105] Hostetter, *Movement Matters*, 83.   [106] Massie, *Loosing the Bonds*, 560.

Black Caucus and TransAfrica were out in front and militant."[107] By late 1984, more members of Congress began to call for stronger measures against apartheid as South African repression escalated and protests continued.[108] Dellums recalls how quickly the climate in Washington changed and how suddenly colleagues from both parties and of all races would "scramble to get arrested in front of the South African embassy and introduce sanctions bills."[109] The activism of FSAM and the rest of the anti-apartheid movement heightened pressure on congressional Democrats to demonstrate their opposition to apartheid.[110] It now appeared to be good politics to support anti-apartheid policy. Moreover, growing dissatisfaction with Reagan's foreign policy in general, most notably his support for the Nicaraguan Contras and rightwing dictators in Central America, made Democrats increasingly antagonistic toward the administration. Consequently, leading liberal Democrats, such as Edward Kennedy (D-MA) became more active in opposing apartheid from late 1984. Testifying before the Senate Foreign Relations Committee on September 26, 1984, in one of several hearings on the human rights situation in South Africa, Kennedy lamented the repressive violence in South Africa, noting, "More than sixty deaths have already resulted from the recent violence, and hundreds more have been injured."[111] In January 1985, Kennedy visited South Africa, conducting his own diplomacy and drawing increased media attention to apartheid. Upon his return, he declared himself firmly committed to ending constructive engagement.[112]

Moderate Republicans, who had previously supported constructive engagement, began to feel the need to position themselves against apartheid. In December 1984, senators Richard Lugar (R-IN) and Nancy Kassebaum (R-KS) sent a public letter to Reagan that argued that constructive engagement had failed and called for a stronger policy against apartheid.[113] This change was particularly important because

---

[107] Memo, Staffer to Stephen Solarz, November 1984, Box 1080, Stephen Solarz Papers, Robert D. Farber University Archives and Special Collections, Brandeis University.

[108] US Congress, Committee on Foreign Affairs, *Congress and Foreign Policy – 1985–1986*, 14, Klotz, *Norms in International Relations*, 100.

[109] Dellums quoted in Tillery, "Foreign Policy Activism," 100.   [110] Ibid., 100–101.

[111] US Congress, Senate, Committee on Foreign Relations, *U.S. Policy on South Africa: Hearing before the Subcommittee on African Affairs of the Committee on Foreign Relations*, 98th Congress, 2nd Session, September 26, 1984, 4.

[112] Adam Clymer, *Edward M. Kennedy: A Biography* (New York: Morrow, 1999), 353–365; Massie, *Loosing the Bonds*, 564. This was just one of several examples of congressional diplomacy on apartheid through interaction with foreign leaders.

[113] US Congress, Committee on Foreign Affairs, *Congress and Foreign Policy – 1985–1986*, 15.

Kassebaum chaired the Senate Subcommittee on Africa and Lugar would become the chair of the Senate Foreign Relations Committee in 1985. Even more conservative Republicans in the House, such as representatives Newt Gingrich (R-GA), Robert Walker (R-PA), and their fellow members of the Conservative Opportunity Society voiced opposition to apartheid. The day after Lugar and Kassebaum's public letter, Walker personally delivered a letter to the South African ambassador from thirty-five self-proclaimed conservative members of Congress. In the letter, they expressed concern about the South African government's willingness to move toward "real human rights reforms" and warned that they would recommend restrictions on investment and other economic sanctions "unless certain economic and civil rights guarantees for all persons are in place."[114] According to Walker, the group wanted "South Africa to understand that there is no significant political or philosophical base in this country supporting apartheid."[115] Walker further argued that while the national media had perceived the letter as a significant change in position for some conservatives, he believed, "many conservatives had been long abhorrent of the apartheid system, but simply had not spoken up loudly and clearly enough about it."[116] Public opposition to apartheid and support for racial equality and human rights in South Africa made a growing number of Republicans anxious to publicly express disapproval of apartheid.[117]

The increased public protest and the criticism from within the Republican Party prompted Reagan to appear more receptive to the criticism of apartheid. On December 7, 1984, the president hosted South African Bishop Desmond Tutu at the White House.[118] During the meeting, Tutu, who had received the Nobel Peace Prize two months earlier, scolded Reagan's South Africa policy and urged the president to impose economic sanctions. Reagan, in turn, rejected the criticism by arguing that his policy worked and had achieved "sizable progress" in encouraging

---

[114] Letter inserted in congressional hearing US Congress, House, Committee on Foreign Affairs, *The Anti-Apartheid Act of 1985 Hearings and Markup before the Subcommittees on International Economic Policy and Trade and on Africa of the Committee on Foreign Affairs*, 99th Congress, 1st Session, April 17, 18, 30, May 2, 1985, 157–158.

[115] Ibid., 154.   [116] Ibid.

[117] Klotz, *Norms in International Relations*, 104–105. As pointed out by Lindsay, congressional foreign policy activity is often reactive as members of Congress are sensitive to public opinion. Lindsay, *Congress and the Politics of U.S. Foreign Policy*, 48. Once an issue such as apartheid becomes salient among constituents, members of Congress have an incentive to address it.

[118] Memo, Robert C. McFarlane to Ronald Reagan, Dec. 6, 1984, Folder 'South Africa General 1985-87 1of14 (8853),' RAC Box 10, African Affairs Directorate, NSC: Records, RPL.

reform of apartheid.[119] In his diary, Reagan described Tutu as "naive" in his belief that sanctions would bring about change in South Africa.[120] Three days later, on International Human Rights Day (December 10), Reagan gave his strongest public criticism of the South African government to date, when he rebuked the practices of forced removals, detentions without trial, and lengthy imprisonments of black leaders. Characteristically for Reagan's rhetoric on South Africa, however, the three paragraphs devoted to South Africa did not include the term "human rights." He likewise refrained from condemning the South African government's use of violence and instead urged whites and blacks to engage in a constructive dialogue.[121]

The Tutu meeting and the International Human Rights Day remarks were some of several initiatives recommended by a State Department report to improve public perceptions of Reagan's South Africa policy.[122] The initiatives, however, did little to improve the growing perception that the administration's policy toward South Africa was failing to achieve its stated objectives. Tutu left the White House meeting with a feeling that Reagan was out of reach.[123] Botha responded to Reagan's new rhetorical criticism and the meeting with Tutu with an angry assertion that South Africa would not yield to external pressure.[124] On January 7, 1985, Reagan sent Botha a letter in which he reassured him that the new rhetoric did not reflect a change in policy. The administration still preferred quiet diplomacy and would continue to oppose economic sanctions, Reagan wrote. However, he cautioned that the current debates over apartheid in the United States reflected the genuine feelings of the American public and it was likely that Congress would pursue new sanctions. Therefore, Reagan urged Botha to moderate his actions and to demonstrate to the American people that he was a reformer by

---

[119] Ronald Reagan, Remarks and a Question-and-Answer Session with Reporters on Foreign and Domestic Issues, December 7, 1984. Online by Gerhard Peters and John T. Woolley, The American Presidency Project, accessed August 7, 2019, www.presidency.ucsb.edu/node/261178.

[120] Reagan and Brinkley, *The Reagan Diaries*, 285.

[121] Ronald Reagan, Remarks on Signing the International Human Rights Day Proclamation, December 10, 1984. Online by Gerhard Peters and John T. Woolley, The American Presidency Project, accessed August 7, 2019, www.presidency.ucsb.edu/node/261207.

[122] Memo, Phillip Ringdahl to Robert McFarlane, December 17, 1984, Folder 'South Africa Working Files #3(8) October 1984–June 86 (8828),' RAC Box 9, African Affairs Directorate, NSC: Records, RPL.

[123] Massie, *Loosing the Bonds*, 562.

[124] "South African Leader Denies U.S. Won Release of Jailed Dissidents," *The New York Times*, December 14, 1984, www.nytimes.com/1984/12/14/world/south-african-leader-denies-us-won-release-of-jailed-dissidents.html.

pursuing constructive domestic reforms.[125] In other words, Reagan asked his South African counterpart to give him some assistance to counter the rising domestic pressure.

The Anti-Apartheid Act of 1985 and Reagan's Executive Order

While Reagan was trying to mend relations with the South African government, the pressure for economic sanctions grew in Congress. By early 1985, a consensus had emerged among the vast majority of Democrats and many Republicans that Congress ought to change US policy toward South Africa by imposing some form of sanctions, and numerous bills were introduced to this effect.[126] Again, the increasingly influential CBC was leading the way. In the 99th Congress (1985–1987), the twenty members of the CBC wielded more formal institutional influence than ever before, with its members chairing no less than five standing committees, two select committees, and sixteen subcommittees.[127] In March, members of the CBC agreed to cosponsor legislation on South Africa introduced by a fellow CBC member to signal a unified front.[128]

The most prominent sanctions bill introduced in the House was the Anti-Apartheid Act of 1985. In March 1985, senators Kennedy and Lowell Weicker (R-CT) and representatives Gray, Wolpe, and Solarz introduced the bill simultaneously in the Senate and the House. The Anti-Apartheid Act had three major components: banning new bank loans to the South African government, banning all new investment by American companies in South Africa, and prohibiting the import of Krugerrands.[129] The bill was carefully crafted to appeal to Republicans in the Senate. To make it palatable to conservatives, who were skeptical of singling out South Africa, the bill also included sanctions against other countries based on their human rights violations, such as Cuba, Vietnam, and Romania. While the CBC understood the necessity of such a

---

[125] Letter, Ronald Reagan to Pieter Botha, January 7, 1985, Folder 'South Africa Working Files #3(10) October 1984–June 86 (9315),' RAC Box 9, African Affairs Directorate, NSC: Records, RPL.

[126] US Congress, Committee on Foreign Affairs, *Congress and Foreign Policy – 1985–1986*, 18.

[127] Nadine Cohodas, "Black House Members Striving for Influence," *Congressional Quarterly* 43, no. 15 (1985): 675. This increased influence was in part a result of CBC members accruing seniority aided by their continuous reelection through reasonably secure seats. See Singh, *The Congressional Black Caucus*, 130.

[128] Mickey Leland to CBC Members, March 25, 1985, Box 375, Folder 4, WFP.

[129] US Congress, Committee on Foreign Affairs, *Congress and Foreign Policy – 1985–1986*, 18.

strategy, it worried that it might shift the debate away from South Africa.[130] Lobbying his colleagues to support his bill, Gray called apartheid "abhorrent to anyone who believes in basic human rights and equality" and referred to the brutality of the South African government citing police killings of civilians.[131] At the same time, Gray made sure to present his bill as a limited, measured response to apartheid, pointing out that it would not end apartheid overnight but would simply "get us out of the business of financing it."[132] The proponents of sanctions were keenly aware of the need for Republican support.

In an attempt to signal distance from apartheid without passing as comprehensive sanctions as proposed by the Anti-Apartheid Act, some Republicans introduced milder sanction bills. In March 1985, Walker introduced a bill that would put sanctions on both South Africa and the Soviet Union at the same time. Walker's bill conditioned new investments in South Africa on adherence to the Sullivan Principles and at the same time introduced a wide range of human rights-related bans on countries in the Eastern Bloc. In a letter to his colleagues, Walker argued that his bill offered members of Congress a way to voice "moral repugnance" over apartheid without adopting the "meat-ax" approach to the issue that Democrats were advocating. Walker further declared that his bill would build upon and expand the Reagan administration's constructive engagement.[133] Representative Mark Siljander (R-MI) introduced another bill that would postpone sanctions for three years while a commission evaluated South African progress. House Republicans, however, were too divided over apartheid for Walker's or Siljander's proposals to find sufficient support to challenge the Anti-Apartheid Act. Some preferred comprehensive sanctions while others sided with Reagan and opposed sanctions altogether. Undoubtedly, public opinion, which was now passionately and overwhelmingly critical of apartheid, contributed to a growing willingness among Republicans to go on record against apartheid.[134] Anti-apartheid demonstrations surged across college

---

[130] Mickey Leland to CBC Members, Memo, February 22, 1985, Box 375, Folder 4, WFP.

[131] Letter, William H. Gray to Silvio O. Conte, March 6, 1985, Box 66, Silvio O. Conte Papers (MS 371). Special Collections and University Archives, W. E. B. Du Bois Library, University of Massachusetts Amherst. William H. Gray, Dear Colleague, March 21, 1985, Box 66, Silvio O. Conte Papers (MS 371). Special Collections and University Archives, W. E. B. Du Bois Library, University of Massachusetts Amherst.

[132] News Release, "News from Congressman Bill Gray," June 5, 1985, Box 17, Folder 'Press Releases,' WHG.

[133] Robert Walker, "Dear Colleague," March 8, 1985, Box 17, Folder 'CDI,' WHG.

[134] For public opinion, see Cambridge Reports/Research International. Cambridge Reports National Omnibus Survey, January 1985. USCAMREP.85JAN.R151.

campuses, and groups such as FSAM lobbied heavily for the passage of the Anti-Apartheid Act.[135] Faced with the option of doing nothing or voting for the Anti-Apartheid Act, fifty-six Republicans chose to do the latter and voted with their Democratic counterparts to pass the bill on June 5, 1985.[136] The House had passed a law that would fundamentally alter US policy toward South Africa if it could find its way through the Senate.[137]

During 1985, Senate Republicans began introducing legislation of their own, but these proposals tended to be less substantial than the ones introduced in the House. Most Senate Republicans wanted to send a signal to Pretoria, but they did not want to pass sanctions that would hurt American companies or the South African economy too much.[138] Proponents of this approach argued, in agreement with the administration, that sanctions would hurt South African blacks and would not have the desired effect on the South African government's willingness to reform.[139] Eventually, however, moderate Republican senators introduce bills of a more substantial nature. Ultimately, a bill introduced in April by Senate Majority Leader Robert Dole (R-KS), Senate Foreign Relations Committee chair Lugar, and Charles Mathias (R-MD) combined many of the previous proposals. The bill called for economic sanctions unless the South African government made "significant progress" by March 1, 1987. Moreover, it requested that all US corporations subscribe to the Sullivan Principles, and offered a scholarship fund for black education.[140] In his memoirs, Crocker argues that Lugar and others began to moderate their views in favor of sanctions, amid

---

Cornell University, Ithaca, NY: Roper Center for Public Opinion Research, iPOLL, accessed August 6, 2019. Asked in January 1985: Do you think the United States should continue to do business with South Africa or not? Only 33 percent answered "Yes," while 42 percent said "No," and 25 percent were "Not sure." In the following months leading up to the vote on Gray's bill in June, the public attention to apartheid only intensified.

[135] "Free South Africa Movement: Anti-Apartheid Act of 1985," May 14, 1985, Box 17, Folder 10, Ronald V. Dellums Congressional Papers, African American Museum & Library at Oakland, Oakland Public Library.

[136] US Congress, Committee on Foreign Affairs, *Congress and Foreign Policy – 1985–1986*, 19.

[137] At the same occasion, the House rejected an even stronger bill introduced by Dellums. Dellums and Halterman, *Lying Down*, 130.

[138] US Congress, Committee on Foreign Affairs, *Congress and Foreign Policy – 1985–1986*, 19.

[139] 131 *Congressional Record*, 99th Congress, 1st Session, 18831 (July 11, 1985). "Sanctions Will Not Help: Excerpts from a March 29 Interview with Assistant Secretary of State Chester A. Crocker," *Africa News*, April 8, 1985.

[140] S995 – Anti-Apartheid Action Act of 1985, accessed August 6, 2019, www.congress.gov/bill/99th-congress/senate-bill/995.

"a confused rush for cover among legislators of both parties."[141] When the Senate Foreign Relations Committee considered the bill in June, it voted to add additional provisions, most notably a ban on new bank loans, sales of nuclear technology and restrictions on the sale of computer technology.[142] On July 11, 1985, the Senate comfortably passed the bill with an 80–12 vote.

Human rights were front and center of the debates over the sanctions bills in both the House and the Senate. Rising in support of the Anti-Apartheid Act during a hearing in the House Subcommittee on Africa in April 1985, CBC member Hayes argued that the bill would "stop the split tongue approach to civil and human rights" where the United States would speak out on Central America but not on South Africa.[143] Another member of the CBC, George W. Crockett (D-MI) issued a press release stating that the South African government "has failed to move in any meaningful way to redress the human rights abuses it has visited upon its Black population."[144] In a press release in May, Dellums roared against "the single most important human rights issue of our time, the unspeakable evil system of apartheid," before blaming constructive engagement for contributing to hold the apartment system together and concluding, "I can think of nothing more urgent than this ultimate human rights issue."[145] During the Senate's consideration of sanctions in July, conservative Republican Steven Symms (R-ID) criticized the "enlightened beltway liberals" for their persistent concern with "human rights and the apartheid policy in South Africa."[146] One of those who might have fallen under Symms's term "enlightened beltway liberals" was Gary Hart (D-CO), who motivated his vote for sanctions by declaring, "There can be no question that the evils of apartheid encompass the most serious human rights abuses known today."[147]

By the end of July 1985, the conferees of the House and Senate had agreed to a joint version of the Anti-Apartheid Act. The bipartisan

---

[141] Crocker, *High Noon*, 264.
[142] US Congress, Committee on Foreign Affairs, *Congress and Foreign Policy – 1985–1986*, 20.
[143] US Congress, House, Committee on Foreign Affairs, *The Anti-Apartheid Act of 1985 Hearings and Markup*, 40.
[144] George W. Crockett News, April 1985, Box 57, Folder 'South Africa General,' George W. Crockett Papers, Manuscript Division, Moorland-Spingarn Research Center, Howard University.
[145] Ronald Dellums, press release, May 17, 1985, Box 18, Ronald V. Dellums Congressional Papers, African American Museum & Library at Oakland, Oakland Public Library.
[146] 131 *Congressional Record*, 99th Congress, 1st Session, 18326 (July 10, 1985).
[147] 131 *Congressional Record*, 99th Congress, 1st Session, 18778 (July 11, 1985).

support for the bill and the framing of apartheid as a human rights issue was aptly summarized by Gingrich, who proclaimed, "Today we stand with the Black Caucus on behalf of human rights in South Africa."[148] All that remained for the bill to arrive on the president's table to be signed into law was a final vote in both chambers on the conference version. Conservative senators Helms and Wallop, however, threatened a filibuster that would have delayed the Senate's recess.[149] To avoid a filibuster, Dole rescheduled the vote for when Congress reconvened in September. The postponement of the final vote on the Anti-Apartheid Act gave the Reagan administration a month to come up with a strategy to prevent the bill's passage. Assuming the House was a lost cause, the Reagan administration focused its efforts on the Senate, investing substantial time and energy in lobbying senators to vote against the bill and by seeking to influence public opinion.[150]

These efforts of the Reagan administration were significantly complicated on July 20, when P. W. Botha declared a state of emergency in some districts in South Africa, which quickly resulted in hundreds of detentions. The state of emergency destroyed the illusion that constructive engagement was working and made it difficult to persuade senators to reject a sanctions bill. Solarz called the state of emergency "the final nail in the coffin of the policy of constructive engagement."[151] Fauntroy, Robinson, Berry, and other FSAM leaders returned to the South African embassy to protest, getting arrested once again.[152] Yet, Reagan himself remained convinced that sanctions were not the answer to end apartheid and would hurt rather than help South African blacks.[153]

On August 15, 1985, as the administration was hard at work lobbying key Senate votes, Botha delivered a speech that all but cemented the vote in favor of sanctions. Before an international audience of 200 million, Botha delivered a highly anticipated address on the situation in South

---

[148] 131 *Congressional Record*, 99th Congress, 1st Session, 22521 (August 1, 1985).

[149] A filibuster is a procedure that allows a Senator to block or delay a vote on a bill, amendment, or resolution by giving a prolonged talk on the Senate floor during which the Senator does not have to cede the floor.

[150] Memo, "Southern Africa: Diplomatic, Legislative and Public Diplomacy Strategy," July 29, 1985, Folder 'South Africa Working Files #3(4) October 1984–June 86,' RAC Box 9, African Affairs Directorate, NSC: Records, RPL.

Congressional Quarterly, "Reagan Averts a Confrontation on South Africa," September 14, 1985, Series II, Box LEG-151, Folder 1, 'Foreign Policy: South Africa 1983–1986,' PRP.

[151] Sara Fritz, "Reagan Prepares to Review Policy toward Pretoria," *Los Angeles Times*, July 25, 1985, www.latimes.com/archives/la-xpm-1985-07-25-mn-5857-story.html.

[152] Walter E. Fauntroy news release, July 23, 1985, Box 97, Folder 32, WFP.

[153] "Friday, July 26, 1985," Ronald Reagan and Douglas Brinkley, *The Reagan Diaries*, 345.

Africa that irrevocably destroyed the illusions of progress. The international community was expecting reforms and the possible release of Mandela; instead, it was presented with a raging Botha who declared his determination to uphold apartheid.[154] Throughout the spring of 1985, the administration, led by Crocker, had sought to persuade Pretoria that it needed to deliver reform and human rights improvements to prevent the imposition of sanctions. In a meeting with the Reagan administration in Vienna in April, South African foreign minister Pik Botha had reassured that reforms were underway.[155] However, P. W. Botha's speech on August 15 made it hard for anyone but the most optimistic of optimists to believe in South African reforms.

The American and international reaction to Botha's speech was overwhelmingly negative. Combined with the state of emergency, the speech led even more people to conclude that Botha was unwilling to reform. As the South African government's bank loans began to dry up, and multinational companies pulled out, a growing number of Democrats and Republicans alike called for action.[156] Botha's speech even became too much for members of the Reagan administration, with Crocker recalling how he, Shultz, and McFarlane were deeply disturbed by the speech.[157] McFarlane, who had previously been strongly opposed to sanctions, recalled how the speech turned him around to favor sanctions.[158] Yet, Reagan himself stood by Botha, and gave a radio interview where he maintained that the South African government was reformist. He went as far as to declare that all racial segregation in South Africa had already ended and blaming the Soviet Union for spurring unrest in the country.[159] Realizing the political damage of such statements, the White House immediately sought to retract the president's statements and some weeks later Reagan even personally apologized for the remarks.[160]

In light of this situation, Reagan decided that the only way to prevent congressionally imposed sanctions was to issue an executive order, which

---

[154] Pieter W. Botha, "Address by State President P. W. Botha at the Opening of the National Party Natal Congress Durban, South Africa, August 15, 1985," accessed August 6, 2019, https://omalley.nelsonmandela.org/omalley/index.php/site/q/03lv01538/04lv01600/05lv01638/06lv01639.htm.

[155] Massie, *Loosing the Bonds*, 585.

[156] Baker, "The United States and South Africa," 105.   [157] Crocker, *High Noon*, 276.

[158] Massie, *Loosing the Bonds*, 587.

[159] "Reagan Portrays Pretoria's Rulers as Seeking Change," *The New York Times*, August 27, 1985, Nexis Uni.

[160] Bernard Weinraub, "Reagan Apologizes for Asserting That Pretoria Segregation Is Over," *The New York Times*, September 7, 1985, www.nytimes.com/1985/09/07/world/reagan-apologizes-for-asserting-that-pretoria-segregation-is-over.html.

enacted most of the sanctions while retaining presidential control over US policy toward South Africa. On September 9, 1985, only five hours before Congress was scheduled to vote, Reagan signed an executive order that imposed limited sanctions on South Africa. The executive order among other things banned bank loans to the South African government, banned the export of nuclear technology, banned sales of computers and high technology, encouraged US companies to comply with the Sullivan Principles, and increased funding for US human rights programs in South Africa. Announcing his executive order, Reagan declared that he would veto the pending sanctions bill if put on his desk, as he believed it would hurt the black South Africans the United States was trying to help.[161] During a subsequent press conference, Reagan rejected labeling his executive order as an economic sanction and argued that the administration's policy had only changed to an "active" constructive engagement.[162] The Reagan administration was anxious to show that the executive order was not a break with constructive engagement. Nevertheless, regardless of what Reagan called his executive order, it was, in essence, a milder version of the economic sanctions agreed to by the House and the Senate shortly before.

The executive order by no means reflected a change of heart by the Reagan administration. It was an adaption to a changed political reality. Internal memos from the administration reveal that the executive order was part of a strategy to avoid a situation whereby the president would risk having a veto overridden by the Senate.[163] An executive order, officials argued, was advantageous over congressionally imposed sanctions, for several reasons. First, in terms of content, it would allow the administration to exclude the most severe sanctions in the congressional bill. Second, on a tactical level, the president could revoke it without congressional approval. Finally, it offered a way to maintain executive control over US–South Africa policy.[164] The administration constructed

---

[161] Ronald Reagan, "Remarks of the President on Signing Executive Order Regarding South Africa," September 9, 1985, SA01894, South Africa: The Making of U.S. Policy, 1962–1989, Digital National Security Archive.

[162] George P. Shultz, "Presidential Actions Regarding South Africa," Press Conference, September 9, 1985, SA01891, South Africa: The Making of U.S. Policy, 1962–1989, Digital National Security Archive.

[163] Memo, Patrick Buchanan to Robert C. McFarlane, August 20, 1985, ID# 275835, CO141 WHORM: Subject File, RPL.

[164] Memo, Phillip Ringdahl to Robert C. McFarlane, August 27, 1985, Folder "South Africa Working Files #3 October 1984–June 86(2)," RAC Box 9, African Affairs Directorate, NSC: Records, RPL; Crocker, *High Noon*, 261. According to Crocker, "The fundamental issue underlying the debate was a struggle over control of U.S. policy toward South Africa."

the executive order in close dialogue with Senate leaders Lugar and Dole to ensure that the Senate would drop the sanctions bill in return.[165]

The National Security Decision Directive 187 (NSDD187) adopted two days earlier on September 7 confirmed the administration's commitment to continue its policy of constructive engagement. NSDD187 declared US policy would continue to rely on constructive engagement to promote reforms in South Africa, while also seeking to enhance regional security and increase funding for human rights initiatives. Furthermore, the NSDD187 laid out a program for a South Africa Public Diplomacy Campaign aimed at convincing the American public of the merits of constructive engagement.[166] It was clear that the administration had no intention of breaking with its existing policy.

The executive order was far from the sanctions bills that the CBC desired and it did have a limited immediate impact on US–South African relations. Contemporary observers estimated that the sanctions would have only a limited impact on the South African economy.[167] Yet, despite the intentions of the Reagan administration and skepticism toward the effect of the executive order, the bottom line was that members of Congress had forced a significant concession from the executive branch. Congressional opponents of apartheid had succeeded in forcing an administration hostile to economic sanctions to impose the first US sanctions ever against South Africa.

In the short term, the executive order had the desired effect of halting congressional sanctions initiatives. In a final attempt to save the sanctions bill, members of the CBC, on September 11, 1985, walked across Capitol Hill to the Senate offices to plead for the bill's passage, but the Senate stood firm.[168] Moderate Republicans such as Kassebaum

---

[165] Crocker, *High Noon*, 277; Congressional Quarterly, "Reagan Averts a Confrontation on South Africa," September 14, 1985, Series II, Box LEG-151, Folder 1, 'Foreign Policy: South Africa 1983–1986,' PRP. The collaboration between the administration and the Republican leadership in Congress illustrates Lindsay's point about how alliances often form across branches of government. There is no indication, however, of a similar collaboration between moderates in the administration and sanctions advocates in Congress, although Kassebaum's attempt to persuade Crocker to get Reagan to address sanctions represents an attempt of collaboration on a centrist position. Lindsay, *Congress and the Politics of U.S. Foreign Policy*, 7.

[166] "National Security Decision Directive 187: US Policy toward South Africa," September 7, 1985, accessed August 6, 2019, https://fas.org/irp/offdocs/nsdd/nsdd-187.htm.

September 7, 1985, SA01888, South Africa: The Making of U.S. Policy, 1962–1989, Digital National Security Archive.

[167] Bernard Weinraub, "Reagan, in Reversal, Orders Sanctions on South Africa; Move Causes Split in Senate; an Executive Act," *The New York Times*, September 10, 1985.

[168] Dellums and Halterman, *Lying Down*, 131.

declared that they were satisfied with the president taking action against apartheid and expressed hope for a unified executive–legislative policy going forward.[169] The push for sanctions in the Senate weakened, and conservatives such as Helms and Wallop were able to prevent the passage of the conference version of the Anti-Apartheid Act. In the House, most Democrats remained unimpressed with the executive order. Speaker Thomas "Tip" O'Neill (D-MA) described the executive order as "chock-full of loopholes."[170] Gray, the chief architect of the Anti-Apartheid Act, argued that these loopholes essentially rendered the executive order meaningless.[171] Still, the mood in Congress had changed with moderate Republicans declaring themselves satisfied with Reagan taking a stand against apartheid. The administration had conceded a blow by accepting the imposition of sanctions through the executive order, but it had thwarted congressional efforts to gain control over its South Africa policy.

Defeating Reagan: The Comprehensive Anti-Apartheid Act of 1986

Opposition to further sanctions prevailed in Congress by the opening of the second session of the 99th Congress in January 1986. However, in the late spring of 1986, the actions of the South African government once again inadvertently assisted the sanctions advocates. On May 19, Pretoria conducted a series of military operations against alleged guerrillas in Botswana, Zimbabwe, and Zambia.[172] The attacks received strong international criticism and revived congressional interest in passing economic sanctions. Less than a month later, on June 12, the South African government issued another state of emergency and detained more than 1,000 people.[173] The same day, the Eminent Persons Group, a group established by the Commonwealth of Nations to examine South African apartheid, issued a long-awaited report. The report recommended that the international community implement economic sanctions and noted

---

[169] 131 *Congressional Record*, 99th Congress, 1st Session, 23294, (September 11, 1985).
[170] George de Lama and Dorothy Collin, "Reagan Slaps S. Africa's Wrist: Limited Sanctions Ordered," *Chicago Tribune*, September 10, 1985, 1.
[171] Congressional Quarterly, September 14, 1985: 1801.
[172] Alan Cowell, "Pretoria's Forces Raid 3 Neighbors in Move on Rebels," *The New York Times*, May 20, 1986, www.nytimes.com/1986/05/20/world/pretoria-s-forces-raid-3-neighbors-in-move-on-rebels.html.
[173] Alan Cowell, "State of Emergency Imposed Throughout South Africa; More Than 1,000 Rounded Up," *The New York Times*, June 13, 1986, www.nytimes.com/1986/06/13/world/state-of-emergency-imposed-throughout-south-africa-more-than-1000-rounded-up.html.

the importance of including the ANC in negotiations over the future of South Africa.[174] Two days later, reflecting the salience of the issue, more than 40,000 people demonstrated against apartheid in New York City on the tenth anniversary of the 1976 Soweto uprising, in which the massacre of hundreds of students led to nationwide protests in South Africa.[175]

In direct reaction to the events in South Africa, Gray, Kennedy, and Weicker introduced new sanctions legislation in both the House and the Senate on June 18. The foundation for these sanctions was the Anti-Apartheid Act of 1985. When the House debated the bill, Dellums offered an amendment that included even stronger sanctions, including total divestment and a trade embargo. To the surprise of everyone, the Dellums Amendment passed the House by a voice vote because Representative Siljander, who managed the bill for the Republicans, abstained from asking for a recorded vote.[176] Dellums recalls, he was so surprised he "almost fainted on the floor."[177] Subsequently, Siljander maintained that he let the Dellums bill pass because he thought it was so extreme that the Senate would easily reject it.[178] Dellums himself argued that Republicans abstained from counting the votes because they could not afford to go on record in support of apartheid.[179] In his memoirs, Dellums's CBC colleague Charles Rangel supports Dellums's explanation.[180] By contrast, Solarz argues in his memoirs that a recorded vote most likely would have killed the Dellums Amendment and describes Siljander's failure to ask for one as an outright tactical blunder.[181] Regardless of Siljander's motivations, the Dellums Amendment attached to the Anti-Apartheid Act of 1986 passed the House on June 18, becoming by far the most radical South Africa sanctions bill to date.

---

[174] Commonwealth Group of Eminent Persons, *Mission to South Africa: The Commonwealth Report* (London: Penguin, 1986); Gleijeses, *Visions of Freedom*, 286–290.

[175] Lyle V. Harris, "New York Rally Protests Apartheid," *The Washington Post*, June 15, 1986, A21.

[176] Massie, *Loosing the Bonds*, 608.

[177] Transcript, Ronald V. Dellums Oral History Interview, February 10, 2000, 5, by Harry Kreisler, Conversations with History; Institute of International Studies, UC Berkeley, accessed October 22, 2018, http://globetrotter.berkeley.edu/people/Dellums/dellums-con0.html.

[178] Edward Walsh, "House Would Require U.S. Disinvestment from South Africa," *The Washington Post*, June 19, 1986, A1; Dellums and Halterman, *Lying Down*, 133.

[179] James R. Dickenson, "Dellums: Exoneration Is His: Passage of Anti-Pretoria Sanctions Marks Milestone for Hill Veteran," *The Washington Post*, June 20, 1986, A17.

[180] Charles B. Rangel and Leon E. Wynter, *And I Haven't Had a Bad Day Since: From the Streets of Harlem to the Halls of Congress* (New York: Thomas Dunne/St. Martin's, 2007), 232.

[181] Solarz, *Journeys to War & Peace*, 84.

Again, the language used by sanctions advocates during the congressional debates and in public statements was heavily dominated by human rights and historical references that sought to magnify the moral significance of the issue. Introducing the Gray bill in a House subcommittee hearing on June 10, 1986, Representative Fernand St. Germain (D-RI) argued that the bill "mobilizes America's greatest strength – moral leadership in the arena of human rights."[182] In a statement on June 19, the day after the House passed the Comprehensive Anti-Apartheid Act of 1986, Dellums proclaimed, "The struggle for personal freedom and human dignity for the Black majority in South Africa is a moral imperative for the global community of conscience. It is a universal human rights issue – one that transcends national boundaries and political ideologies."[183] Dellums continued to argue that the Anti-Apartheid Act of 1986 was the first step toward putting the United States on the right side of history and in accordance with its own Bill of Rights. In a press release the same day, Senator Alan Cranston (D-CA) noted that just as the United States once decided it would not do business with Hitler, so it had now decided that it would not do business with apartheid.[184] At a press conference at the NGO, the Washington Office on Latin America (WOLA), Jesse Jackson made even more direct use of the historical analogy, declaring "There is Nazi apartheid in South Africa [...] Botha is the successor to Hitler."[185] Gray told the *Washington Post* that the bill was a reaction to "the carnage and the violations of human rights that have occurred in the last ten days."[186] In a Senate hearing on sanctions in July 1986, Kennedy argued, "Congress must act to put the United States back on the right side of history and human rights."[187] The most ardent proponents of sanctions clearly made a conscious effort to present apartheid as a human rights issue of historical proportions that required a principled US policy true to American values.

The House passage of the Dellums Amendment and the situation in South Africa led the Reagan administration to conduct a formal review

[182] US Congress, House, Committee on Banking, Finance, and Urban Affairs, *Anti-Apartheid Act of 1986: Hearing before the Subcommittee on Financial Institutions Supervision, Regulation, and Insurance of the Committee on Banking, Finance, and Urban Affairs*, 99th Congress, 2nd Session, June 10, 1986, 1.

[183] Ronald Dellums, Statement "Brothers and Sisters in the Struggle for Human Rights and Social Justice," June 19, 1986, Box 154, Ronald V. Dellums Congressional Papers, African American Museum & Library at Oakland, Oakland Public Library.

[184] Alan Cranston, Press Release, June 19, 1986, Box 262, ACP.

[185] Jesse Jackson, WOLA Press Conference, June 19, 1986, Box 22, Folder 'Anti-Apartheid Act II 1985-86,' WHG.

[186] Walsh, "House Would Require U.S. Disinvestment from South Africa."

[187] Edward M. Kennedy, "The Sanctions Debate," *Africa Report* 31, no. 5 (1986): 37.

of its South Africa policy. On July 22, 1986, in the aftermath of this review, Reagan delivered a speech in which he defended South African reforms and blamed the state of emergency on the ANC, whom he also deemed unfit for negotiations. Reagan sent a clear message to Congress that he remained opposed to further sanctions, which he argued would hurt black South Africans, discard US diplomatic leverage, and deepen the crisis.[188] In the preceding days, the content of the speech had been the subject of fierce controversy between the moderates Crocker and Shultz and the hardliner Pat Buchanan, a battle that Buchanan won.[189] As historian Robert Massie observes, Crocker found himself lobbying the administration in much the same way as external critics were lobbying him.[190]

The speech provoked outrage in Congress from both Democrats and moderate Republicans. In the official Democratic response to Reagan's speech, Gray rejected Reagan's argument that blacks would suffer because of sanctions, arguing instead that blacks were suffering because of apartheid. Gray also took issue with Reagan's concern that a violent end to apartheid might damage US strategic interests, by arguing that the status quo was hurting such interests by forcing black Africans to look elsewhere for support.[191] The CBC responded that Reagan had reaffirmed his position as the nation's leading apologist for apartheid, calling constructive engagement "morally bankrupt."[192] The Republican leadership in the Senate expressed disappointment that Reagan had not included any of their recommendations in the speech, with Weicker stating, "I don't think the president speaks for the United States on this issue."[193] Desmond Tutu perhaps articulated the negative reception of Reagan's speech most clearly, when he told the West to "go to hell."[194]

---

[188] Ronald Reagan, Remarks to Members of the World Affairs Council and the Foreign Policy Association, July 22, 1986. Online by Gerhard Peters and John T. Woolley, The American Presidency Project, accessed August 7, 2019, www.presidency.ucsb.edu/node/259098.

[189] Gleijeses, *Visions of Freedom*; Shultz, *Turmoil and Triumph*, 1,122. In his memoirs, Shultz recalls losing this internal turf war to Buchanan and decries the impact of the speech.

[190] Massie, *Loosing the Bonds*, 615.

[191] William H. Gray to Peter Rodino, "Official Democratic Response to the President's South African Address, July 22, 1986," July 23, 1986, Series II, Box LEG-151, Folder '1 Foreign Policy: South Africa 1983–1986,' PRP.

[192] CBC press release "CBC Assails Reagan," July 22, 1986, Box 307, Folder 20, WFP.

[193] Steven J. Roberts, "Reaction in Congress to Speech Is Mostly Negative," *The New York Times*, July 23, 1986, www.nytimes.com/1986/07/23/world/reaction-in-congress-to-speech-is-mostly-negative.html.

[194] "Reagan Rejects Sanctions; Tutu Tells West: Go to Hell: 'Emotional Clamor' Hit in Speech," *Los Angeles Times*, July 22, 1986, www.latimes.com/archives/la-xpm-1986-07-22-mn-30949-story.html.

The day after the speech, Shultz sought to exert damage control in a testimony before the Senate Foreign Relations Committee. In his testimony, Shultz sought to reassure Congress of the administration's commitment to ending apartheid, while maintaining that further sanctions would not be the right way to bring about such change.[195] His efforts proved unsuccessful. In a heated exchange with Shultz, an agitated Senator Joseph Biden (D-DE) expressed understanding of Tutu's frustration and scolded the administration for not doing enough to bring about an end to apartheid.[196] Several other senators, including Chairman Lugar and Senator John Kerry (D-MA) expressed concern that the administration was failing to take new steps to put pressure on the South African government.[197] In case Reagan's speech was not enough to convince Congress that sanctions were needed to force a change in US policy toward South Africa, a few weeks later it was revealed that the administration had signed a new textile agreement with South Africa. O'Neill declared that the agreement "demonstrated a strange disregard for American jobs and American values."[198] The revelation strengthened the widespread perception that the administration was insensitive to the anti-apartheid position.

On August 15, 1986, the Senate sent a clear signal of its disapproval of both apartheid and constructive engagement by passing a sanctions bill introduced by Lugar with overwhelming bipartisan support in an 84–14 vote. Thirty-seven Republican senators joined all forty-seven Democrats in voting in favor of sanctions. The Lugar bill was much weaker than the Dellums bill passed by the House but stronger than the Anti-Apartheid Act that the Senate had passed the previous summer before it was derailed by Reagan's executive order. Essentially, the Lugar bill included the content of the executive order plus additional sanctions, such as a ban on new investment in South Africa by American companies, numerous import bans, and a set of punitive measures against the South African government.[199] Legislators introduced several stronger bills resembling the Gray and Dellums bills, but they all failed to generate enough support to pass the Senate Foreign Relations Committee. Kennedy, however, succeeded in adding an amendment to Lugar's bill, which significantly

[195] US Congress, Senate, Committee on Foreign Relations, *Situation in South Africa: Hearings before the Committee on Foreign Relations*, 99th Congress, 2nd Session, July 22–24, and 29, 1986, 76–88.

[196] Ibid., 94–96.   [197] Ibid., 88, 109.

[198] Thomas P. O'Neill, Statement, July 29, 1986, Series II, Box LEG-151, Folder 1, 'Foreign Policy: South Africa 1983–1986,' PRP.

[199] Memo, Memorandum for John Poindexter, August 1, 1986, Folder "South Africa 1986," Box OA15539, Dean C. McGrath Files, RPL.

strengthened the bill by barring the import of South African agricultural products, iron, and steel and prohibited US exports of oil and petroleum products to South Africa.[200]

During the floor debate, senators made comparisons to US foreign policy toward other countries and the human rights records of these to argue both for and against sanctions. Lending his support to sanctions, the moderate Senator David Pryor (D-AR) referred to US policy toward Nicaragua. In an obvious jab at Reagan's description of the Nicaraguan Contras as freedom fighters, Pryor described South African blacks as the real freedom fighters and argued that if the United States could interfere in Nicaragua, surely it could speak out against South Africa.[201] By contrast, the archconservative Senator Gordon Humphrey (R-NH) attacked what he perceived as the "double standards" of passing sanctions against South Africa when the United States was improving relations with the Soviet Union, which he viewed to be a far worse human rights violator.[202] In a committee hearing a month before, Wallop had gone as far as to claim, "There are scores of countries, including many of those in southern Africa, that deny fundamental human freedoms to their people in a far more repressive and systematic way than South Africa."[203] These arguments illustrate how the broader foreign policy views of liberals and conservatives shaped their views on human rights issues from country to country, as well as the extent to which debates over human rights in US policy toward one country sometimes spilled over into debates about another.

The passage of sanctions bills in both the House and Senate put the administration and sanctions opponents in Congress under maximum pressure. House Republicans urged Reagan to "raise the moral level of the discussion" by calling for constitutional reform and urging negotiations between the South African government and South African blacks.[204] This desire from House Republicans should be seen in the light of public opinion where a year earlier a survey showed that 63 percent of Americans found it immoral for the United States to support the

---

[200] 1986 "Hill Overrides Veto of South Africa Sanctions," in *CQ Almanac 1986*, 42nd edn., 259–373 (Washington, DC: Congressional Quarterly, 1987), 8.

[201] 132 *Congressional Record*, 99th Congress, 2nd Session, 21855 (August 15, 1986).

[202] 132 *Congressional Record*, 99th Congress, 2nd Session, 21818–21819 (August 15, 1986).

[203] Testimony by Malcolm Wallop before the Senate Committee on Foreign Relations, July 22, 1986, Box 186, Folder 11, Malcolm Wallop papers, 1965–1995, Collection Number 08011, American Heritage Center, University of Wyoming.

[204] Letter, Robert S. Walker and others to Ronald Reagan, August 15, 1986, ID #422269, CO141, WHORM Subject File, RPL.

South African government.[205] The administration, however, responded by declaring that it was not for the United States to write the South African constitution.[206] Once again, the administration proved unsympathetic to the sentiments of its Republican allies on Capitol Hill, who clearly felt the pressure for a stronger Republican stance against apartheid.

Rather than seeking to shift the focus of the debate on apartheid, the administration pooled its efforts to build enough support in the Senate to prevent an override of a presidential veto. Officials in the NSC conceded that the only way the administration could hope to secure enough support to prevent the Senate from overriding a veto would be to produce a strong executive order. By doing so, the NSC hoped to convince moderate senators to reach the conclusion that overriding a veto to get minor improvements in sanctions was not worth the downside of damaging presidential authority.[207] The NSC thus essentially adopted the same strategy that had been used the year before for the executive order and the Anti-Apartheid Act of 1985. Simultaneously, in another attempt to win votes for the veto, Pat Buchanan proposed internally a "Reagan Plan," which presented a new vision for southern Africa, aimed at securing reforms and an end to the violence without the imposition of economic sanctions (Figure 6).[208]

In the House, supporters of the Dellums bill were faced with a dilemma. Should they try to push the stricter Dellums bill on the Senate, with the risk of delaying a decision on the bill in a conference session that could give Reagan the option to "pocket veto" the bill?[209] Or should they give up on the Dellums bill and accept the more moderate Lugar bill, which would secure them a bill to put on Reagan's table in time to force him to sign or veto? Dellums advocated for his stronger bill but, eventually, he caved under pressure from Democrats and activists who favored

---

[205] Louis Harris & Associates. Harris Survey, September 1985. USHARRIS.091285.R04. Cornell University, Ithaca, NY: Roper Center for Public Opinion Research, iPOLL, accessed August 6, 2019. Opinion polls over the 1980s generally testified to increased public opposition to apartheid.

[206] Letter, Edward Fox to Jim Courter, September 3, 1986, ID #422269, CO141, WHORM Subject File, RPL.

[207] Memo, Clark Murdock to John Poindexter, September 6, 1986, Folder 09-01-1986–09-15-1986, Box 90668, Rodney B. McDaniel Files, RPL.

[208] Memo, Pat Buchanan to Donald Regan and John Poindexter, September 10, 1986, ID #426189, CO141, WHORM Subject File, RPL.

[209] The Constitution gives the president ten days to sign into law a bill presented to him by Congress. If Congress prevents the bill's return by being out of session during those ten days, and the president does not sign the bill, then a "pocket veto" occurs and the bill fails to become law.

Figure 6 Representatives William Gray, Stephen Solarz, and Ronald Dellums review legislation to impose economic sanctions on South Africa over its practice of apartheid, September 1, 1986.
Terry Ashe/The LIFE Images Collection via Getty Images.

accepting the Lugar bill to avoid the risk of a "pocket veto."[210] Reluctantly casting his vote in favor of accepting the Lugar version, Dellums declared the need to keep the momentum going forward to bring down "the greatest human rights issue of our time."[211] In return for the House support of his bill, Lugar pledged to defend it against both another executive order and a veto.[212] Consequently, on September 12, a little less than one month after the Senate passed the Lugar bill, the House approved the same bill with a 308–77 vote.

The House's passage of the Lugar bill put maximum pressure on the Reagan administration to secure enough support in the Senate to sustain a veto. The administration focused on Senate foreign affairs leaders, Dole and Lugar. Memos from the administration testify to comprehensive efforts to garner support for a veto through personal lobbying

[210] Dellums and Halterman, *Lying Down*, 136–137.
[211] 132 *Congressional Record*, 99th Congress, 2nd Session, 23145 (September 12, 1986).
[212] US Congress, Committee on Foreign Affairs, *Congress and Foreign Policy – 1985–1986*, 29.

of individual senators as well as the enlistment of interest groups to put pressure on Congress. These memos also indicate that the administration was skeptical about the chances of success.[213] Crocker recalls in his memoirs that hardliners in the White House, such as Buchanan and Don Regan, were unwilling to offer serious concessions to Senate Republicans and proposals from himself and Shultz at the State Department were ignored.[214] Ultimately, Dole agreed to lobby to sustain a veto in the Senate in return for a promise from the administration to issue a new stronger executive order.[215] Dole, however, was fighting a losing battle on Capitol Hill, where most legislators had lost faith in the administration's willingness to act.[216]

When the deadline for signing the sanctions bill came on September 26, 1986, Reagan presented his veto without any clear indications that it could be sustained. Reagan stated that although he shared the viewpoint that "Apartheid is an affront to human rights," he did not believe that sanctions were the solution.[217] He repeated the familiar argument that sanctions would hurt the black South Africans they were designed to help. He then added that sanctions would diminish US economic leverage, constrict diplomatic freedom, and infringe upon his constitutional prerogatives to articulate foreign policy.[218] In a last-minute effort to secure support for his veto, Reagan sent letters to Speaker O'Neill and Senate Majority Leader Dole on September 29, in which he presented his proposal for an executive order and offered assurances that he was committed to the goal of a democratic southern Africa with respect for human rights.[219] O'Neill promptly rejected Reagan's letter, arguing that Reagan's proposal would be a softening of US policy toward apartheid. House Minority Leader, the conservative Republican Robert H. Michel (R-IL), described the administration's handling of the sanctions issue as

---

[213] Memo, Clark Murdock to John Poindexter, September 13, 1986, ID #461064, CO141, WHORM Subject File, RPL.
   Memo, Mildred Webber to Mari Maseng, September 23, 1986, Folder 16591, Box 12, Carl Anderson Files, RPL.
[214] Crocker, *High Noon*, 328–329.
[215] US Congress, Committee on Foreign Affairs, *Congress and Foreign Policy – 1985–1986*, 29.
[216] Crocker, *High Noon*, 328.
[217] Press release, Ronald Reagan to the House of Representatives, September 26, 1986, Folder 16591, Box 12, Carl Anderson Files, RPL.
[218] Ibid.
[219] Letter, Ronald Reagan to Robert Dole, September 29, 1986, Folder 16591, Box 12, Carl Anderson Files, RPL.
   Letter, Ronald Reagan to Thomas O'Neill, September 29, 1986, ID #420014, CO141, WHORM: Subject File, RPL.

"less than brilliant."[220] Later that same day, the House overrode the veto with a comfortable 313–83 vote.

In the Senate, a clash ensued between conservative Republicans, headed by Dole, who sought to sustain the veto and moderate Republicans, headed by Lugar, who sought to override the veto. Senate Democrats unanimously favored overriding the veto. Two days before the Senate vote, Lugar and Kassebaum wrote an op-ed article in the *Washington Post* under the headline "Override the President's Veto," in which they stated that they regretted having to defy the president, but argued that they had to uphold "the basic principles that are the very foundation of our democracy."[221] Conservative senators such as Wallop and Helms not only favored sustaining the veto, but also complained that Reagan's proposed executive order was too harsh on the South African government.[222] In a highly unusual move, the South African government also intervened, in an attempt to uphold the veto. Through the mediation of Helms, South African foreign minister Pik Botha called senators Edward Zorinsky (D-NE) and Charles Grassley (R-IA), threatening them that sanctions would result in the cancellation of a grain order that would adversely affect their districts.[223] However, the effort backfired, as it failed to convince Zorinsky and Grassley to support the veto and enraged the rest of the Senate when it became known that Pik Botha had attempted to "blackmail" US senators.[224] On October 2, the Senate easily overruled Reagan's veto with a 78–21 vote to make the Comprehensive Anti-Apartheid Act (CAAA) the law of the land.

While the economic sanctions imposed by the United States was not the decisive factor in ending apartheid, they were the most impactful sanctions, due to the economic and strategic relationship between the two countries. The CAAA alone reduced American imports from South Africa by 50 percent.[225] US sanctions also provided momentum for the transnational anti-apartheid movement. Shortly after the passage of the CAAA, the Commonwealth, Japan, Canada, and several European countries passed similar economic sanctions and the Scandinavian countries went a step further, banning all trade with South Africa in

---

[220] Edward Walsh, "House Easily Overrides Veto of South Africa Sanctions," *The Washington Post*, September 30, 1986, A1.

[221] Richard Lugar and Nancy Landon Kassebaum, "Override the President's Veto," *The Washington Post*, September 30, 1986, A15.

[222] Letter, Malcolm Wallop to Ronald Reagan, September 30, 1986, Box 70, Folder 48, Malcolm Wallop papers, 1965–1995, Collection Number 08011, American Heritage Center, University of Wyoming.

[223] Massie, *Loosing the Bonds*, 619.

[224] 132 *Congressional Record*, 99th Congress, 2nd Session, 27859 (October 2, 1986).

[225] Fieldhouse, *Anti-Apartheid*, 70.

1986 and 1987.[226] These sanctions exerted significant economic pressure on the South African government and, combined with internal factors such as continued uprisings in townships, they forced the South African economy to its knees and maximized pressure on the government to reform.

Multiple factors converged to create the momentum for sanctions in Congress during the summer and fall of 1986. Most importantly, the South African government's continued resistance to political reform and its use of brute force against domestic protesters and neighboring countries alike was pivotal in securing support for sanctions. Several members of Congress, who had not previously supported sanctions, cited media coverage of South African violence as the reason they changed their mind.[227] Rising in favor overriding Reagan's veto in the Senate, Biden referred to the "dramatic increase in frustration and violence" in South Africa and argued that sanctions were necessary to prevent "an ugly, bloody civil war."[228] Regarding the South African government's arrests and violence against protesters, Claiborne Pell (D-RI) argued, "We must say no to a government that represses the basic human rights of 21 million of its people."[229] In the House, Dixon lamented South Africa's denial of human rights to its black population, accentuating how the regime "sends police to break up funerals – funerals – and to gas, beat, and shoot those who attend."[230] Proponents of sanctions repeatedly returned to the escalating violence in South Africa, emphasizing how it constituted a violation of basic human rights that warranted a response from the United States.

Moreover, the Reagan administration failed to convince members of Congress and the American public that its policy of constructive engagement was working and that it was truly committed to ending apartheid. Reagan's failure to distance the United States from the actions of the Botha regime caused widespread resentment and discomfort among members of Congress. Moderate Republicans, in particular, were dissatisfied with the administration's lack of willingness to compromise on South Africa. An otherwise loyal Reagan supporter, Senator Mitch McConnell (R-KY) switched from supporting Reagan in 1985 to opposing the 1986 veto, decrying Reagan's failure to act on apartheid, "I do not feel I made a decision to act, so much as the president made a decision

[226] Gleijeses, *Visions of Freedom*, 293.
[227] US Congress, Committee on Foreign Affairs, *Congress and Foreign Policy – 1985–1986*.
[228] 132 *Congressional Record*, 99th Congress, 2nd Session, 27827 (October 2, 1986).
[229] 132 *Congressional Record*, 99th Congress, 2nd Session, 27829 (October 2, 1986).
[230] 132 *Congressional Record*, 99th Congress, 2nd Session, 27652 (October 1, 1986).

not to act."[231] The administration's failure to nurture its allies on Capitol Hill eventually led them to pursue alternative measures to demonstrate their opposition to apartheid.

The existence of a strong and vocal anti-apartheid movement with ties to members of Congress, most notably in the CBC, also played an important role in the imposition of sanctions. The growing strength of the anti-apartheid movement and the lobbying efforts of groups such as FSAM, WOLA, and TransAfrica put pressure on members of Congress to distance themselves from apartheid. From around 1984, the events in South Africa and the activism of committed members of Congress and the anti-apartheid movement raised the issue salience of apartheid to unprecedented levels.[232] In 1986, the *New York Times* published no less than 1,100 articles on South Africa.[233] This rise in issue salience and the continued debate over sanctions helped change the discussion from *whether* the United States should impose sanctions to *what kind* of sanctions it should impose. In seeking to answer this question, members of the CBC played essential roles by introducing numerous sanction bills and driving the push for congressional action. In the Senate, Lugar and Kassebaum played key roles, using their committee positions to persuade moderate Republicans to join their Democratic colleagues in favoring sanctions.[234]

South African violence, the failure of the Reagan administration's policy, and the growing anti-apartheid movement combined to sway public opinion, which ultimately changed the political calculus on apartheid. By 1986, the salience of the issue made it a force to be reckoned with in the November midterm elections, and supporting sanctions had become good politics for most members of Congress due to the massive opposition to apartheid. A July 1986 survey found that only 36 percent of Americans believed that the administration's efforts to put an end to apartheid had been "excellent/pretty good," while 60 percent believed it had been "only fair/poor."[235] In light of the public opinion, several Republican members of Congress felt it necessary to distance themselves from the administration on apartheid.

---

[231] 132 *Congressional Record*, 99th Congress, 2nd Session, 27832 (October 2, 1986). See also Nancy Kassebaum: 132; *Congressional Record*, 99th Congress, 2nd Session, 27843–27844 (October 2, 1986).

[232] Baker, "Getting It Right," 116.   [233] Massie, *Loosing the Bonds*, 606.

[234] It is evident from Crocker's memoirs that the administration viewed Lugar and Kassebaum as some of the congressional leaders when it came to shaping the sanctions effort. Crocker, *High Noon*, 264, 304–305.

[235] Louis Harris & Associates. Harris Survey, July 1986. USHARRIS.072886.R6. Cornell University, Ithaca, NY: Roper Center for Public Opinion Research, iPOLL, accessed August 6, 2019.

An anonymous Republican source told the *Washington Post* on July 17, 1986, that South Africa "hits home more than any other foreign policy issue" and that "a few percentage points vote by blacks could make the difference" in close Senate races.[236] Kassebaum called Crocker, urging him to get Reagan to show initiative on South Africa in order not to lose the support of Senate Republicans, who were worried about the issue damaging their chances in the upcoming midterm elections.[237] Electoral concerns were unquestionably an important factor behind the increasing support for sanctions among moderate Republicans, although they made sure to motivate their views by referring to higher principles, such as upholding American values.[238] Several members of the CBC, on the contrary, had been dedicated to sanctions well before it became a prominent political issue, having long felt a strong moral and often personal obligation to protest apartheid.[239]

Regardless of the motivations of individual members of Congress, the passage of the CAAA marked a watershed moment in US–South Africa policy, as it shattered the administration's policy of constructive engagement and manifested the role of Congress as the predominant American actor on apartheid. Throughout the rest of Reagan's presidency, Congress was in the driver seat on South Africa, having taken the lead on both policy and the national debate on the issue. With the passage of the CAAA, Congress did more than impose sanctions on South Africa. It enumerated policy goals that the United States should pursue in South Africa. It listed a number of demands to be fulfilled for sanctions to be lifted, including the release of Mandela and all other political prisoners and a repeal of the state of emergency and fundamental apartheid laws. Congress, hereby, put pressure on the Reagan administration to work with South Africa toward achieving these objectives. The CAAA also provided substantial funding for anti-apartheid forces in

---

[236] Edward Walsh, "Shultz Tries to Head Off Sanctions," *The Washington Post*, July 17, 1986, Box 198, Folder 2, WFP.

[237] Crocker, *High Noon*, 304–305. Author's interview with Chester Crocker, June 6, 2016. Crocker believes that Lugar and Kassebaum caved to public pressure: "They were looking for the president to give them cover, and by which I mean they were looking for strong symbolic leadership of the kind that the right speech might have given. And they didn't get it. So they ducked and they ran. They were prepared to go with the CAAA."

[238] Lugar and Kassebaum, "Override the President's Veto"; Nancy Kassebaum, "Tougher Action against S. Africa Is Necessary Now," *Kansas City Times*, September 13, 1986, 12, Box 154, Folder 6, The Kansas State Historical Society, Library and Archives Division, Manuscript Collections, Senator Nancy Landon Kassebaum Papers.

[239] Dellums and Halterman, *Lying Down*. Interviews in Tillery, *Between Homeland and Motherland*.

South Africa, including funding earmarked for human rights programs and scholarships for black South Africans.[240] The CAAA, thereby, helped push through engagement with black South Africa and forced human rights concerns into future US policy toward South Africa.

The CAAA's impact on the Reagan administration became evident almost immediately.[241] The administration stopped using the term "constructive engagement" and became more willing to condemn apartheid in public. In accordance with the CAAA, the administration began to engage black anti-apartheid groups in South Africa.[242] This engagement included a meeting between Shultz and ANC president Oliver Tambo in Washington in January 1987.[243] In May, the administration issued National Security Decision Directive 273, which stated that the United States would increase its contact with the ANC.[244]

Yet, there were also limits to the CAAA's impact on the administration, as was illustrated by instances of noncompliance. A prominent example occurred in February 1987 when the United States vetoed a UN Security Council Resolution modeled after the CAAA calling for stronger sanctions. This veto was in direct violation of the CAAA's requirement that the United States should pursue wider international sanctions.[245] Instances like this led to continued contestation between Congress and the administration.[246] Nevertheless, they did not disrupt the overall picture that the CAAA inaugurated a decisive break in US policy toward South Africa. It brought about changes in the US–South African relations that went beyond the imposition of economic sanctions to affect the target, tactics, and instruments of US policy.[247] Historian Alex Thomson has shown that the CAAA actually made the Reagan administration's South Africa policy more effective, as it pushed the administration to

---

[240] US Congress, Committee on Foreign Affairs, *Congress and Foreign Policy – 1985–1986*, 30.

[241] Schmitz, *The United States and Right-Wing Dictatorships, 1965–1989*, 231.

[242] Memo, Nancy Stetson and Tom Boney to Members of the Committee on Foreign Relations, "US Policy Options Toward South Africa," Box 264, ACP.

[243] US Library of Congress, Congressional Research Service, *South Africa: US Policy after Sanctions*, by Brenda M. Branaman, IB87128, (1990), Box 19, Folder 'CRS Info Pack,' WHG.

[244] "National Security Decision Directive 273: US Policy towards South Africa," May 7, 1987, SA02301, South Africa: The Making of U.S. Policy, 1962–1989, Digital National Security Archive.

[245] Peter J. Schraeder, *United States Foreign Policy toward Africa: Incrementalism, Crisis, and Change* (Cambridge, UK: Cambridge University Press, 1994), 233.

[246] Alex Thomson, "A More Effective Constructive Engagement: US Policy towards South Africa after the Comprehensive Anti-Apartheid Act of 1986," *Politikon: South African Journal of Political Studies* 39, no. 3 (2012): 376.

[247] Baker, "Getting It Right," 113.

engage broader aspects of South African society, leading to increasing influence on developments in the country.[248]

The success of the CAAA did not make members of the CBC and their allies in the anti-apartheid movement rest on their laurels. Rather, they continued to advocate for further sanctions and sought to draw attention to human rights violations in South Africa. In March 1987, TransAfrica launched a yearlong campaign called "Faces Behind Apartheid," which attacked Americans, such as singer Frank Sinatra and Shell Oil president John Bookout, for failing to distance themselves from apartheid.[249] TransAfrica also attacked senators opposed to sanctions, such as Dole and Helms, by placing advertisements in newspapers in their states with pictures of the senators next to black South Africans carrying a coffin.[250] In Congress, members of the CBC continued to introduce legislation aimed at bringing an end to apartheid. In December 1987, Rangel secured an amendment to the Omnibus Budget and Reconciliation Act to prohibit "foreign tax credit" for US companies operating in South Africa to compensate for taxes paid to the apartheid regime. The Rangel Amendment increased the tax rate from 58 percent to 72 percent, and as a result increased the cost of doing business in South Africa for the last remaining US companies.[251] A former civil rights activist and a decorated veteran from the Korean War, Rangel had become one of the most powerful Democrats in the House, when O'Neill made him Deputy Majority Whip in 1983. Although he belonged firmly in the liberal camp, Rangel's pragmatic outlook helped him rise through the ranks of the Democratic Party.[252] Although the Rangel Amendment received limited press coverage at the time, its impact was significant. The largest US company still operating in South Africa by the end of 1987, the oil giant Mobil Corporation, cited the tax hike as a major reason for its withdrawal from South Africa in April 1989.[253] When Rangel met Mandela for his

---

[248] Thomson, "A More Effective Constructive Engagement."

[249] Memo, Randall Robinson to TransAfrica Board of Directors, Box 109, Folder 15, TransAfrica Collection, Manuscript Division, Moorland-Spingarn Research Center, Howard University.

[250] "Newspaper Ad Blasts Helms," *The Asheville Citizen*, March 6, 1987; "Activists Make US Policy toward South Africa a Campaign Issue," *The Christian Science Monitor*, April 20, 1987, Box 109, Folder 14, TransAfrica Collection, Manuscript Division, Moorland-Spingarn Research Center, Howard University.

[251] Rangel had been working to end foreign tax credit to US companies in South Africa for years. Charles Rangel, "Dear Colleague," March 7, 1985, Box 66, Silvio O. Conte Papers (MS 371). Special Collections and University Archives, W.E.B. Du Bois Library, University of Massachusetts Amherst.

[252] Unfortunately, the private papers of Charles B. Rangel are not yet available for research.

[253] Nancy H. Kreisler, "Mobil Is Quitting South Africa, Blaming 'Foolish' Laws in U.S.," *The New York Times*, April 29, 1989, www.nytimes.com/1989/04/29/business/mobil-is-quitting-south-africa-blaming-foolish-laws-in-us.html.

inauguration as president of South Africa in 1994, Mandela told him that the apartheid regime had commonly referred to his amendment as the "bloody Rangel amendment."[254]

Even the Reagan administration's greatest victory in southern Africa, the signing of the New York Accords in December 1988, appears not to have been the result of constructive engagement, but rather, at least in part, the result of congressional sanctions. The signing of the New York Accords by Angola, Cuba, and South Africa achieved Crocker's long-standing goals of Cuban withdrawal from Angola and Namibian independence. At the time, observers generally celebrated the agreement as a victory for Crocker and constructive engagement. The *Wall Street Journal* called it "one of the most significant foreign policy achievements of the Reagan administration."[255] However, historian Piero Gleijeses has shown that the peace agreement did not come about because of constructive engagement or Crocker's strategy of linkage. Rather, Gleijeses argues, South Africa agreed to the New York Accords because of the rising power of the ANC, the military strength of Cuba in Angola, and the threat of further sanctions.[256] This assertion thus lends further claim to the significance of economic sanctions and the failure of constructive engagement.

Conclusion

Opposition to apartheid and the Reagan administration's policy of constructive engagement toward South Africa constituted one of the most extensive and intensive cases of congressional human rights activism in the 1980s. By the end of 1986, members of Congress took the highly unusual action of overruling a presidential veto to force sanctions on the South African apartheid regime. The passage of the CAAA represented the climax of years of activism against apartheid, which had built up slowly for decades and picked up pace in the mid-1980s. Members of Congress pursued a broad range of activities in their attempt to prevent human rights abuses in South Africa, such as writing letters to the South African government, meeting with activists, and participating in protests. Yet more than any other activity, congressional human rights activism on apartheid centered on changing US foreign policy through legislation. Under the leadership of the CBC, members of Congress combined legislative efforts with extra-institutional activities such as protests

---

[254] Rangel and Wynter, *And I Haven't Had a Bad Day Since*, 233. In his memoirs, Ronald Dellums also highlights the significance of the Rangel Amendment. Dellums and Halterman, *Lying Down*, 138.
[255] Cited in Gleijeses, *Visions of Freedom*, 503.   [256] Ibid., 503–508.

through FSAM and other activist efforts to mobilize support for economic sanctions.

The language of human rights was not the only framework used by members of Congress to advocate for the passage of sanctions and to protest the system of apartheid. Stefan-Ludwig Hoffmann has argued that the opposition to apartheid was not about human rights, but rather a democratic revolution and the reassertion of national sovereignty and that the international anti-apartheid movement was primarily run on an anti-racist agenda.[257] Members of Congress did express their opposition to apartheid in an anti-racist framework. Perhaps not surprisingly, this was often done in the context of America's own recent experience with racial segregation and its troubled history of racism dating back to slavery. As African Americans living through the era of the civil rights movement, in which several of them had played important roles, the members of the CBC naturally saw a connection between apartheid and their own lived experience with racial segregation. Republicans who came to favor sanctions also made the connection to America's past. Declaring his support for sanctions in May 1985, Representative Jim Leach (R-IA) argued, "Ending apartheid in this century is as great a moral imperative as ending slavery was in the last."[258] According to Lugar in the fall of 1986, "[South Africa] is a foreign policy issue strongly tied to our own troubled racial history [...] It evokes the memory of racial conflict in our own country and recalls how recently blacks were denied equal opportunity. Americans emphasize with South African blacks and embrace them as suffering brothers."[259] Racism and the American experience with racial segregation were important frameworks for anti-apartheid protest in Congress.

Yet, members of Congress opposing apartheid, including members of the CBC, also embraced universal human rights to further their agenda. As this chapter has demonstrated, human rights constituted a vital framework in the American debate over apartheid, and human rights concerns played an important role in the imposition of sanctions. Framing apartheid and US support for the system as a human rights violation offered opponents of apartheid several advantages. Since the Reagan administration had adopted at least a rhetorical commitment to uphold and promote human rights as part of its foreign policy, framing apartheid as a human rights issue made it possible for members of Congress to challenge the administration's rhetoric. By comparing the

---

[257] Hoffmann, "Human Rights and History," 10.
[258] Jim Leach, Statement, May 21, 1986, Box 307, Folder 26, WFP.
[259] Richard G. Lugar, "Making Foreign Policy: The Congress and Apartheid," *Africa Report* 31 (September–October 1986): 33–34.

administration's condemnation of the human rights situation in countries such as the Soviet Union and Nicaragua with its continued support for the apartheid regime, members of Congress effectively used human rights to highlight the inconsistency in the administration's foreign policy.[260] Human rights also constituted a powerful language for members of Congress because of the tangible institutionalization of human rights concerns in both the bureaucracy and legislation of US foreign policy. The State Department's Human Rights Bureau, for instance, was tasked with compiling annual reports on the human rights records of countries and how US foreign policy was addressing abuses. General legislation passed in the 1970s put restrictions on US foreign aid to countries found to be gross violators of human rights. Framing apartheid as a human rights issue thus problematized constructive engagement as potentially violating American commitment to protect human rights. Finally, framing apartheid as a universal human rights issue allowed members of Congress to enlarge their coalition by associating themselves with a growing circle of human rights NGOs and human rights advocates in Congress, such as the CHRC.

The CAAA and other sanctions legislation against South Africa also contributed to bolstering the position of human rights concerns in US foreign policy. In a very concrete way, the legislation made US relations with South Africa contingent upon the latter's respect for the human rights of its black citizens. The CAAA also included funding for human rights programs in South Africa, making human rights promotion part of US policy toward the country. The sanctions thus constituted country-specific legislation with a significant human rights component, adding another example to the growing body of US legislation passed since the 1970s that inserted human rights concerns into American foreign relations. Moreover, the contestation between the administration and members of Congress over how the United States should deal with apartheid drew national attention to the role of human rights concerns in US foreign policy. Just as human rights language was important for the American struggle against apartheid, the latter helped strengthen the role of human rights concerns in American foreign relations.

---

[260] See, for instance, US Congress, House, Committee on Banking, Finance, and Urban Affairs, *Anti-Apartheid Act of 1986*, 46. NGOs also criticized such inconsistency. See, for instance, an op-ed by the Campaign for Peace and Democracy: *The New York Times*, "Just Say No to the U.S. War against Nicaragua," December 19, 1986; Campaign for Peace and Democracy Records, TAM 462; 3, Tamiment Library/Robert F. Wagner Labor Archives, New York University.

6   Two Tales of Human Rights
US Policy toward Nicaragua

Few foreign policy issues drew more attention in the United States during the 1980s than US policy toward Nicaragua. The small Central American country with a population of 3.3 million became the key battleground for the Reagan administration's attempt to roll back communism in Central America. It also became the focus of a bitter struggle between the administration and liberal members of Congress, which culminated in the most severe foreign policy crisis of the decade, the Iran-Contra Affair. A host of factors drove this struggle, among them partisan politics, congressional dissatisfaction with presidential unilateralism, anti-war sentiments fueled by the fear of "another Vietnam," and religious divides.[1] It also became a vital battleground in the contestation over the appropriate role of human rights concerns in American foreign relations.

In the fall of 1981, the Reagan administration began supporting a group of Nicaraguan guerrillas known as the *contra-revolucionarios*, or simply the Contras. The Contras were fighting the leftist Nicaraguan government headed by the Frente Sandinista de Liberación Nacional (FSLN) – known as the Sandinistas, which had overthrown the US-friendly, authoritarian Somoza regime in 1979.[2] The administration's support for the Contras began as a covert operation, but by December 1982, the *New York Times* called it "The Worst-Kept Secret War."[3] Suddenly, the administration found itself fighting a two-front war. Abroad, it supported the Contra rebels and conducted covert CIA

---

[1] Roger C. Peace, "Winning Hearts and Minds: The Debate over U.S. Intervention in Nicaragua in the 1980s," *Peace & Change* 35, no. 1 (2010): 1–38; Roger C. Peace, *A Call to Conscience: The Anti/Contra War Campaign* (Amherst: University of Massachusetts Press, 2012).

[2] For Jimmy Carter's Nicaragua policy, see Robert A. Pastor, *Not Condemned to Repetition: The United States and Nicaragua* (Boulder, CO: Westview, 2002), 155–188; Schmidli, "The Most Sophisticated Intervention We Have Seen," 66–86.

[3] Editorial, "The Worst-Kept Secret War," *The New York Times*, December 8, 1982, www.nytimes.com/1982/12/08/opinion/the-worst-kept-secret-war.html.

operations against the Sandinistas in Nicaragua. At home, it waged a public diplomacy war to gain support for its policy. In both wars, human rights issues emerged as important factors. Liberal Democrats, seeking to restrict or end support for the Contras, pointed to the atrocities by the Contras. The administration, conversely, labeled the Contras as freedom fighters and instead criticized the human rights record of the Sandinistas.

Reflecting the importance contemporaries ascribed to US Nicaragua policy and its dramatic implications for the presidency through the Iran-Contra Affair, the issue has received considerable attention from historians.[4] Congress figures prominently in several of the broader accounts and historians have also examined the role of key individual members of Congress, such as Thomas "Tip" O'Neill (D-MA) and Jesse Helms (R-NC).[5] While human rights concerns figure in most of these studies, they are rarely at the center of attention. This chapter specifically examines how human rights concerns informed the contestation over US Nicaragua policy among members of Congress and the Reagan administration. Relying on numerous private collections of individual members of Congress, several of which have never been used to study this topic, the chapter introduces a number of important, but previously neglected, members of Congress to the history of US foreign policy toward Nicaragua.[6] Based on these sources, the chapter demonstrates that human rights concerns featured more prominently in debates among the administration and its congressional critics and supporters than described in the existing scholarship. Specifically, the sources allow for an examination of the following questions: How did congressional opponents of Contra aid use human rights concerns to frame their opposition to US Nicaragua policy? How did the administration and its congressional allies use human rights concerns to justify its policy? How did the struggle

---

[4] For US Nicaragua policy in the 1980s, see LeoGrande, *Our Own Backyard*; Robert Kagan, *A Twilight Struggle: American Power and Nicaragua, 1977–1990* (New York: Free Press, 1996); Carothers, *In the Name of Democracy*, 77–116; Grow, *U.S. Presidents*, 114–136. For the Iran–Contra Affair, see Theodore Draper, *A Very Thin Line: The Iran–Contra Affairs* (New York: Hill & Wang, 1991); Malcolm Byrne, *Iran–Contra: Reagan's Scandal and the Unchecked Abuse of Presidential Power* (Lawrence: University Press of Kansas, 2014).

[5] James M. Scott, *Deciding to Intervene: The Reagan Doctrine and American Foreign Policy* (Durham, NC: Duke University Press, 1996); Stead, "What You Know"; Theresa Keeley, "Reagan's Real Catholics vs. Tip O'Neill's Maryknoll Nuns: Gender, Intra-Catholic Conflict, and the Contras," *Diplomatic History* 40, no. 3 (2015): 530–558.

[6] These include the private collections of Senators Robert Dole (R-KS), Alan Cranston (D-CA), Jesse Helms (R-NC), Charles Mathias (R-MD), William Proxmire (D-WI), and Malcolm Wallop (R-WY) and Representatives Thomas O'Neill (D-MA), Peter Rodino (D-NJ), and Jack Kemp (R-NY).

affect US policy toward Nicaragua? What was the long-term effect of the Nicaragua debate on the role of human rights in US foreign policy?

The Reagan Doctrine: Rolling Back Communism and Promoting Human Rights?

The Reagan administration was convinced that the Soviet Union was determined to expand its influence in Central America and that this represented a serious threat to US national security.[7] In accordance with the Reagan Doctrine of supporting guerrillas fighting communist regimes, the administration became strongly committed to supporting the Nicaraguan Contras' struggle against the Sandinistas. The administration also gave foreign assistance to authoritarian regimes friendly to the United States, such as Honduras and El Salvador, without much concern for their severely blemished human rights records.[8] Members of Congress concerned with human rights criticized such policy, but in most cases had limited success in altering it.[9] At the same time, the administration oversaw a significant redirection of US foreign assistance to the region, replacing economic assistance with military assistance in an effort to bolster anti-communist regimes.

Although primarily concerned with fighting communism, the Reagan administration also presented its Central America policy as a way to promote human rights.[10] Following the administration's understanding of human rights as political and civil rights, the promotion of human rights was perceived as practically interchangeable with the promotion of democracy.[11] Describing the administration's regional strategy in a hearing before the Foreign Operations Subcommittee of the House Appropriations Committee in March 1983, Secretary of State George P. Shultz, declared, "The first and critical component is support for democracy, reform, and the protection of human rights."[12] NSC staffer

---

[7] US Department of State, *Foreign Relations of the United States, 1981–1988, Volume III, Soviet Union, January 1981–January 1983*, Document 10. LeoGrande, *Our Own Backyard*, 35–37, 580; Rabe, *The Killing Zone*, 149.

[8] See Sikkink, *Mixed Signals*, 159–174. During the Reagan presidency, the United States provided $5 billion in economic and military aid to Central American countries.

[9] Don Bonker and Michael D. Barnes to Thomas Enders, July 22, 1981, Box 96 & 97, Folder 11, House Foreign Affairs Committee Subcommittee on Human Rights. Don Bonker, Testimony before the House Foreign Affairs Committee Subcommittee on Inter-American Affairs, February 2, 1982, Box 96 & 97, Folder 11, House Foreign Affairs Committee Subcommittee on Human Rights.

[10] Zelizer, *Arsenal of Democracy*, 311.   [11] Sikkink, *Mixed Signals*, 150.

[12] George P. Shultz, Testimony before the Foreign Operations Subcommittee House Appropriations Committee, March 16, 1983, Box 125, Folder 5, JKP.

Oliver North even referred to covertly raised funds for the Contras as "Project Democracy."[13] Following the logic of the Kirkpatrick Doctrine, the administration implemented a human rights policy of minimal criticism of authoritarian regimes and full-out attack of totalitarian ones (i.e., communist). Thus, on the one hand, the administration attempted to diminish the human rights violations of authoritarian allies to allow for continued aid to these, while, on the other hand, it exaggerated the human rights violations of leftist regimes such as Cuba and Nicaragua to gain support for aggressive policies against these. Nowhere was this double standard more apparent than in Nicaragua, where the administration exaggerated the human rights violations of the Sandinista government and neglected the abuses of the Contras.

The administration's decision to integrate a commitment to human rights concerns into its Central America policy was primarily a reaction to congressional and public concern about human rights. The strong insistence by members of Congress, the American public, and NGOs that US foreign policy should reflect a commitment to human rights made it costly for the administration to flat-out reject human rights concerns. As a result, the administration became, as Kathryn Sikkink has argued, at least partially interested in promoting democracy and respect for human rights in Latin America.[14] Improved human rights conditions, real or perceived, in authoritarian allies such as El Salvador, Guatemala, and Honduras made it easier for the administration to obtain congressional and public support for its policy and thereby helped it achieve its objectives. Thus, human rights became an important framework for the administration's efforts to legitimize its Central America policy, including toward Nicaragua.

Initially, El Salvador overshadowed Nicaragua as the administration's key priority in the region. As described in Chapter 1, the administration viewed El Salvador as a test case for its attempt to stop the expansion of communism in Central America, and committed massive economic and military assistance to support José Napoleón Duarte's authoritarian but US-friendly regime. Secretary of State Alexander Haig explained the appeal of El Salvador by telling Reagan, "Mr. President, this is one you can win."[15] Nicaragua, by contrast, was perceived as a testament to the failed human rights policy of the Carter administration and, therefore,

---

[13] *The Contras, Cocaine, and Covert Operations*, National Security Archive Electronic Briefing Book No. 2, Oliver North to John Poindexter, August 23, 1986, accessed August 17, 2016, http://nsarchive.gwu.edu/NSAEBB/NSAEBB2/docs/doc07.pdf.
[14] Sikkink, *Mixed Signals*, 177.
[15] Rabe, *The Killing Zone*, 158; Cannon, *President Reagan*, 298.

was the Democratic Party's problem.[16] The goal of the Reagan administration's El Salvador policy was to prevent the country from falling to communism the way Nicaragua had done following the overthrow of Anastasio Somoza in 1979 by the leftist Sandinistas.[17] The situations in the two countries, however, were closely entwined and, with the Nicaraguan Sandinistas supporting leftist guerrilla forces in El Salvador, the administration's attention quickly turned to Nicaragua.

The initial focus on El Salvador was by no means an indication that the administration was not concerned with Nicaragua. Reagan entered the White House deeply hostile toward the Sandinistas. As a presidential candidate, Reagan had advocated termination of all aid to Nicaragua and argued that the Sandinistas were Marxist-Leninists puppets of the Soviet Union bent on subverting Central America.[18] The majority of Republicans and conservatives shared Reagan's perception of the Sandinistas. The 1980 Republican Party platform condemned the Sandinista coup, deplored Carter's subsequent aid for the regime, and declared its intention to support the Nicaraguan people in establishing a free and independent government.[19] The wording was inserted in the platform at the behest of Helms, who played an important role in the wider anti-Sandinista community underpinning the Reagan administration's Nicaragua policy.[20]

The administration's portrayal of the Sandinistas did not come out of thin air. FSLN founder Carlos Fonseca, as well as his intellectual heirs, the brothers Daniel and Humberto Ortega, were all self-proclaimed Marxist-Leninists committed to a communist revolution. The FSLN, however, spanned a variety of political leanings, consisting primarily of anti-American radicals and nativists. Despite this political mixture, the Sandinistas found common ground in a strong commitment to supporting fellow revolutionary movements in the region.[21] Initially, the FSLN tried to create a mixed economy and maintain a nonaligned political stance, but this strategy proved increasingly difficult as the Contra War escalated and damaged the Nicaraguan economy. The Sandinistas did have ties with Cuba, the Soviet Union, and Eastern European countries, which they looked to for inspiration, support, and protection. The

---

[16] For an elaboration of this view, see Kirkpatrick, "U.S. Security & Latin America."

[17] Grow, *U.S. Presidents*, 128.

[18] James M. Scott, "Interbranch Rivalry and the Reagan Doctrine in Nicaragua," *Political Science Quarterly* 112, no. 2 (1997): 239.

[19] Republican Party Platforms: "Republican Party Platform of 1980," July 15, 1980.

[20] Stead, "What You Know," 59–60.

[21] Odd Arne Westad, *The Global Cold War: Third World Interventions and the Making of Our Times* (Cambridge, UK: Cambridge University Press, 2007), 341.

Sandinistas viewed the Cuban revolution as their most important role model and they were heavily reliant on Cuban advice and assistance. They were, however, cautious about establishing too strong relations with the Soviet Union, out of fear of provoking an American reaction. The Kremlin shared this concern and was skeptical about getting too involved in what it viewed as an uncertain revolution.[22] Consequently, the Soviets provided aid primarily through the Cubans, and they made it clear to the Sandinistas that they had no intention of defending Nicaragua in case of a US invasion. Thus, at the time Reagan entered office, the Sandinistas were not the Soviet puppets that he made them out to be, nor were they as nonaligned and independent from Soviet influence as they declared.[23]

When Nicaragua began to feature more prominently on the administration's agenda in the spring of 1981, it was specifically because of its role in El Salvador. In his memoirs, Reagan recalls how shortly after his inauguration he was presented with intelligence that proved that the Sandinistas were transferring Soviet arms from Cuba to guerrilla groups in El Salvador.[24] Referring to this intelligence, Reagan suspended loan payments to Nicaragua and terminated all US assistance on April 1, 1981.[25] The decision followed an intensive lobbying campaign by American conservatives, such as Helms, urging the administration to do exactly this.[26] The administration made the decision despite reports that the flow of arms from Nicaragua into El Salvador had diminished and possibly even come to a halt.[27] The administration's approach to Nicaragua was shaped by the views of conservative Catholics, who believed that communism was spiritually evil and, as a consequence, had to be defeated at all costs. This view resonated with Reagan's personal philosophy and several conservative Catholics in the administration, such as Haig and CIA Director William J. Casey.[28]

Merely cutting off foreign assistance to Nicaragua, however, did not satisfy the Reagan administration. During 1981, it considered three options for dealing with the regime in Managua: military intervention, diplomacy, and covert intervention through paramilitary forces. From

---

[22] Ibid., 343.   [23] Grow, *U.S. Presidents*, 114–118.

[24] Ronald Reagan, *An American Life* (New York: Simon & Schuster, 1990), 238.

[25] A year later in May 1982, the Soviet Union granted Nicaragua around $170 million in aid over a five-year period.

[26] "U.S. Halts Economic Aid to Nicaragua," *The New York Times*, April 2, 1981, www.nytimes.com/1981/04/02/world/us-halts-economic-aid-to-nicaragua.html. See also Letter, Alexander Haig to Jesse Helms, December 8, 1981, Box 87, The Jesse A. Helms Papers, The Jesse Helms Center Archives, Wingate, NC

[27] Carothers, *In the Name of Democracy*, 82–83.

[28] Keeley, "Reagan's Real Catholics," 534.

the onset, there was considerable disagreement on which policy to pursue. Haig argued for a direct US military intervention against Nicaragua to demonstrate American resolve, and even publicly floated the idea of military action against both Nicaragua and Cuba.[29] Haig found little support for his policy inside the administration, where both the Pentagon and the White House staff opposed direct military intervention, knowing it would be unpopular with the public and Congress.[30] As a result, Haig and other hardliners found themselves marginalized in the debate, which instead turned to politically less costly options. The State Department, under the leadership of Assistant Secretary for Inter-American Affairs Thomas Enders, was permitted to pursue diplomatic negotiations with the Sandinistas. In the face of continued reports of Sandinista arms transfers over the summer of 1981, Enders went to Managua in August for a secret meeting with Daniel Ortega, then-leader of the Nicaraguan junta. Here, Enders proposed a nonaggression treaty and held out the promise of renewed economic assistance in return for an end to Sandinista arms transfers into El Salvador.[31] Ortega rejected the proposal, proclaiming that the Sandinistas would continue to support revolutions in Central America and would be willing to face any US military attack head-on.[32] Back home, hardliners such as Casey, Caspar Weinberger, and Jeane Kirkpatrick opposed the initiative as much as Ortega did, arguing that such a settlement would lose Nicaragua to communism once and for all.[33]

With a direct military intervention and a diplomatic solution both scuttled, only the option of covert intervention through paramilitary forces remained. The idea of setting up a paramilitary group first surfaced in a National Security Planning Group meeting between Haig, Weinberger, Casey, Allen, and Kirkpatrick in March 1981.[34] Firmly committed to stopping the Sandinistas, Casey played a dominant role through the CIA in defining the administration's policy toward Nicaragua.[35] During the summer and fall of 1981, the CIA held meetings with Latin American allies to discuss the situation in Nicaragua and the possible support of the anti-Sandinista group, Fuerza Democrática Nicaragüense (FDN). The FDN was one of the groups that would become publicly known as the Contras.[36] In August, a CIA official

---

[29] LeoGrande, *Our Own Backyard*, 139.   [30] Grow, *U.S. Presidents*, 129.
[31] Scott, "Interbranch Rivalry," 242.   [32] Grow, *U.S. Presidents*, 131.
[33] LeoGrande, *Our Own Backyard*, 91.   [34] Scott, "Interbranch Rivalry," 241.
[35] Weiner, *Legacy of Ashes*, 379–381.
[36] For an overview of the different Contra groups, see US Library of Congress, Congressional Research Service, *U.S. Assistance to Nicaraguan Guerrillas: Issues for the Congress*, by Nina Serafino, IB84139 (1987), Box 118, Folder 9, JKP.

declared US support for the FDN in a meeting with Honduran military officials, Argentine advisers, and FDN leadership. Casey and the chief of staff of the Argentine military agreed on a scheme in which Argentina would manage the training of the Contras and the United States would provide money and weapons.[37] With diplomatic talks scuttled and intervention politically unfeasible, the administration settled for the paramilitary option.

On November 17, 1981, Reagan approved support for a paramilitary operation when he signed the National Security Decision Directive 17 on Cuba and Central America (NSDD17). The NSDD17 allocated $20 million to organize anti-Sandinista Nicaraguans against the Sandinista regime and the Cuban presence in the region.[38] Two weeks later on December 1, 1981, Reagan signed another presidential finding, which authorized the CIA to organize a military force of Nicaraguans to overthrow the Sandinista government.[39] The CIA's first support to the Contras went through its Argentine and Honduran allies, but the agency quickly became directly involved in the support. Strengthened by US support, the Contras expanded and intensified their attacks into Nicaragua throughout the spring and summer of 1982.

Challenging the Reagan Doctrine: Congress and the Boland Amendment

A clear advantage of the paramilitary approach through covert aid had been that it could be carried out in secrecy without having to persuade the war-skeptical American public and members of Congress. Until the spring of 1982, US support to the Contras went largely unnoticed by both the American public and most members of Congress. Although the administration did report the Contra aid program to Congress in closed-door hearings before the congressional intelligence committees in December 1981, the information did not leave the committees. However, as the Contra operations expanded over the spring of 1982, they gained the attention of the American press and soon became a hotly contested foreign policy issue. The secret war became public

---

[37] Rabe, *The Killing Zone*, 160; Carothers, *In the Name of Democracy*, 83. For Argentina's role in training the Contras, see Ariel C. Armony, *Argentina, the United States, and the Anti-Communist Crusade in Central America, 1977–1984* (Athens: Ohio University Centre for International Studies, 1997).

[38] "National Security Decision Directive 17: Cuba and Central America," January 4, 1982, accessed August 6, 2019, https://fas.org/irp/offdocs/nsdd/nsdd-17.pdf.

[39] National Security Archive, Ronald Reagan Presidential Finding on Covert Operations in Nicaragua, December 1, 1981, NI01414.

knowledge.[40] Suddenly, the administration found itself fighting a two-front war on Nicaragua. In Central America, it supported the Contra rebels and conducted covert CIA operations against Sandinista Nicaragua. In the United States, it waged a public diplomacy war to gain public and congressional support for its policy. Human rights became an essential issue in both of these as the human rights records of the Contras and the Sandinistas became key issues in the public diplomacy war.

Winning public support for Contra aid was complicated by the existence of a large and vibrant movement against US intervention in Central America, consisting of a mixture of leftists, labor unions, church organizations, and peace groups.[41] Reflecting the diversity of the groups involved, the various factions of the movement relied on arguments based in religion, anti-imperialism, human rights language, and anti-war sentiments rooted in fear of "another Vietnam." By the mid-1980s, such non-governmental groups constituted a strong and outspoken opposition to the administration's Nicaragua policy. The groups developed transnational connections between the United States and Nicaragua through the establishment of sister cities, study trips for Americans to Nicaragua, and other initiatives. In 1983, the Evangelical left launched the so-called Pledge of Resistance, with thousands of people pledging to resist the US policies toward Central America through civil disobedience and protest.[42] Leftist Catholic groups in Latin America, such as the Maryknoll Sisters, also strongly opposed Reagan's policy of military assistance to rightwing regimes and the Contras.[43] Such leftist Catholics advocated "liberation theology," which sought to apply religious faith to alter the socioeconomic structures causing social injustice by aiding the poor and oppressed through involvement in political and civic affairs. This decentralized but comprehensive movement

---

[40] LeoGrande, *Our Own Backyard*, 285.

[41] For a survey of this movement and their arguments, see Peace, "Winning Hearts and Minds"; Smith, *Resisting Reagan*.

[42] Between 1983 and 1986, some 80,000 people signed the pledge. David R. Swartz, *Moral Minority: The Evangelical Left in an Age of Conservatism* (Philadelphia: University of Pennsylvania Press, 2012), 235–239. The strategy included the occupation of the offices of members of Congress in case of a US intervention. 1984 Voting Record of Rep. McHugh on Central America, undated; Nicaragua Solidarity Network of Greater New York Records, TAM 580, Box 3; Tamiment Library/Robert F. Wagner Labor Archives, New York University. The Pledge of Resistance also received support from peace groups such as the Committee for Non-Intervention in Central America. See, for instance, Flyer, Committee for Non-Intervention in Central America (undated); Committee for Non-Intervention in Central America, TAM 649, 2, Publications P, Tamiment Library/Robert F. Wagner Labor Archives, New York University.

[43] Keeley, "Reagan's Real Catholics"; LeoGrande, *Our Own Backyard*, 454–455.

against US intervention in Central America offered considerable support for congressional critics of the administration's Nicaragua policy.

As with congressional opposition to the administration's South Africa policy, congressional activism on Nicaragua mostly came from the Democrat-controlled House, where the Democratic leadership became heavily involved. Undoubtedly, this involvement was motivated by the political salience of the issue and the opportunity for Democrats to challenge the administration on a foreign policy topic that was widely unpopular with the American public. Yet, as it was often the case with congressional human rights activism, some of the most engaged individuals were also driven by personal convictions and experiences. While African Americans had been among the most active on apartheid, East Coast Catholics and anti-war liberals fearful of US military involvement in the region dominated opposition to Reagan's Central American policy. No one better personified the combination of these motivations than did Speaker O'Neill. As the most powerful leader of the Democratic Party, O'Neill repeatedly confronted Reagan on both domestic and foreign policy issues. In addition, O'Neill became deeply involved with Nicaragua due to the reports of human rights abuses he received from the Maryknoll Sisters, including Sister Peggy Healy.[44] In his memoirs, O'Neill explains that his passion for Central America was due to the Maryknoll religious, whom he believed were reliable sources because of their supposed disinterest in politics.[45] He was also motivated by his general skepticism of military interventions rooted in his longstanding opposition to the Vietnam War and the views of his friend Eddie Kelly, a former Marine, who had participated in the US occupation of Nicaragua in the 1920s and opposed new interventions in the country.[46]

Several other leading Democrats shared O'Neill's viewpoints and interest in Nicaragua. House Majority Leader and later O'Neill's successor as speaker, Jim Wright (D-TX) became a strong opponent of the Reagan administration's Nicaragua policy and in 1987 he took a highly controversial decision to negotiate with the Nicaraguan government directly, circumventing the administration. Aside from his policy

---

[44] WOLA to Keith O'Donnell, May 13, 1983, Box 19, Folder 2, TOP. Keeley, "Reagan's Real Catholics," 530–537; LeoGrande, *Our Own Backyard*, 454. O'Neill's aunt, Annie Tolan, was a highly placed member in the Maryknoll order and played an important role in connecting him with the other members.

[45] Tip O'Neill and William Novak, *Man of the House: The Life and Political Memoirs of Speaker Tip O'Neill* (New York: Random House, 1987), 370.

[46] John A. Farrell, *Tip O'Neill and the Democratic Century* (Boston, MA: Little, Brown, 2001).

differences with Reagan, Wright had long wanted to alter the balance of power in American government by making the speaker more equal with the president.[47] A long-serving member of Congress by the time he ascended to the role of speaker, Wright was not afraid to twist arms in the pursuit of this agenda and he took a more assertive approach than his predecessor before he was forced to resign in a politicized ethics scandal in June 1989.[48] Since the focal point of struggle between the administration and congressional Democrats became US assistance to the Contras and the role of the CIA, the appropriations committees, tasked with authorizing aid and the intelligence committees, tasked with oversight of the use of aid and the actions of the CIA, became key actors.[49] The chair of the House Select Committee on Intelligence from 1977 to 1985, Edward Boland (D-MA), played a particularly prominent role, not least through the Boland Amendments.[50] A Catholic of Irish descent from Massachusetts, Boland was a close friend of O'Neill, with whom he shared an apartment in Washington, DC[51] Boland's successor, the more moderate Lee H. Hamilton (D-IN), who served on the House Foreign Affairs Committee throughout his thirty-four years in Congress, also engaged with the issue as part of his strong interest in foreign affairs.[52] In the Republican-controlled Senate intelligence committee, the archconservative Barry Goldwater (R-AZ) remained supportive of the Reagan administration throughout his period as chair from 1981 to 1985, despite occasional frustration over not being informed of secret CIA activities. By the 1980s, the former 1964 presidential candidate was widely acknowledged as the founder of the conservative movement that had paved the way for the Reagan Revolution and as such was trusted by the administration.[53] Goldwater's replacement by the more moderate Senator David Durenberger (R-MN) in 1985 caused some concern in the administration, as Durenberger had declared his opposition to

---

[47] John M. Barry, *The Ambition and the Power* (New York: Penguin, 1990), 4.

[48] J. Brooks Flippen, *Speaker Jim Wright: Power, Scandal, and the Birth of Modern Politics* (Austin: University of Texas Press, 2018). For Wright's time as speaker, see 349–372. For Wright's resignation, see 373–387.

[49] For more on the role of these committees, see Lindsay, *Congress and the Politics of U.S. Foreign Policy*, 61–67.

[50] Unfortunately, access to the private papers of Edward Boland is currently restricted.

[51] O'Neill and Novak, *Man of the House*, 146–147.

[52] According to Vic Johnson, Staff Director of the House Subcommittee on the Western Hemisphere from 1981 to 1993, the most important congressional opponents of Contra aid in addition to Michael D. Barnes were Lee Hamilton, David Bonior, and Speaker Jim Wright. Author's interview with Vic Johnson, June 11, 2016.

[53] It was a speech delivered on behalf of Goldwater during the 1964 presidential campaign that brought Reagan to national prominence and helped propel his political career.

Contra aid in December 1984, expressing his dissatisfaction with Reagan's reliance of covert military action.[54]

Several other liberal Democrats, many of them Catholic, played important roles as active opponents of the administration's Nicaragua policy. Michael D. Barnes (D-MD) used his position as chair of the Subcommittee on the Western Hemisphere in the House Foreign Affairs Committee to hold several hearings on Nicaragua from 1981 to 1987.[55] Barnes's criticism of Reagan's Central America policy led the *New York Times* to call him "the leading Democratic Party voice on human rights and democracy in Latin America."[56] Yet, he has not previously received sustained attention from historians of US Nicaragua policy. Other key figures in the House included Edward Markey (D-MA) and Peter Rodino (D-NJ), who played important roles due to their committee positions and their special interest in Central America. In the Senate, Edward Kennedy (D-MA), Christopher Dodd (D-CT), and Alan Cranston (D-CA) were among the most active. These liberal Democrats were united in their discomfort with American alliances with rightwing dictators, and while they were not blind to the threat of communism, they wanted the United States to do more to encourage political reforms. Moreover, most of them had been critical of the Vietnam War and harbored a lingering skepticism of US military involvement abroad. Instead, they preferred to address issues in Central America through diplomacy and development assistance aimed at promoting respect for human rights and democracy (Figure 7).[57] Finally, Markey, Kennedy, Dodd, and Rodino were all liberal Catholics, who, as Theresa Keeley has demonstrated in her analysis of the intra-Catholic conflict over US Nicaragua policy, tended to share the views of the Maryknoll Sisters.[58]

The vast majority of Republicans in both the House and Senate generally remained supportive of the administration's Nicaragua policy,

---

[54] M. B. Oglesby to James A. Baker and Robert McFarlane, Nicaragua Legislative Strategy, January 10, 1985, ID#297413, CO114, WHORM: Subject File, RPL; Joanne Omang, "Senator Hits 'Contra' Aid," *The Washington Post*, November 30, 1984.

[55] The whereabouts of Michael D. Barnes's papers in unknown, including to Barnes himself. However, I was able to partially make up for this through an interview with him.

[56] "Michael D. Barnes," Truman Center, accessed August 6, 2019, http://trumancenter.org/team-view/michael-d-barnes/.

[57] For an example summarizing the view of liberal Democrats that the United States should push for democratic reform and respect for human rights to prevent the spread of communism in Central America, see Press Release, William Proxmire (D-WI), July 28, 1983, Digital Identifier: BPPRPt3, Senator William Proxmire Papers, Wisconsin Historical Society, http://digital.library.wisc.edu/1711.dl/wiarchives.uw-whs-mss00738.

[58] Keeley, "Reagan's Real Catholics."

Figure 7 Chair of the Subcommittee on the Western Hemisphere in the House Foreign Affairs Committee, Representative Michael D. Barnes, greets Assistant Secretary Elliott Abrams before his testimony on US aid to the Nicaraguan Contras, April 1986.
Terry Ashe/The LIFE Images Collection via Getty Images.

testifying to the significant partisan divide. In the Senate, Helms used his position as chair of the Senate Foreign Relations Committee's Subcommittee on the Western Hemisphere to hold hearings that drew attention to Sandinista human rights abuses. Helms and his staff had cultivated an extensive network in Central America, including among the Contras, which he relied on for information and witnesses to deliver testimonies.[59] In the House, Jack Kemp (R-NY) was one of the most active and outspoken advocates of the need to support the Contras to fight communism in Central America. In November 1983, for instance, Kemp stated that the Contras were "inspired by the same beliefs and principles of Jefferson, Madison, and Washington."[60] When Barnes introduced a resolution to support Afghan rebels fighting the Soviets while opposing aid to the Contras, Kemp remarked, "I think he should extend his

[59] Stead, "What You Know," 57–66.
[60] Jack Kemp to Henry Kissinger, "Views of the Honorable Jack Kemp Presented to the National Bipartisan Commission on Central America," November 21, 1983, Box 118, Folder 8, JKP.

principle of helping the fight for human rights to this hemisphere."[61] To conservatives such as Helms and Kemp, Cold War allegiance was the defining factor in any Third World conflict. Moderate Republicans, such as Charles H. Percy (R-IL), Nancy Kassebaum (R-KS), and Charles Mathias (R-MD) were much less categorical in their support for the administration. They favored a diplomatic solution to the conflict in Nicaragua and consequently voted against several of Reagan's requests for Contra aid.

Throughout 1981 and 1982, Congress paid only limited attention to the administration's Nicaragua policy and instead focused more on other aspects of the administration's Central America policy, including countering human rights violations in El Salvador.[62] As mentioned above, the intelligence committees received a briefing about the Contra aid program in December 1981 and through these committees, Congress even approved initial secret funding of $19 million in covert military assistance to the Contras to be managed by the CIA.[63] However, as reports of US support for the Contras and various schemes to overthrow the Sandinista government began to surface in the media, members of Congress started calling for an end to US involvement in Nicaragua.

On February 14, 1982, the *Washington Post* reported that the Reagan administration was supporting the Contras through the covert CIA program, and a month later, the newspaper confirmed that Reagan had authorized the allocation of the funding.[64] Around the same time, a copy of Reagan's authorization of Contra funding was slipped under the door to Barnes's office overnight.[65] The revelation of such information led more members of Congress to begin questioning the goals of the administration's support for the Contras. The administration maintained as it had from its first briefing of Congress that the purpose of its support for the Contras was to interdict arms flowing from Nicaragua into El Salvador.[66] Members of Congress, however, became concerned that the

---

[61] 130 *Congressional Record*, 98th Congress, 2nd Session (April 12, 1984); "Jack Kemp Supports Freedom Fighters in Nicaragua," Box 118, Folder 8, JKP.

[62] US Congress, Committee on Foreign Affairs, *Congress and Foreign Policy – 1982*, Committee Print (Washington, DC: US Government Printing Office, 1983), 84. See, for instance, 128 *Congressional Record*, 97th Congress, 2nd Session, H717-H720, March 8, 1982, Legislation to prohibit further military assistance to El Salvador, *Moakley Archive & Institute*, accessed August 8, 2019, https://moakleyarchive.omeka.net/items/show/8897.

[63] "Contra Aid," *Congressional Digest* 67, no. 3 (1988): 68.

[64] Patrick E. Tyler and Bob Woodward, "U.S. Approves Covert Plan in Nicaragua," *The Washington Post*, March 10, 1982, Nexis Uni.

[65] Author's interview with Representative Michael D. Barnes, May 22, 2016.

[66] Robert A. Pastor, *Whirlpool: U.S. Foreign Policy toward Latin America and the Caribbean* (Princeton, NJ: Princeton University Press, 1992), 69.

administration intended to destabilize and maybe even overthrow the Nicaraguan government and feared that the situation might lead to US military involvement. As a result, Democrats introduced bills prohibiting US involvement in military or paramilitary actions against Nicaragua without congressional approval.[67] While Congress did not adopt any of these bills, they signified the concern that would eventually lead to the passing of the Boland Amendment.

At the same time, supporters of Reagan's policy on Capitol Hill sought to draw attention to the Sandinista regime's repression to justify continuing support for the Contras. On February 25, 1982, Helms chaired a hearing in the Senate Foreign Relations Committee's Subcommittee on the Western Hemisphere entitled "Human Rights in Nicaragua." Helms opened the hearing by referring to conversations he had had with religious and political leaders in Central America about atrocities committed by the Sandinistas, including killings of Miskito Indians. The hearing also included testimony from the Reagan administration in the form of Assistant Secretary for Human Rights Elliott Abrams and Ambassador to the United Nations Jeane Kirkpatrick. Abrams declared that the Sandinistas had failed on their promise for human rights and democracy in Nicaragua and instead had become a "threatening Marxist-Leninist oligarchy."[68]

Democrats, on the other hand, used the hearing to challenge the administration's Nicaragua policy in light of its broader policy toward the region. Senator Edward Zorinsky (D-NE), a conservative Democrat and former Republican, asked how the administration could justify supporting countries like Guatemala and El Salvador, which Assistant Secretary Thomas Enders had admitted was more repressive than Nicaragua, while terminating aid for Nicaragua. Senator Dodd questioned the administration's reports on Sandinista repression, suggesting that they might suffer from over-reliance on a report by the watchdog organization Freedom House, which took a very critical stance on the leftist regime.[69] He continued by noting that this report awarded Nicaragua roughly the same human rights score as Argentina, Chile, El Salvador, and Guatemala, and he further questioned how Abrams could justify continued aid for these but not Nicaragua. Abrams responded that the difference in policy was justified because countries such as El Salvador

---

[67] See, for instance, Clement Zablocki, "Dear Colleague," March 24, 1982, Box 96 & 97, Folder 10, House Foreign Affairs Committee Subcommittee on Human Rights.

[68] US Congress, Senate, Committee on Foreign Relations, *Human Rights in Nicaragua: Hearings before the Subcommittee on Western Hemisphere Affairs of the Committee on Foreign Relations, United States Senate*, 97th Congress, 2nd Session, February 25 and March 1, 1982, 4.

[69] Carter and Scott, *Choosing to Lead*, 124.

and Guatemala were striving to build democracy, while the Marxist-Leninist leaders in Nicaragua were aiming to destroy it and were guilty of exporting revolution.[70]

Senator Paul Tsongas (D-MA) quite accurately described the situation at hand when, on the second day of the hearing, he proclaimed, "I think one of the problems with the discussion of human rights in this country is that conservatives enjoy speaking out against human rights violations of leftwing governments and liberals enjoy speaking out against human rights violations of rightwing governments. Consistently, human rights is not an issue in and of itself with its own worth, but rather it is used as a weapon to make a point on either one side or the other."[71] The staff director of the House Subcommittee on the Western Hemisphere at the time, Vic Johnson, offers a similar interpretation. Taking aim at the Reagan administration, Johnson recalls, "As an anti-communist regime with a leftist opposition, South Africa, in the administration's world view, was exempt from human rights criticism or, perhaps more accurately, was deemed to be a human rights-respecting democracy by virtue of the fact that it was anti-communist. Nicaragua was the mirror image of that as a revolutionary regime purporting to institute socialism, it was automatically a human rights violator, and its opposition was not. This was all about ideology; it had nothing to do with human rights in any empirical sense."[72] As these quotes illustrate, the elusive nature of human rights meant that they could be adapted selectively to claim moral authority for preexisting policy goals.

In months that followed, congressional concern about the administration's intentions in Nicaragua continued to grow. In the summer of 1982, the House Intelligence Committee attached classified language to the Intelligence Authorization Act, which prohibited the use of CIA funds for overthrowing the Sandinista government. The language passed both the House and the Senate in September.[73] In November, Congress learned that its concerns about the CIA's operations in Nicaragua were justified. A *Newsweek* article entitled "America's Secret War: Nicaragua" revealed that the CIA had been working covertly to overthrow the Sandinista government.[74] In response, seventeen House Democrats,

---

[70] US Congress, Senate, Committee on Foreign Relations, *Human Rights in Nicaragua*, 16–23.

[71] Ibid., 61.   [72] Author's interview with Vic Johnson, June 11, 2016.

[73] US Congress, Senate, *Report of the Select Committee on Intelligence, January 1, 1983, to December 31, 1984* (Washington, DC: US Government Printing Office, 1985), 2–3.

[74] John Brecher, "A Secret War for Nicaragua," *Newsweek*, November 8, 1982, Central Intelligence Agency Electronic Reading Room, Doc. No. CIA-RDP84B00049R001202830014–6.

including Harkin and Barnes, created a "Democratic Alternative" to US Central America policy based on respect for human rights, an expanded development program, diplomacy, and an end to Contra aid. Motivating their proposal, they argued that Reagan's policy of military aid and quiet diplomacy on human rights issues had failed to accomplish its object-ives.[75] The alternative was merely a statement, but it would prove indica-tive of Democratic preferences on Nicaragua in the coming years.

Congress did not limit itself to statements, however, but immediately set out to halt the administration's attempt to overthrow the Nicaraguan government. In December 1982, the House passed the Boland Amend-ment to the defense appropriations bill, which the Senate subsequently accepted. The Boland Amendment echoed the language passed by the intelligence committees in September, stipulating that no money could be used for overthrowing the Sandinista regime.[76] The congressional debate over the Boland Amendment reflected a variety of concerns about the administration's support for the Contras. A dominant theme was the fear that the United States was getting involved in "another Vietnam" in Central America. As Representative Robert Dornan (R-CA) observed with disapproval, "The debate so far is rife with repeated references to the past horrors of Vietnam war."[77] Some liberals, such as Ronald Dellums (D-CA), invoked international law by pointing out that covert operations against Nicaragua, "cannot be justified by strict national security criteria," since the Sandinistas have never committed a hostile act against the United States.[78] James Oberstar (D-MN), another liberal Democrat with strong links to the Maryknoll Sisters, acknowledged that the Sandinistas were far from perfect but pointed out that, apparently, the administration had no problem supporting regimes in El Salvador and Honduras guilty of massive human rights violations.[79] While human rights concerns were not the dominant argument for the Boland Amend-ment, congressional proponents of the legislation did reject the adminis-tration's argument that Nicaragua's human rights record justified US military action against the regime.

Reagan signed the Boland Amendment into law as part of the defense appropriations bill on December 21, 1982, after the amendment had passed through Congress with significant Republican support. Some

---

[75] Tom Harkin, Central America Policy: A Democratic Alternative, 1982, Box 96 & 97, Folder 10, House Foreign Affairs Committee Subcommittee on Human Rights.
[76] US Congress, Committee on Foreign Affairs, *Congress and Foreign Policy – 1982*, 87–88.
[77] 128 *Congressional Record* 97th Congress, 2nd Session, 29464 (December 8, 1982).
[78] 128 *Congressional Record* 97th Congress, 2nd Session, 29461 (December 8, 1982).
[79] 128 *Congressional Record* 97th Congress, 2nd Session, 29460–29461 (December 8, 1982). Keeley, "Reagan's Real Catholics," 544.

Republicans had justified their vote in favor of the amendment by arguing that it was meaningless, since Reagan had never declared it US policy to seek regime change in Nicaragua in the first place.[80] Another important factor was a tactical calculation that failure to pass the Boland Amendment might lead to the adoption of a stronger amendment by Harkin, which would have prohibited funds for any operations in or against Nicaragua altogether.[81] At first, Republican calculations appeared to have been justified as the Boland Amendment had little practical impact on US policy. The administration continued to support the Contras, arguing that the amendment did not bar the administration from such support as long as it was not a US objective to overthrow the Nicaraguan government.[82] The amendment, however, added a new element to the debate on Contra aid by tasking Congress with keeping oversight over whether the administration complied with the law. More importantly, it was only the first warning shot in an increasingly bitter struggle between the administration and liberals in Congress over US Nicaragua policy.

Struggle over Contra Aid: "Freedom Fighters" and Human Rights Violations

The Reagan administration responded to the congressional assertiveness on Nicaragua by introducing three new initiatives in 1983 intended to galvanize support for its Central America policy and to secure Contra aid. Reagan commissioned the National Bipartisan Commission on Central America, popularly known as the Kissinger Commission, to come up with the foundations for a bipartisan policy.[83] The administration launched the Caribbean Basin Initiative, offering trade and tariff benefits to several Caribbean and Central American countries, to counter the notion that US policy toward the region lacked an economic component.[84] Finally, the administration established the Office of Public Diplomacy for Latin America and the Caribbean (S/LPD) to oversee a public diplomacy war for public opinion. The S/LPD engaged in a comprehensive campaign

---

[80] Cynthia Arnson, *Crossroads: Congress, the Reagan Administration, and Central America* (New York: Pantheon, 1989), 111.

[81] LeoGrande, *Our Own Backyard*, 303.

[82] The Boland Amendment, Non-Classified, Report, April 6, 1983, #IC00087, National Security Archive.

[83] The initiative for the Kissinger Commission came from Michael D. Barnes and Jack Kemp. Author's interview with Rep. Michael D. Barnes, May 22, 2016.

[84] "Special report Central America, 1981–1984 overview," Congress and the Nation, 1981–1984, vol. 6 (Washington, DC: CQ, 1985).

aimed at promoting public and congressional support for the administration's Nicaragua policy but was eventually terminated in 1987, when its activities were declared to be illegal propaganda.

In addition to these efforts, the Reagan administration publicly declared its support for the so-called Contadora peace plan, which sought to end the crisis of military conflicts in Central America. Conceived by the foreign ministers of Colombia, Mexico, Venezuela, and Panama in January 1983, the plan quickly received the support of the United Nations as well as of several members of Congress .[85] This declaration of support, however, was for congressional consumption only, as hardliners in the administration had no desire to pursue diplomatic efforts. A 1982-NSC document published in the *New York Times* on April 7, 1983, showed that hardliners suggested the administration declare support for the negotiations to avoid congressional interference on the issue.[86] Reagan later declared himself in agreement with this observation.[87] In his memoirs, Shultz similarly notes that the hardliners had no interest in a diplomatic solution.[88]

Two actions by the administration during 1983 contributed to strengthening the perception among its critics that it might be contemplating a military rather than a diplomatic solution to the situation in Nicaragua. The first action occurred in February, when the United States intensified its military presence in Honduras, conducting large-scale military exercises on the border with Nicaragua.[89] In March, American newspapers reported that the Contras would be able to overthrow the Sandinistas by December.[90] Reagan denied that it was US policy to overthrow the Sandinistas and maintained that support for the Contras simply aimed at stopping Nicaraguan support for leftist guerrillas in El Salvador. Nonetheless, members of Congress grew increasingly concerned about the escalating presence of the United States in the region and about the administration's explanations for its policy. The other action was the US invasion of Grenada in October. By the request of the Organization of Eastern Caribbean States, the United States intervened to overturn a Marxist coup against President Maurice Bishop.

---

[85] US Congress, Committee on Foreign Affairs, *Congress and Foreign Policy – 1983*, Committee Print (Washington, DC: US Government Printing Office, 1984), 46.
[86] "National Security Council Document on Policy in Central America and Cuba," *The New York Times*, April 7, 1983, www.nytimes.com/1983/04/07/world/national-security-council-document-on-policy-in-central-america-and-cuba.html.
[87] Minutes, National Security Planning Group Meeting on Central America, June 25, 1984, National Security Archive Collection.
[88] Shultz, *Turmoil and Triumph*, 305.
[89] US Congress, Committee on Foreign Affairs, *Congress and Foreign Policy – 1983*, 43–44.
[90] Ibid., 44.

Justifying the intervention, the administration also referred to it as a rescue mission aimed at securing the safety of six hundred American students on the island.[91] The intervention led to increased concern, among the Sandinistas as well as American opponents of the Contra War, about whether a US military intervention against Nicaragua was forthcoming.[92] To the hardliners in the administration, who had advocated for the invasion, and to most conservatives, Grenada was a great foreign policy success that demonstrated American's resolve to fight communism in the Third World.[93]

The Reagan administration's public diplomacy war focused on three themes to justify its support for the Contras. The first theme held that support for the Contras was important for US national security and the regional security of Central America. This theme rested on the claim that the Sandinistas, with the support of the Soviet Union and Cuba, were exporting revolution to its neighbors and overseeing the largest military buildup in the region. The first claim represented a "Cold War security framework," informed by the Kirkpatrick Doctrine. The second theme concerned the nature of the Sandinista government. The administration consistently exaggerated the political repression and abuses by the Sandinistas and ignored any improvements to the human rights situation in Nicaragua. It also ignored the fact that US support for the Contras was deliberately contributing to increase Sandinista repression, as the Contra attacks destabilized the country and undermined its economy. The third theme concerned the nature of the Contras, who the administration presented as a group of democracy-loving "freedom fighters" that the United States had a moral obligation to support.[94] Moreover, the administration consciously refrained from publicly using the term "Contra," sticking instead to the official name of the Contra umbrella organization, "United Nicaraguan Opposition" and later the "Nicaraguan Democratic Resistance." The latter two themes were extensively framed in human rights terms and became increasingly dominant as the Reagan administration failed to convince the American public and Congress that Nicaragua constituted a threat to US national security.

Congressional opponents of US support for the Contras responded to the administration's public diplomacy campaign by seeking to disqualify the administration's arguments. Here, human rights violations in the

---

[91] Pach, "Sticking to His Guns," 99.   [92] Loveman, 324–325

[93] Westad, *The Global Cold War*, 345; Carothers, *In the Name of Democracy*, 115.

[94] Peace, "Winning Hearts and Minds," 8–10. Jack Kemp to Henry Kissinger, November 21, 1983, Box 118, Folder 8, JKP.

Nicaraguan conflict played a paramount role as Congress sought to challenge the administration's portrayal of the Contras and at least partially rehabilitate the image of the Sandinistas. Edward Kennedy pointed to how support for the Contras had "escalated the level of violence in Nicaragua" and led to the "killing of hundreds of innocent civilians."[95] The debate over Contra aid thus became one of competing human rights narratives, especially once the administration's Cold War security framework failed to convince skeptics in Congress. Members of Congress also warned against the risk of direct US military involvement in the conflict and urged a diplomatic solution. "On each day we slip closer to another mistake, another quagmire, another Vietnam," Markey wrote to Rodino in October 1983.[96] This public diplomacy war over US Nicaragua policy played out in congressional hearings and the public space of newspaper op-eds and press releases.

Human rights NGOs and religious groups played an important role in these hearings on human rights, as members of Congress used their reports to challenge the administration's policy. Human rights NGOs focused on exposing the facts and largely refrained from challenging policies.[97] Congressional opponents of Contra aid, however, looking for ammunition to challenge the administration's policy, deliberately used the reports and testimonies of human rights NGOs and religious groups to support their viewpoint. Amnesty International, the International League for Human Rights, the Washington Office on Latin America (WOLA), Americas Watch, and a host of religious groups all submitted evidence of Contra human rights violations to congressional hearings.[98] The general message was that the Sandinistas were guilty of human rights abuses, but that these dwindled in comparison with the atrocities committed by the Contras. A WOLA report from June 1986 concluded that abuses committed by the Nicaraguan armed forces were "relatively isolated cases," while the Contras were responsible for a "systematic pattern of gross violations of the laws of war [...] indiscriminate attacks against civilian targets, kidnappings, rapes,

---

[95] Edward Kennedy, "Dear Colleague," September 19, 1984, Box 264, ACP.

[96] Edward Markey to Peter Rodino, October 14, 1983, Series II, Box B.LEG-150, Folder 3 'Foreign Policy: Central America,' PRP.

[97] Peck, *Ideal Illusions*, 104.

[98] See reports and testimonies in US Congress, House, Committee on Foreign Affairs, *Human Rights in Nicaragua: Hearing before the Subcommittee on Human Rights and International Organizations of the Committee on Foreign Affairs*, 98th Congress, 1st Session, September 15, 1983; US Congress, House, Committee on Foreign Affairs, *U.S. Support for the Contras: Hearing before the Subcommittee on Western Hemisphere Affairs of the Committee on Foreign Affairs*, 99th Congress, 1st Session, April 16–18, 1985.

assassinations, mutilations, and other forms of violence."[99] Providing statistical evidence to back up such claims as well as horrifying stories of the atrocities, such reports offered powerful ammunition for congressional attacks on the administration's support for the Contras. The administration also used reports from human rights NGOs to bolster its claims, but it generally found few reports that supported its views.[100] For instance, a report by Americas Watch comparing the human rights situation in Guatemala, Honduras, El Salvador, and Nicaragua concluded, "the Reagan administration has attempted to create a distorted impression of the actual human rights situation in Central America" to further its geopolitical goals.[101] The administration in return charged human rights NGOs with being biased and victims of Sandinista propaganda.[102]

Finding most human rights NGOs unsympathetic to its cause, the administration increased its own production of reports to support its views. Between 1983 and 1987, the S/LPD produced a steady stream of reports and White House Digests, which countered the reports of the human rights community.[103] Another avenue was the State Departments' *Country Reports on Human Rights Practices*, which became increasingly politicized during the Reagan years. In the case of Central America, the reports devoted considerable attention to human rights violations by the Sandinistas.[104] Furthermore, Nicaragua featured prominently in reports on its neighbors, where it was charged with contributing to the worsening human rights situations there.[105] When it came to reporting on the human rights abuses of the Contras, the reports stated that it had been "extremely difficult to obtain objective independent verification of

---

[99] Report, Washington Office on Latin America, February 19, 1986, Records of the United States Senate, Record Group 46; Dockery and Sklar Files, Box 92, Center for Legislative Archives, National Archives, Washington, DC.

[100] The main exception was Freedom House, which produced numerous reports on Sandinista human rights abuses. See for instance: Report, Freedom House, February 22, 1982, ID#097002, CO114, WHORM: Subject File, RPL.

[101] Americas Watch, "Human Rights in Central America," April 27, 1983, Box 19, Folder 2, TOP. According to Aryeh Neier's memoirs, the Reagan administration grossly exaggerated the violations by the Sandinistas and "used human rights information as an instrument of warfare." Neier, *Taking Liberties*, 217.

[102] See, for instance, A Disinformation Campaign, Box 19, Folder 3, TOP.

[103] See, for instance, White House Digest, Nicaragua's Sandinistas: Having It All Ways, June 01, 1983, ID#165053, CO114, WHORM: Subject File, RPL; White House Digest, Persecution of Christian Groups in Nicaragua, February 29, 1984, ID#198611, CO114, WHORM: Subject File, RPL.

[104] See, for instance, US Department of State, *Country Reports on Human Rights Practices for 1984* (Washington, DC: US Government Printing Office, 1985), 608–625.

[105] See, for instance, US Department of State, *Country Reports on Human Rights Practices for 1983*, 550.

these charges."[106] Quite clearly, the Reagan administration and its critics did not see eye to eye on the human rights situation on the ground, but the administration accepted that it would have to frame its policy in human rights terms.

Throughout the debates over US Nicaragua policy, both the administration and its critics in Congress selectively employed experts and witnesses who were sympathetic to their views. The administration enlisted private Nicaraguans critical of the Sandinistas to provide accounts favorable to its policy.[107] It also relied on the support of conservative think tanks such as the Heritage Foundation. A 1983 report from the Heritage Foundation entitled "The Sandinista War on Human Rights," accused the Sandinistas of an "all-out war on the human rights of all those who oppose the regime."[108] The politicization of the Human Rights Bureau's human rights reporting during the 1980s conversely contributed to increasing Congress's reliance on reports from human rights NGOs.[109]

In a hearing on the administration's policy toward Honduras and Nicaragua in March 1983, Barnes opened the floor by arguing US policy toward Nicaragua was "making a bad situation into what could be a disaster."[110] Characteristically of the wider public diplomacy war, the hearing that ensued unfolded as a war on words, where Nicaraguans, human rights NGOs, and academics provided testimonies about the human rights situation in Nicaragua, which often outright contradicted one another. Professor John A. Booth argued that Sandinista Nicaragua had a "vastly superior human rights record in almost every respect" compared to the Somoza regime it had disposed of as well, as its neighboring countries El Salvador and Guatemala.[111] Adriana Guillen, a former Nicaraguan government official who had broken with the Sandinistas and since moved on to work in Washington, DC, declared herself in complete disagreement with Booth's assessment of the situation.[112]

---

[106] US Department of State, *Country Report on Human Rights Practices for 1986* (Washington, DC: US Government Printing Office, 1987), 569.

[107] For more on the Reagan administration's efforts to manipulate public opinion, see Greg Grandin, *Empire's Workshop: Latin America, the United States, and the Rise of the New Imperialism* (New York: Metropolitan, 2006), 124–133, 228.

[108] The Heritage Foundation, "The Sandinista War on Human Rights," July 19, 1983, Box 125, Folder 8, JKP. The report emphasized the Sandinistas restrictions on free movement and association, the use of torture, the denial of a due process, and a general lack of freedom of thought and religion, paying special attention to minorities, such as Miskito Indians and Jews.

[109] Forsythe, *Human Rights and U.S. Foreign Policy*, 125–126.

[110] US Congress, House, Committee on Foreign Affairs, *U.S. Policy in Honduras and Nicaragua: Hearing before the Subcommittee on Western Hemisphere Affairs of the Committee on Foreign Affairs*, 98th Congress, 1st Session, March 15, 1983, 1.

[111] Ibid., 114.   [112] Ibid., 115.

The main issue of congressional concern, however, was whether the United States supported the Contra attacks in Nicaragua and, if so, whether this constituted a violation of the Boland Amendment. In late March 1983, thirty-seven members of Congress sent Reagan a letter expressing their concern that CIA activities were violating the Boland Amendment. Shortly after, on April 1, Senator Daniel P. Moynihan (D-NY) told the *New York Times*, "a growing number of my colleagues question whether the CIA is complying with the law."[113] This concern was strengthened two days later when press reports delivered the first solid evidence that the Reagan administration was, in fact, supporting the Contras with weapons, intelligence, and advice.[114] On April 12, the Senate Foreign Relations Committee held a hearing to investigate the situation. Not surprisingly, however, the hearing failed to generate any definitive answers, as the administration continued to deny its intentions to overthrow the Sandinistas and refused to reveal US support for the Contras by referring to the classified nature of such information. In his opening statement, Claiborne Pell (D-RI) posed the rhetorical question of how the United States could criticize others (Cuba) for supporting guerrillas in El Salvador and elsewhere while doing the same in Nicaragua. When Pell followed up later in the hearing by questioning Assistant Secretary Thomas Enders about whether the administration supported the Contras, Enders declined to reveal such classified information in a public forum.[115] Enders, however, was more than willing to discuss his interpretation of the Boland Amendment. According to the assistant secretary, the amendment's prohibition of support for regime change did not prevent the United States from putting pressure on the Sandinistas.[116] Meanwhile, on the same day, Barnes's House Subcommittee on the Western Hemisphere voted in favor of banning all support for the Contras.[117]

While such hearings and subcommittee votes had no direct impact on US policy, it helped push the House and Senate Intelligence Committees

[113] Philip Taubman, "Moynihan Questions CIA's Latin Role," *The New York Times*, April 1, 1983, www.nytimes.com/1983/04/01/world/moynihan-questions-cia-s-latin-role.html.

[114] Christopher Dickey, "Nothing Ragtag about Nicaraguan Rebels," *The Washington Post*, April 3, 1983, Nexis Uni; Raymond Bonner, "U.S. Ties to Anti-Sandinists Are Reported to Be Extensive," *The New York Times*, April 3, 1983, www.nytimes.com/1983/04/03/world/us-ties-to-anti-sandinists-are-reported-to-be-extensive.html.

[115] US Congress, Senate, Committee on Foreign Relations, *U.S. Policy toward Nicaragua and Central America: Hearing before the Committee on Foreign Relations*, 98th Congress, 1st Session, April 12, 1983, 2, 21.

[116] Ibid., 24–25.

[117] Arnson, *Crossroads*, 127. The subcommittee attached the ban as an amendment to the foreign aid authorization bill but later removed it.

to address the issue. The day after the Subcommittee on the Western Hemisphere had voted to ban all support for the Contras, the House Intelligence Committee agreed to demand that the administration explain what it was doing in Nicaragua. Democratic members of the Senate Intelligence Committee also expressed concern about the administration's activities in Nicaragua with the liberal Senator Gary Hart (D-CO) introducing a proposal to tighten the language of the Boland Amendment.[118] Ultimately, however, Senate Republicans came to the administration's rescue. After a meeting with Casey the day before, the Committee's Chairman Barry Goldwater (R-AZ) stated that he had concluded that US operations in Nicaragua did not violate the Boland Amendment.[119] Consequently, Congress failed to pass new legislation that seriously challenged the administration's Central America policy.

Nonetheless, the growing congressional concern with Central America prompted the administration to react. On April 27, 1983, amid protests against US involvement in Central America on the National Mall, Reagan took the highly unusual action of delivering a televised speech before a joint session of Congress devoted solely to Central America. Normally, speeches before a joint session of Congress are reserved for State of the Union addresses and national emergencies.[120] In his speech, the president blamed Nicaragua for being the cause of instability and conflict in the region. He repeated his attacks on the Sandinistas for failing to deliver democracy at home and for continuing its "export of subversion and violence" to its neighbors. He reiterated, however, that the United States did not seek to overthrow the Sandinistas. Rather, US policy toward Central America, Reagan declared, would center on four basic goals: democracy, dialogue, development, and defense, since simplified as the "four Ds." As had become the norm, Reagan spoke of human rights in general terms without getting specific. He acknowledged that El Salvador still faced "major problems regarding human rights," but stressed his commitment to see democracy thrive in that country as well as in Nicaragua. "We will work at human rights problems," Reagan continued, "not walk away from them." He did not elaborate on what this work implied. Reagan ended his speech by beating the drum of national security, arguing, "the national security of all the Americas is

---

[118] Patrick E. Tyler and Don Oberdorfer, "Nicaragua Activities Questioned: Rep. Boland Says U.S. Role There May Be Illegal," *The Washington Post*, April 14, 1983, Nexis Uni.

[119] "Nicaragua Covert Aid Issue Compromised," in *CQ Almanac 1983*, 39th edn., 123–132 (Washington, DC: Congressional Quarterly, 1984), http://library.cqpress.com/cqalmanac/cqal83-1198446.

[120] The speech marked only the thirteenth time in the previous thirty years that a president had used a joint session of Congress to address a single topic.

at stake in Central America" and maintaining that if the United States failed to defend itself there, "our credibility would collapse, our alliances would crumble, and the safety of our homeland would be put in jeopardy."[121] Once again, Reagan emphasized the fatal consequences of defeat in Central America in an attempt to put maximum pressure on Congress to get behind his policy in the region.

Reagan's speech received mixed reviews. Supporters of the administration applauded the speech and expressed hope that it would foster a bipartisan consensus on Central America.[122] However, where it mattered most, among Democrats on Capitol Hill, the reception was chilling. In the official Democratic response, Senator Dodd called Reagan's approach to Central America a militaristic formula for failure that would lead to endless intervention. The real cause for instability in the region, Dodd proclaimed, was not communism but poverty and deprivation under dictatorships that had "stifled democracy and destroyed human rights." Dodd went on to contrast the administration's policy with the American tradition of shining "the light of liberty before the world," referring to how "Lincoln once spoke of an America leading the way to human progress and human rights."[123] Reagan's warning about the dangers of communist subversion in Central America failed to persuade the majority of the American public, which instead sided with House Democrats. Asked in an *ABC News/Washington Post* poll in May 1983, "Which do you think is the greater cause of unrest in Central America today: subversion from Cuba, Nicaragua and the Soviet Union, or poverty and the lack of human rights in the area?" only 22 percent answered "subversion," while 57 percent responded "poverty and the lack of human rights."[124]

On Capitol Hill, support for Contra aid remained very much a partisan issue. Twice in the second half of 1983, the Democrat-controlled House voted to end to all US support for military groups in Nicaragua, but in

---

[121] Ronald Reagan, Address before a Joint Session of the Congress on Central America, April 27, 1983. Online by Gerhard Peters and John T. Woolley, The American Presidency Project, accessed August 7, 2019, www.presidency.ucsb.edu/node/262883. Numerous *White House Digests* repeated the message. *White House Digest*, "Soviet Threat Caribbean, July 6, 1983, ID #198661, CO114, WHORM: Subject File, RPL.

[122] US Congress, Committee on Foreign Affairs, *Congress and Foreign Policy – 1983*, 46.

[123] Democratic Response to President Reagan's Speech to Joint Session of Congress, April 27, 1983, Box 18, Folder 4, TOP. "Transcript of Democrat's Response to Reagan Speech on Central America," *The New York Times*, April 28, 1983, Nexis Uni.

[124] *ABC News/Washington Post*, ABC News/Washington Post Poll, May 1983. USABCWP.75.R40. Cornell University, Ithaca, NY: Roper Center for Public Opinion Research, iPOLL, accessed August 6, 2019. The remaining answers were 8 percent "both equally" and 13 percent "do not know/no opinion."

both cases, Republicans in the Senate saved the administration. In July, a bill introduced by Boland and Clement Zablocki (D-WI) made it through the House but was bottled up in the Senate Intelligence Committee. In October, a similar measure passed the House, but once again the Senate turned it down, with conservative Republicans like Wallop arguing that a ban on Contra aid would make Nicaragua a sanctuary for communist military action.[125] In November, the two chambers reached a compromise on a bill that provided Reagan $24 million in continued Contra aid, but prohibited the CIA from using contingency funds to support the Contras. The bill also stipulated that future funds would have to be allocated by Congress, offering opponents of Contra aid an opportunity to block the program the following year. The compromise also committed the administration to pursue a negotiated settlement in Nicaragua.[126] The decision effectively ended the Boland Amendment by allocating the first openly approved funding for the Contras, effectively transforming the Contra program from covert to overt.[127] Although support for the Contras remained contested and restrictions remained in place, the approval of overt military assistance to the Contras was a significant victory for the administration.

In January 1984, the Kissinger Commission issued its report aimed at forging a bipartisan consensus on Central America. The report rejected the notion that there was a tradeoff between human rights and security, and argued that the United States had to advance both issues simultaneously. Applying this assumption to Nicaragua, the report argued that the Contras' struggle was a struggle for human rights. The report also advocated for tying military aid to progress on human rights.[128] However, Kemp, who was one of the commissioners, specified that concern for human rights should not be allowed to impair US security interests.[129]

Just as it was the case with the issues of Soviet Jewry and South African apartheid, members of Congress did not limit their activity to legislative efforts. On March 20, 1984, ten members of Congress, including Wright, Barnes, and Boland, sent a letter to Nicaraguan President Daniel Ortega, declaring their opposition to official US policy. The letter encouraged Ortega to seek continued reform in Nicaragua but also

---

[125] Malcolm Wallop, Statement on the Floor of the US Senate (undated), Box 65, Folder 35, Malcolm Wallop papers, 1965–1995, Collection Number 08011, American Heritage Center, University of Wyoming.

[126] "Nicaragua Covert Aid Issue Compromised," in *CQ Almanac*, 1983.

[127] Carothers, *In the Name of Democracy*, 85–86.

[128] United States, *Report of the National Bipartisan Commission on Central America* (Washington, DC: Government Printing Office, 1984).

[129] Jack Kemp News Release, January 11, 1983, Box 125, Folder 11, JKP.

expressed hope for friendly relations and pledged their willingness to enter into dialogue.[130] Through such a letter, members of Congress bypassed the administration to engage in their own diplomacy with the head of a foreign country, challenging the president's foreign policy powers.[131] The significance of such an action was not lost on the administration and its supporters. In a letter to Reagan, Representative Newt Gingrich (R-GA) lamented that the letter undercut US foreign policy and violated the executive branch's prerogative of negotiation with foreign governments by offering Ortega talks with members of Congress. By appealing to Ortega to pursue reforms, Gingrich argued, the signatories of the letter were seeking to use Nicaraguan behavior to further the cause of the anti-Contra movement in the United States, and thus manipulating America politics. "Historians will look upon this letter," Gingrich proclaimed, "as a model of how Congress undercut and crippled the capacity of the US Government to pursue a stable foreign policy."[132] In its response to Gingrich, the administration declared itself in agreement with Gingrich's observations and pointed out that the Wright letter failed to mention the presence of Soviet and Cuban forces in Nicaragua.[133] Barnes, one of the signatories, later recalled how "the right wing just had a field day going after all of us who had signed the letter."[134] Despite his views on the Ortega letter, later the same year Gingrich would put his own signature on a letter to the South African ambassador threatening economic sanctions unless the human rights situation in the country improved.[135] For Gingrich, as for several of his colleagues, the proper role of Congress in diplomacy apparently varied according to political and ideological circumstances.

In April 1984, a bombshell hit the debate over Contra aid and brought renewed momentum to the congressional opposition. Newspapers reported that the CIA had placed mines in Nicaraguan harbors, and the *Wall Street Journal* since reported that the CIA had instructed the Contras to claim the credit.[136] Ignoring congressional restrictions and in

---

[130] Members of Congress to Daniel Ortega, March 20, 1984, Box 127, Folder 2, JKP
[131] Lindsay, *Congress and the Politics of U.S. Foreign Policy*, 120.
[132] Letter, Newt Gingrich to M. B. Oglesby, April 16, 1984, ID #213488, CO114, WHORM: Subject File, RPL. As a curiosity, it can be noted that Gingrich holds a PhD in history from Tulane University (1971).
[133] Letter, Michael K. Deaver to Newt Gingrich, August 17, 1984, ID #222951, CO114, WHORM: Subject File, RPL.
[134] Author's interview with Rep. Michael D. Barnes, May 22, 2016.
[135] Letter inserted in congressional hearing US Congress, House, Committee on Foreign Affairs, *The Anti-Apartheid Act of 1985 Hearings and Markup*, 157–158.
[136] David Rogers, "U.S. Role in Mining Nicaraguan Harbors Reportedly Is Larger Than First Throught," *Wall Street Journal*, April 6, 1984, 6.

anticipation of future limits on Contra aid, the administration had stepped up its covert operations in Nicaragua over the fall of 1983, and by early January 1984 the National Security Planning Group had given the CIA the green light to mine the harbors.[137] Nicaragua responded by filing a suit against the United States at the International Court of Justice (ICJ). The administration, however, decided to boycott the court after unsuccessfully contesting its jurisdiction in the matter.[138]

The revelation of the harbor mining sent shockwaves throughout Congress, where members expressed anger over the unlawful activity of the CIA and over learning about US operations in Central America through the press once again. Barnes declared that he was "shocked that the president shows so little respect for international law" and promised to hold a hearing on the matter. Senator Robert Byrd (D-WV) called the mining "an act of terrorism."[139] Speaker O'Neill proclaimed, "I have contended that the Reagan administration's secret war against Nicaragua was morally indefensible. Today it is clear that it is legally indefensible as well."[140] Admittedly, the House Intelligence Committee had been briefed about the mining but had failed to share the information with its Senate counterpart. A report submitted to the Senate Intelligence Committee by Casey in mid-March also included a sentence about the harbor mining, but it did not mention any CIA involvement in the action. Even the administration's key allies on Capitol Hill had been left in the dark. Chairman of the Senate Foreign Relations Committee Charles H. Percy publicly complained that he and other Republican leaders had to learn about such activities through the press.[141] Goldwater kept his criticism private, but gave Casey a piece of his mind in an April 9 letter: "I am pissed off! [...] Bill, how can we back his foreign policy when we don't know what the hell he is doing? [...] In the future, if anything like this

---

[137] US Congress, House, Select Committee to Investigate Covert Arms Transactions with Iran and Senate, Select Committee on Secret Military Assistance to Iran and the Nicaraguan Opposition, *Report of the Congressional Committees Investigating the Iran-Contra Affair: With Supplemental, Minority, and Additional Views*, 100th Congress, 1st session (Washington, DC: US Government Printing Office, 1987), 36.

[138] US Congress, Committee on Foreign Affairs, *Congress and Foreign Policy – 1984*, 32. In 1986, the International Court of Justice ruled that the United States had violated the sovereignty of Nicaragua.

[139] *The Washington Post*, April 10, 1984, Robert J. Dole Senate Papers, Nicaragua 1983–1984, Box N/A, Folder N/A, Robert J. Dole Archive and Special Collections, University of Kansas.

[140] Philip Taubman, "House to Block Aid for Rebels, O'Neill Asserts," *The New York Times*, April 10, 1984, Nexis Uni.

[141] *The Washington Post*, April 10, 1984, Robert J. Dole Senate Papers, Nicaragua 1983-1984, Box N/A, Folder N/A, Robert J. Dole Archive and Special Collections, University of Kansas.

happens, I'm going to raise one hell of a lot of fuss about it in public."[142] The administration's secrecy had caused significant blowback.

The revelations prompted a monumental shift in congressional attitudes toward the administration's Nicaragua policy. Both the House and Senate immediately passed nonbinding resolutions condemning the harbor mining, and opponents of Contra aid began working on reintroducing restrictions. Staunch supporters of Contra aid, such as Dick Cheney (R-WY), remained unaffected and immediately denounced any restrictions, arguing they would destroy the Contras' ability as a fighting force.[143] Yet moderate Republicans and conservative Democrats, who had previously found a ban on Contra aid too extreme a measure, changed their mind after the harbor mining and gave the bill the necessary support. Consequently, in May 1984, the House passed the second Boland Amendment, which Senate Republicans reluctantly accepted, in part also because it was tied to a popular jobs bill.[144] The second Boland Amendment, which became law on October 10, 1984, contained much stronger and more precise language than had its predecessor and unambiguously prohibited the use of funds for any military or paramilitary operations in Nicaragua of any kind. Congress could choose to revoke the amendment if the president submitted evidence that the Sandinistas were providing military assistance to guerrilla groups in El Salvador.[145]

Attempts to prevent the passage of the second Boland Amendment had been complicated by another shocking revelation on October 1, 1984. *The Associated Press* reported that the CIA had provided the Contras with a manual entitled *Psychological Operations in Guerilla Warfare*, which provided instructions on how to make selective killings of Nicaraguan government officials and how to terrorize civilians to deter them from collaborating with the Sandinista government.[146] The manual became known as the Contra "murder manual," and its revelation marked the beginning of intensified interest in Contra human rights

---

[142] Felton, John. "Hill Presses Reagan on Central America Policy," *CQ Weekly* (April 14, 1984): 831–833.
    http://library.cqpress.com/cqweekly/WR098402494. Lindsay, *Congress and Politics of U.S. Foreign Policy*, 67.
[143] Charlie Savage, *Takeover: The Return of the Imperial Presidency and the Subversion of American Democracy* (New York: Little, Brown, 2007), 53.
[144] LeoGrande, *Our Own Backyard*, 343–344.
[145] US Congress, *Public Law 98-473 H.J.Res. 648; Continuing Appropriations, 1985 – Comprehensive Crime Control Act of 1984 including section 8066(a), Boland Amendment II*, October 12, 1984, accessed August 9, 2019, www.brown.edu/Research/ Understanding_the_Iran_Contra_Affair /documents/d-all-39.pdf.
[146] LeoGrande, *Our Own Backyard*, 363; Tayacán and Library of Congress, Language Services Section, *Psychological Operations in Guerrilla Warfare* (Washington, DC: Congressional Research Service, 1984).

violations in the mainstream media.[147] Boland argued that the manual "points to the wisdom of Congressional action to cut off funding for the secret war."[148] Moreover, the revelation came at a sensitive time for Reagan, who was facing Walter Mondale in a presidential election debate less than a week later.[149] The administration, therefore, reacted by placing the responsibility for the manual with low-level agency employees in an attempt to keep Reagan and top officials free from blame.

Terrorists or "Gentlemen under Arms": From Reagan Victory to Iran–Contra

The struggle over Contra aid, and US policy toward Nicaragua in general, continued throughout Reagan's second term as the administration sought to navigate congressional restrictions. The struggle took place at the highest level, with the direct involvement of both the president and senior foreign policy officials and the Democratic leadership in Congress. Reagan's was personally strongly committed to resuming Contra aid. In January 1985, he told National Security Advisor Robert McFarlane "to do everything possible to reverse the course of the Congress, and get the funding renewed."[150]

Put on the defensive by the revelations of unlawful CIA activities and the passage of the second Boland Amendment, the administration revised its strategy on Nicaragua. First, the administration modified its legislative strategy and intensified its public diplomacy campaign to garner support for the resumption of Contra aid. Second, it launched alternative programs to secure funding for the Contras and moved operational support for the Contras from the CIA and the Department of Defense to the NSC, to circumvent the second Boland Amendment. The former strategy would ultimately prove successful as it secured the resumption of military aid to the Contras in the fall of 1986, although it failed to persuade the majority of the American public and the strongest opponents in Congress. The second strategy, however, would end up undermining the administration's Nicaragua policy and prove nearly fatal for Reagan's presidency as is escalated into the Iran–Contra Affair.

The administration invested an extraordinary amount of time and energy in its attempt to secure support for its Nicaragua policy, with

---

[147] Peace, "Winning Hearts and Minds," 18.
[148] Edward Boland to Thomas Downey, October 17, 1984, Box 19, Folder 8, TOP.
[149] Peck, *Ideal Illusions*, 120.
[150] US Congress, House, Senate, Select Committees, *Report of the Congressional Committees Investigating the Iran–Contra Affair*, 45.

the personal involvement of Reagan and other key officials. Reagan gave more speeches on Nicaragua during 1986 than he gave about all of the South American countries combined in his entire presidency.[151] The administration conducted a carefully planned lobbying campaign targeted at selected members of Congress, keeping detailed lists of members and timelines of congressional votes. Reagan, Vice President George H. W. Bush, and others personally phoned and met with selected members of Congress to persuade them to support the continuation of Contra aid.[152] Moreover, Reagan and key officials of the administration gave several speeches on Capitol Hill. In his 1985 State of the Union address, Reagan repeated his support for the Contras, calling them "freedom fighters" and urged, "we must not break faith with those who are risking their lives – on every continent, from Afghanistan to Nicaragua – to defy Soviet-supported aggression and secure rights which have been ours from birth."[153]

The administration, however, was convinced that direct lobbying on Capitol Hill was not enough to sway the mood of Congress on Contra aid. Therefore, it combined such lobbying with a comprehensive public diplomacy campaign aimed at influencing public opinion. According to a White House memo, the key issue was that members of Congress only received constituent pressure from people opposed to Contra support. This was the case, the memo continued, because the public got most of its information from reports written by human rights NGOs and religious organizations that lacked an understanding of Nicaragua's strategic importance to the United States. To increase public support for Contra aid, the memo recommended that such aid be presented as part of a broader effort aimed at encouraging democratic reforms in both Nicaragua and El Salvador.[154]

The administration invested extensive resources in its public diplomacy campaign. As with its legislative lobbying campaign, it kept detailed

---

[151] Carothers, *In the Name of Democracy*, 142.

[152] M. B. Oglesby by to James A. Baker III and Robert McFarlane, Nicaragua Legislative Strategy, January 10, 1985, ID #297413, CO114, WHORM: Subject File, RPL. See, for instance, Reagan's meeting with members of Congress on April 22, 1985; Reagan and Brinkley, *The Reagan Diaries*, 318; Max Friedersdorf and M. B. Oglesby to Ronald Reagan, April 15, 1985, Folder "Congressman Hamilton," Box OA 17439, White House Office of Legislative Affairs, RPL; Max Friedersdorf and M. B. Oglesby to Ronald Reagan, April 17, 1985, Folder 'Selected House Republicans,' Box OA 17439, White House Office of Legislative Affairs, RPL.

[153] Ronald Reagan, "Address before a Joint Session of the Congress on the State of the Union February 6, 1985," accessed August 1, 2019, www.reaganlibrary.gov/research/speeches/20685e.

[154] M. B. Oglesby to James A. Baker III and Robert McFarlane, Nicaragua Legislative Strategy, January 10, 1985, ID #297413, CO114, WHORM: Subject File, RPL.

lists of key newspapers, TV shows, and private sector leaders to target.[155] The State Department issued a staggering number of White House Digests through the S/LPD between 1983 and 1986, seeking to reinvigorate the image of the Contras and draw attention to the human rights violations of the Sandinistas.[156] The administration also enlisted Nicaraguans hostile toward the Sandinistas to sell its message, sending them on lobbying tours around the United States. In internal memos, the S/LPD bragged about the success of its "white propaganda." An S/LPD memo from March 1985 described a *Washington Post* editorial as the direct result of such a lobbying tour and called it an excellent example of the approach "to capture moderates and liberals on the Hill for the President's Nicaragua problem."[157]

At the same time, the administration initiated a backup plan to secure alternative funding for the Contras in case efforts to restore official funding should fail.[158] First, North and Abrams were tasked with soliciting funds from third parties, such as private individuals and the governments of foreign allies, including Saudi Arabia, Taiwan, and Brunei, which was not explicitly forbidden by the second Boland Amendment. Second, the administration sold arms to Iran in exchange for help with the release of American hostages in Beirut and then funneled the proceeds from these sales to the Contras, thereby violating US law by breaking a ban on arms sales to Iran and going against Reagan's declaration that the United States does not negotiate with terrorists.[159] Third, the administration moved the operational support for the Contras to the NSC, which was not explicitly mentioned in the Boland Amendment.

Multiple concerns drove congressional opposition to Contra aid in 1985–1986. The dominating concern, shared by both Democrats and Republicans, was that the administration's activities in Nicaragua were violating the Boland Amendment and thereby breaking US law.[160] At the same time, concern for "another Vietnam" remained strong. Senator

[155] "No title," April 16, 1985, ID #231909, CO114, WHORM: Subject File, RPL.

[156] *White House Digest*, "Nicaraguan Repression of Labor Unions," August 24, 1983, ID #198611, CO114, WHORM: Subject File, RPL; *White House Digest*, "Persecution of Christians," February 29, 1984, ID #198611, CO114, WHORM: Subject File, RPL; *White House Digest*, "Sandinista Violations of Human Rights," May 24, 1984, ID #204608, CO114, WHORM: Subject File, RPL.

[157] Jonathan Miller to Pat Buchanan, Editorial in the *Washington Post*, March 18, 1985, ID #273247, CO114, WHORM: Subject File, RPL.

[158] Robert McFarlane, Top Secret, Memorandum "[With Tabs – "Approve" Box Initialed by Robert McFarlane]," January 15, 1985, IC00725, The Iran–Contra Affair: The Making of a Scandal, 1983–1988, Digital National Security Archive.

[159] Zelizer, *Arsenal of Democracy*, 336–337.

[160] Peace, "Winning Hearts and Minds," 12.

Cranston feared that the administration might be dragged into a war in Nicaragua, although Reagan did not intend to get involved.[161] Liberal anti-war Democrats, such as Harkin and Cranston, in particular, stressed their preference for a diplomatic solution to the conflict, urging the administration to genuinely support regional peace proposals such as the Contadora process.[162] Another, less broadly quoted concern was international law. In June 1986, the ICJ confirmed that the United States had violated the sovereignty of Nicaragua by placing mines in its harbors.[163] Finally, human rights violations by the Sandinistas and the Contras continued to be an essential part of the debate.

Congressional opponents of Contra aid were initially successful in blocking further aid. In April 1985, the Senate approved a request by Reagan for the release of $14 million in aid, only to see the House reject it the following day.[164] Reagan had coupled his request with a proposal for a cease-fire and support for Sandinista–Contra negotiations to make the request more palatable for its critics in Congress.[165] The majority of Congress, however, remained unconvinced of the administration's commitment to negotiations, continued to fear a direct military intervention, and remained concerned with Contra human rights abuses. Ahead of the vote, the Subcommittee on the Western Hemisphere held a three-day-long hearing on "U.S. Support for the Contras." In the words of Barnes, the purpose of the hearing was to establish the truth of claims of human rights violations on both sides. Officials from the administration argued that violations were taking place on both sides. Representative Samuel Gejdenson (D-CT) contested this assessment, claiming that no legitimate group had made substantial allegations of human rights abuses by the Sandinistas.[166] In reality, several human rights NGOs, including Amnesty International and Freedom House, had reported on human rights abuses by the Sandinistas.[167] Nevertheless, most witnesses at the

---

[161] Alan Cranston, Talking Paper for Nicaragua Press Conference, April 18, 1985, Box 272, ACP.

[162] Tom Harkin et al. to Ronald Reagan, February 10, 1986, Box 264, ACP.

[163] The International Court of Justice, *Summary of the Judgment of 27 June 1986. Case Concerning the Military and Paramilitary Activities in and against Nicaragua (Nicaragua v. United States of America)*, accessed August 1, 2019, https://www.icj-cij.org/files/case-related/70/6505.pdf.

[164] Congress had put the $14 million on hold through previous legislation, but eventually released it in August 1985 earmarked for "humanitarian purposes."

[165] US Congress, House, Committee on Foreign Affairs, *U.S. Support for the Contras*, 191–198.

[166] Ibid., 236.

[167] See, for instance, News from Freedom House, February 22, 1982, ID #097002, CO114, WHORM: Subject File, RPL; *Newsweek*, "Nicaragua and Human Rights: A Double Standard?"August 18, 1986, Box IV.1.6 260, Folder 9, AIUSA; Letter and

hearing agreed that Sandinista abuses dwindled in comparison to those by the Contras. The so-called Brody Report, based on a five-month fact-finding mission by lawyer Reed Brody, found that the Contras committed systematic attacks and atrocities against civilian targets.[168] The report strongly contradicted the Reagan administration's description of the Contras and led Reagan to attack Brody for being a Sandinista sympathizer. Yet several human rights NGOs overwhelmingly confirmed the accuracy of the report.[169] Liberal senators also issued press releases ridiculing Reagan's description of the Contras as freedom fights. Senator Proxmire, for instance, proclaimed, "The Nicaraguan rebels we support have repeatedly committed serious human rights violations," before listing rape, torture, and murder of civilians among the abuses.[170]

The floor debates in April 1985 ahead of the vote in both the House and the Senate also centered on human rights abuses. Opponents of Contra aid focused on Contra human rights violations. In the Senate, Harkin argued, "No, the Contras are not freedom fighters, who reflect the ideals and values of the American people. They are terrorists whose atrocities have been documented by respected human rights organizations."[171] In the House, Lee Hamilton (D-IN) speculated that the human rights violations committed by the Contras were probably no worse than those by the Sandinistas, but argued that the main difference was that the United States financed the Contras and therefore had to answer for their atrocities.[172] Representative Mel Levine (D-CA) referred to the Contras' record of a "terribly disturbing pattern of attacks on civilian targets resulting in the killing on unarmed men, women, children, and the elderly: premeditated acts of brutality including rape, beatings, mutilation, and torture" documented by human rights groups.[173] While focusing primarily on the threat of communism, Contra aid supporters also invoked human rights language. Ahead of the Senate vote, Helms opened his statement by declaring that Congress had to "decide whether the United States wants to support freedom and human

---

Report, Amnesty International USA to George P. Shultz, December 8, 1986, Box IV.1.6 260, Folder 9, AIUSA.

[168] US Congress, House, Committee on Foreign Affairs, *U.S. Support for the Contras*, 346–356.

[169] Ibid., 315.

[170] Press Release, William Proxmire, April 14, 1985, Digital Identifier: BPPRPt4, Senator William Proxmire Papers, Wisconsin Historical Society, http://digital.library.wisc.edu/1711.dl/wiarchives.uw-whs-mss00738.

[171] 131 *Congressional Record*, 99th Congress, 1st Session, 8831 (April 23, 1985). Previously a representative, Tom Harkin was elected to the Senate in 1984.

[172] 131 *Congressional Record*, 99th Congress, 1st Session, 9015 (April 23, 1985).

[173] 131 *Congressional Record*, 99th Congress, 1st Session, 9007 (April 23, 1985).

rights, or whether one more nation will fall by default to Marxism-Leninism."[174] Senator Jeremiah Denton (R-AL), a conservative anti-communist, argued that the Contras were committed to improving their human rights record, citing from a Nicaraguan Democratic Force manual: "FDN means enforcement of human rights: above all."[175] In the House, Minority Leader Robert H. Michel (R-IL) similarly stated his belief that the Sandinistas were "ideologically committed to human rights violations as a matter of Marxist-Leninist principle."[176] Evidently, both sides in the debate included references to human rights concerns as part of their argumentation.

The day after the House had rejected the resumption of aid, the media reported that Nicaraguan President Daniel Ortega was traveling to Moscow, where he received Soviet assurances of further foreign aid. Although the trip was not Ortega's first to the Soviet Union, it added strength to Reagan's claims of a Moscow–Managua alliance and as such put pressure on opponents of Contra aid, while also adding to their discontent with the Sandinistas. This situation, along with the perception that the administration had shown its willingness to compromise by supporting Sandinista–Contra negotiations, helped shift the political climate in favor of supporting the Contras.[177] The administration immediately seized the moment to ramp up its pressure on both the Sandinista and the domestic opponents of Contra aid. On May 1, 1985, Reagan imposed a trade embargo on Sandinista Nicaragua through an executive order.[178] Announcing the embargo to Congress, Reagan listed his demands for Nicaragua to halt subversive activities in neighboring countries, cut military ties to the Soviet Union and Cuba, cease its arms buildup, and adhere to "democratic pluralism and observance of full political and human rights."[179] The administration pointed out that the embargo ought not to be considered a substitute for Contra aid.[180]

---

[174] 131 *Congressional Record*, 99th Congress, 1st Session, 99, 8837 (April 23, 1985).

[175] 131 *Congressional Record*, 99th Congress, 1st Session, 99, 8862 (April 23, 1985).

[176] 131 *Congressional Record*, 99th Congress, 1st Session, 99, 8965 (April 23, 1985).

[177] Arnson, *Crossroads*, 183.

[178] Ronald Reagan, Executive Order 12513—Prohibiting Trade and Certain Other Transactions Involving Nicaragua, May 1, 1985. Online by Gerhard Peters and John T. Woolley, The American Presidency Project, accessed August 7, 2019, www.presidency.ucsb.edu/node/259383.

[179] Ronald Reagan, Message to the Congress on Economic Sanctions Against Nicaragua, May 1, 1985. Online by Gerhard Peters and John T. Woolley, The American Presidency Project, accessed August 7, 2019, www.presidency.ucsb.edu/node/259384.

[180] Ronald Reagan, Statement by Principal Deputy Press Secretary Speakes on Economic Sanctions against Nicaragua, May 1, 1985. Online by Gerhard Peters and John T. Woolley, The American Presidency Project, accessed August 7, 2019, www.presidency.ucsb.edu/node/259385.

The embargo came at a time when the administration was vehemently resisting congressional pressure for economic sanctions against South Africa.

In the increasingly hostile climate, moderate Democrats like Dave McCurdy (D-OK) became concerned that rejecting Contra aid made them look supportive of communism and consequently introduced a bill for nonlethal aid of $27 million.[181] Ahead of the House vote, Reagan used a national radio address to challenge House Democrats by asking: "Will you support those struggling for democracy? Will you resist the Soviets' brazen attempt to impose communism on our doorstep or won't you?"[182] Reagan also sent a letter to McCurdy that was distributed on the House floor the day of the vote, stating that the US government accepted special responsibility for the human rights record of the Contras including "proper treatment of prisoners and the civilian population."[183] The pressure proved successful, as the fear of appearing soft on communism triumphed over the desire to halt Contra abuses. "Nobody wants to be portrayed as friendly toward Communism," Wright reasoned after both chambers of Congress approval of the resumption of Contra aid in June 1985.[184] The restored Contra aid was only a partial victory for Reagan, however. The $27 million was strictly earmarked for humanitarian aid, CIA or Defense Department involvement was prohibited, and Congress required that aid be used as leverage to push for peace talks.[185] To comply with the restrictions, the administration had to establish a new agency, the Nicaraguan Humanitarian Assistance Office, to oversee the distribution of Contra aid.

Despite its partial victories on Capitol Hill, the administration failed to win the public diplomacy war. An NSC memo from June 1985 conceded that the administration was failing to generate public support for its

---

[181] Reagan had met with McCurdy five days before in an attempt to persuade him to support the resumption of Contra aid. Max Friedersdorf and M. B. Oglesby to Ronald Reagan, April 18, 1985, Folder "Congressman McCurdy," Box OA 17439, White House Office of Legislative Affairs, RPL.

[182] Ronald Reagan, Radio Address to the Nation on United States Assistance for the Nicaraguan Democratic Resistance, June 8, 1985. Online by Gerhard Peters and John T. Woolley, The American Presidency Project, accessed August 7, 2019, www.presidency.ucsb.edu/node/260206.

[183] Report, Washington Office on Latin America, February 19, 1986, Records of the United States Senate, Record Group 46, Dockery and Sklar Files, Box 92, Center for Legislative Archives, National Archives, Washington, DC.

[184] Steven J. Roberts, "House Reverses Earlier Ban on Aid to Nicaragua Rebels; Passes $27 Million Package," The New York Times, June 13, 1985, Nexis Uni.

[185] "Congress Votes to Resume Nicaragua Rebel Aid," in CQ Almanac 1985, 41st edn., 61–80 (Washington, DC: Congressional Quarterly, 1986), http://library.cqpress.com/cqalmanac/cqal85-1147212.

policy and that Reagan's ability to influence public opinion had reached its limit. Consequently, the memo recommended that the administration seek to shift public focus away from military activities in Nicaragua and onto diplomatic and economic initiatives in Central America more broadly.[186] Already on March 15, 1985, Reagan wrote in his diary, "Our communications on Nicaragua have been a failure."[187] Opinion polls confirmed the president's analysis. In May 1985, a Harris Survey asked the American public which side they took in recent disagreements between Reagan and Congress over, "Sending military aid to the Contra rebels in Nicaragua, which is favored by Reagan and opposed by Congress?" Thirty-four percent answered that they sided with Reagan, while 59 percent sided with Congress.[188] Two months later, the numbers were 28 percent with Reagan and 64 percent with Congress.[189] There could be no doubt that public opinion was firmly on the side of Congress in opposing military aid to the Contras.

Still not allowed to supply the Contras with arms, Reagan returned to Congress in February 1986 with a new request, this time for $100 million in military aid. To make the request palatable to its critics in Congress, the administration framed the request as part of a wider diplomatic effort aimed at forcing the Sandinistas to the negotiating table to secure a peaceful end to the conflict.[190] The request also earmarked $3 million to improve respect for human rights among the Contras. Before Congress voted on the request, Abrams assured the Senate Foreign Relations Committee that the Contras were determined to improve their human rights record.[191] Such rapprochements to congressional concerns were accompanied by fierce partisan attacks on Democrats. White House Director of Communications Pat Buchanan went as far as to state, "With the Contra vote, the Democratic Party will reveal whether is stands with

---

[186] Rodney McDaniel to Robert McFarlane, Public Opinion Re U.S. Policy toward Nicaragua, June 3, 1985, ID #337438, CO114, WHORM: Subject File, RPL.

[187] Reagan and Brinkley, *The Reagan Diaries*, 308.

[188] Louis Harris & Associates. Harris Survey, May 1985. USHARRIS.060685.R4. Cornell University, Ithaca, NY: Roper Center for Public Opinion Research, iPOLL, accessed August 6, 2019.

[189] Louis Harris & Associates. Harris Survey, July 1985. USHARRIS.281285.R6. Cornell University, Ithaca, NY: Roper Center for Public Opinion Research, iPOLL, accessed August 6, 2019.

[190] Ronald Reagan, Message to the Congress Transmitting a Request for Assistance for the Nicaraguan Democratic Resistance, February 25, 1986. Online by Gerhard Peters and John T. Woolley, The American Presidency Project, accessed August 7, 2019, www.presidency.ucsb.edu/node/258023.

[191] US Congress, Senate, Committee on Foreign Relations, *U.S. Policy toward Nicaragua: Aid to Nicaraguan Resistance Proposal: Hearings before the Committee on Foreign Relations*, 99th Congress, 2nd Session, February 27 and March 4, 1986, 37–39.

Ronald Reagan and the resistance – or Daniel Ortega and the communists."[192] Conservative pro-Contra groups also ran attack ads against Democrats opposed to Contra aid, such as Barnes, who was at the time running for a Senate seat. The ads questioned Barnes's loyalty to the United States and drew support from conservatives Republicans such as Gingrich, who called Barnes "an ideological radical," while moderate Republicans such as Mathias denounced it as a smear campaign.[193] Despite the ferocious attacks questioning their patriotism, Democrats in the House turned down the request in a close-cut vote on March 20, justifying their position by arguing that military aid to the Contras was not going to solve the conflict.

The Reagan administration unaffectedly continued its lobbying efforts over the spring, as developments in Nicaragua offered a helping hand. A few days after the House vote, the Sandinistas raided a Contra camp inside Honduras, providing the administration an additional argument for the need to support the Contras. The Senate responded by narrowly approving Reagan's $100 million request as part of a bill introduced by Richard Lugar (R-IN), although moderate Republicans such as Mathias voted against, arguing that more weapons would not contribute to a diplomatic solution to the conflict.[194] Still, Democrats in the House stood firm, rejecting a proposal for limited aid introduced by McCurdy in April.[195] The administration and its allies continued to intensify pressure on Democrats, making extensive use of human rights language. In a letter to members of Congress, the administration argued that the Sandinista raid into Honduras and the regimes continued repression of Miskito Indians demonstrated their "belligerent approach to internal and regional conflict."[196] The administration attached documents by the Contra leadership, which it claimed demonstrated "a clear commitment

---

[192] Patrick Buchanan, "The Contras Need Our Help," *The Washington Post*, March 5, 1986, A19.

[193] "A Message to Congressman Mike Barnes," *The Washington Times*, March 17, 1986, 5A; Sandra Sugawara, "Conservative Gop Congressmen Blasts Barnes," *The Washington Post*, March 13, 1986, C1; Press Release, "Maryland Legislators Deplore Smear Campaign Tactics," June 27, 1986, Box 17, Folder 'Barnes,' Charles McC Mathias Papers Ms. 150, Special Collections, Milton S. Eisenhower Library, The Johns Hopkins University. Barnes was unsuccessful in his attempt to win the Senate seat left vacant by the retirement of Mathias, but there is no evidence to suggest that the ads were responsible, since another liberal Democrat, Barbara Mikulski (D-MD), won the seat.

[194] Press Release, "Mathias Opposes Military Aid to Nicaraguan Contras," March 26, 1986, Box 29, Folder 'Nicaragua 1986,' Charles McC Mathias Papers Ms. 150, Special Collections, Milton S. Eisenhower Library, The Johns Hopkins University.

[195] Scott, "Interbranch Rivalry," 252.

[196] Department of State to Congress, April 11, 1986, Box 19, Folder 5, TOP.

to democratic objectives and respect for human rights." Among the documents was a Contra "Code of Conduct" which stated that every soldier had an obligation to "conduct himself as a gentleman under arms."[197] Although the administration realized that the majority of Americans did not see the Contras as "freedom fighters," it relentlessly sought to rehabilitate their image by claiming they respected human rights.[198]

In June 1986, moderate Democrats in the House finally caved in under the mounting pressure and voted to grant the $100 million, while liberal Democrats dissented. Representative Lane Evans (D-IL) dismissed Contra efforts to rebrand themselves as respectful of human rights as a mere "public relations ploy."[199] Representative George Miller (D-CA) expressed a viewpoint shared by most liberals when he summarized the situation surrounding the request: "When former Sandinistas say that the Sandinistas are violating human rights, Ronald Reagan says we should invade them. When Contra leaders say that the Contras are violating human rights, Ronald Reagan says reward them with $100 million."[200] Yet, most representatives complied with Reagan's request, and in August the Senate followed suit. After agreeing to a joint resolution in October, Congress reestablished military aid to the Contras effective from November 1. The resolution also lifted most Boland restrictions, including allowing the CIA to once again manage the funds. The bill did include a provision barring aid to any group retaining individuals engaged in gross human rights abuses, drug smuggling, or significant misuse of public or private funds. The provision, however, was without teeth because its enforcement was left to the administration.[201]

The victory on Contra aid, however, was short lived. The Iran–Contra Affair had begun to unfold in parallel with the debate over Contra aid, and by the end of 1986, it threatened not only to terminate support for the Contras but also to destabilize the administration entirely.[202] On October 5, the Sandinistas shot down a cargo plane carrying arms to the Contras, capturing one of its American pilots. A few days later, American newspapers reported that the pilot had been carrying out the

---

[197] Code of Conduct: FDN, Box 19, Folder 5, TOP.

[198] The administration applied a similar strategy to El Salvador, arguing that the regime was improving its human rights record by instituting a code of conduct. Renouard, *Human Rights in American Foreign Policy*, 187–188.

[199] 132 *Congressional Record*, 99th Congress, 2nd Session, 15461 (June 25, 1986).

[200] Ibid.

[201] "Congress Agrees to Renew Contra Arms Aid," in *CQ Almanac 1986*, 42nd edn., 394–414 (Washington, DC: Congressional Quarterly, 1987), http://library.cqpress .com/cqalmanac/cqal86–1149114.

[202] For a more extensive account of the Iran–Contra Affair, see Draper, *A Very Thin Line*; Byrne, *Iran–Contra*.

operation as part of a CIA supply mission for the Contras. Subsequently, the Senate Foreign Relations Committee held a briefing with the CIA to investigate these claims.[203] Abrams and other administration officials at first denied any connection, but in Iran–Contra hearings would later confirm that the plane was part of a CIA operation. Then on November 3, the day before the 1986 midterm elections, a Lebanese newspaper revealed that the administration had sold weapons to Iran in exchange for hostages. The administration initially denied the allegations, but as further evidence emerged, it acknowledged on November 25 that officials had funneled money from the Iranian weapons sale to the Contras. On the same date, Reagan announced the resignation of Admiral John Poindexter from his position as deputy national security advisor and the dismissal of NSC staffer Lieutenant Colonel Oliver North, who had been responsible for keeping the Contras alive.[204]

The administration's confessions did not prevent further scrutiny of the affair but rather signified the beginning of several thorough investigations. Reagan appointed a special review board, known as the Tower Commission from its chair Senator John Tower (R-TX), to examine the activities of the NSC. In addition, an independent counsel, Lawrence Walsh, was appointed to investigate the legal issues of the affair. In March 1987, the House and Senate set up special committees to investigate the affair, conducting extensive, TV-covered public hearings with key officials lasting forty-one days. The hearings offered Congress a leading role in the investigations of the affair. The Democratic Party's recapturing of control over the Senate in the 1986 midterm elections left the administration extra vulnerable to the congressional onslaught.[205]

The investigations delivered a rough judgment on Reagan and the NSC but failed to place definitive responsibility with Reagan. The Tower Commission concluded that White House staffers had broken the law by using funds from the Iran weapon sales and foreign donors to arm the Contras. However, it maintained that the president had been unaware of this scheme, limiting itself to rebuking Regan for his managerial style and

[203] Memorandum, Mark Falcoff and Barry Sklar to Members of the SFRC, October 9, 1986, Records of the United States Senate, Record Group 46; Dockery and Sklar Files, Box 93, Center for Legislative Archives, National Archives, Washington, DC; "Captured American Says CIA ran Supply Missions," *Washington Post*, October 10, 1986, Records of the United States Senate, Record Group 46; Dockery and Sklar Files, Box 93, Center for Legislative Archives, National Archives, Washington, DC.

[204] Ronald Reagan, Remarks Announcing the Review of the National Security Council's Role in the Iran Arms and Contra Aid Controversy, November 25, 1986. Online by Gerhard Peters and John T. Woolley, The American Presidency Project, accessed August 7, 2019, www.presidency.ucsb.edu/node/258235.

[205] Byrne, *Iran–Contra*. For the congressional investigations, see 279–306.

for failing to oversee the activities of his administration.[206] On March 4, 1987, the day before the congressional investigations began; Reagan took responsibility for selling weapons to Iran in exchange for hostages, but he denied knowing about the funneling of money to the Contras.[207] The congressional investigations as well as the independent counsel, Lawrence Walsh, concluded that the responsibility for the Iran–Contra Affair ultimately rested with the president, yet they failed to provide evidence of Reagan explicitly giving orders to violate the law.[208] Historian Malcolm Byrne has since demonstrated that Reagan was the driving force behind the decisions that led to the scandal and argued that the actions amounted to an abuse of presidential power.[209]

Reagan eventually recovered politically by delivering progress on negotiations with the Soviet Union, but the Iran–Contra Affair significantly weakened the administration's ability to dictate policy on Nicaragua.[210] Despite lacking decisive evidence to place responsibility for Iran–Contra with Reagan, members of Congress and others involved with the investigations generally agreed that the activities were in line with Reagan's policies and general instructions.[211] In the court of public opinion, the verdict was also unfavorable to Reagan. As the Iran-Contra Affair unraveled before the eyes of millions of Americans watching the televised investigations during the summer of 1987, Reagan's popularity plummeted to around the mid-forties throughout 1987.[212]

Congress used the situation to seize the initiative on US Nicaragua policy, effectively taking control over US policy during the last years of

---

[206] John Tower, Edmund Muskie, and Brent Scowcroft, *The Tower Commission Report* (New York: Bantam Books, 1987).

[207] Ronald Reagan, Address to the Nation on the Iran Arms and Contra Aid Controversy, March 4, 1987. Online by Gerhard Peters and John T. Woolley, The American Presidency Project, accessed August 7, 2019, www.presidency.ucsb.edu/node/252209.

[208] US Congress, House, Senate, Select Committees, *Report of the Congressional Committees Investigating the Iran–Contra Affair*, 149; Lawrence E. Walsh and Office of Independent Counsel, *Iran–Contra: The Final Report* (New York: Times, 1994), 443–445.

[209] Byrne, *Iran–Contra*, 331–333.

[210] Several key officials from the NSC, including North, McFarlane, and Poindexter, were convicted of a number of criminal offenses, including withholding information from Congress and providing false statements. President George H. W. Bush pardoned McFarlane, North was granted immunity in return for his testimony, and Poindexter's sentence was overturned. Casey was hospitalized before the hearings began and died in 1987. Weinberger was also indicted but was pardoned by George H. W. Bush.

[211] US Congress, House, Senate, Select Committees, *Report of the Congressional Committees Investigating the Iran–Contra Affair*, 69; Walsh and Office of Independent Counsel, *Iran–Contra: The Final Report*, 562.

[212] Jeffrey M. Jones, Frank Newport, and Lydia Saad, *Ronald Reagan from the People's Perspective: A Gallup Poll Review*, accessed August 9, 2019, www.gallup.com/poll/11887/ronald-reagan-from-peoples-perspective-gallup-poll-review.aspx.

the Reagan administration.[213] Under the leadership of Speaker Wright, Democrats worked to prevent further military aid to the Contras and to reach a diplomatic solution to the conflict. Liberals wanted to cut off all aid to the Contras, and in March 1987, the House tried to block the release of the remainder of the funds authorized for 1987. Their efforts, however, were obstructed by the Senate, where conservative Republicans such as Wallop continued to support the Contra aid.[214] Nevertheless, Congress did reject Reagan's requests for new military aid, agreeing only to allocate $14 million for humanitarian aid by the end of the year. In February 1988, House Democrats defeated another Reagan request for $36 million in new military and nonmilitary aid in a close 211–219 vote.[215] Congress approved a request for humanitarian aid the following month but continued to reject military aid throughout the rest of Reagan's tenure.

Simultaneously, congressional Democrats such as Wright, Dodd, and Byrd stepped up their efforts to commit the United States to a diplomatic solution to the conflict, often conducting their own diplomacy without administration approval. Byrd, for instance, corresponded with Nicaraguan officials and subsequently sought to persuade the administration to engage in direct negotiations with the Sandinistas.[216] After the Contadora peace plan talks broke down in the summer of 1986, four Central American presidents had united behind the new peace initiative under the leadership of Costa Rican President Oscar Arias.[217] Congress enthusiastically supported the peace initiative, adopting with an overwhelming majority a resolution calling for the administration to support it.[218] Shultz later recalled, "Dodd conducted his own negotiations, making suggestions that undercut" the administration's positions by encouraging much more extensive talks that Reagan desired.[219]

---

[213] Lindsay, *Congress and the Politics of U.S. Foreign Policy*, 89.
[214] Letter, Malcolm Wallop to Frank Carlucci, February 25, 1987, Box 65, Folder 35, Malcolm Wallop Papers, 1965–1995, Collection Number 08011, American Heritage Center, University of Wyoming.
[215] "Hill, Reagan Struggle over Aid to Contras," in *CQ Almanac 1987*, 43rd edn., 112–135 (Washington, DC: Congressional Quarterly, 1988). http://library.cqpress.com/cqalmanac/cqal87–1144546.
[216] Letter, Ambassador Carlos Tunnermann to Robert Byrd, August 12, 1986; Letter, Robert Byrd to George P. Shultz, August 14, 1986, Records of the United States Senate, Record Group 46; Dockery and Sklar Files, Box 85, Center for Legislative Archives, National Archives, Washington, DC.
[217] President Arias won the 1987 Nobel Peace Prize for his efforts.
[218] Statement, Claiborne Pell, March 12, 1987, Records of the United States Senate, Record Group 46; Dockery and Sklar Files, Box 85, Center for Legislative Archives, National Archives, Washington, DC; Linda Greenhouse, "Senate Backs Costa Rican Peace Plan," *The New York Times*, March 13, 1987, www.nytimes.com/1987/03/13/world/senate-backs-costa-rican-peace-plan-881.html.
[219] Shultz, *Turmoil and Triumph*, 955.

The congressional advocacy for diplomatic negotiations succeeded on August 5, 1987, when Wright got Reagan's support for a peace proposal that called for a cease-fire and a sixty-day suspension of both US military aid to the Contras and Soviet military aid to the Sandinistas. Two days later, however, the Arias peace initiative resulted in the agreement with the Sandinistas known as the Esquipulas I, which required regional cease-fires, negotiations, and preparations for elections. Wright immediately endorsed Esquipulas I and began pressuring the Reagan administration to do the same.[220] On November 9, the administration reluctantly threw its support behind the peace plan. In a further demonstration of congressional power over US Nicaragua policy, Wright met with the Sandinistas and the Contra leaders in the following days, trying to bring the two parties together.[221] The meeting represented another act of Lone Ranger diplomacy, where Congress assumed a role normally reserved for the executive branch. Wright received substantial criticism for infringing the president's foreign policy prerogatives, but the power balance in the wake of the Iran–Contra Affair made such congressional assertiveness possible. Congress's rejection of Reagan's request for renewed military aid in February 1988 underscored this new reality. The following month, the Sandinistas and the Contras signed a cease-fire agreement.

Reagan's replacement with H. W. Bush, who did not share his predecessor's deep commitment to the Contras, improved the working relationship between the executive branch and Congress tremendously and contributed to unifying American support for the peace initiative.[222] Within two months of his tenure, Bush had signed the Bipartisan Accord on Central America with the congressional leadership, which effectively made Contra aid a non-issue by banning military aid, while allowing humanitarian aid. Bush's Secretary of State, James A. Baker III, recalls that he told Dodd in a private meeting in 1989 that although he preferred military aid, "We realize that's not in the cards, so I'm not even going to ask for it."[223] Congressional assertiveness had stymied the executive branch's willingness to fight for Contra aid and on February 25, 1990, democratic elections achieved what the Contras had failed to do by putting the Sandinistas out of power.

---

[220] "Hill, Reagan Struggle over Aid to Contras," in *CQ Almanac 1987*.

[221] Lindsay, *Congress and the Politics of U.S. Foreign Policy*, 120.

[222] "Nicaragua Policy Shifts under Bush," in *CQ Almanac 1989*, 45th edn., 569–585 (Washington, DC: Congressional Quarterly, 1990), http://library.cqpress.com/cqalmanac/cqal89–1139520.

[223] James Addison Baker and Thomas M. DeFrank, *The Politics of Diplomacy: Revolution, War, and Peace, 1989–1992* (New York: G. P. Putnam's, 1995), 56.

Conclusion

Human rights concerns figured prominently as the Reagan administration and members of Congress struggled to shape US Nicaragua policy in the 1980s. Liberal Democrats and other members of Congress opposed to Contra aid invoked the human rights violations of the Contras as one of several arguments to terminate aid for these. The administration and its congressional allies partially motivated their support for the Contras as a way to end Sandinista human rights abuses. The most important vehicle for congressional human rights concerns was the imposition of bans on Contra aid through legislation such as the Boland Amendments. Closely connected to these efforts was a public diplomacy war over American public opinion, where the human rights records of the Contras and the Sandinistas again figured prominently. Some members of Congress, such as Wright, also bypassed the administration through Lone Ranger diplomacy with the Sandinista government. Congressional activism on Nicaragua was comprehensive, made extensive use of human rights language, and received active support from the Democratic leadership.

The shifting fortunes in the power struggle between the administration and members of Congress resulted in an inconsistent foreign policy. Congressional restrictions on aid constrained the administration's ability to legally provide the Contras with the aid it preferred and consequently hampered its objective of overthrowing the Sandinistas. Through such aid restrictions members of Congress successfully used structural policy to impede the strategic policy of the executive branch.[224] Their pressure also forced the administration to show more support for negotiations than it would have preferred. Ultimately, congressional restrictions on aid made the administration pursue illegal alternatives to fund the Contras, resulting in the Iran–Contra Affair. Congressional opposition to Contra aid also led the administration to devote significant time and resources to swaying congressional and popular opinion. The extensive focus on human rights abuses in the conflict also led to the formalized integration of human rights concerns into US Nicaragua policy, for instance by earmarking funds to train the Contras to respect human rights.

The Reagan administration's decision to engage its opponents in a public diplomacy war over the human rights situation in Nicaragua shaped American attention to human rights in the 1980s in important ways. While the administration and its critics in Congress disagreed, sometimes ferociously, about the facts, the intense struggle over human

---

[224] Lindsay, *Congress and the Politics of U.S. Foreign Policy*, 157.

rights at the highest level of government elevated the salience of human rights concerns on the national agenda. Had the administration insisted on solely discussing the Nicaraguan conflict within a framework of anti-communism, such a comprehensive discussion of human rights would have been impossible. Whereas the struggle between members of Congress and the administration during the first months had centered on whether human rights had a role in US foreign policy, the debate over Nicaragua contributed to shifting the discussion to what role human rights ought to play.[225] This situation also reflected a significant change from the 1970s, when the Nixon and Ford administrations refused to recognize human rights concerns as a legitimate foreign policy issue. Importantly, the administration's insistence on attacking the human rights record of the Sandinistas also underscored its selective concern for human rights and made it vulnerable to criticism of hypocrisy and double standards. More than most other country-specific cases, the administration's demonizing of the Sandinistas and canonizing of the Contras demonstrated its failure to apply human rights standards consistently. The administration's human rights criticism of Sandinista Nicaragua also called into question US support for repressive regimes with more grievous human rights records. The willingness to impose sanctions on Nicaragua while fighting sanctions on South Africa was a case in point referred to by several liberal Democrats. The public diplomacy war over the situation in Nicaragua both contributed to the prominence of human rights as a moral language and underlined the ambiguity of the concept.

---

[225] Neier, *Taking Liberties*, 193. As Neier recalls about Americas Watch, "After Reagan's first year in office, we did not debate administration officials about the importance of human rights [...] We disputed them on the facts."

Conclusion

The contestation among members of Congress and the Reagan administration over the role of human rights concerns in US foreign policy was the defining factor shaping American attention to human rights in the 1980s. Having been at the forefront of the breakthrough of human rights concerns in the United States the 1970s, members of Congress played a vital role in the persistence of these during the Reagan era. Ronald Reagan came into office determined to break with Jimmy Carter's human rights-based foreign policy, but within a year rejection had made way for reform. Members of Congress were essential to this turnaround in Reagan's approach to human rights, as they pressured the administration to reconsider its initial intention to downgrade human rights concerns. The standout episode was the Senate Foreign Relations Committee's bipartisan rejection of the nomination of Ernest Lefever as head of the Human Rights Bureau in June 1981 on the grounds that he was viewed as unsupportive of human rights. The episode underscored the broad congressional support for human rights and made it clear to the administration that failing to address human rights issues could hurt support for the its foreign policy agenda.

The congressional assertion on human rights led the administration to co-opt human rights concerns into its overarching foreign policy strategy, constructing a conservative human rights policy centered on fighting communism and promoting democracy. To liberals in Congress, this cooptation of human rights into an anti-communist agenda was an unintended consequence of their initial criticism of the administration. The seeds for a conservative human rights policy, however, were already present among lower-level officials inside the administration before the Senate rejected Lefever. As early as February 1981, NSC staffer Carnes Lord warned National Security Advisor Richard V. Allen that the administration ought to take a more proactive approach to human rights. Crucially, however, the voices inside the administration calling for coopting human rights concerns did not prevail until their warnings were supported by strong manifestations of congressional and public support for human rights. The implementation of the new approach was shaped by two important personnel changes in the year following the Lefever hearing: The appointment of Elliott Abrams as head of the Human Rights Bureau in December 1981 and the replacement of Alexander Haig with George P. Shultz as secretary of state in July 1982. Under the leadership of Abrams, in an attempt to roll back communism the administration sought to redefine US human rights policy as essentially the promotion of democracy.

After the administration's turnaround on human rights, members of Congress continued to engage it in an ongoing contestation over the appropriate role of human rights in US foreign policy. The administration's commitment to human rights was strategic, highly selective, and only truly enthusiastic when combined with anti-communism. Yet the fact that the administration did address human rights changed the debate over human rights from whether human rights concerns should have a place in US foreign policy to what role they should play. Similarly, the invocation of human rights concerns by liberals as well as by conservatives established a near consensus that the United States should promote human rights in the abstract. The main disagreement thus became how and where to promote human rights concerns in practice and how to balance these against economic and security interests. As reflected in the activities of the Congressional Human Rights Caucus (CHRC) and the issue of Soviet Jewish emigration, certain issues such as the mistreatment of dissidents and minorities in the Soviet Bloc could muster bipartisan support. The CHRC's focus on civil and political rights and its omission of any substantial activism on behalf of economic, social, and cultural rights reflected another consensus in American attention to human rights.

Oftentimes, however, human rights issues proved highly contentious, reflecting the varied motivations that informed American attention to human rights. While liberals were particularly concerned with human rights violations in rightwing regimes supported by the United States, conservatives believed the United States should limit its human rights criticism on the Soviet Union and its allies. This led to heated confrontation over how to deal with human rights abuses in countries that sided with the United States in the Cold War, such as South Africa. In addition to ideology, a host of factors such as partisanship, race, ethnicity, and religion also shaped how Americans viewed human rights issues abroad. For particularly dedicated individuals, personal background and experiences were often key drivers. These different motivations contributed to the creation of shifting alliances among members of Congress and officials in the administration. Moreover, inside the administration moderates and hardliners often clashed on the relative importance ascribed to human rights concerns and whether promoting human rights was in America's best interest. On South African apartheid, African American members of Congress took the lead on calling for economic sanctions, eventually receiving support from moderate Republicans. Fearful of a communist takeover, the administration and its most conservative allies in Congress conversely prioritized economic and security interests over human rights concerns. In the case of Nicaragua, liberal Catholics and anti-war advocates in the Democratic Party were among the most outspoken opponents of US support for the Contras. Conversely, the administration and most congressional Republicans, including conservative Catholics, believed that support for the Contras was necessary to fight communism in Central America. Yet both sides referred extensively to human rights abuses in Nicaragua to claim moral authority for their opposing policy preferences.

The struggle among the Reagan administration and members of Congress over the appropriate role for human rights concerns in US foreign policy impacted US human rights policy beyond the Cold War era in two important ways. First, this contestation between the executive and legislative branches of government helped secure human rights as the key moral language in American foreign relations. Human rights language was pervasive in a range of different foreign policy debates, as evident in the scope of the CHRC's bipartisan human rights activities and the case studies examined. Members of Congress strengthened existing human rights institutions in Congress and created new ones, such as the CHRC, which have since gained the status of a permanent commission. Moreover, congressional pressure led the administration to strengthen human rights institutions in the executive branch, such as the State Department's Human Rights Bureau, rather than to follow its initial impulse to eliminate or downgrade these. While the 1980s could have seen a downgrade in the US government's commitment to human rights following the election of Reagan, instead it witnessed the increasingly ubiquitous presence of human rights concerns in both the debates and institutions that shaped US foreign policy.

Second, the contestation among members of Congress and the administration moved American policymakers further away from a consensus on the content of US human rights policy and underlined the ambiguity and elusiveness of the concept of human rights. The range of positions taken on human rights issues in this book testifies to how human rights was fundamentally a political language that policymakers invoked to claim moral authority when it was beneficial to their cause. Universal human rights principles were coopted by policymakers for their parochial political agendas. Partisanship, ideology, race, religion, and a range of personal preferences and ambitions informed and often determined positions on human rights. As Tsongas observed in 1982, "Conservatives enjoy speaking out against human rights violations of leftwing governments and liberals enjoy speaking out against human rights violations of rightwing governments. Consistently, human rights is not an issue in and of itself with its own worth, but rather it is used as a weapon to make a point on either one side or the other."[1] As a growing number of political actors invoked human rights as a moral language to support their positions on a host of foreign policy issues, they stretched the meaning of the concept beyond any consensus. The flexibility and ambiguity of human rights as a moral language that is easily adapted to diverse political causes meant that it became increasingly politicized.

The increasingly ubiquitous presence of human rights as well as their growing politicization due to the conceptual ambiguity of human rights has continued with undiminished force in the post–Cold War era. Human rights remain the language of choice for American policymakers advocating for a moral component in US foreign policy, although the degree to which such a moral component has been deemed desirable has fluctuated. The end of the Cold War led to human rights being portrayed as part of the project of the West, associated with the triumph of liberal democracy that had supposedly brought about the end of history, but it has remained an ambiguous concept.[2] Human rights have been used to advocate for US participation in international organizations such as the United Nations as well as the unilateral use of force without broad-based support from the international community. Just as in the 1980s, today the United States continues to invoke human rights concerns to claim moral authority for its foreign policy, but the goals pursued in the name of human rights are so diverse that it threatens to deprive the concept of any true meaning and bred accusations of hypocrisy.

Demonstrating the extensive human rights activism of members of Congress during the 1980s, this book challenges the perception of congressional deference to the executive branch on foreign policy during the twentieth century. While the power of the executive branch most certainly has increased dramatically during this period, members of Congress became increasingly willing to challenge presidential administrations on foreign policy from the early 1970s. Political scientists Ralph G. Carter and James M. Scott have demonstrated through quantitative analysis that Congress became both more active and assertive on foreign policy issues during the 1970s and 1980s.[3] Historian Robert "KC" Johnson has

---

[1] US Congress, Senate, Committee on Foreign Relations, *Human Rights in Nicaragua*, 61.
[2] Francis Fukuyama, *The End of History and the Last Man* (New York: Free Press, 1992).
[3] Carter and Scott, *Choosing to Lead*, 115–153.

likewise demonstrated that Congress was a much more active player in US foreign policymaking during the Cold War than the traditional narrative would have it.[4] The members of Congress challenging the Reagan administration on human rights issues in this book adds further support to this observation.

Members of Congress undertook a range of efforts to advance human rights concerns in the 1980s, often in defiance of the administration. Importantly, they created new institutions to address human rights issues, most notably the CHRC, while continuing to rely on existing ones, such as the US Helsinki Commission and the House Subcommittee on Human Rights. Established in 1983, the CHRC and its spin-off initiatives expanded and systematized congressional human rights activism, while forging new links between members of Congress, human rights activists, and NGOs. Legislation also remained a popular avenue for those seeking to insert human rights concerns into US foreign policy. Upholding the Jackson–Vanik Amendment and passing legislation such as the Comprehensive Anti-Apartheid Act of 1986 and the Boland Amendments contributed to assert the will of Congress and promote human rights concerns on US foreign policy.[5] Moreover, members of Congress passed numerous nonbinding resolutions stating its commitment to human rights issues. Through the Senate Foreign Relations Committee, Congress also used its power of "advice and consent" to reject the nomination of Lefever as head of the Human Rights Bureau, signaling that it would not tolerate a downgrading of human rights concerns.

Nonlegislative actions, such as hearings, consultations, correspondence, and oversight activities, represented another avenue for members of Congress to draw attention to human rights. They used hearings to draw attention to human rights issues, challenge the administration's policy, and give voice to human rights activists and NGOs. They sought to influence the administration through consultations and entered the realm of what has traditionally been perceived as presidential foreign policy prerogatives by engaging in human rights diplomacy with foreign officials. On Soviet Jewry, such diplomacy happened with the administration's blessings, when members of Congress participated in the CSCE follow-up meetings through the US Helsinki Commission. At other times, members of Congress conducted their own diplomacy in defiance of the executive branch, such as Wright's Lone Ranger diplomacy on Nicaragua. They also wrote extensively to foreign leaders to urge them to

---

[4] Johnson, *Congress and the Cold War.*
[5] Members of Congress increasingly placed restrictions on foreign aid in the 1980s. Lindsay, *Congress and the Politics of U.S. Foreign Policy*, 86.

improve the human rights situation in their respective countries. Members of Congress carried out wide-ranging oversight over the administration's compliance with human rights legislation. Through the US Helsinki Commission, they even monitored foreign countries' compliance with the human rights principles outlined in the Helsinki Accords. Finally, members of Congress also descended from Capitol Hill to participate in human rights activism through activities traditionally reserved for activists, such as protests and demonstrations. Members of the Congressional Black Caucus (CBC) and other opponents of apartheid participated in protests and even staged arrests in front of the South African embassy through the Free South Africa Movement (FSAM) from December 1984. Members of Congress hosted and participated in numerous events to draw attention to Soviet Jewish emigration, including a demonstration before the Washington Summit in 1987. The comprehensiveness of such congressional human rights activism highlights the willingness of members of Congress to shape foreign policy on human rights issues during the 1980s.

The contestation among the administration and members of Congress over the appropriate role of human rights affected US foreign policy very differently in the three case studies examined in this book. Members of Congress had the biggest impact on US human rights policy when they found themselves in accordance with public opinion and supported by strong NGOs.[6] Under such circumstances, motivated members of Congress could successfully challenge the administration, particularly if they used Congress's significant influence over structural policy and ability to frame the national debate to force a change in strategic policy. The implementation of sanctions against South Africa constituted an example of this. However, such alignment of the stars was rare. Most of the time, members of Congress experienced significant limitations in their ability to decisively influence human rights policy if the administration resisted interference.

In the case of Soviet Jewish emigration, the generally constructive collaboration between members of Congress and the administration strengthened US foreign policy. Members of Congress and the administration generally shared the goal of advancing Jewish emigration, resulting in executive–legislative cooperation, with disagreements revolving mostly around tactics. Both liberals and conservatives in both branches of government shared the perception that the issue constituted an important

---

[6] For similar arguments about the importance of public opinion to congressional influence on foreign policy, see Andrew Johnstone and Helen Laville, *The US Public and American Foreign Policy* (London: Routledge, 2010), 87–91; Ole Holsti, "Public Opinion on Human Rights in American Foreign Policy," in *The United States and Human Rights: Looking Inward and Outward*, ed. David P. Forsythe (2000), 131–174.

human rights issue. Congressional activism for Soviet Jewish emigration provided the administration with significant political backing to raise the issue in negotiations with Mikhail Gorbachev and conversely increased the political costs of remaining quiet. Of crucial importance, it also allowed Reagan to use congressional opinion as leverage to push Gorbachev on Soviet Jewry, adding an extra weapon to the president's arsenal. It is also possible to view congressional human rights activism as an important step in the overall improvement in US–Soviet relations. Congressional criticism of Soviet human rights abuses hurt US–Soviet relations in the short run, but eventually progress on Jewish emigration and other human rights issues contributed to an overall improvement in bilateral relations between the two countries that spilled over to other issues, such as arms control and trade. While members of Congress must share credit for this development with Reagan and Gorbachev, there is no denying that they played an essential role for putting human rights and Jewish emigration at the center of the agenda.

In the case of South African apartheid, the tumultuous relationship between the administration and its congressional critics changed the direction of US foreign policy. Shared abhorrence for the apartheid system and the human rights violations it committed did not translate into shared policy objectives. As more members of Congress came to favor economic sanctions over the administration's policy of constructive engagement, the two branches of government were increasingly pitched against each other. Congressional advocacy for sanctions started with the CBC and a few liberal allies and developed into one of the most dramatic executive–legislative foreign policy showdowns of the decade, when the support of moderate Republicans led to the passage of the Comprehensive Anti-Apartheid Act in October 1986. By overruling a presidential veto to pass sanctions, members of Congress forced the most extensive change in US foreign policy toward South Africa in the Cold War era and asserted their will on US foreign policy. History has proven that this policy change helped the United States obtain its goal of ending apartheid without losing South Africa to communism.

In the case of the conflict in Nicaragua, the relationship among members of Congress and the administration was also characterized by escalating confrontation, as liberal Democrats sought to restrict – and later terminate – the administration's support for the Nicaraguan Contras. Both the administration and its opponents in Congress motivated their positions on US Nicaragua policy in part by referring to the human rights violations taking place in Nicaragua, but they strongly disagreed about which side in the conflict was guilty of the worst abuses. Unlike the South African case, members of Congress failed to conclusively alter the administration's policy. The reason for this failure was in part due to lacking congressional unity on the issue, but more importantly it resulted from the administration's disregard for congressional restrictions. The consequence was an inconsistent foreign policy, with US support for the Contras fluctuating according to the alternating power balance between the executive and legislative branches of government. For the administration, the consequence was its most damaging scandal in the form of the Iran–Contra Affair.

Although members of Congress could point to significant results of their efforts to impose human rights concerns into US foreign policy in the 1980s, they often had to defer to the executive branch. For all its direct and indirect influence on foreign policy, especially on human rights issues, Congress often could not match the foreign policy power of the presidency. However, when assessing congressional influence on foreign policy, it is important to keep in mind that policymaking is almost always the result of compromise. Only rarely does congressional influence on foreign policy manifest itself in landmark legislation such as the Comprehensive Anti-Apartheid Act. Rather, a "congressional victory," as Stanley Heginbotham points out, "is achieved when restrictive legislation loses, but Congress extracts some policy compromises reflecting congressional concerns."[7] This scenario was the situation for most congressional human rights activism examined in this book. Only rarely did members of Congress succeed in dictating US human rights policy against the will of the administration, but the administration often felt compelled to compromise in order to accommodate congressional concerns. Reagan's increased willingness to link progress on Jewish emigration to progress on other issues in US–Soviet negotiations, his executive order on South Africa in 1985, and his decision to seek to legitimize Contra support with human rights concerns are all examples of compromises reflecting congressional concerns.

As such, to fully comprehend US human rights policy, one needs to examine the ongoing interactions between the two branches of government that shape US foreign policy. Accounts that focus too narrowly on the presidency are likely to fail to capture the broader political environment in which US human rights policy is created. Therefore, historians of American foreign relations would be wise to include members of Congress in their examinations, alongside presidential administrations and NGOs. Individual members of Congress not only led the way for human rights in the 1970s, but they were also crucial for the persistence of human

---

[7] Quoted in Lindsay, *Congress and the Politics of U.S. Foreign Policy*, 98.

rights as a language of morality in debates over US foreign policy in the 1980s. Therefore, attention to such mid-level actors is crucial to understanding the history of human rights in American foreign relations.

As the declassification of archives progresses, historians of human rights will undoubtedly expand the research on the 1980s. An already fast-growing body of scholarship on human rights in American foreign relations during the 1980s continues to demonstrate how the decade was pivotal for shaping contemporary US human rights policy. As historians embark on this task, some areas appear particularly worthy of research. Examining the merger between human rights and democracy promotion during the Reagan years would enhance our understanding of the role of both of these concepts in US foreign policy.[8] Related to this merger is the largely untold history of economic and social rights and how these have been deliberately downgraded in US foreign policy since the 1980s, resulting in a narrow conception of human rights as civil and political rights. Examining this conception of human rights and its potential connections with the simultaneous rise of neoliberalism in an increasingly unequal world appears to be vital for our understanding of human rights in a globalized world.[9] Addressing the neglect of economic, social, and cultural rights in historical scholarship, including in American foreign relations, would also give us a fuller account of the history of human rights.[10] Further case studies of US human rights policy toward specific countries during the 1980s would be another welcome addition to the human rights historiography, as the role of human rights in several of the United States' bilateral relationships remain unexamined. Finally, tracing the transition into the early post–Cold War period promises to offer a better understanding of the role of human rights in a world dominated by the United States. Specifically, such examinations could help clarify how

---

[8] For recent research on the topic, see William Michael Schmidli and Robert Pee (eds.), *The Reagan Administration, the Cold War and the Transition to Democracy Promotion* (New York: Palgrave Macmillan, 2019).

[9] For human rights and economic inequality, see Moyn, *Not Enough*; Christian O. Christiansen and Steven L. B. Jensen (eds.), *Histories of Global Inequality: New Perspectives* (Switzerland: Palgrave Macmillan, 2019).

[10] For historical research on economic and social rights, including in American foreign relations, see Daniel J. Whelan and Jack Donnelly, "The West, Economic and Social Rights, and the Global Human Rights Regime: Setting the Record Straight," *Human Rights Quarterly* 29, no. 4 (2007): 908–949; Daniel J. Whelan, "'Under the Aegis of Man': The Right to Development and the Origins of the New International Economic Order," *Humanity* 6, no. 1 (2015): 93–108; Roland Burke, "Competing for the Last Utopia? The NIEO, Human Rights, and the World Conference for the International Women's Year, Mexico City, June 1975," *Humanity* 6, no. 1 (2015): 47–61. For the downgrade of economic and social rights by the Reagan administration, see Søndergaard, "A Positive Track of Human Rights Policy."

human rights have been fused with military interventions to prevent genocide and the proliferation of international human rights law.[11]

Although the end of the Cold War is commonly dated to the dissolution of the Soviet Union on December 26, 1991, in many respects the Cold War had already come to an end in 1989. The year of 1989 witnessed the fall of communism across Eastern Europe as country after country overthrew their communist governments without any interference from Moscow. At their Malta Summit in December 1989, Gorbachev and President George H. W. Bush officially declared an end to the Cold War.[12] Sarah B. Snyder has suggested that the close of the CSCE Vienna Review Meeting on January 19, 1989, could be an alternative date as the endpoint for the Cold War.[13] The year thus represented a milestone in superpower relations and in international politics. In the United States, the year marked the end of the Reagan presidency as well as the end of the 100th Congress in January 1989, making the year the natural endpoint for this book.

Although Bush had been Reagan's vice president for eight years, he was cut from a different cloth than his predecessor, when it came to his views on human rights in US foreign policy. In 1991, Bush famously proclaimed a "new world order," where the absence of Cold War hostility would allow for "a world in which freedom and respect for human rights find a home among all nations."[14] In practice, however, the Bush administration was guided by realistic prudence and showed little interest in aggressively promoting human rights and democracy, prioritizing stability over transformation despite the power vacuum left after the fall of the Soviet Union. In the 1991 Persian Gulf War, for instance, Bush resisted the temptation to continue to Baghdad and overthrow Saddam Hussein's regime after liberating Kuwait.[15] To a host of human rights activists, policymakers,

---

[11] For thoughts about human rights in the 1990s, see Hoffmann, "Human Rights and History"; Frederick Cooper, "Afterword: Social Rights and Human Rights in the Time of Decolonization," *Humanity* 3, no. 3 (2012): 473–492.

[12] "The Malta Summit; Transcript of the Bush–Gorbachev News Conference in Malta," *The New York Times*, December 4, 1989, A12.

[13] Snyder, *Human Rights Activism*, 244.

[14] George Bush, Address before a Joint Session of the Congress on the Cessation of the Persian Gulf Conflict, March 6, 1991. Online by Gerhard Peters and John T. Woolley, The American Presidency Project, accessed August 7, 2019, www.presidency.ucsb.edu/node/265314.

[15] For Bush's foreign policy, see Jeffrey A. Engel, *When the World Seemed New: George H. W. Bush and the End of the Cold War* (New York: Houghton Mifflin Harcourt, 2017); Brands, *Making the Unipolar Moment*, 274–335. For Bush's reluctance to push human rights at the CSCE, see Sarah B. Snyder, "Beyond Containment? The First Bush Administration's Sceptical Approach to the CSCE," *Cold War History* 13, no. 4 (2013): 483–484.

and scholars, the end of the Cold War brought optimistic expectations of a world where respect for human rights would finally dominate international relations. Several contemporaries hoped to see the United States take a more active role in promoting human rights and democracy, but the Bush administration took a much more restrained approach.[16]

Bush's successor, Bill Clinton, campaigned on idealist rhetoric and included several human rights advocates in his staff, raising expectations of a revival of Carter's call for a human rights-based foreign policy. However, once in office, Clinton generally prioritized the expansion of markets over concerns for democracy and human rights whenever such issues collided. Moreover, during Clinton's presidency, the international community failed to prevent genocide in Rwanda and ethnic cleansing in Bosnia. In reaction to these tragedies, however, liberal internationalists urged so-called humanitarian interventions to prevent massive human rights abuses, leading to the intervention in Kosovo in 1999.[17] The Clinton administration motivated interventions in Haiti and Kosovo by linking democracy and human rights to US national security, creating a discourse that helped to legitimize a gradual move toward a more militaristic foreign policy based on moral claims.[18] In the 1980s, Reagan and Bush had made similar motivations for their interventions in Grenada in 1983 and Panama in 1989, respectively. Where human rights concerns in the 1960s and 1970s had emerged as the weapon of the weak against repressive governments, by the 1990s they increasingly served as a justification for powerful states to intervene in other states to prevent atrocities. Eventually, this form of humanitarian intervention was enshrined in the doctrine of the Responsibility to Protect adopted by the United Nations in 2005.[19] In a remarkable development, individual human rights had emerged to challenge the state sovereignty on which the international system had been based since the Treaty of Westphalia in 1648.[20]

---

[16] For contemporary examples advocating for the assertive promotion of human rights and democracy as the new mission for US foreign policy, see Joshua Muravchik, *Exporting Democracy: Fulfilling America's Destiny* (Washington, DC: American Enterprise Institute, 1991); Robert Kagan, "Global Mission," *Commentary* 92, no. 2 (1991): 54–65.

[17] Stefan-Ludwig Hoffmann argues that the Kosovo intervention was the first war conducted in the name of human rights to prevent genocide. Hoffmann, "Human Rights and History," 292.

[18] Rasmus Sinding Søndergaard, "Bill Clinton's 'Democratic Enlargement' and the Securitisation of Democracy Promotion," *Diplomacy & Statecraft* 26, no. 03 (2015): 534–551.

[19] United Nations, *Responsibility to Protect* (2005), accessed August 1, 2019, www.un.org/en/genocideprevention/about-responsibility-to-protect.shtml.

[20] For the history of humanitarian interventions, see Gary Jonathan Bass, *Freedom's Battle: The Origins of Humanitarian Intervention* (New York: Alfred A. Knopf, 2008); Brendan Simms and David J. B. Trim, *Humanitarian Intervention a History* (Cambridge, UK:

In the wake of the terrorist attacks of September 11, 2001, the George W. Bush administration invoked human rights language to justify military interventions and nation-building in the Middle East.[21] Yet, at the same time, in the war on terror, the Bush administration displayed a profound disregard for the standards of international law for humanitarian treatment in war outlined in the Geneva Conventions, and as a consequence severely damaged the international image of the United States as a human rights promoter.[22] The Bush administration's invocation of human rights testifies to the extraordinary flexibility of the concept as a moral language in foreign policy, while also demonstrating how easily human rights can be manipulated as justification for less-noble causes. President Barack Obama went out of his way to distance himself from the legacy of his predecessor, but despite a more restrained foreign policy, he continued some human rights violations of the previous administration, most notably targeted drone killings. Obama also significantly toned down the rhetorical emphasis on human rights and moralistic language in general.[23] In a 2016 interview with the *Atlantic*, he professed his belief that the United States should promote democracy and human rights but cautioned that the world is "a tough, complicated, messy, mean place" and that "there are going to be times where our security interests conflict with our concerns about human rights."[24] Yet, on notable occasions, such as in his Cairo speech in June 2009 and his Nobel Peace Prize acceptance speech later that year, Obama invoked human rights in his attempt to signal a new beginning in the United

---

Cambridge University Press, 2011). For US humanitarian interventions in the 1990s, see Karin Von Hippel, *Democracy by Force, U.S. Military Intervention in the Post–Cold War World* (Cambridge, UK: Cambridge University Press, 2000).

[21] See, for instance, George W. Bush, Address to the United Nations General Assembly in New York City, September 12, 2002. Online by Gerhard Peters and John T. Woolley, The American Presidency Project, accessed August 7, 2019, www.presidency.ucsb.edu/node/213436.

[22] According to George W. Bush's White House counsel Alberto Gonzales, the new type of war in the age of terrorism "renders obsolete Geneva's strict limitations on questioning of enemy prisoners." Memorandum, Alberto Gonzales to George W. Bush, January 25, 2002, National Security Archive, The Interrogation Documents: Debating U.S. Policy and Methods, accessed September 19, 2016, http://nsarchive.gwu.edu/NSAEBB/NSAEBB127/02.01.25.pdf.

[23] For an argument that Obama's human rights policy has been an inconsistent "muddling through," see David P. Forsythe, "U.S. Foreign Policy and Human Rights: Situating Obama," *Human Rights Quarterly* 33, no. 3 (2011): 767–789. For an argument that Obama's human rights policy has been a limited approach to secure the most basic human right, the right to life, see Amitai Etzioni, "Obama's Implicit Human Rights Doctrine," *Human Rights Review* 12, no. 1 (2011): 93–107.

[24] Jeffrey Goldberg, "The Obama Doctrine," *The Atlantic*, April (2016), www.theatlantic.com/magazine/archive/2016/04/the-obama-doctrine/471525/.

States' relationship to the world.[25] Despite the stains on American human rights promotion left by the war on terror and some policymakers' desire to take US foreign policy in a less moralistic direction, human rights remains the most popular language for expressing moral visions for America's role in the world.

Throughout the shifting presidential administrations of the post–Cold War period, members of Congress have remained important actors in shaping US human rights policy. Congressional assertiveness on foreign policy increased in the 1990s, as the disappearance of the Soviet threat provided members of Congress with greater leeway to challenge presidential foreign policy.[26] While the terrorist attacks on September 11, 2001, virtually ended this congressional assertiveness overnight, a few years later members of Congress were again willing to challenge the executive branch on foreign policy.[27] In 2012, for instance, Congress passed the Sergei Magnitsky Rule of Law Accountability Act sanctioning Russian human rights violators. This occurred against the will of the Obama administration, which feared that the law would compromise the president's ability to manage relations with Russia. When the administration of Donald J. Trump made a move to lift these sanctions, Congress passed legislation that further strengthened the sanctions, with overwhelming bipartisan support. Members of Congress remain willing to contest the role of human rights in US foreign policy and to use human rights concerns as a means to constrain the president's foreign policy prerogatives. The American public also continues to support human rights as a foreign policy objective in broad terms. In a Harris poll from December 2015, 77 percent of Americans answered positively to the statement, "The US should be the world's leader in promoting human rights around the world."[28] While the content of US human rights policy continues to be contested, human rights remain the most powerful language for expressing morality in US foreign policy. As it was the case in the 1980s, relations between the executive and legislative branches of government are likely to be crucial for shaping the role of human rights in American foreign relations in the future.

---

[25] Barack Obama, *Remarks by the President at Cairo University, June 4, 2009*, accessed August 1, 2019, https://obamawhitehouse.archives.gov/the-press-office/remarks-president-cairo-university-6-04-09. Barack Obama, *Remarks by the President at the Acceptance of the Nobel Peace Prize, December 10, 2009*, accessed August 1, 2019, https://obamawhitehouse.archives.gov/the-press-office/remarks-president-acceptance-nobel-peace-prize.

[26] Carter and Scott, *Choosing to Lead*, 15–16.

[27] Ibid., 205–220.

[28] Harris Poll, *Human Rights First*, December 9, 2015, accessed August 9, 2019, www.humanrightsfirst.org/sites/default/files /HumanRightsFirstHarrisPoll.pdf.

Bibliography

Archival Collections

American Heritage Center, University of Wyoming, WY
  Malcolm Wallop Papers
American Jewish Historical Society, Center for Jewish History, NY
  National Conference on Soviet Jewry
  Union of Councils for Soviet Jews
Bancroft Library, Berkeley, CA
  Alan Cranston Papers
  Tom Lantos Papers
Center for Legislative Archives, National Archives, Washington, DC
  Commission on Security and Cooperation in Europe (US Helsinki
    Commission)
  Dockery and Sklar Files (Senate Foreign Relations Committee)
  Galbraith Files (Senate Foreign Relations Committee)
  House Foreign Affairs Committee, Subcommittee on Human Rights
    and International Organizations
The Center for Human Rights Documentation & Research, Columbia
  University, NY
  Amnesty International USA
  Human Rights Watch Records (Helsinki Watch and Africa Watch
    Collections)
Gelman Library, George Washington University, Washington, DC
  Walter E. Fauntroy Papers
The Hoover Institution, Stanford, CA
  Richard V. Allen Papers
  William J. Casey Papers
Houghton Library, Andrei Sakharov Archives, Harvard University, Boston,
  MA
  Human Rights Collection
John J. Burns Library, Boston College, Boston, MA
  Thomas P. O'Neill, Jr. Congressional Papers
The Kansas State Historical Society, Library and Archives Division, Manu-
  script Collections, Topeka, KS
  Nancy Landon Kassebaum Papers
Milton S. Eisenhower Library, The Johns Hopkins University, Baltimore, MD
  Charles McCurdy Mathias Papers

Minnesota Historical Society, MN
    Donald M. Fraser Papers
Mooland-Springarn Research Center, Howard University, Washington DC
    George W. Crockett Papers
    TransAfrica Collection
National Archives, College Park, MD
    Records of the Department of State
Oakland Public Library, Oakland, CA
    Ronald V. Dellums Papers
Robert D. Farber University Archives and Special Collections, Brandeis University, MA
    Stephen Solarz Papers
Robert J. Dole Archive and Special Collections, Robert J. Dole Institute of Politics, Lawrence, KS
    Robert J. Dole Senate Papers
The Rodino Archives, Seton Hall University, NJ
    Peter Rodino Papers
Ronald Reagan Presidential Library, Simi Valley, CA
Office files:
    African Affairs Directorate, NSC: Records, 1981–1989
    Anderson, Carl Files, 1985–1987
    Coordination office, NSC: Records, 1983–1989
    Dolan, Anthony "Tony" R. Files, 1981–1989
    European and Soviet Affairs Directorate, NSC: Records, 1983–1989
    Green, Max, 1985–1988
    Ledsky, Nelson C. Files, 1987–1989
    Legislative Affairs, White House Office of, 1981–1988
    Matlock, Jack F. Jr. Files, 1983–1986
    McDaniel, Rodney B. Files, 1985–1987
    McGrath, Dean C. Files, 1986–1988
WHORM Subject files:
    Country Files: Nicaragua (CO114), Republic of South Africa (CO141), Union of Soviet Socialist Republics (USSR) (CO165)
    Foreign Affairs (FO)
    Human Rights (HU)
Schomburg Center for Research in Black Culture, New York Public Library, NY
    William H. Gray III Congressional Records
Tamiment Library, New York University, NY
    The Campaign for Peace and Democracy
    The Committee for Non-Intervention in Central America
    The Nicaragua Solidarity Network of Greater New York
The Library of Congress, Washington, DC
    Jack Kemp Papers
University of Massachusetts, Amherst, MA
    Silvio O. Conte Papers
University of Miami, Miami, FL
    Dante B. Fascell Papers

University of Rhode Island, Providence, RI
   Claiborne Pell Papers
Wright State University, Special Collections and Archives, Dayton, OH
   Tony Hall Papers

Online Archives

Benson Latin American Collection, University of Texas Libraries, the University of Texas at Austin, https://legacy.lib.utexas.edu/taro/utlac/00188/lac-00188.html
   George Lister Papers
Central Intelligence Agency, Freedom of Information Act Electronic Reading Room, www.cia.gov/library/readingroom/home
Congress.gov, www.congress.gov/
Moakley Archive & Institute, Digital Collections, www.moakleyarchive.omeka.net
   Joseph Moakley Papers
National Security Archive, the George Washington University, Washington, DC
   Nicaragua: The Making of U.S. Policy, 1978–1990
   South Africa: The Making of U.S. Policy, 1962–1989
   The Philippines: U.S. Policy During the Marcos Years, 1961–1986
Roper Center for Public Opinion Research, University of Connecticut, https://ropercenter.cornell.edu
   Opinion polls (iPOLL)
The American Presidency Project, www.presidency.ucsb.edu
University of Massachusetts, Lowell Library, Digital Collection, https://libguides.uml.edu/ptsongasuml
   Paul E. Tsongas Papers
Wisconsin Historical Society, Digital Collections, http://digital.library.wisc.edu/1711.dl/wiarchives.uw-whs-mss00738
   William Proxmire Papers

Government Publications

Congressional Human Rights Caucus. Human Rights Violations in Kuwait, C-SPAN. 1990 (accessed August 5, 2019), www.c-span.org/search/?searchtype=All&query=human +rights+caucus+kuwait.
United Nations General Assembly. *Universal Declaration of Human Rights.* December 10, 1948 (accessed August 13, 2019), www.un.org/en/universal-declaration-human-rights/.
United Nations. *Responsibility to Protect.* 2005 (accessed August 1, 2019), www.un.org/en/genocideprevention/about-responsibility-to-protect.shtml.
United States. *Report of the National Bipartisan Commission on Central America.* Washington, DC: Government Printing Office, 1984.
US Commission on Security and Cooperation in Europe. "President Reagan in Helsinki." *CSCE Digest,* May 1988.

"Statement by Representative Steny H. Hoyer." *CSCE Digest*, November 11, 1988.

"Chairman DeConcini Opposes Waiver of Jackson-Vanik." *CSCE Digest*, August 1989.

US Congress. *Human Rights in the World Community: A Call for U.S. Leadership.* Washington, DC: US Government Printing Office, 1974.

US Congress, Committee on Foreign Affairs. *Congress and Foreign Policy 1981*, Committee Print. Washington, DC: US Government Printing Office, 1982.

Congress and Foreign Policy 1982, Committee Print. Washington, DC: US Government Printing Office, 1983.

Congress and Foreign Policy 1983, Committee Print. Washington, DC: US Government Printing Office, 1984.

Congress and Foreign Policy 1984, Committee Print. Washington, DC: US Government Printing Office, 1985.

Congress and Foreign Policy 1985–1986, Committee Print. Washington, DC: US Government Printing Office, 1988.

Congress and Foreign Policy 1988, Committee Print. Washington, DC: US Government Printing Office, 1989.

US Congress, House, Commission on Security and Cooperation in Europe. *Hearing before the Commission on Security and Cooperation in Europe on Basket III: Implementation of the Helsinki Accords*, 96th Congress, 2nd Session, April 29, 1980. Washington, DC: US Government Printing Office, 1980.

Soviet Jewry Hearing and Markup before the Subcommittee on Human Rights and International Organizations of the Committee on Foreign Affairs and the Commission on Security and Cooperation in Europe, 98th Congress, 1st Session, June 23 and 28, 1983. Washington, DC: US Government Printing Office, 1984.

Implementation of the Helsinki Accords: Hearing before the Commission on Security and Cooperation in Europe, the Ottawa Human Rights Experts Meeting and the Future of the Helsinki Process, 99th Congress, 1st Session, June 25, 1985. Washington, DC: US Government Printing Office, 1985.

Implementation of the Helsinki Accords Hearing before the Commission on Security and Cooperation in Europe, 99th Congress, 1st Session, October 3, 1985. Washington, DC: US Government Printing Office, 1986.

Implementation of the Helsinki Accords: Hearing before the Commission on Security and Cooperation in Europe: Soviet and East European Emigration Policies, 99th Congress, 2nd Session, April 22, 1986. Washington, DC: US Government Printing Office, 1986.

Implementation of the Helsinki Accords: Hearing before the Commission on Security and Cooperation in Europe, Glasnost: The Soviet Policy of "Openness," 100th Congress, 1st Session, March 4, 1987. Washington, DC: US Government Printing Office, 1987.

Implementation of the Helsinki Accords: Hearing before the Commission on Security and Cooperation in Europe, Soviet Jewry Struggle, 100th Congress, 1st Session, December 4, 1987. Washington, DC: US Government Printing Office, 1987.

US Congress, House, Committee on Foreign Affairs. *U.S. Policy in Honduras and Nicaragua: Hearing before the Subcommittee on Western Hemisphere Affairs of the*

Committee on Foreign Affairs, 98th Congress, 1st Session, March 15, 1983. Washington, DC: US Government Printing Office, 1983.

US Congress, House, Committee on Banking, Finance, and Urban Affairs. *To Increase the U.S. Quota in the International Monetary Fund and Related Matters: Hearings before the Subcommittee on International Trade, Investment, and Monetary Policy of the Committee on Banking, Finance, and Urban Affairs*, 98th Congress, 1st Session, April 7–28 and May 3, 1983. Washington, DC: US Government Printing Office, 1983.

United States–Philippines Relations and the New Base and Aid Agreement: Hearings before the Subcommittee on Asian and Pacific Affairs of the Committee on Foreign Affairs, 98th Congress, 1st Session, June 17–28, 1983. Washington, DC: US Government Printing Office, 1983.

Human Rights in Nicaragua: Hearing before the Subcommittee on Human Rights and International Organizations of the Committee on Foreign Affairs, 98th Congress, 1st Session, September 15, 1983. Washington, DC: US Government Printing Office, 1984.

U.S. Support for the Contras: Hearing before the Subcommittee on Western Hemisphere Affairs of the Committee on Foreign Affairs, 99th Congress, 1st Session, April 16–18, 1985. Washington, DC: US Government Printing Office, 1985.

The Anti-Apartheid Act of 1985 Hearings and Markup before the Subcommittees on International Economic Policy and Trade and on Africa of the Committee on Foreign Affairs, 99th Congress, 1st Session, April 17, 18, 30 and May 2, 1985. Washington, DC: US Government Printing Office.

The Human Rights Situation in South Africa, Zaire, the Horn of Africa, and Uganda: Hearings before the Subcommittee on Human Rights and International Organizations and the Subcommittee on Africa of the Committee on Foreign Affairs, 98th Congress, 2nd Session, June 21, August 9, 1984. Washington, DC: US Government Printing Office, 1985.

Religious Persecution in the Soviet Union. Part I – Soviet Jewry. Hearing Before the Subcommittees on Europe and the Middle East and on Human Rights and International Organizations of the Committee on Foreign Affairs, 99th Congress, 1st Session, September 11, 1985. Washington, DC: US Government Printing Office, 1985.

US Congress, House, Committee on Banking, Finance, and Urban Affairs. *Anti-Apartheid Act of 1986: Hearing before the Subcommittee on Financial Institutions Supervision, Regulation, and Insurance of the Committee on Banking, Finance, and Urban Affairs*, 99th Congress, 2nd Session, June 10, 1986. Washington, DC: US Government Printing Office, 1986.

U.S. Human Rights Policy toward the Soviet Union: Pre-Summit Assessment and Update: Hearings and Markup before the Committee on Foreign Affairs and Its Subcommittee on Human Rights and International Organizations, 100th Congress, 2nd Session, May 4, 11, and 18, 1988. Washington, DC: US Government Printing Office, 1988.

US Congress, Senate, Committee on Foreign Relations. *Hearings before the Committee on Foreign Relations on Nomination of Ernest W. Lefever, to Be Assistant Secretary of State for Human Rights and Humanitarian Affairs*, 97th

Congress, 1st Session, May 18, 19, June 4, and 5, 1981. Washington, DC: US Government Printing Office, 1981.

Hearing before the Committee on Foreign Relations on Nomination of Elliott Abrams, of the District of Columbia, to Be Assistant Secretary of State for Human Rights and Humanitarian Affairs, 97th Congress, 1st Session, November 17, 1981. Washington, DC: US Government Printing Office, 1982.

Human Rights in Nicaragua: Hearings before the Subcommittee on Western Hemisphere Affairs of the Committee on Foreign Relations, United States Senate, 97th Congress, 2nd Session, February 25 and March 1, 1982. Washington, DC: US Government Printing Office, 1982.

U.S. Policy toward Nicaragua and Central America: Hearing before the Committee on Foreign Relations, 98th Congress, 1st Session, April 12, 1983. Washington, DC: US Government Printing Office, 1983.

United States-Soviet Relations: Hearings before the Committee on Foreign Relations, 98th Congress, 1st Session, June 15, 16, 21, 22, and 23, 1983. Washington, DC: US Government Printing Office, 1983.

Hearing before the Committee on Foreign Relations, United States Senate on the Promotion and Protection of Human Rights in Eastern Europe and the Soviet Union, 98th Congress, 1st Session, November 9, 1983. Washington, DC: US Government Printing Office, 1984.

U.S. Policy on South Africa: Hearing before the Subcommittee on African Affairs of the Committee on Foreign Relations, 98th Congress, 2nd Session, September 26, 1984. Washington, DC: US Government Printing Office, 1985.

U.S. Policy toward Nicaragua: Aid to Nicaraguan Resistance Proposal: Hearings before the Committee on Foreign Relations, 99th Congress, 2nd session, February 27 and March 4, 1986. Washington, DC: US Government Printing Office, 1986.

Situation in South Africa: Hearings before the Committee on Foreign Relations, 99th Congress, 2nd Session, July 22–24 and 29, 1986. Washington, DC: US Government Printing Office, 1986.

US Department of State. *Foreign Relations of the United States, 1969–1976, Volume E–3, Documents on Global Issues, 1973–1976*. Washington, DC: US Government Printing Office, 2009.

Foreign Relations of the United States, 1969–1976, Volume I, Foundations of Foreign Policy, 1969–1972. Washington, DC: US Government Printing Office, 2003.

Foreign Relations of the United States, 1969–1976, Volume XXXVIII, Part 1, Foundations of Foreign Policy, 1973–1976. Washington, DC: US Government Printing Office, 2012.

Foreign Relations of the United States, 1977–1980, Volume II, Human Rights and Humanitarian Affairs. Washington, DC: US Government Printing Office, 2013.

Foreign Relations of the United States, 1977–1980, Volume VI, Soviet Union. Washington, DC: US Government Printing Office, 2013.

Foreign Relations of the United States, 1977–1980, Volume I, Foundations of Foreign Policy. Washington, DC: US Government Printing Office, 2014.

Foreign Relations of the United States, 1981–1988, Volume III, Soviet Union, January 1981–January 1983. Washington, DC: US Government Publishing Office, 2016.

Foreign Relations of the United States, 1981–1988, Volume XII, Global Issues II. Washington, DC: US Government Publishing Office, 2017.

Country Reports on Human Rights Practices for 1979. Washington, DC: US Government Printing Office, 1980.

Country Reports on Human Rights Practices for 1981. Washington, DC: US Government Printing Office, 1982.

Country Reports on Human Rights Practices for 1982. Washington, DC: US Government Printing Office, 1983.

Country Reports on Human Rights Practices for 1983. Washington, DC: US Government Printing Office, 1984.

Country Reports on Human Rights Practices for 1984. Washington, DC: US Government Printing Office, 1985.

Country Report on Human Rights Practices for 1986. Washington, DC: US Government Printing Office, 1987.

Country Report on Human Rights Practices for 1987. Washington, DC: US Government Printing Office, 1988.

Country Reports on Human Rights Practices for 1989. Washington, DC: US Government Printing Office, 1990.

US Library of Congress, Congressional Research Service. *Human Rights and US Foreign Policy,* by Vita Bite, IB81125 (1982).

U.S. Assistance to Nicaraguan Guerrillas: Issues for the Congress, by Nina Serafino, IB84139 (1987).

Emigration and Human Rights in the USSR: Is There a New Approach? (1988).

South Africa: US Policy after Sanctions, by Brenda M. Branaman, IB87128 (1990).

Congressional Member Organizations: Their Purpose and Activities, History, and Formation, by Robert Jay Dilger and Jessica C. Gerrity, R40683 (2013).

"Dear Colleague" Letters in the House of Representatives: Past Practices and Issues for Congress (2017).

Tayacán and Library of Congress, Language Services Section, *Psychological Operations in Guerrilla Warfare.* Washington, DC: Congressional Research Service, Library of Congress, 1984.

Oral Histories

Transcript, Chester Crocker Oral History Interview, June 5, 2006, by Charles Stuart Kennedy, the Association for Diplomatic Studies and Training Foreign Affairs Oral History Project. www.adst.org/OH%20TOCs/Crocker,%20Chester%20Arthur.toc.pdf.

Transcript, George P. Shultz Interview, December 18, 2002, Reagan Presidential Oral History Project, Miller Center, University of Virginia, Charlottesville, Virginia. www.millercenter.org/the-presidency/presidential-oral-histories/george-p-shultz-oral-history-secretary-state.

Transcript, Patricia Derian Oral History Interview, March 12, 1996, by Charles Stuart Kennedy, the Association for Diplomatic Studies and Training Foreign Affairs Oral History Project. www.adst.org/wp-content/uploads/2013/12/Derian-Patricia.19961.pdf.

Transcript, Robert Hunter Oral History Interview, February 11, 2009, by Janet Heininger, Edward M. Kennedy Oral History Project, Miller Center, University of Virginia. www.emkinstitute.org/resources/robert-hunter-oral-history-foreign-policy-adviser-edward.

Transcript, Ronald V. Dellums Oral History Interview, February 10, 2000, by Harry Kreisler, Conversations with History; Institute of International Studies, UC Berkeley. http://globetrotter.berkeley.edu/people/Dellums/dellums-con0.html.

Interviews

Arriaga, Alexandra, staff director of the Congressional Human Rights Caucus (1987–1995). June 8, 2018.

Barnes, Michael D., Representative (D-MD) (1979–1986). May 22, 2016.

Crocker, Chester, Assistant Secretary of State for African Affairs (1981–1989). June 9, 2016.

Johnson, Vic, staff director of the House Subcommittee on the Western Hemisphere (1981–1993). June 11, 2016.

Laber, Jeri, executive director, Helsinki Watch (1978–1995). November 6, 2015.

Matlock, Jack, advisor on the National Security Council (1983–1987) and US Ambassador to the Soviet Union (1987–1991). December 24, 2015.

Neier, Aryeh, co-founder and executive director of Helsinki Watch (1978–1990). October 15, 2015.

Oliver, Spencer, Chief of Staff of the US Helsinki Commission (1976–1985). July 8, 2014.

Philips, David L., president of the Congressional Human Rights Foundation (1988–1995). July 30, 2015.

Porter, John E., Representative (R-IL) (1980–2001). October 17, 2018.

Schifter, Richard, Assistant Secretary for Human Rights (1985–1989). May 30, 2016.

Schrayer, Elizabeth, staffer for Representative John E. Porter (R-IL) (1980,1982). Spring 2015.

References

Adamishin, A. L., and Richard Schifter. *Human Rights, Perestroika, and the End of the Cold War*. Washington, DC: United States Institute of Peace Press, 2009.

Aldrich, John H., John L. Sullivan, and Eugene Borgida. "Foreign Affairs and Issue Voting: Do Presidential Candidates 'Waltz before a Blind Audience?'" *The American Political Science Review* 83, no. 1 (1989): 123–141.

Altshuler, Stuart. *From Exodus to Freedom: A History of the Soviet Jewry Movement*. Lanham, MD: Rowman & Littlefield, 2005.

American Association for the International Commission of Jurists. *Human Rights and United States Foreign Policy, the First Decade, 1973–1983*. Geneva: International Commission of Jurists, 1984.

Apodaca, Clair. *Understanding U.S. Human Rights Policy: A Paradoxical Legacy.* New York: Routledge, 2006.

Armony, Ariel C. *Argentina, the United States, and the Anti-Communist Crusade in Central America, 1977–1984.* Athens, OH: Ohio University Centre for International Studies, 1997.

Arnson, Cynthia. *Crossroads: Congress, the Reagan Administration, and Central America.* New York: Pantheon Books, 1989.

Baker, James Addison, and Thomas M. DeFrank. *The Politics of Diplomacy: Revolution, War, and Peace, 1989–1992.* New York: G. P. Putnam's, 1995.

Baker, Pauline. "Getting It Right. U.S. Policy in South Africa." In *Implementing U.S. Human Rights Policy: Agendas, Policies, and Practices,* edited by Debra Liang-Fenton, 85–112. Washington, DC: Institute of Peace, 2004.

"The United States and South Africa: Persuasion and Coercion." In *Honey and Vinegar: Incentives, Sanctions and Foreign Policy,* edited by Richard N. Hass and Meghan O'Sullivan, 95–121. Washington, DC: Brookings Institute, 2000.

Barry, John M. *The Ambition and the Power.* New York: Penguin Books, 1990.

Bass, Gary Jonathan. *Freedom's Battle: The Origins of Humanitarian Intervention,* 1st edition. New York: Alfred A. Knopf, 2008.

Bassano, David. *Fight and Flight: The Central America Human Rights Movement in the United States in the 1980s.* Newcastle upon Tyne: Cambridge Scholars, 2016.

Beckerman, Gal. *When They Come for Us, We'll Be Gone: The Epic Struggle to Save Soviet Jewry.* Boston, MA: Houghton Mifflin Harcourt, 2010.

Bíró, Anna-Mária, and Katrina Lantos-Swett, eds. *The Noble Banner of Human Rights: Essays in Memory of Tom Lantos.* Leiden, NL: Brill Nijhoff, 2018.

Bon Tempo, Carl J. *Americans at the Gate: The United States and Refugees during the Cold War, Politics and Society in Twentieth-Century America.* Princeton, NJ: Princeton University Press, 2008.

"From the Center-Right: Freedom House and Human Rights in the 1970s and 1980s." In *The Human Rights Revolution: An International History,* edited by Petra Goedde and William Hitchcock, 223–244. New York: Oxford University Press, 2012.

"Human Rights and the U.S. Republican Party in the Late 1970s." In *The Breakthrough. Human Rights in the 1970s,* edited by Jan Eckel and Samuel Moyn, 146–165. Philadelphia: University of Pennsylvania Press, 2014.

Bonner, Raymond. "U.S. Ties to Anti-Sandinists Are Reported to Be Extensive." *The New York Times,* April 3, 1983.

Borgwardt, Elizabeth. *A New Deal for the World: America's Vision for Human Rights.* Cambridge, MA: Harvard University Press, 2005.

Botha, Pieter W. "Address by State President P. W. Botha at the Opening of the National Party Natal Congress Durban." August 15, 1985.

Bradley, Mark Philip. *The World Reimagined: Americans and Human Rights in the Twentieth Century.* New York: Cambridge University Press, 2016.

Brands, H. W. *Reagan: The Life.* New York: Doubleday, 2015.

Brands, Hal. *Making the Unipolar Moment: U.S. Foreign Policy and the Rise of the Post-Cold War Order.* Ithaca, NY: Cornell University Press, 2016.

Brazinsky, Gregg. *Nation Building in South Korea: Koreans, Americans, and the Making of a Democracy, The New Cold War History*. Chapel Hill: University of North Carolina Press, 2007.

Brecher, John. "A Secret War for Nicaragua." *Newsweek*, November 8, 1982.

Brier, Robert. "Beyond the Quest for a 'Breakthrough': Reflections on the Recent Historiography on Human Rights." *European History Yearbook* 16 (2015): 155–173.

Brinkley, Douglas. *The Unfinished Presidency: Jimmy Carter's Journey beyond the White House*. New York: Viking, 1998.

Broder, David S. "A Sharp Right Turn." *The Washington Post*, November 6, 1980, 2.

Brown, Archie. "Gorbachev, Perestroika, and the End of the Cold War." In *Reagan and the World: Leadership and National Security, 1981–1989*, edited by Bradley Lynn Coleman and Kyle Longley, 111–126. Lexington: The University Press of Kentucky, 2017.

Brownlee, W. Elliot. "Introduction: Revisiting the "Reagan Revolution." In *The Reagan Presidency: Pragmatic Conservatism and Its Legacies*, edited by W. Elliot Brownlee and Hugh Davis Graham, 1–13. Lawrence: University Press of Kansas, 2003.

Buchanan, Patrick. "The Contras Need Our Help." *The Washington Post*, March 5, 1986, A19.

Burke, Roland. "Competing for the Last Utopia?: The NIEO, Human Rights, and the World Conference for the International Women's Year, Mexico City, June 1975." *Humanity* 6, no. 1 (2015), 47–61.

Decolonization and the Evolution of International Human Rights. Philadelphia: University of Pennsylvania Press, 2010.

Burt, Richard. "Presidential Candidates Stake Out Divergent Ground on Foreign Policy." *The New York Times*, October 19, 1980, 1.

Burton-Hafner, Emilie M. "Sticks and Stones: Naming and Shaming the Human Rights Enforcement Problem." *International Organization* 62 (2008), 689–716.

Busch, Andrew. *Reagan's Victory: The Presidential Election of 1980 and the Rise of the Right, American Presidential Elections Series*. Lawrence: University Press of Kansas, 2005.

Byrne, Malcolm. *Iran-Contra: Reagan's Scandal and the Unchecked Abuse of Presidential Power*. Lawrence: University Press of Kansas, 2014.

Cannon, Lou. *President Reagan: The Role of a Lifetime*. New York: Public Affairs, 2000.

Cannon, Lou, and Edward Walsh. "War, Peace Dominate Debate War and Peace Theme Dominates Carter-Reagan Debate." *The Washington Post*, October 29, 1980.

Carleton, David, and Michael Stohl. "The Foreign Policy of Human Rights: Rhetoric and Reality from Jimmy Carter to Ronald Reagan." *Human Rights Quarterly* 7, no. 2 (1985): 205–229.

Carothers, Thomas. *In the Name of Democracy: U.S. Policy toward Latin America in the Reagan Years*. Berkeley: University of California Press, 1991.

Carter, Ralph G., and James M. Scott. *Choosing to Lead: Understanding Congressional Foreign Policy Entrepreneurs*. Durham, NC: Duke University Press, 2009.

Christian, Shirley. "Helms, in Chile, Denounces U.S. Envoy." *The New York Times*, July 14, 1986, A03.

Christiansen, Christian O., and Steven L. B. Jensen, eds. *Histories of Global Inequality: New Perspectives*. Switzerland: Palgrave Macmillan, 2019.

Clymer, Adam. *Edward M. Kennedy: A Biography*. New York: Morrow, 1999.

Cmiel, Kenneth. "The Emergence of Human Rights Politics in the United States." *Journal of American History* 86, no. 3 (1999): 1231–1250.

Cohen, Pamela B., and Micah Naftalin."Congress Should Save Human Rights Caucus." *The New York Times*, December 6, 1994, A22.

Cohen, Stephen B. "Conditioning U.S. Security Assistance on Human Rights Practices." *American Journal of International Law* 76, no. 2 (1982): 246–279.

Cohodas, Nadine. "Black House Members Striving for Influence." *Congressional Quarterly* 43, no. 15 (1985): 675–681.

Commonwealth Group of Eminent Persons. *Mission to South Africa: The Commonwealth Report*. London: Penguin, 1986.

"Contra Aid." *Congressional Digest* 67, no. 3 (1988): 67–96.

Cooper, Frederick. "Afterword: Social Rights and Human Rights in the Time of Decolonization." *Humanity* 3, no. 3 (2012): 473–492.

Copson, Raymond W. *The Congressional Black Caucus and Foreign Policy*. New York: Novinka, 2003.

Cowell, Alan. "Pretoria's Forces Raid 3 Neighbors in Move on Rebels." *The New York Times*, May 20, 1986. www.nytimes.com/1986/05/20/world/pretoria-s-forces-raid-3-neighbors-in-move-on-rebels.html.

"State of Emergency Imposed throughout South Africa; More Than 1,000 Rounded Up." *The New York Times*, June 13, 1986. www.nytimes.com/1986/06/13/world/state-of-emergency-imposed-throughout-south-africa-more-than-1000-rounded-up.html.

Craig, Campbell, and Fredrik Logevall. *America's Cold War: The Politics of Insecurity*. Cambridge, MA: Harvard University Press, 2009.

Crocker, Chester A. *High Noon in Southern Africa: Making Peace in a Rough Neighborhood*. New York: W. W. Norton, 1992.

"South Africa: Strategy for Change." *Foreign Affairs* 59, no. 2 (1980): 323–351.

Crossette, Barbara. "Strong U.S. Human Rights Policy Urged in Memo Approved by Haig." *The New York Times*, November 5, 1981. www.nytimes.com/1981/11/05/world/strong-us-human-rights-policy-urged-memo-approved-haig-excerpts-memo-page-a10.html.

Cullen, Robert B. "Soviet Jewry." *Foreign Affairs* 65, no. 2 (1986): 252–266.

de Lama, George, and Dorothy Collin. "Reagan Slaps S. Africa's Wrist: Limited Sanctions Ordered." *Chicago Tribune*, September 10, 1985.

de Neufville, Judith Innes. "Human Rights Reporting as a Policy Tool: An Examination of the State Department Country Reports." *Human Rights Quarterly* 8, no. 4 (1986): 681–699.

Dellums, Ronald V., and H. Lee Halterman. *Lying Down with the Lions: A Public Life from the Streets of Oakland to the Halls of Power*. Boston, MA: Beacon Press, 2000.

Dickenson, James R. "Dellums: Exoneration Is His: Passage of Anti-Pretoria Sanctions Marks Milestone for Hill Veteran." *The Washington Post*, June 20, 1986, A17.

Dickey, Christopher. "Nothing Ragtag about Nicaraguan Rebels." *The Washington Post*, April 3, 1983, Nexis Uni.

"Disinvestment Is Still a Threat to SA's Euphoria over Reagan." *Cape Times*, November 10, 1984.

Dobrynin, Anatoly. *In Confidence: Moscow's Ambassador to America's Six Cold War Presidents (1962–1986)*, 1st edition. New York: Random House, 1995.

Domber, Gregory F. *Empowering Revolution: America, Poland, and the End of the Cold War, The New Cold War History*. Chapel Hill: University of North Carolina Press, 2014.

Draper, Theodore. *A Very Thin Line: The Iran–Contra Affairs*. New York: Hill & Wang, 1991.

Dubow, Saul. *South Africa's Struggle for Human Rights: The History of Rights in South Africa*. Athens: Ohio University Press, 2012.

Dumbrell, John. *The Carter Presidency: A Re-Evaluation*. Manchester: Manchester University Press, 1995.

Eckel, Jan. "The International League for the Rights of Man, Amnesty International, and the Changing Fate of Human Rights Activism from the 1940s through the 1970s." *Humanity* 4, no. 2 (2013): 183–214.

Eckel, Jan, and Samuel Moyn, eds. *The Breakthrough: Human Rights in the 1970s*, 1st edition, *Pennsylvania Studies in Human Rights*. Philadelphia: University of Pennsylvania Press, 2014.

Editorial. "Deception on Capitol Hill." *The New York Times*, January 15, 1992, A20.

"Semantic Antics over Human Rights." *The New York Times*, May 24, 1981, 18. www.nytimes.com/1981/05/24/opinion/semantic-antics-over-human-rights.html.

"Wrong Turns on Human Rights." *The New York Times*, February 6, 1981. www.nytimes.com/1981/02/06/opinion/wrong-turns-on-human-rights.html.

Engel, Jeffrey A. *When the World Seemed New: George H. W. Bush and the End of the Cold War*. New York: Houghton Mifflin Harcourt, 2017.

Etzioni, Amitai. "Obama's Implicit Human Rights Doctrine." *Human Rights Review* 12, no. 1 (2011): 93–107.

"Excerpts from State Department Memo on Human Rights." *The New York Times*, November 5, 1981, A10.

Farnsworth, Clyde H. "Dole Proposes Suspension of Law Restricting Soviet Trade." *The New York Times*, April 25, 1986. www.nytimes.com/1986/04/25/world/dole-proposes-suspension-of-law-restricting-soviet-trade.html.

Farrell, John A. *Tip O'Neill and the Democratic Century*, 1st edition. Boston, MA: Little, Brown, 2001.

Fenno, Richard F. *Home Style: House Members in Their Districts*. Boston, MA: Little, Brown, 1978.

Fieldhouse, Roger. *Anti-Apartheid: A History of the Movement in Britain: A Study in Pressure Group Politics*. London: Merlin, 2005.

Fischer, Beth A. *The Reagan Reversal: Foreign Policy and the End of the Cold War*. Columbia: University of Missouri Press, 1997.

Flippen, J. Brooks. *Speaker Jim Wright: Power, Scandal, and the Birth of Modern Politics*. Austin: University of Texas Press, 2018.

Forsythe, David P. *Human Rights and U.S. Foreign Policy: Congress Reconsidered*. Gainesville: University of Florida Press, 1988.

"U.S. Foreign Policy and Human Rights: Situating Obama." *Human Rights Quarterly* 33, no. 3 (2011): 767–789.

Forsythe, David P., and David Beetham. "Human Rights and US Foreign Policy: Two Levels, Two Worlds." *Political Studies* 43, no. 4 (1995): 111–130.

Forsythe, David P., and Patrice C. McMahon. *American Exceptionalism Reconsidered: US Foreign Policy, Human Rights, and World Order, International Studies Intensives.* New York: Routledge, 2017.

Fukuyama, Francis. *The End of History and the Last Man.* New York: Free Press, 1992.

Galey, Margaret E. "Congress, Foreign Policy and Human Rights Ten Years after Helsinki." *Human Rights Quarterly* 7, no. 3 (1985): 334–372.

Gargan, Edward A. "Chinese Report Protest by Lamas to Free Tibet." *The New York Times,* October 1, 1987, A8.

Geoghegan, Kate. "A Policy in Tension: The National Endowment for Democracy and the U.S. Response to the Collapse of the Soviet Union." *Diplomatic History* 42, no. 5 (2018): 772–801.

Gleijeses, Piero. *Visions of Freedom: Havana, Washington, Pretoria and the Struggle for Southern Africa, 1976–1991, The New Cold War History.* Chapel Hill: The University of North Carolina Press, 2013.

Glen, Stovall James. "Foreign Policy Issue Coverage in the 1980 Presidential Campaign." *Journalism Quarterly* 59, no. 4 (1982): 531–540.

Glendon, Mary Ann. *A World Made New: Eleanor Roosevelt and the Universal Declaration of Human Rights,* 1st edition. New York: Random House, 2001.

Goldberg, Jeffrey. "The Obama Doctrine." *The Atlantic,* April 2016. www.the atlantic.com/magazine/archive/2016/04/the-obama-doctrine/471525/.

Goldstone, Richard. "Ambiguity and America: South Africa and US Foreign Policy." *Social Research* 72, no. 4 (2005): 811–824.

Grandin, Greg. *Empire's Workshop: Latin America, the United States, and the Rise of the New Imperialism,* 1st edition. New York: Metropolitan, 2006.

Granieri, Ronald J. "Beyond Cap the Foil. Caspar Weinberger and the Reagan-Era Defense Buildup." In *Reagan and the World: Leadership and National Security, 1981–1989,* edited by Bradley Lynn Coleman and Kyle Longley, 51–79. Lexington: The University Press of Kentucky, 2017.

Greenberger, Robert S. "U.S. Looks to Jewish Leaders for Cues on Prodding Soviets over Emigration." *Wall Street Journal,* May 18, 1987, 22.

Greenhouse, Linda. "Senate Backs Costa Rican Peace Plan." *The New York Times,* March 13, 1987. www.nytimes.com/1987/03/13/world/senate-backs-costa-rican-peace-plan-881.html.

Grow, Michael. *U.S. Presidents and Latin American Interventions: Pursuing Regime Change in the Cold War.* Lawrence: University Press of Kansas, 2008.

Guilhot, Nicolas. *The Democracy Makers: Human Rights & International Order.* New York: Columbia University Press, 2005.

Gwertzman, Bernard. "U.S. Jewish Group Shifts on Soviet." *The New York Times,* May 25, 1986, 15.

Haig, Alexander Meigs, and Clare Boothe Luce. *Caveat: Realism, Reagan, and Foreign Policy.* New York: Macmillan, 1984.

Hamilton, Lee H. "Congress and the Presidency in American Foreign Policy." *Presidential Studies Quarterly* 18 (Summer 1988): 507–511.

Hammond, Susan Webb. *Congressional Caucuses in National Policy Making*. Baltimore, MD: Johns Hopkins University Press, 1998.

Hannum, Hurst, Dinah Shelton, S. James Anaya, and Rosa Celorio. *International Human Rights: Problems of Law, Policy, and Practice*, 6th edition. *Aspen Casebook Series*. New York: Wolters Kluwer, 2018.

Harris, Lyle V. "New York Rally Protests Apartheid." *The Washington Post*, June 15, 1986, A21.

Hartmann, Hauke. "US Human Rights Policy under Carter and Reagan, 1977–1981." *Human Rights Quarterly* 23, no. 2 (2001): 402–430.

Hartz, Louis. *The Liberal Tradition in America; an Interpretation of American Political Thought since the Revolution*, 1st edition. New York: Harcourt, 1955.

Heginbotham, Stanley J. "Dateline Washington: The Rules of the Games." *Foreign Policy* no. 53 (1983): 157–172.

Helms, Jesse. *Here's Where I Stand: A Memoir*, 1st edition. New York: Random House, 2005.

Hersman, Rebecca K. C. *Friends and Foes: How Congress and the President Really Make Foreign Policy*. Washington, DC: Brookings Institution, 2000.

Herszenhorn, David M. "Tom Lantos, 80, Is Dead; Longtime Congressman." *The New York Times*, February 12, 2008, D6.

Hess, Stephen, and Michael Nelson. "Foreign Policy: Dominance and Decisiveness in Presidential Elections." In *The Election of 1984*, edited by Michael Nelson, 129–154. Washington, DC: Congressional Quarterly, 1985.

Hoffmann, Stefan-Ludwig. "Human Rights and History." *Past & Present* 232, no. 1 (2016): 279–310.

"Introduction: Genealogies of Human Rights." In *Human Rights in the Twentieth Century*, edited by Stefan-Ludwig Hoffmann, 1–26. New York: Cambridge University Press, 2010.

ed. *Human Rights in the Twentieth Century*. New York: Cambridge University Press, 2010.

Holsti, Ole. "Public Opinion on Human Rights in American Foreign Policy." In *The United States and Human Rights: Looking Inward and Outward*, edited by David P. Forsythe, 131–174. Lincoln: University of Nebraska Press, 2000.

Hopgood, Stephen. *Keepers of the Flame: Understanding Amnesty International*. Ithaca, NY: Cornell University Press, 2006.

Hostetter, David. *Movement Matters: American Antiapartheid Activism and the Rise of Multicultural Politics, Studies in African American History and Culture*. New York: Routledge, 2006.

Hudson, Cheryl, and Gareth Davies, eds. *Ronald Reagan and the 1980s: Perceptions, Policies, Legacies*. New York: Palgrave Macmillan, 2008.

Ignatieff, Michael, ed. *American Exceptionalism and Human Rights*. Princeton, NJ: Princeton University Press, 2005.

The International Court of Justice. 1986. Summary of the Judgment of 27 June 1986. Case Concerning the Military and Paramilitary Activities in and against Nicaragua (*Nicaragua v. United States of America*). Accessed August 1, 2019, www.icj-cij.org/files/case-related/70/6505.pdf.

Iriye, Akira, Petra Goedde, and William I. Hitchcock, eds. *The Human Rights Revolution: An International History, Reinterpreting History*. Oxford: Oxford University Press, 2012.

Irwin, Ryan M. *Gordian Knot: Apartheid and the Unmaking of the Liberal World Order, Oxford Studies in International History*. Oxford: Oxford University Press, 2012.

Jackson, Thomas F. *From Civil Rights to Human Rights: Martin Luther King, Jr., and the Struggle for Economic Justice, Politics and Culture in Modern America*. Philadelphia: University of Pennsylvania Press, 2007.

Jacobs, Meg, and Julian E. Zelizer. *Conservatives in Power: The Reagan Years, 1981–1989: A Brief History with Documents, Bedford Series in History and Culture*. Boston, MA: Bedford/St. Martin's, 2011.

Jacoby, Tamar. "The Reagan Turnaround on Human Rights." *Foreign Affairs* 64, no. 5 (1986): 1066–1086.

Jensen, Steven L. B. *The Making of International Human Rights: The 1960s, Decolonization, and the Reconstruction of Global Values*. New York: Cambridge University Press, 2016.

Jones, Jeffrey M., Frank Newport, and Lydia Saad. *Ronald Reagan from the People's Perspective: A Gallup Poll Review*. Accessed August 9, 2019, www .gallup.com/poll/11887/ronald-reagan-from-peoples-perspective-gallup-poll-review.aspx.

Johnson, Robert David. "Congress and the Cold War." *Journal of Cold War Studies* 3, no. 2 (2001): 76–100.

Congress and the Cold War. New York: Cambridge University Press, 2006.

Johnstone, Andrew, and Helen Laville. *The US Public and American Foreign Policy, Routledge Studies in US Foreign Policy*. London: Routledge, 2010.

Kagan, Robert. *A Twilight Struggle: American Power and Nicaragua, 1977–1990*. New York: Free Press, 1996.

"Global Mission." *Commentary* 92, no. 2 (1991): 54–56.

Karnow, Stanley. "Reagan and the Philippines: Setting Marcos Adrift." *The New York Times*, March 19, 1989. www.nytimes.com/1989/03/19/magazine/rea gan-and-the-philippines-setting-marcos-adrift.html.

Kaufman, Robert Gordon. *Henry M. Jackson: A Life in Politics*. Seattle: University of Washington Press, 2000.

Keck, Margaret E., and Kathryn Sikkink. *Activists beyond Borders: Advocacy Networks in International Politics*. Ithaca, NY: Cornell University Press, 1998.

Keeley, Theresa. "Reagan's Real Catholics vs. Tip O'Neill's Maryknoll Nuns: Gender, Intra-Catholic Conflict, and the Contras." *Diplomatic History* 40, no. 3 (2015): 530–558.

Kelly, Patrick William. *Sovereign Emergencies: Latin America and the Making of Global Human Rights Politics, Human Rights in History*. New York: Cambridge University Press, 2018.

Kennedy, Edward M. "The Sanctions Debate." *Africa Report* 31, no. 5 (1986).

Keys, Barbara J. "Anti-Torture Politics: Amnesty International, the Greek Junta, and the Origins of the Human Rights 'Boom' in the United States." In *The Human Rights Revolution: An International History*, edited by Akira Iriye, Petra Goedde, and William I. Hitchcock, 201–250. Oxford: Oxford University Press, 2012.

"Congress, Kissinger, and the Origins of Human Rights Diplomacy." *Diplomatic History* 34, no. 3 (2010): 823–851.

"Harnessing Human Rights to the Olympic Games: Human Rights Watch and the 1993 'Stop Beijing' Campaign." *Journal of Contemporary History* 53, no. 2 (2016): 415–438.

Reclaiming American Virtue: The Human Rights Revolution of the 1970s. Cambridge, MA: Harvard University Press, 2014.

"The Telephone and Its Uses in 1980s U.S. Activism." *The Journal of Interdisciplinary History* 48, no. 4 (2018): 485–509.

King, Jr., Martin Luther. "Letter from Birmingham Jail." *The Atlantic Monthly* 212, no. 2 (1963): 78–88.

Kirkpatrick, Jeane J. "Dictatorships and Double Standards." *Commentary* 68, no. 5 (1979): 34–45.

"U.S. Security & Latin America." *Commentary* 71, no. 1 (1981): 29–40.

Klotz, Audie. *Norms in International Relations: The Struggle against Apartheid, Cornell Studies in Political Economy*. Ithaca, NY: Cornell University Press, 1995.

Knoblauch, William M. *Nuclear Freeze in a Cold War: The Reagan Administration, Cultural Activism, and the End of the Arms Race, Culture and Politics in the Cold War and Beyond*. Amherst: University of Massachusetts Press, 2017.

Krauss, Clifford. "Congressman Says Girl Was Credible." *The New York Times*, January 12, 1992. www.nytimes.com/1992/01/12/world/congressman-says-girl-was-credible.html.

Krauthammer, Charles. "The Reagan Doctrine." *Time Magazine*, April 1, 1985.

Kreisler, Nancy H. "Mobil Is Quitting South Africa, Blaming 'Foolish' Laws in U.S." *The New York Times*, April 29, 1989. www.nytimes.com/1989/04/29/business/mobil-is-quitting-south-africa-blaming-foolish-laws-in-us.html.

LaFeber, Walter. *Inevitable Revolutions: The United States in Central America*. New York: W. W. Norton, 1993.

Lazin, Fred A. *The Struggle for Soviet Jewry in American Politics: Israel versus the American Jewish Establishment*. Lanham, MD: Lexington, 2005.

Lefever, Ernest W. *Morality and Foreign Policy: A Symposium on President Carter's Stance, Monograph Series – Ethics and Public Policy Center, Georgetown University*. Washington, DC: Ethics and Public Policy Center, Georgetown University, 1977.

LeoGrande, William M. *Our Own Backyard: The United States in Central America, 1977–1992*. Chapel Hill, NC: University of North Carolina Press, 1998.

Levin, Geoffrey P. "Before Soviet Jewry's Happy Ending: The Cold War and America's Long Debate over Jackson–Vanik, 1976–1989." *Shofar* 33, no. 3 (2015): 63–85.

Lewis, Ann Jo. "Deep in the Art of Russia." *The Washington Post*, July 13, 1983, D3.

Lindsay, James M. *Congress and the Politics of U.S. Foreign Policy*. Baltimore, MD: Johns Hopkins University Press, 1994.

Loomis, Burdett A. *The Contemporary Congress*. New York: St. Martin's, 1998.

Loveman, Brian. *No Higher Law: American Foreign Policy and the Western Hemisphere since 1776*. Chapel Hill: University of North Carolina Press, 2010.

Lugar, Richard G. "Making Foreign Policy: The Congress and Apartheid." *Africa Report* 31 (September–October 1986): 33–34.

Lugar, Richard G., and Nancy Landon Kassebaum. "Override the President's Veto." *The Washington Post*, September 30, 1986, A15.

MacArthur, John R. "Remember Nayirah, Witness for Kuwait?" *The New York Times*, January 6, 1992, A15.

"The Malta Summit; Transcript of the Bush–Gorbachev News Conference in Malta." *The New York Times*, December 4, 1989, A12.

Marriott, Michel, and Karlyn Barker. "1960s Tactics Revived for Embassy Sit-Ins." *The Washington Post*, November 29, 1984, Nexis Uni.

Mason, Robert. "The Domestic Politics of War and Peace: Jimmy Carter, Ronald Reagan, and the Election of 1980." In *US Presidential Elections and Foreign Policy*, 250–270. Lexington: University Press of Kentucky, 2017.

Massie, Robert. *Loosing the Bonds: The United States and South Africa in the Apartheid Years*. New York: Doubleday, 1997.

Matlock, Jack F. *Autopsy on an Empire: The American Ambassador's Account of the Collapse of the Soviet Union*. New York: Random House, 1995.
   Reagan and Gorbachev: How the Cold War Ended, 1st edition. New York: Random House, 2004.

Matusow, Allen J. *The Unraveling of America, The New American Nation Series*. New York: Harper & Row, 1984.

Mayhew, David R. *Congress: The Electoral Connection, Yale Studies in Political Science*. New Haven, CT: Yale University Press, 1974.

Maynard, Edwin S. "The Bureaucracy and Implementation of US Human Rights Policy." *Human Rights Quarterly* 11, no. 2 (1989): 175–248.

Mazower, Mark. "The Strange Triumph of Human Rights, 1933–1950." *Historical Journal* 47, no. 2 (2004): 379–398.

McCormick, Evan D. "Breaking with Statism? U.S. Democracy Promotion in Latin America, 1984–1988★." *Diplomatic History* 42, no. 5 (2017): 745–771.
   "Freedom Tide? Ideology, Politics and the Origins of Democracy Promotion in U.S. Central America Policy, 1980–1984." *Journal of Cold War Studies* 16, no. 4 (2014): 60–109.

McCormick, James M., and Neil J. Mitchell. "Commitments, Transnational Interests, and Congress." *Political Research Quarterly* 60, no. 4 (2007): 579–592.

McMahon, Robert J. "Diplomatic History and Policy History: Finding Common Ground." *Journal of Policy History* 17, no. 1 (2005): 93–109.

"A Message to Congressman Mike Barnes." *The Washington Times*, March 17, 1986, 5A.

Miller, G. Wayne. *An Uncommon Man: The Life & Times of Senator Claiborne Pell*. Lebanon, NH: University Press of New England, 2011.

Miller, Judith. "A Neoconservative for Human Rights Post." *The New York Times*, October 31, 1981, 7.

Mohr, Charles. "Coalition Assails Reagan's Choice for State Dept. Human Rights Job." *The New York Times*, February 25, 1981, www.nytimes.com/1981/02/25/world/coalition-assails-reagan-s-choice-for-state-dept-human-rights-job.html.

Monshipouri, Mahmood, ed. *Information Politics, Protests, and Human Rights in the Digital Age*. New York: Cambridge University Press, 2016.

Montgomery, Paul L. "Throngs Fill Manhattan to Protest Nuclear Weapons." *The New York Times*, June 13, 1982, 1.

Morley, Morris, and Chris McGillion. *Reagan and Pinochet: The Struggle over U.S. Policy toward Chile*. New York: Cambridge University Press, 2015.

"Soldiering On: The Reagan Administration and Redemocratisation in Chile, 1983–1986." *Bulletin of Latin American Research* 25, no. 1 (2006): 1–22.

Mower, A. Glenn. *Human Rights and American Foreign Policy: The Carter and Reagan Experiences*. New York: Greenwood, 1987.

Moyn, Samuel. "The End of Human Rights History." *Past & Present* 233, no. 1 (2016): 307–322.

The Last Utopia: Human Rights in History. Cambridge, MA: Harvard University Press, 2010.

Not Enough: Human Rights in an Unequal World. Cambridge, MA: Harvard University Press, 2018.

"Substance, Scale, and Salience: The Recent Historiography of Human Rights." *Annual Review of Law and Social Science* 8 (2012): 123–140.

Muravchik, Joshua. *Exporting Democracy: Fulfilling America's Destiny, AEI Studies*. Washington, DC: American Enterprise Institute, 1991.

The Uncertain Crusade: Jimmy Carter and the Dilemmas of Human Rights Policy. Lanham, MD: Hamilton, 1986.

Murdie, Amanda M., and David R. Davis. "Shaming and Blaming: Using Events Data to Assess the Impact of Human Rights INGOs." *International Studies Quarterly* 56, no.1 (2012): 1–16.

Mydans, Seth. "Bahais Seek the Glare of Publicity." *The New York Times*, April 27, 1984, A16.

Myers, David S. "Editorials and Foreign Affairs in Recent Presidential Campaigns." *Journalism Quarterly* 59, no. 4 (1982): 541–547.

"National Security Council Document on Policy in Central America and Cuba." *The New York Times*, April 7, 1983. www.nytimes.com/1983/04/07/world/national-security-council-document-on-policy-in-central-america-and-cuba.html.

Nau, Henry R. *Conservative Internationalism: Armed Diplomacy under Jefferson, Polk, Truman, and Reagan*. Princeton, NJ: Princeton University Press, 2013.

Neier, Aryeh. "Of Reagan and Rights." *The New York Times*, November 12, 1981. www.nytimes.com/1981/11/12/opinion/of-reagan-and-rights.html.

Taking Liberties: Four Decades in the Struggle for Rights. New York: Public Affairs, 2003.

Nesbitt, Francis Njubi. *Race for Sanctions: African Americans against Apartheid, 1946–1994, Blacks in the Diaspora*. Bloomington: Indiana University Press, 2004).

"New Human Rights Group Formed." *Jewish Telegraph Agency*, June 14, 1983. www.jta.org/1983/06/30/archive/new-human-rights-group-formed.

"Newspaper Ad Blasts Helms." *The Asheville Citizen*, March 6, 1987.

Novak, Michael, and Richard Schifter. *A Conversation with Michael Novak and Richard Schifter: Human Rights and the United Nations: Held on April 3, 1981, Studies in Philosophy, Religion, and Public Policy*. Washington, DC: American Enterprise Institute for Public Policy Research, 1981.

Obama, Barack. *Remarks by the President at Cairo University, June 4, 2009*. Accessed August 1, 2019, https://obamawhitehouse.archives.gov/the-press-office/remarks-president-cairo-university-6-04-09.

Remarks by the President at the Acceptance of the Nobel Peace Prize, December 10, 2009. Accessed August 1, 2019, https://obamawhitehouse.archives.gov/the-press-office/remarks-president-acceptance-nobel-peace-prize.

Omang, Joanne. "Senator Hits 'Contra' Aid." *The Washington Post*, November 30, 1984.

O'Neill, Thomas. "Tip," and William Novak. In *Man of the House: The Life and Political Memoirs of Speaker Tip O'Neill*. New York: Random House, 1987.

Oyen, Meredith. *The Diplomacy of Migration: Transnational Lives and the Making of U.S.-Chinese Relations in the Cold War*. Ithacha, NY: Cornell University Press, 2016.

Pace, Eric. "Rep. Dante B. Fascell, 81; Headed Foreign Affairs Panel." *The New York Times*, November 30, 1998. www.nytimes.com/1998/11/30/us/rep-dante-b-fascell-81-headed-foreign-affairs-panel.html.

Pach, Chester. "Sticking to His Guns: Reagan and National Security." In *The Reagan Presidency: Pragmatic Conservatism and Its Legacies*, edited by W. Elliot Brownlee and Hugh Davis Graham, 85–112. Lawrence: University Press of Kansas, 2003.

Pastor, Robert A. *Not Condemned to Repetition: The United States and Nicaragua*. Boulder, CO: Westview Press, 2002.

Whirlpool: U.S. Foreign Policy toward Latin America and the Caribbean. Princeton, NJ: Princeton University Press, 1992.

Patterson, James T. *Restless Giant: The United States from Watergate to Bush v. Gore*. New York: Oxford University Press, 2005.

Peace, Roger C. *A Call to Conscience: The Anti/Contra War Campaign, Culture, Politics, and the Cold War*. Amherst: University of Massachusetts Press, 2012.

"Winning Hearts and Minds: The Debate over U.S. Intervention in Nicaragua in the 1980s." *Peace & Change* 35, no. 1 (2010): 1–38.

Pearson, Richard. "Florida Congressman Dante B. Fascell Dies." *The Washington Post*, November 30, 1998.

Peck, James. *Ideal Illusions: How the U.S. Government Co-Opted Human Rights, American Empire Project*. New York: Metropolitan, 2010.

Pee, Robert. *Democracy Promotion, National Security and Strategy: Foreign Policy under the Reagan Administration*. London: Routledge, 2015.

Peters, B. Guy, Jon Pierre, and Desmond S. King. "The Politics of Path Dependency: Political Conflict in Historical Institutionalism." *Journal of Politics* 67, no. 4 (2005): 1275–1300.

Peterson, Christian Philip. "'Confronting' Moscow: The Reagan Administration, Human Rights, and the Final Act." *Historian* 74, no. 1 (2012): 57–86.

Globalizing Human Rights: Private Citizens, the Soviet Union, and the West, Routledge Studies on History and Globalization. New York: Routledge, 2012.

Podhoretz, Norman. "The Present Danger." *Commentary* 69, no. 3 (1980): 27–40.

Poll, Harris. *Human Rights First*, December 9, 2015. Accessed August 9, 2019, www.humanrightsfirst.org/sites/default/files/HumanRightsFirstHarrisPoll.pdf.

Preston, Andrew. *Sword of the Spirit, Shield of Faith: Religion in American War and Diplomacy*, 1st edition. New York: Alfred A. Knopf, 2012.

Rabe, Stephen G. *The Killing Zone: The United States Wages Cold War in Latin America*. New York: Oxford University Press, 2012.

Ramirez, Zachary Steven. "International Human Rights Activism in the United States during the Cold War." PhD dissertation, University of California, Berkeley, 2013.

Rangel, Charles B., and Leon E. Wynter. *And I Haven't Had a Bad Day Since: From the Streets of Harlem to the Halls of Congress*. New York: Thomas Dunne Books/St. Martin's, 2007.

"Reagan Rejects Sanctions; Tutu Tells West: Go to Hell: 'Emotional Clamor' Hit in Speech." *Los Angeles Times*, July 22, 1986, www.latimes.com/archives/la-xpm-1986-07-22-mn-30949-story.html.

Reagan, Ronald. *An American Life*. New York: Simon & Schuster, 1990.

"Tactics for Détente." *Wall Street Journal*, February 13, 1976, 8.

Reagan, Ronald, and Douglas Brinkley. *The Reagan Diaries*, 1st edition. New York: Harper Collins, 2007.

"Rejects Assertion Jackson-Vanik Law Harmed Soviet Jewish Immigration." *Jewish Advocate*, June 2, 1983.

Renouard, Joe. *Human Rights in American Foreign Policy: From the 1960s to the Soviet Collapse, Pennsylvania Studies in Human Rights*. Philadelphia: University of Pennsylvania Press, 2016.

Riding, Alan. "Olympics: 2000 Olympics Go to Sydney in Surprise Setback for China." *The New York Times*, September 24, 1993, A01.

Roberts, Steven J. "House Reverses Earlier Ban on Aid to Nicaragua Rebels; Passes $27 Million Package." *The New York Times*, June 13, 1985, Nexis Uni.

"Reaction in Congress to Speech Is Mostly Negative." *The New York Times*, July 23, 1986. www.nytimes.com/1986/07/23/world/reaction-in-congress-to-speech-is-mostly-negative.html.

Roberts, Steven V. "Foreign Policy: Lot of Table Thumping Going On." *The New York Times*, May 29, 1985. www.nytimes.com/1985/05/29/us/foreign-policy-lot-of-table-thumping-going-on.html.

Robinson, Randall. *Defending the Spirit: A Black Life in America*. New York: Dutton, 1998.

Rodgers, Daniel T. *Age of Fracture*. Cambridge, MA: Harvard University Press, 2011.

Rogers, David. "U.S. Role in Mining Nicaraguan Harbors Reportedly Is Larger Than First Throught." *Wall Street Journal*, April 6, 1984, 6.

Sanchez, Rene. "Dalai Lama Urges Tibetan Freedom." *The Washington Post*, September 22, 1987, Nexis Uni.

"Sanctions Will Not Help: Excerpts from a March 29 Interview with Assistant Secretary of State Chester A. Crocker." *Africa News*, April 8, 1985.

Santese, Angela. "Ronald Reagan, the Nuclear Weapons Freeze Campaign and the Nuclear Scare of the 1980s." *The International History Review* 39, no. 3 (2016): 1–25.

Sargent, Daniel. *A Superpower Transformed: The Remaking of American Foreign Relations in the 1970s*. Oxford: Oxford University Press, 2015.

Savage, Charlie. *Takeover: The Return of the Imperial Presidency and the Subversion of American Democracy.* New York: Little, Brown, 2007.

Schaller, Michael. "Reagan and the Puzzles of 'So-Called Communist China' and Vietnam." In *Reagan and the World: Leadership and National Security, 1981–1989,* edited by Bradley Lynn Coleman and Kyle Longley, 191–209. Lexington: The University Press of Kentucky, 2017.

 Right Turn: American Life in the Reagan–Bush Era, 1980–1992. New York: Oxford University Press, 2007.

Schmemann, Serge. "What It Means for Moscow and the Refuseniks." *The New York Times,* February 9, 1986. www.nytimes.com/1986/02/09/weekinreview/what-it-means-for-moscow-and-the-refuseniks.html.

Schmidli, William Michael. "Institutionalizing Human Rights in U.S. Foreign Policy: U.S.–Argentine Relations, 1976–1980." *Diplomatic History* 35, no. 2 (2011): 351–377.

 "'The Most Sophisticated Intervention We Have Seen': The Carter Administration and the Nicaraguan Crisis, 1978–1979." *Diplomacy & Statecraft* 23, no. 1 (2012): 66–86.

 The Fate of Freedom Elsewhere: Human Rights and U.S. Cold War Policy toward Argentina. Ithaca, NY: Cornell University Press, 2013.

Schmidli, William Michael, and Robert Pee, eds. *The Reagan Administration, the Cold War and the Transition to Democracy Promotion, Security, Conflict and Cooperation in the Contemporary World.* New York: Palgrave Macmillan, 2019.

Schmitz, David F. *The United States and Right-Wing Dictatorships, 1965–1989.* New York: Cambridge University Press, 2006.

Schmitz, David F., and Vanessa Walker. "Jimmy Carter and the Foreign Policy of Human Rights: The Development of a Post-Cold War Foreign Policy." *Diplomatic History* 28, no. 1 (2004): 113–143.

Schraeder, Peter J. *United States Foreign Policy toward Africa: Incrementalism, Crisis, and Change.* Cambridge: Cambridge University Press, 1994.

Scott, James M. *Deciding to Intervene: The Reagan Doctrine and American Foreign Policy.* Durham, NC: Duke University Press, 1996.

 "Interbranch Rivalry and the Reagan Doctrine in Nicaragua." *Political Science Quarterly* 112, no. 2 (1997): 237–260.

Shaw, John. *Richard G. Lugar, Statesman of the Senate: Crafting Foreign Policy from Capitol Hill.* Bloomington: Indiana University Press, 2012.

Shcharansky, Anatoly. *The Case for Democracy: The Power of Freedom to Overcome Tyranny and Terror.* New York: Public Affairs, 2004.

Shultz, George Pratt. *Turmoil and Triumph: My Years as Secretary of State.* New York: Maxwell Macmillan International, 1993.

Sikkink, Kathryn. *Mixed Signals: U.S. Human Rights Policy and Latin America.* Ithaca, NY: Cornell University Press, 2004.

Simms, Brendan, and David J. B. Trim. *Humanitarian Intervention a History.* New York: Cambridge University Press, 2011.

Singh, Robert. *The Congressional Black Caucus: Racial Politics in the U.S. Congress, Contemporary American Politics.* Thousand Oaks, CA: Sage, 1998.

 "The Rise and Fall of Legislative Service Organisations in the United States Congress." *The Journal of Legislative Studies* 2, no. 2 (1996): 79–102.

Slezkine, Peter. "From Helsinki to Human Rights Watch: How an American Cold War Monitoring Group Became an International Human Rights Institution." *Humanity* 5, no. 3 (2014): 345–370.

Smith, Christian. *Resisting Reagan: The U.S. Central America Peace Movement.* Chicago, IL: University of Chicago Press, 1996.

Smith, Gaddis. *Morality, Reason, and Power: American Diplomacy in the Carter Years*, 1st edition. New York: Hill & Wang, 1986.

Smith, Hedrick. "A Turning Point Seen." *The New York Times*, November 6, 1980, A1.

Smith, Tony. *America's Mission: The United States and the Worldwide Struggle for Democracy in the Twentieth Century, Princeton Studies in International History and Politics.* Princeton, NJ: Princeton University Press, 1994.

Foreign Attachments: The Power of Ethnic Groups in the Making of American Foreign Policy. Cambridge, MA: Harvard University Press, 2000.

Snyder, Sarah B. "'A Call for U.S. Leadership': Congressional Activism on Human Rights." *Diplomatic History* 37, no. 2 (2013): 372–397.

"Beyond Containment? The First Bush Administration's Sceptical Approach to the CSCE." *Cold War History* 13, no. 4 (2013): 463–484.

"The CSCE and the Atlantic Alliance: Forging a New Consensus in Madrid." *Journal of Transatlantic Studies* 8, no. 1 (2010): 56–68.

"The Defeat of Ernest Lefever's Nomination: Keeping Human Rights on the United States Foreign Policy Agenda." In *Challenging U.S. Foreign Policy: America and the World*, edited by Bevan Sewell and Scott Lucas, 136–161. Basingstoke: Palgrave Macmillan, 2011.

From Selma to Moscow: How Human Rights Activists Transformed U.S. Foreign Policy. New York: Columbia University Press, 2018.

"The Foundation for Vienna: A Reassessment of the CSCE in the Mid-1980s." *Cold War History* 10, no. 4 (2010): 493–512.

Human Rights Activism and the End of the Cold War: A Transnational History of the Helsinki Network, Human Rights in History. New York: Cambridge University Press, 2011.

"Human Rights and U.S. Foreign Relations: A Historiographical Review." *Passport: The Newsletter of the SHAFR* 44 (2013): 16–21.

"The Rise of Human Rights during the Johnson Years." In *Beyond the Cold War*, edited by Francis J. Gavin and Mark Atwood Lawrence, 237–260. Oxford: Oxford University Press, 2014.

Solarz, Stephen J. *Journeys to War & Peace: A Congressional Memoir.* Waltham, MA: Brandeis University Press, 2011.

Søndergaard, Rasmus Sinding. "Bill Clinton's 'Democratic Enlargement' and the Securitisation of Democracy Promotion." *Diplomacy & Statecraft* 26, no. 3 (2015): 534–551.

"The Congressional Human Rights Caucus and the Plight of the Refuseniks." In *The Cold War at Home and Abroad: Domestic Politics and U.S. Foreign Policy since 1945*, edited by Andrew L. Johns and Mitchell B. Lerner, 224–246. Lexington: University Press of Kentucky, 2018.

"'A Positive Track of Human Rights Policy': Elliott Abrams, the Human Rights Bureau and the Conceptualization of Democracy Promotion." In

The Reagan Administration, the Cold War and the Transition to Democracy Promotion, edited by William Michael Schmidli and Robert Pee, 31–50. New York: Palgrave Macmillan, 2019.

The Committee for the Free World and the Defense of Democracy." *Journal of Cold War Studies* (in press).

"South African Leader Denies U.S. Won Release of Jailed Dissidents." *The New York Times*, December 14, 1984. www.nytimes.com/1984/12/14/world/south-african-leader-denies-us-won-release-of-jailed-dissidents.html.

Stead, Andrew. "What You Know and Who You Know: Senator Jesse Helms, the Reagan Doctrine and the Nicaraguan Contras." *49th Parallel* 33 (Winter 2014): 55–93.

Steinmetz, Sara. *Democratic Transition and Human Rights: Perspectives on U.S. Foreign Policy*. Albany: State University of New York Press, 1994.

Stevens, Simon. "'From the Viewpoint of a Southern Governor': The Carter Administration and Apartheid, 1977–81." *Diplomatic History* 36, no. 5 (2012): 843–880.

Stuckey, Mary E. *Jimmy Carter, Human Rights, and the National Agenda*. College Station: Texas A&M University Press, 2008.

Sugawara, Sandra. "Conservative Gop Congressmen Blasts Barnes." *The Washington Post*, March 13, 1986, C1.

Swain, Carol M. *Black Faces, Black Interests: The Representation of African Americans in Congress*. Lanham, MD: University Press of America, 2006.

Swartz, David R. *Moral Minority: The Evangelical Left in an Age of Conservatism, Politics and Culture in Modern America*. Philadelphia: University of Pennsylvania Press, 2012.

Swett, Katrina Lantos. "An Indispensable Catalyst. Congress, Human Rights and American Foreign Policy." PhD dissertation, University of Southern Denmark, 2007.

Taubman, Philip. "House to Block Aid for Rebels, O'Neill Asserts." *The New York Times*, April 10, 1984, NExis Uni.

"Moynihan Questions CIA's Latin Role." *The New York Times*, April 1, 1983. www.nytimes.com/1983/04/01/world/moynihan-questions-cia-s-latin-role.html.

"Soviet Offers East–West Rights Talks in Moscow." *The New York Times*, November 6, 1986. www.nytimes.com/1986/11/06/world/soviet-offers-east-west-rights-talks-in-moscow.html.

Thatcher, Gary. "Activists Make US Policy toward South Africa a Campaign Issue." *The Christian Science Monitor* , April 20, 1987.

Thomas, Daniel C. *The Helsinki Effect: International Norms, Human Rights, and the Demise of Communism*. Princeton, NJ: Princeton University Press, 2001.

Thomson, Alex. "A More Effective Constructive Engagement: US Policy towards South Africa after the Comprehensive Anti-Apartheid Act of 1986." *Politikon: South African Journal of Political Studies* 39, no. 3 (2012): 371–389.

U.S. Foreign Policy towards Apartheid South Africa, 1948–1994: Conflict of Interests. Basingstoke: Palgrave Macmillan, 2008.

Thompson, Kenneth W. *Foreign Policy in the Reagan Presidency: Nine Intimate Perspectives: Sterling Kernek, Caspar Weinberger, Max M. Kampelman, Dwight*

Ink, Paul H. Nitze, John C. Whitehead, Elliott Abrams, Paul H. Nitze, Don Oberdorfer. Lanham, MD: University Press of America, 1993.

Thörn, Håkan. Anti-Apartheid and the Emergence of a Global Civil Society. Basingstoke: Palgrave Macmillan, 2006.

Thornberry, Patrick. Indigenous Peoples and Human Rights, Melland Schill Studies in International Law. Manchester: Manchester University Press, 2002.

Tillery, Alvin B. Between Homeland and Motherland: Africa, U.S. Foreign Policy, and Black Leadership in America. Ithaca, NY: Cornell University Press, 2011.

"Foreign Policy Activism and Power in the House of Representatives: Black Members of Congress and South Africa, 1968–1986." Studies in American Political Development 20, no. 1 (2006): 88–103.

Timerman, Jacobo. Prisoner without a Name, Cell without a Number. New York: Knopf, 1981.

Tower, John, Edmund Muskie, and Brent Scowcroft. The Tower Commission Report. New York: Bantam Books, 1987.

"Transcript of Democrat's Response to Reagan Speech on Central America." The New York Times, April 28, 1983, Nexis Uni.

Troy, Gil. Morning in America: How Ronald Reagan Invented the 1980s. Princeton, NJ: Princeton University Press, 2005.

Tucker, Robert W. "America in Decline: The Foreign Policy of 'Maturity.'" Foreign Affairs 58, no. 3 (1980): 449–484.

Turek, Lauren F. To Bring the Good News to All Nations: Evangelicals, Human Rights, and U.S. Foreign Relations. New York: Cornell University Press, in press.

"To Support a 'Brother in Christ': Evangelical Groups and U.S.–Guatemalan Relations during the Ríos Montt Regime." Diplomatic History 39, no. 4 (2015): 689–719.

Tyler, Patrick E., and Don Oberdorfer. "Nicaragua Activities Questioned: Rep. Boland Says U.S. Role There May Be Illegal." The Washington Post, April 14, 1983, Nexis Uni.

Tyler, Patrick E., and Bob Woodward. "U.S. Approves Covert Plan in Nicaragua." The Washington Post, March 10, 1982, Lexis Uni.

United Nations Commission on the Truth for El Salvador. "From Madness to Hope: The 12-Year War in El Salvador: Report of the Commission on the Truth for El Salvador." UN Document No. S/25500 (1993).

"U.S. Acts to Ease Trade with East Bloc." In CQ Almanac 1990. Washington, DC, United States: Congressional Quarterly, 1991.

"U.S. Halts Economic Aid to Nicaragua." The New York Times, April 2, 1981. www.nytimes.com/1981/04/02/world/us-halts-economic-aid-to-nicaragua .html.

Vaïsse, Justin. Neoconservatism: The Biography of a Movement. Cambridge, MA: Harvard University Press, 2010.

Von Hippel, Karin. Democracy by Force: U.S. Military Intervention in the Post-Cold War World. New York: Cambridge University Press, 2000.

Walsh, Edward. "Carter to Return to 'Peace or War' Issue." The Washington Post, September 28, 1980, Nexis Uni.

"House Easily Overrides Veto of South Africa Sanctions." The Washington Post, September 30, 1986, A1.

"House Would Require U.S. Disinvestment from South Africa." *The Washington Post*, June 19, 1986, Nexis Uni.

Walsh, Lawrence E., and United States. Office of Independent Counsel. *Iran–Contra: The Final Report*. New York: Times Books, 1994.

Weiner, Tim. *Legacy of Ashes: The History of the CIA*. New York: Doubleday, 2007.

Weinraub, Bernard. "President Links Rights in Soviet to Summit Success." *The New York Times*, October 8, 1986, A6.

Weintraub, Richard M. "Members of Congress Fight IMF Loan to South Africa." *The Washington Post*, November 2, 1982, Nexis Uni.

Westad, Odd Arne. *The Global Cold War: Third World Interventions and the Making of Our Times*. Cambridge, UK: Cambridge University Press, 2007.

Whelan, Daniel J. "'Under the Aegis of Man': The Right to Development and the Origins of the New International Economic Order." *Humanity* 6, no. 1 (2015): 93–108.

Whelan, Daniel J., and Jack Donnelly. "The West, Economic and Social Rights, and the Global Human Rights Regime: Setting the Record Straight." *Human Rights Quarterly* 29, no. 4 (2007): 908–949.

"Wives' Group: 'Not Just John Q. Citizens.'" *The New York Times*, February 21, 1986. www.nytimes.com/1986/02/21/us/wives-group-not-just-john-q-citizens .html.

Worland, Gayle. "Congressional Maverick." *Illinois Issues*, July/August 1997, 16–21.

"The Worst-Kept Secret War," *The New York Times*, December 8, 1982. www.nytimes.com/1982/12/08/opinion/the-worst-kept-secret-war.html.

Zeiler, Thomas W. "The Diplomatic History Bandwagon: A State of the Field," *Journal of American History* 95, no. 4 (2009): 1053–1073.

Zelizer, Julian E. *Arsenal of Democracy: The Politics of National Security from World War II to the War on Terrorism*. New York: Basic, 2010.

"Conservatives, Carter, and the Politics of National Security." In *Rightward Bound: Making America Conservative in the 1970s*, edited by Bruce J. Schulman and Julian E. Zelizer, 265–287. Cambridge, MA: Harvard University Press, 2008.

Index